D0323234

Diversity, Equity and Inclusion in Sport and Leisure

Despite the mythology of sport bringing people together and encouraging everyone to work collectively to succeed, modern sport remains a site of exclusionary practices that operate on a number of levels. Although sports participation is, in some cases at least, becoming more open and meritocratic, at the management level it remains very homogenous; dominated by western, white, middle-aged, able-bodied men. This has implications both for how sport develops and how it is experienced by different participant groups, across all levels. Critical studies of sport have revealed that, rather than being a passive mechanism and merely reflecting inequality, sport, via social agents' interactions with sporting spaces, is actively involved in producing, reproducing, sustaining and indeed, resisting, various manifestations of inequality. The experiences of marginalised groups can act as a resource for explaining contemporary political struggles over what sport means, how it should be played (and by whom), and its place within wider society. Central to this collection is the argument that the dynamics of cultural identities are contextually contingent; influenced heavily by time and place and the extent to which they are embedded in the culture of their geographic location. They also come to function differently within certain sites and institutions, be it in one's everyday routine or leisure pursuits, such as sport. Among the themes and issues explored by the contributors to this volume are: social inclusion and exclusion in relation to class, 'race' and ethnicity, gender and sexuality, social identities and authenticity, social policy, deviance and fandom.

This book was originally published as a special issue of *Sport in Society*.

Thomas Fletcher is a Senior Lecturer within Carnegie Faculty at Leeds Metropolitan University. Thomas's research interests include: 'race'/ethnicity, social identities, heritage, and equity and diversity in sport and leisure. Thomas's book, *Sports Events, Society and Culture* (co-edited with Katherine Dashper and Nicola McCullough) is due to be published by Routledge in 2014.

Katherine Dashper is a Senior Lecturer within Carnegie Faculty at Leeds Metropolitan University. Her research interests include gender, sexuality, social identities and human-animal studies, and she specialises in rural sport, leisure and tourism. She has two edited books – *Sports Events, Society and Culture* (with Thomas Fletcher and Nicola McCullough) and *Rural Tourism: An International Perspective* – due for publication in 2014/15.

Diversity, Equity and Inclusion in Sport and Leisure

Edited by
Thomas Fletcher and Katherine Dashper

Routledge
Taylor & Francis Group

LONDON AND NEW YORK

First published 2014
by Routledge
2 Park Square, Milton Park, Abingdon, Oxon, OX14 4RN, UK

and by Routledge
711 Third Avenue, New York, NY 10017, USA

Routledge is an imprint of the Taylor & Francis Group, an informa business

British Library Cataloguing in Publication Data
A catalogue record for this book is available from the British Library

ISBN 13: 978-0-415-74781-3

Typeset in Times New Roman
by Taylor & Francis Books

Publisher's Note
The publisher accepts responsibility for any inconsistencies that may have arisen during the conversion of this book from journal articles to book chapters, namely the possible inclusion of journal terminology.

Disclaimer
Every effort has been made to contact copyright holders for their permission to reprint material in this book. The publishers would be grateful to hear from any copyright holder who is not here acknowledged and will undertake to rectify any errors or omissions in future editions of this book.

Contents

Sport in the Global Society – Contemporary Perspectives

Series Editor: Boria Majumdar

The social, cultural (including media) and political study of sport is an expanding area of scholarship and related research. While this area has been well served by the *Sport in the Global Society* series, the surge in quality scholarship over the last few years has necessitated the creation of *Sport in the Global Society: Contemporary Perspectives*. The series will publish the work of leading scholars in fields as diverse as sociology, cultural studies, media studies, gender studies, cultural geography and history, political science and political economy. If the social and cultural study of sport is to receive the scholarly attention and readership it warrants, a cross-disciplinary series dedicated to taking sport beyond the narrow confines of physical education and sport science academic domains is necessary. *Sport in the Global Society: Contemporary Perspectives* will answer this need.

Titles in the Series

Australian Sport
Antipodean Waves of Change
Edited by Kristine Toohey and
*   Tracy Taylor*

Australia's Asian Sporting Context
1920s and 1930s
Edited by Sean Brawley and Nick Guoth

Bearing Light: Flame Relays and the
**   Struggle for the Olympic Movement**
Edited by John J. MacAloon

'Critical Support' for Sport
Bruce Kidd

Disability in the Global Sport Arena
A Sporting Chance
Edited by Jill M. Clair

Diversity, Equity and Inclusion in Sport
**   and Leisure**
Edited by Thomas Fletcher and
*   Katherine Dashper*

Documenting the Beijing Olympics
Edited by D.P. Martinez and
*   Kevin Latham*

Ethnicity and Race in Association Football
Case Study analyses in Europe, Africa and the USA
Edited by David Hassan

Exploring the cultural, ideological and economic legacies of Euro 2012
Edited by Peter Kennedy and Christos Kassimeris

Fan Culture in European Football and the Influence of Left Wing Ideology
Edited by Peter Kennedy and David Kennedy

Football in Southeastern Europe
From Ethnic Homogenization to Reconciliation
Edited by John Hughson and Fiona Skillen

Football Supporters and the Commercialisation of Football
Comparative Responses across Europe
Edited by Peter Kennedy and David Kennedy

Forty Years of Sport and Social Change, 1968-2008
"To Remember is to Resist"
Edited by Russell Field and Bruce Kidd

Global Perspectives on Football in Africa
Visualising the Game
Edited by Susann Baller, Giorgio Miescher and Ciraj Rassool

Global Sport Business
Community Impacts of Commercial Sport
Edited by Hans Westerbeek

Governance, Citizenship and the New European Football Championships
The European Spectacle
Edited by Wolfram Manzenreiter and Georg Spitaler

Indigenous People, Race Relations and Australian Sport
Edited by Christopher J. Hallinan and Barry Judd

Olympic Reform Ten Years Later
Edited by Heather Dichter and Bruce Kidd

Reflections on Process Sociology and Sport
'Walking the Line'
Joseph Maguire

Soccer in Brazil
Edited by Martin Curi

Soccer in the Middle East
Edited by Alon Raab and Issam Khalidi

South Africa and the Global Game
Football, Apartheid and Beyond
Edited by Peter Alegi and Chris Bolsmann

Sport – Race, Ethnicity and Identity
Building Global Understanding
Edited by Daryl Adair

Sport and Communities
Edited by David Hassan and Sean Brown

Sport, Culture and Identity in the State of Israel
Edited by Yair Galily and Amir Ben-Porat

Sport in Australian National Identity
Kicking Goals
Tony Ward

Citation Information

The chapters in this book were originally published in *Sport in Society*, volume 16, issue 10 (December 2013). When citing this material, please use the original page numbering for each article, as follows:

Please direct any queries you may have about the citations to
clsuk.permissions@cengage.com

Introduction: diversity, equity and inclusion in sport and leisure

Katherine Dashper and Thomas Fletcher

School of Events, Tourism and Hospitality, Carnegie Faculty, Leeds Metropolitan University, Leeds, UK

When even an Old Etonian Conservative Prime Minister makes public statements condemning racism in British football, as David Cameron did in February 2012, the most sceptical of us can see both the importance of sport in everyday lives and the inequity of modern sport itself.[1] Despite the mythology of sport bringing people together and encouraging everyone to work together to success, modern sport remains a site of exclusionary practices that operate on a number of levels. Although sports participation is, in some cases at least, becoming more open and meritocratic, at the management level it remains very homogenous; dominated by western, white, middle-aged, able-bodied men. This has implications for both how sport develops and how it is experienced by different participant groups, across all levels.

Within sociology and sports studies, the concept of inequality has been widely defined and has been applied to various political ideologies. Inequality, as defined from the right, is inevitable, or is necessary for society to function well. In contrast, from the left, inequality is a social ill and should be eradicated by democratic or revolutionary means. According to Donnelly, 'Sport, by its very nature, produces and reveals inequalities'.[2] Early studies suggested that sport reflected existing inequalities – i.e. it acted as a microcosm of society. However, more critical studies of sport have since revealed that, rather than being a passive mechanism and merely reflecting inequality, sport, via social agents' interactions with sporting spaces, is actively involved in producing, reproducing, sustaining and indeed, acts as a site for resistance.

'In social terms however, sport has often been considered the great social *leveller*' (see Van Slobbe et al., this volume).[3] In fact, sport continues to be cited as an exemplar par excellence of an agent of personal and social change (see Chamberlain, Dacombe, this volume).[4] Numerous studies articulate the possibility of sport acting as a legitimate space for political struggle, resistance and change, and as a modality for 'self-actualization and the reaffirmation of previously abject identities'.[5] Thus, the experiences of marginalized groups can act as a resource for explaining contemporary political struggles over what sport means, how it should be played (and by whom), and its place within wider society. However, most people do not engage in sport to achieve certain societal ends. Instead, their participation is more leisure-focused, for enjoyment, health or to spend time with friends and family.[6]

Sport's structural, cultural and institutional inequalities have been well rehearsed.[7] In our own research exploring gender, sexuality and class in equestrian sport, and 'race' and ethnicity in cricket for example, we argue that sport is heavily implicated in the (re)production of inequalities, but it may also offer opportunities for challenge, and possibly transformation (see Watson et al., this volume).[8] However, although that potential is there, the reality of achieving this is limited. As a number of the contributions to this volume illustrate, the role of sport cannot be considered in isolation from wider social structures and discourses: sport is a representation of these social relations. The challenge facing academics, policy-makers and practitioners in sport is leveraging sport's potential for positive action. In other words, we find ourselves revisiting 'old' ground in conceptualizing the relationship between democratization through sport and democratization of sport. The problem with this is the lack of evidence pertaining to sport, and 'the absence of an understanding of processes and mechanisms which either produce, or are assumed to produce, particular impacts and outcomes'.[9]

Central to the theoretical framework of this volume is the argument that the dynamics of cultural identities are contextually contingent; influenced heavily by time and place and the extent to which they are embedded in the culture of their geographic location. They also come to function differently within certain sites and institutions; be it in one's everyday routine or leisure pursuits, such as sport. As Bauman observes, in late modernity identity is fluid, continually negotiated and (re)constructed in the interactions of everyday life.[10] Such identity work is, however, subject to fractures and dissonances, where fluid notions of identity only go so far – choices about sport participation and leisure more generally, for instance, become conflated with hegemonic struggles over what sporting activities are everyday, what are normal, and what are acceptable.[11] Individuals have some agency to make sense of their own place in the wider networks of society, but all the while they are negotiating their identities and legitimacy within sporting spaces.

The inspiration for this volume of *Sport in Society* came from the 2012 launch of the 'Institute for Sport, Physical Activity and Leisure' (ISPAL) at Leeds Metropolitan University in the UK. One of the five research centres within ISPAL is the 'Centre for Diversity, Equity and Inclusion' (DEI) (see http://www.leedsmet.ac.uk/research/centre-for-diversity-equity-and-inclusion.htm). The DEI Research Centre brings together researchers with a shared concern for critical social research within the broad areas of sport, physical education, leisure and culture. Currently (Spring 2013), there are 22 researchers within the DEI. Collectively, their research practice is underpinned by principles of equity and social justice and reflects a commitment to examining inequities resulting from gender, 'race', sexuality, class, disability, age or religion and their intersections. Some of this work is showcased in contributions to this volume (see Norman, Watson et al.). The launch of ISPAL and the DEI provided us with the opportunity to (re)consider pertinent diversity, equity and inclusion issues within sport and leisure.

Overview of the volume

The 13 papers have been grouped into five broad sections: inclusionary politics and active recreation, sport, policy and inclusion, gender and sexuality, 'race' and ethnicity and watching and supporting sport. Assigning papers to these sections was a difficult task, and we acknowledge that there was scope for cross categorization. This is both a strength and weakness of the process and was done purely for clarity, but may underplay the interconnectedness of the issues expressed here. In this collection, there are two 'Research Insight' papers. The purpose of these was to offer an opportunity for early career researchers to showcase their work, and due to their shorter format (4000–5000 words) provide an accessible outlet for research dissemination.

Section 1: Inclusionary politics and active recreation

Section 1 begins with Rebecca Watson, Lee Tucker and Scarlett Drury's paper 'Can we make a difference? Examining the transformative potential of sport and active recreation'.

Watson, Tucker and Drury consider if and how sport can be transformative for those involved, both participants and coaches and managers. The authors draw upon three individual case studies of gay-and-lesbian-identified football clubs, grass roots football and young men and dance to argue that research into the transformative potential of sport and active recreation needs to be empirically driven, focusing on change and transformation on a variety of levels: at the macro, sport-wide level; at the meso level, within individual sports clubs and organizations and at the level of individual athletes and participants. Following this, in his paper 'The civilised skateboarder and the sports funding hegemony', Daniel Turner critically investigates public funding of the alternative and niche sport of skateboarding. He argues that sports funding and policy decisions are based on a hegemonic conceptualization of sport (and its benefits), which may be at odds with the ethos of participation in alternative sports. He problematizes the compromises that skateboarding has to make in order to fit within what he terms the 'sports funding hegemony' and questions the implications of this for the identities of skateboarders.

Section 2: Sport, policy and inclusion

Rod Dacombe opens section 2 with his paper 'Sports clubs and civic inclusion: Rethinking the poverty of association'. Dacombe argues that, despite the position of sports clubs acting as a 'community resource' – for example, a hub for social networks, generating information and promoting trust – has long been acknowledged, sports clubs have been largely neglected in scholarly discussion of civic participation and deprivation. He suggests that sport is marginalized from discussion of policy, and challenges the view of many political scientists who tend to treat the role of sport in the activities of government as an irrelevance. Some of the issues addressed by Dacombe are examined further, from a different perspective, by Martyn Chamberlain's paper 'Sports-based intervention and the problem of youth offending: a diverse enough tool for a diverse society?' Chamberlain questions the evidence-base supporting the efficacy of sports-based interventions for preventing youth crime and reoffending. He calls for more methodologically robust evidence to support the argument that participation in sporting activity can directly lead to a reduction in antisocial and offending behaviour and thus, to change the lives of some young people for the better.

Section 3: Gender and sexuality

The third section of this collection shifts focus to questions of everyday manifestations of gender and sexuality in sport. Alex Channon begins by considering the transformative potential of sex integration within martial arts in his paper 'Enter the discourse: exploring the discursive roots of inclusivity in mixed-sex martial arts'. He contends that the discursive framing of martial arts in contemporary Western culture is significant in the generation and normalization of mixed-sex inclusivity in these settings. Through an exploration of everyday training practices he explores how sex integration becomes normalized and accepted within this milieu. Deborah Butler continues these themes in her paper 'Not a job for "girly girls": horseracing, gender and work identities' where she analyzes the experiences of female 'lads' in the male-dominated working environment of horse racing. Butler argues that female 'lads' are in a contradictory position: forced to embody masculinity in their everyday working lives, yet denied the status and opportunity to race ride, due to their female bodies. Leanne Norman also centralizes female voices in her paper 'The concepts underpinning everyday gendered homophobia based upon the experiences of lesbian coaches', and in so doing, further advances discussion of everyday inequalities. Her concept of 'everyday gendered homophobia' highlights how gender and sexuality intersect in the experiences of lesbian coaches. In distinguishing this from other forms of homophobia she argues that everyday gendered homophobia is the integration of gendered homophobia into daily situations through practices that initiate and sustain unequal power relationships between lesbians and dominant social groups.

Section 4: 'Race' and ethnicity

In the fourth section of this collection we provide three diverse case studies. Marcelo Almeida, Janelle Joseph, Alexandre Palma and Antonio Jorge Soares' paper 'Marketing strategies within an African-Brazilian martial art' centralizes the African Brazilian martial art of capoeira and examines the ways in which contemporary marketing of capoeira has arguably diluted its cultural authenticity. They contend that the symbols of capoeira, and African Brazilian culture more generally, that are marketed worldwide are based on the legends of the physical activity's history and origins. These symbols are promoted as 'authentically Brazilian', increasing the value of the capoeira 'product' by demonstrating proximity to a history of struggles for equality and celebrations of multiculturalism in Brazil, when in reality the 'product' is relatively new, relying heavily on invented traditions. Michel van Slobbe, Jeroen Vermeulen and Martijn Koster's paper 'The making of an ethnically diverse management: contested cultural meanings in a Dutch amateur football club' examines pertinent issues of 'race' and ethnicity within the context of the management of a recreational football club in the Netherlands. They trace the evolution of the club's ethnic composition from predominantly white Dutch to becoming more ethnically diverse. They document how changes in the organizational structure and culture of the club led to racially and culturally motivated antagonisms resulting in the inveterate and institutionalized 'us' and 'them' dynamic which came to characterize the organizational culture of the club. Next, Souvik Naha provides the first of two 'Research Insights'. In 'Sport controversy, the media and Anglo-Indian cricket relations: the 1977 "Vaseline incident" in retrospect' he problematizes postcolonial Anglo-Indian relationships through an interpretation of British and Indian media coverage of the 'Vaseline incident'. He suggests that the incident had two overarching consequences. First, that it called into question the moral virtue of the England players and managers, specifically John Lever, the England bowler accused of applying Vaseline to the ball and second, that the English cricketing establishment then embarked on an unfounded witch hunt against India captain, Bishan Singh Bedi, who had been a staunch critic of the England team and management throughout the process. Bedi's negativity, he argues, stirred anti-English sentiment amongst the Indian public and media commentators.

Section 5: Supporting and watching sport

In his paper 'Social inclusion through football fandom: opportunities for learning-disabled people' Kris Southby centralizes the voices of learning-disabled football fans which have previously been silent within sociological studies of fandom. In so doing, he problematizes romanticized views of social inclusion as a simple matter of 'creating routes back into society and giving people a chance to integrate' into their communities. His ethnographic study of learning-disabled football fans suggests that football fandom provides learning-disabled people with an identity and sense of community and belonging beyond being 'disabled', but that the transformative potential of such experiences fall short of the social inclusion characterized by governments. Andy Harvey and Piotrowska Agnieszka also centralize the complexity of football fandom in their paper 'Intolerance and joy, violence and love among male football fans: towards a psychosocial explanation of "excessive" behaviours'. In their provocative Research Insight, Harvey and Agnieszka suggest that psychoanalytic theory may provide useful tools for understanding the predilection of some football fans for excessive behaviour, ranging from aggression and the use of intolerant language to acts of spontaneous and unrestrained joy and love, including same-sex hugging and kissing, and which make up an important, if under-researched, aspect of fandom. Finally, Matthew Kobach and Robert Potter's paper 'The role of mediated sports programming on implicit racial stereotypes' provides an innovative methodological approach for understanding how racial stereotypes of athletes become internalized by consumers of sport-related images and media commentaries. They apply a version of the Implicit Association Test (IAT). The IAT asks participants to rapidly pair various stimuli objects and traits and demonstrates how participants rely on associations that have been learned and reinforced through repetitive exposure to media commentaries. Kobach and Potter draw upon cultivation theory and social reality theory to argue that there is a relationship between overall time spent with mediated sports and the participants' notions of athletic ability, as defined by one's 'race'.

To many critical scholars of sport and leisure the issues raised in this volume are nothing new, but the range of case studies and discussions presented here reaffirms the contemporary relevance of the concepts of diversity, equity and inclusion within the fields of sport and leisure. The content of this volume covers a lot of ground, theoretically, empirically and geographically, but inevitably possesses limitations in its scope and trajectory and therefore must, as with all scholarship, be seen as part of a broader discourse. We thank the authors for their contributions and hope their papers spark interest and provoke further discussion.

Notes

1. Sparrow, 'David Cameron Calls Football'.
2. Donnelly, 'Approaches to Social Inequality', 221.
3. Ibid.
4. Spaaij, 'Social Impact of Sport'.
5. Carrington, *Race, Sport and Politics*, 36.
6. Spaaij, 'Social Impact of Sport'.
7. Bourdieu, 'Sport and Social Class'; Jarvie, *Sport, Racism and Ethnicity*; Hargreaves, *Sporting Females*; Griffin, *Strong Women, Deep Closets*; Messner, *Taking the Field*; Thomas and Smith, *Disability Sport and Society* and Long and Spracklen, *Sport and Challenges to Racism*.
8. Fletcher, '"Aye, But It were Wasted on Thee"'; Dashper, 'Dressage is Full of Queens!'; Dashper, 'Together, Yet Still Not Equal?' and Fletcher and Spracklen, 'Cricket, Drinking and Exclusion?'.
9. Coalter, *Wider Social Role for Sport*, 2, 3.
10. Bauman, *Identity*.
11. Fletcher and Spracklen, 'Cricket, Drinking and Exclusion?'.

References

Bauman, Zygmunt. *Identity*. Cambridge: Polity, 2004.
Bourdieu, Pierre. 'Sport and Social Class'. *Social Science Information* 17, no. 6 (1978): 819–40.
Carrington, Ben. *Race, Sport and Politics: The Sporting Black Diaspora*. London: Sage, 2010.
Coalter, Fred. *A Wider Social Role for Sport: Who's Keeping the Score?* London: Routledge, 2007.
Dashper, Katherine. 'Dressage is Full of Queens! Masculinity, Sexuality and Equestrian Sport'. *Sociology* 46, no. 6 (2012): 1109–24.

Dashper, Katherine. 'Together, Yet Still Not Equal? Sex Integration in Equestrian Sport'. *Asia Pacific Journal of Health, Sport and Physical Education* 3, no. 3 (2012): 213–25.

Donnelly, Peter. 'Approaches to Social Inequality in the Sociology of Sport'. *Quest* 48, no. 2 (1996): 221–42.

Fletcher, Thomas. '"Aye, But It were Wasted on Thee": Cricket, British Asians, Ethnic Identities, and the "Magical Recovery of Community"'. *Sociological Research Online* 16, no. 4 (2011). doi:10.5153/sro.2468.

Fletcher, Thomas, and Karl Spracklen. 'Cricket, Drinking and Exclusion of British Pakistani Muslims?' *Ethnic and Racial Studies* (2013). doi:10.1080/01419870.2013.790983.

Griffin, Pat. *Strong Women, Deep Closets: Lesbians and Homophobia in Sport*. Champaign, IL: Human Kinetics, 1998.

Hargreaves, Jennifer. *Sporting Females: Critical Issues in the History and Sociology of Women's Sports*. London: Routledge, 1994.

Jarvie, Grant, ed. *Sport, Racism and Ethnicity*. London: Routledge, 1991.

Long, Jonathan and Karl Spracklen, eds. *Sport and Challenges to Racism*. Basingstoke: Palgrave Macmillan, 2011.

Messner, Michael. *Taking the Field: Women, Men and Sports*. Minneapolis: University of Minnesota Press, 2002.

Spaaij, Ramon. 'The Social Impact of Sport: Diversities, Complexities and Contexts'. *Sport in Society* 12, no. 9 (2009): 1109–17.

Sparrow, A. 'David Cameron Calls Football Racism Summit'. 2012. Also available online at: http://www.guardian.co.uk/football/2012/feb/12/football-racism-summit-david-cameron (accessed June 18, 2013).

Thomas, Nigel, and Andy Smith. *Disability Sport and Society: An Introduction*. London: Routledge, 2008.

Can we make a difference? Examining the transformative potential of sport and active recreation

Rebecca Watson, Lee Tucker and Scarlett Drury

School of Sport, Leeds Metropolitan University, Leeds, UK

This paper focuses around the transformative potential of sport and active recreation and is premised on an assertion that sport in its broadest sense is a political project. It draws on three different empirical studies to critically assess ways in which involvement for participants can be (potentially) transformative, transformational and transforming. The first study focuses on gay sport and gay football, the second looks at a recreational football team where the manager is seeking to actualize participation as 'transformational' for players to challenge practices of discrimination including sexism and racism. The third study focuses on dance and masculinity and considers how 'transforming' practices are embodied and expressed in complex ways. We argue that attention needs to be paid to the nature and type of activities being assessed and emphasize the importance of context-specific empirical research to engage more fully with claims pertaining to transformative potential.

Introduction

Making a difference and/or effecting change are often implicit features of interest in diversity, equity and inclusion in sport and leisure. How change occurs is open to question and long-standing debates retain some significance: the potential of sport, for example, to resist and *challenge* social inequalities such as gender and a recognition that sport mirrors and *reproduces* persistent inequalities, such as those associated with social class and a capitalist economy. This paper focuses around the transformative potential of sport and active recreation and is premised on an assertion that sport in its broadest sense is a political project, that is, a site of dynamic interplay of asserting and generating loci for change. It draws on three different empirical studies to critically assess this assertion and considers the ways in which involvement for participants can be (potentially) transformative, transformational and transforming. The three studies offer an insight into the transformative potential of sport and active recreation at macro, meso and micro levels, respectively. The first study focuses on gay sport and gay football and explores how 'transformative' is manifest as a process of challenging hetero- and homonormativities. The second is a study of a recreational football team where the manager is seeking to actualize participation as 'transformational' for players in order to challenge practices of discrimination including sexism and racism. The third study focuses on dance and masculinity and considers how 'transforming' practices are embodied and expressed in often complex ways. All three studies question binary assumptions of exclusion to inclusion and challenge simplistic rhetoric of achieving diversity through participation in sport.

Transformative potential here is conceptualized within a sociological framework that acknowledges agency and the possibility to effect change as an ongoing negotiation of complex subject positions. The paper is not advancing a distinctly 'transformative paradigm', though all three studies reference potential for enhanced social justice, albeit in different ways.[1] Sport activism can instigate social change through its transformative potential, and it is in the context of such activism that these studies are set.[2] Sport itself may be construed as value neutral in some ways yet as Sugden argues, the adoption of a sociological imagination and a progressive attitude to social change for society's most vulnerable groups can provide the basis for human development through the intervention of sport projects and research.[3] Maguire calls for a refocused philosophy that diverts attention and funding away from 'achievement sport' in the 'sports-industrial complex' and back to a humanist tradition that is concerned with 'issues such as morality, equity, participation'.[4] Hargreaves highlights the need for retaining a politics of sport, drawing on feminist praxis, to provide a necessary complement to theorizing centred upon deconstruction.[5] All three studies here engage in some way with these assertions and aim to contribute to a critical analysis of sport and active recreation that enhances our sociological understanding and considers action for change.

It is ambitious to incorporate three studies but we do so in order to argue the need for a multilayered analysis of sport and active recreation's transformative potential, particularly in relation to diversity, equity and inclusion. Our framework insists upon analyses of varying social relations and positions that inform and are interrelated with dynamic subjects, and the potential of social actors to create and transform individual circumstances and, at times, the wider rubric of intersecting social relations. Etymologically we draw loosely on meanings of transformative, transformational and transforming as associated with (potential) change rather making claims for assumed outcomes or distinct changes. Our argument here is generated from empirical data that inform our view that any analysis of transformative potential and actualization can only be gauged through lived experience. The first study refers to 'transformative' and highlights the macro heteronormative context of mainstream football within which gay- and lesbian-identified football teams are positioned. The second study on a 'transformational' context focuses on the process of aiming to bring about change in players' attitudes and behaviours in local, recreational (heterosexual) men's football. The third and final theme of 'transforming' emphasizes how embodiment is crucial to understanding how change might occur, in this instance through a focus on masculinity and dance.

Transformative potential of gay- and lesbian-identified football clubs

Gay- and lesbian-identified sports clubs are understood to be the potential sites of transformation with respect to many of the oppressive practices of mainstream sport.[6] The initial rise of 'gay sports culture' can be attributed to the socio-historic positioning of sport as masculine and the subsequent climate of homophobia and heteronormativity. As such, gay sports spaces offer an alternative, 'inclusive' sports environment in which lesbian, gay, bisexual and transgender (LGBT) sportspeople are able to participate without fear of discrimination. The anti-discrimination ethos of many gay sports organizations, however, is not limited to issues of sexuality. In most, there is a concerted emphasis on tackling other exclusionary boundaries associated with, for instance, ethnicity, gender, physical ability, social class and health status.

Study 1

The rise in gay-identified football clubs has been particularly notable over the last decade.[7] This increase sits alongside a mainstream football culture that continues to be noted for its hostility towards non-heterosexual identities, which is derived in part from the football's influential position as one of the most significant societal institutions involved in the reproduction of dominant forms of masculinity.[8] The limited amount of existing research into gay- or lesbian-identified football spaces points towards the notion of such spaces as an 'alternative' to mainstream football, a football environment that is built around a discourse of inclusion rather than competition.[9] The study referred to here extends analyses of gay football spaces to consider their transformative potential in relation to mainstream football culture. The findings are taken from ethnographic research into the experiences of footballers playing in gay- or lesbian-identified clubs. The project was informed by feminist, post-structural and queer theories of gender, sex and sexuality.

Analysis of the transformative potential of gay sport, as Pronger points out, is no straightforward process.[10] It would be all too easy to assume that gay sports clubs, by virtue of their very existence, transform homophobia and heteronormativity. Clearly, they do provide localized contexts in which such discourses are subverted; the presence and prevalence of homosexual identities coupled with the absence of homophobic shaming within these environments offers evidence of this. But as Pronger identifies, not all gay sports clubs operate in the same ways; some are more closely aligned with mainstream sport, whereas others remain more marginal, which means that the multiple discourses that operate within the broader context of gay sports culture are not without conflict.[11] This makes it difficult to establish the extent to which gay sport as a whole is able to influence, let alone transform, mainstream sports culture.

Yet what remains clear is that regardless of their affiliation with or dislocation from mainstream sport, the discourse of inclusion continues to be a pivotal influence in shaping the overall ethos of gay sports clubs.[12] This emphasis on inclusion means that competitiveness is decentred in favour of a more 'friendly' approach, which allows for the participation of all players regardless of skill or physical prowess. This can be interpreted as a positive transformation of some of the more exclusive practices that dictate the way in which mainstream football is commonly played. Existing research has identified various other processes of transformation existing within gay or lesbian sports spaces.[13] However, there is at present little indication of how this might translate into broader mainstream transformation.

The football clubs involved in the study could be considered transformative in a number of different ways. Many were exemplars of the type of inclusive practices that research has already identified as being prevalent within gay sports settings.[14] The absence of homophobia coupled with the subversion of heteronormativity is perhaps the most obvious factor that contributed to participants' experiences of gay football as an inclusive space. Although very few had turned to gay football as a result of direct experiences of homophobia in mainstream football, many commented that the normalization of homosexual identities within gay leagues allowed them to feel 'free' to compete without the pressures of hiding their sexuality or 'coming out' to team mates.

But the feelings of inclusion described by many participants were not isolated to issues of sexuality. The shared experiences of exclusion in other sports contexts felt by many of the participants resulted in concerted efforts to maintain a sense of inclusion across other boundaries. Emphasis was placed on ensuring the inclusion of players who might otherwise face discrimination on the basis of other axes of difference related to gender identity, age, ethnicity, (dis)ability and social class. This was evident in the apparent diversity of identities present within many of the teams, which was something that was noted by many of the participants as different from the dynamics of mainstream football teams. Emphasis on the inclusion of all participants regardless of physical ability or football prowess was another attribute that was common to the clubs involved. Most were organized in such a way that the social rather than competitive aspects of participation were most emphasized. This meant that for individuals who had previously felt 'alienated' by the heteronormativity of football culture, and, as a result, never had the opportunity to develop an aptitude for the game, gay football provided their first opportunity to play and enjoy football in an environment in which they would not be judged on the basis of skill.

> Chris: We've got people like my friend, who couldn't play football when he was growing up because, well he was obviously gay, nobody would let him play, and he was disenfranchised and disillusioned with the sport, but he loved the game, but let his own lack of involvement in the game affect his physical fitness. And now in his 40s he came to us just to come and watch, and we said 'well you're more than welcome to do so, but there's no reason why you can't play', and now he plays in the league and he gets his 45 min as we all do...

The welcoming, friendly, and supportive environment fostered by gay football teams became a recurrent theme throughout interviews. This was one of the most notable of ways in which gay football was positioned as different from mainstream football. Some participants also spoke about the increasing number of straight players who opted to play for gay-identified teams as a result of their disdain for the over-competitive and hyper-masculine ethos of some mainstream leagues. This for many signified that the inclusive values associated with gay football might have something to offer mainstream sport.

Clearly, this signifies the capabilities of gay football spaces to transform some of the exclusionary boundaries associated with mainstream sport, at least within their own localized contexts. However, the influence that this might have over mainstream sports contexts is more difficult to determine. As other scholars have identified, the separate nature of many gay-identified clubs often provokes criticism surrounding their potential to offer any real challenge to the homophobia, heteronormativity and other oppressive discourses more broadly.[15] This was something that participants were more than aware of; many expressed concerns over the perceived segregation of the gay league, or of criticisms about gay clubs becoming 'enclaves'. Yet they were quick to reassert the need for 'gay space' in an otherwise heteronormative sports culture.

> Dan: It's like why do we have gay bars and why do we have gay clubs and all the rest of it? They don't generally turn straight people away, but it's somewhere where gay people can feel comfortable, and it's the same with the league, you know. We don't turn straight people away but it's somewhere where we can feel comfortable.

> Chris: One of the biggest criticisms of the GFSN [Gay Football Supporters' Network] league and the gay world cup is the perception of exclusivity and self segregation. I think that's a very fair observation, and something we had to watch, but I don't think it's legitimate in that we wouldn't exist if homophobia in football hadn't existed, and homophobia in society hadn't existed.

For these individuals, gay football exists as an inevitable backlash against mainstream hostility, but one that does not necessarily result in the perpetuation of further divisions between 'straight' and 'gay' players. The increased visibility of some of the clubs within mainstream football, through their involvement in competitions and friendlies with mainstream clubs, provided a means of sending out a positive message about LGBT involvement in the game. For the women involved, this was about being acknowledged as a visible and positive presence, and for the men, about challenging stereotypes and dispelling myths about gay men's apparent incompatibility with football.

However, as other research has uncovered, concerns over pushing to increase the visibility of LGBT identities as a means of tackling homophobia and heteronormativity in mainstream sports contexts can often create tensions with the inclusive ethos emphasized within gay sport.[16] This is often linked with the need to create a 'positive' image of LGBT individuals. In the context of gay football, this is manifested in the implicit desire to present gender-normative representations of gay and lesbian identities: lesbian footballers who do not epitomize the 'butch' stereotype, and gay male footballers who embody a more heteronormative ideal of masculinity. Though this strategy may have a positive impact on mainstream LGBT acceptance by 'normalizing' gay identities, it risks compromising the alleged inclusivity of gay-identified teams by re-appropriating some expressions of gender as more hierarchically ascendant than others. This, in turn, means that rather than transforming heteronormativity, gay football may risk merely subverting it and creating instead a 'homonormative' climate, which seeks LGBT assimilation into, rather than transformation of, mainstream football culture.[17]

Given prevailing societal stereotypes of homosexuality, particularly in sport where they are often amplified, it is of course very difficult for gay sports clubs to break free from this tension between fostering an inclusive and transformative sports climate, which may have minimal impact on mainstream sport, and transforming mainstream sports culture, which necessarily results in some level of assimilation. Some of the most transformative clubs with respect to their inclusive and anti-discriminatory values are those that, by necessity, lie furthest away from the centre of mainstream sport.

Aside from these tensions, it is evident that many of the positive and more transformative elements of gay football spaces are capable of being felt by mainstream sport in other ways. Whilst many of the inclusive practices adopted by gay teams may only operate in these localized contexts, their anti-discriminatory message is increasingly reaching a wider audience. The political action spearheaded by those affiliated with gay-identified or anti-homophobia football clubs such as the *Gay Football Supporters' Network* and *The Justin Campaign* has already been influential in challenging homophobic discrimination in football and instigating change at policy level.

Transformational potential in grass roots football

English football is synonymous with white working-class masculine traits including commitment, hard work and aggression.[18] Implicit within this description is a white, non-feminine, heteronormative culture that creates, and is a product of, a particular working-class hegemonic masculine identity. Recent documentaries into issues such as homophobia and racism have highlighted problems within the professional game.[19] However, less has been focused on these issues at a recreational level and, in particular, on what attempts are being made to challenge such discriminatory behaviour. This study is an analysis of how a Sunday league football team within the north-east of England is a site of potential transformational social change. The club, founded in 2009, plays in an adult football league. The majority of its players are aged 22 or under, with only two players over that age regularly playing. This is due to the team being set up by the manager with the intention of providing a team for his son and nephews (and their friends) to continue playing once too old for junior football. The research itself is influenced by an initial year's experience within the club where a lot of interesting issues and situations arose for one of us as a football manager and 'active sociologist'. Empirical data at this stage are based on participant observation and extensive journal entries to assess the transformational potential of the team through the various interactions that members have through different spaces and times.

Study 2

In any form of emancipatory research, there is an implicit intention to impact upon a set of conditions and produce change (or knowledge about necessary change). This resembles an action research approach which Coghlan and Brannick argue aims, not to just know the world, understand it and explain it, but to also change it.[20] This links in with the transformative potential intended within this study. An understanding of the conditions and structures that individual actors are constrained or oppressed by requires an analysis of historical as well as contemporary influences. As Bhaskar points out:

> ... society is both the condition and outcome of human agency and human agency both reproduces and transforms society. However, there is an important asymmetry here: at any moment of time society is pre-given for the individuals who never create it, but merely reproduce or transform it.[21]

So, it is not inevitable that individuals will remain passive recipients of the conditions that affect their lives (e.g. racism, sexism and homophobia). Social structures do not exist independent of human activity and, therefore, it is human activity that has the potential to either reproduce or transform these structures.[22]

The potential for transformational change within the club is generated through one of the authors/researchers (white male) as the manager. An intention from the outset was to not only develop a team that plays good football but also provide an alternative cultural space that contests many of the behaviours and attitudes experienced in many other traditional football clubs. The manager's habitus which Bourdieu conveniently explains as a 'feel for the game' draws upon footballing experiences gained from the same cultural field as others within the team, i.e. playing in teams within the area for the last 30 years.[23] This offers a useful insight into the cultural milieu of the football club environment from which to base my praxis.[24]

The self-appointed role of manager involves a connection to theories around leadership, particularly leadership of change. With the cultural and physical capital as a player/manager has come, the acquisition of necessary symbolic capital to have personal opinions legitimated and, as a consequence, they are, therefore, potentially influential within the club.[25] Part of the role of an authentic transformational leader is to inspire a vision and set high moral and ethical standards.[26] This has always been a driving motivational factor behind the management style of the team. An example of leading this alternative culture is the constitution that was designed to ensure players knew what was expected from them whilst with the club. This includes anti-sexist, anti-racist and anti-homophobic behaviour. The manager discusses this with all new players so that they are aware of what the club stands for. Therefore, the potential transformative process occurs from the outset with ground rules and expectations being made clear.

A sociological imagination is pivotal here in challenging prevalent issues that often occur within the club (and hopefully help to make a difference).[27] Through the constitution, team talks and conversations in the pub or on tour, certain issues are discussed and hopefully new insights provided, for those not cognizant of prejudices faced by marginalized and oppressed people. An example of this awareness raising is highlighted in a pre-match talk on the pitch just before kick-off following an incident from the previous week. Below are the extracts from the journal that explain how the events unfolded:

Sunday 20th January diary entry

There were a couple of comments made in today's game by a player on our side that were homophobic. For him I am sure he perceived it as banter but for me it is something that I feel a need to address. It is not something that I felt compelled to do on the day as I was unsure how I wanted to approach the situation and did not want to feel that I was lecturing people.

Sunday 27th January diary entry

Before the game today I approached the situation of the homophobic comments from last week. I had decided to talk to the team about the comments that I heard (without pointing anyone out) and stating that although maybe considered banter, for me it could be quite damaging to any individual from our team if they were gay in terms of coming out. I expressed the concern that it is difficult enough within society due to oppression and discrimination for individuals to come out to parents, work colleagues, etc. and that I hoped that our club/team is a space and place where they would be able to do so in the comfort that he is a player of our club first and foremost and our constitution supports the anti-discrimination of gay people. I stated that this is what makes us unique compared to all of the other teams playing at the pitches adjacent to us. I also stated that if anyone had strong feelings about this then they can talk to me about it. I asked if this was ok and the person who said yes most positively was the person who I had heard make the comments the previous week. I am not sure if this means he was acknowledging what he had said and was aware that I knew it was him or whether he was wanting it brushed off and get on with the game.

As stated in the journal, there are no guarantees that the player mentioned actually accepted the discrimination in his comments, but this is not something that can ever be confirmed other than by the player himself. However, the open discussion of these issues means that at least a platform is being created for such opinions to be aired. The least it does is to demonstrate to players that the 'institutional language' and 'derogatory vocabulary' used within many (and we suggest most) football clubs is not without resistance via alternative discourse.[28] Without such resistance, then a complicit environment is created which offers a comfort zone of laddishness for dominant males within the group that makes it acceptable for their treatment of women and other men, with less dominant masculinities.[29] There are many other incidents such as the one above that demonstrate the manager's disposition and leadership approach to challenge and resist other examples of discriminatory behaviour and attitude, but obviously there is not sufficient space to do that here. What the above example does is to illustrate how a leader's sociological imagination is pivotal in creating a discourse for transformational change within the sporting spaces they occupy. The potential for such change is partially reliant upon the status that the leader has within the group, a point that requires further investigation.

Transforming masculinities through dance

This section focuses on masculinity and dance and draws on a study of a boys' dance project run in an inner city area in the north of England for 13–18-year-olds. It is important that we consider how masculinity is expressed and embodied in multiple contexts, to assess it as embodied and performed, to acknowledge it as a problematic concept and to assess the opportunities for shifts in its constituent parts as well as in the context of gender relations more broadly.[30] In relation to the research extract included here, for example, the significance of racialized masculinities is informed by research on expressions of black male identities and black feminist standpoint approaches to macro processes of racism, patriarchy and capitalism.[31]

Some authors are beginning to assert the complex nature of masculinity and its intersectional contexts more firmly:

> The constitution and construction of masculinity is, we would argue, a contradictory interweaving of hegemonic and socially marginalised positionings which, from the point of view of societal actors, has started to shake quite dramatically. We need to debate this situation further in theoretical terms, and to explore it empirically with the help of appropriately creative methods, in order to work out what it means for the continuation of masculine domination and of inequalities in gender relations.[32]

Approaching masculinity in such a way helps to inform the recognition that sport and active recreation may exhibit forms beyond traditional, sporting 'orthodox' masculinity and that masculinity may reflect aspects of transforming and reconfiguring.[33] That is, how aspects of hegemonic male power are both present and yet possibly diminishing within the same sphere; charting elements of transforming (masculinity) emphasizes this as *in process* rather than a shift from hegemonic to non-hegemonic forms.[34] However, it is important to note that analyses of masculinity tend to focus on certain aspects, for example, race *or* sexuality (with class often disappearing) and looking intersectionally at masculinity requires further detailed engagement. Re-evaluating hegemonic masculinity in intersectional ways is a relatively new undertaking.[35]

Study 3

This research extract comes from a study of male youth with a mixed range of experience and ability in dance and participants were predominantly from African-Caribbean backgrounds including mixed black and white race/heritage. Key questions here include whether boys who dance are 'transforming' masculinity and to what extent, if any, is masculinity transforming such that boys can experience and develop dance in different ways? In addition, consideration can be given to what changes occur for individuals as a consequence of involvement in dance. Data were gathered via observations, interviews with dance instructors and key dance organization personnel and conversational interaction with participants at dance sessions throughout the 12-week programme. The dance organization receives core funding from the Arts Council England and promotes 'Black British dance' in its mission statements. Research data are taken from one of the interviews with the lead instructor and from diary entries of observations and conversations with the boys. These methods were used to inform analyses of embodied practice and a range of body techniques that contribute to an embodied sociology.[36]

One of the aims of this male-only dance project was to offer a space in which boys could experience dance on male terms – 'to be how the male can be' as the lead instructor put it. This was not a project seeking to change or challenge masculinity through dance though obviously it is often difficult to state that projects and activities explicitly set out to challenge gender relations.[37] There is of course the possibility of participation for enjoyment for its own sake, and/or for aesthetic value, and for involvement in sport for potentially more inclusive aspects of masculinity.[38] The lead instructor was asked his views about the broader potential impacts of dance for the participants including whether dance can make a positive difference in young men's lives.

Interviewer: And do you believe that? That it's possible?

D: Yeah, definitely, (pause), it worked for me, it worked for a lot of dancers I've worked with. You know, you hear people say things like 'If I get ten people, in a group, if I get one person out of that, if I get one person comes (stays) off the street then my job is done' but I think we can get more than that here. You know partly because of the football, those boys are told a lot to respect the people they work with, you know they'll say, respect him, and respect so-and-so and the other guys and I know that they will be saying the same to the boys about us.

He mentioned the football project that a number of dance participants were involved in and made a link to respect and commitment that resonated with his own experiences of involvement in sport and physical activity. This resonates with a discourse of boys' engagement as 'worthwhile' beyond simply taking part, often a crudely functionalist premise of the value of activities as 'diversions'. The funders for this particular work were the Police Authority, and so to some extent there was an implicit theme of activity as diversion yet such an interpretation is of course overly simplistic.[39] Similarly, by their very assertion, such claims commonly rely on and reinforce stereotypes of certain masculinities, particularly black and working-class masculinities, as dangerous and non-normative.[40] Concurrently, this type of 'valuing' of engagement preserves a sporting hegemony that privileges male involvement whilst 'othering' and often subordinating activity such as dance.

The observation data certainly highlight some of the contradictory elements of configurations of masculinity. For instance, there was an evident interplay between hyper-masculinity and heteronormative masculinity which was celebrated and affirmed, yet also arguably disrupted in some ways. From its inception, the project claimed that boys can dance and that dance is not (only) for girls; examining embodied practice including how, for example, the dance space is configured and occupied by participants' bodies is of great significance. 'D', the lead instructor, is a tallish, muscular, black dancer who asserts, through speech and display, a strong and powerful physique and projects a heteronormative sexuality (though arguably this can only be assumed). In the sessions, he made reference, on the one hand, to how he once sought to become a professional football player and linked this to the aspirations of some of the participants. On the other hand, he highlighted his dance training, the need to be graceful and athletic in different ways, to be strong enough to lift and hold other men in dance. He told them that he chose dance over football. His speech and expressions exhibited a hegemonic gender order at times saying, for example, 'stop looking like a girl' if the boys were not perceived to be showing enough physical effort. Yet, he also stated that 'it's not that girls aren't strong, they can be very strong, but they have different strength to boys'. One fairly obvious reading is that, as the instructor, in a position of influence, he was in danger of reproducing essentialist, dichotomous distinctions between boys and girls and their physical capabilities. Another reading is that differentiating boys and girls was not necessarily or automatically detrimental to girls. We cannot offer generalized conclusions about this and it points to further debate, such as whether boys are accessing traditionally 'feminine' activities and the consequences of this. We use selected examples here to argue that the context specific and local expression of masculinities and femininities are crucial to informing analyses of complex configurations of gender.

A number of movements incorporated in the dance workshops were based on martial arts and self-defence techniques, and 'D' outlined several examples of self-defence manoeuvres. He provided some commentary with these such as 'You know you can use this in a protective way, you know when you need to look out for yourself or for someone'. Drawing on the concept of body techniques, it was evident that being able to 'defend oneself' or on occasion 'to fight' is something that the boys take for granted.[41] They had 'play fights', including pushing and mimicking boxing, in ways that were seemingly totally normal to them. Yet the context of the dance project and the African–Caribbean heritage of most of the participants (including 'D') is illuminating with regard to the complexities of masculinity. The positioning of black masculine bodies in the public spaces of the street, for example, makes them vulnerable, and puts their bodies at risk despite dominant discourses of the black male as powerful and to be feared. Black male bodies still get broken (mentally and physically), get shot and get locked up in greater numbers than their white counterparts.[42]

Another example of vulnerability in relation to masculinity within the sessions was when the boys were learning and/or trying out new movements. They took risks amongst the other participants in not always being able to perform physical tasks, including those that required sheer strength (such as full press-ups), those that required some grace and agility (such as cartwheels) or following dance rhythms. Observational data suggest that the boys disrupted dominant sporting, masculine hegemony in that respect; they did not subordinate one another on the grounds of lack of ability and rather, demonstrated support and encouragement, suggesting a different way of being inclusive.[43] They were subverting an accepted 'bad boy' image by engaging in a 'soft' activity such as dance.[44] D's role as an effective leader and instructor engendered a situation through both his embodied presence (being strong and fit at over 40) that resulted in acceptance and adherence to high levels of mutual respect amongst the boys and between the boys and the instructors. The male instructors (across the project) and the boys are products and active constituents in the construction of masculinity and thus are agents in transforming masculinities, however, incremental and localized that may seem.

Assessment and application of masculine hegemony theory can usefully inform our discussion of the transformative potential of sport and active recreation. Critiques of the concept including the alternative terms 'orthodox' and 'inclusive' masculinity as defined by Anderson allow for more nuanced readings of masculinity as embodied practice.[45] However, Anderson's work (by his own admission) is very white-centric. Hegemonic masculinity theory and the associated critique remain sparse in relation to racialized bodies, with some exceptions in sport sociology, though these tend to remain limited in engaging empirical study and embodied practice.[46] Hegemony retains significance across, and within analysis of, sport's transformative potential; not only in relation to configurations of masculinity through dance. It is useful, therefore, to move on to consider some of the interconnections across the three studies and to propose some key aspects of engaging with the premise of transformative potential.

Discussion

The three studies share a respective intention to grapple with existing institutional and structurally conditional aspects of sport and active recreation and the dilemmas this presents to active sociologists when researching various cultural fields. Whether there is an emancipatory outcome in the different examples presented here is debatable though there is certainly a feeling of the possibility for change and hence, the engagement with a notion of transformative potential. Boog states that 'To emancipate means to free oneself from restraint, control or the power of someone else', acknowledging that it applies to the collective as well as the individual.[47] The first study sees direct action from groups of people organizing safe spaces in which to enjoy their recreational activity free from the prejudice and discrimination faced in many mainstream football teams/leagues. As such, it appears as emancipatory and potentially transformative. Gay- and lesbian-identified football here is both a constituent within and an alternative to heteronormative sporting practices. Parameters of inclusion are conditional and contestable and can evidently be imposed from within the alternative community itself. Emphasis is placed on actors within this community to resist the heteronormativities of mainstream football culture whilst perceived desired outcomes of this resistance, for instance in overcoming exclusionary practices, are multilayered and complex. It is, therefore, misleading to state that gay- and lesbian-identified football clubs are transforming homophobic practices in sport in a non-problematic linear fashion.

The power dynamics in the second and third studies considered here are also complex. In the second study, the players within the team are white males who can be regarded, relatively, as a privileged demographic in relation to racialized and heteronormative location. However, the pervasiveness of capitalist economic and social relations informs, and often determines, the life-worlds for many of these working class men whose individual and collective habitus cuts off opportunities via a combination of actual and perceived constraints that limit potential for those involved.[48] Class position and the associated privileges remain significant in sport and intersect with other social factors; it seems a fairly obvious statement to make and yet arguably little research exists on the intersection of different factors in sport and recreation. When assessing advances, or otherwise, in 'diversity' in sport, this point remains pertinent and we would suggest that this requires concerted and consistent engagement with a critical lens onto these issues. Evidently, the second study presented here centralizes different aspects of leadership in sport by focusing on organizational detail within a specific club level and location. Although the study on gay- and lesbian-identified clubs can be regarded here as engaging with transformative potential on a broad macro level, the second study is a good example of assessing transformational potential and practice at a local (micro??) level. Of course, the two are complementary and a key argument proposed is that different 'readings' of sport practice need to be made in order to assess any claims about sport 'transforming lives'.

The third example used in the paper based on a study of masculinity and dance suggests that a more detailed analysis of what is meant by practices and processes of 'transforming' is required. This is twofold and concerns, first, a reticence to accept a simple linear transition from one state to another; that is 'to transform' in this instance transforming, for example, a dominant gender order and/or hegemonic or orthodox masculine practices.[49] Second is recognition that it is the actions of individual agents and how these are evident through embodied practice that is the central dynamic interface between structural features and negotiated processes. In that respect, we would argue it is possible to claim that 'transforming' can and does occur, but it is only meaningful and indeed, purposeful, in relation to the embodiment of body techniques. Embodied masculinities require further attention in research on sport and active recreation as a default position of hegemonic masculinity tends to be employed without sufficient analysis of configurations of masculinity.[50] As indicated above, a failure to analyse intersectional aspects of masculinity persists. In relation to the third study, racialized masculinities are clearly significant; in the second, classed masculinities and in the first, heteronormative masculinities. While these are not discrete or exclusive features, they demonstrate why unravelling context-specific sites are so valuable. When we look across the three studies as a whole, all of these aspects are interrelated and have different consequences for sport and active recreation. If we are to uncover how sport and active recreation needs to change to bring about increased social justice both within and without sport, then we need to pose detailed enough questions to account for different subject positions. Emphasis on participants' practices of embodiment contributes further to understanding the complexities of how people 'do sport', particularly when constructions and the associated pervasive and persistent stereotypes foreground certain social locations, such as black masculinity, 'working class' masculinity, gay and non-heterosexual and so on.

A key point across and within all three studies is the recognition and acknowledgement that social change occurs from within and often from the bottom up. Sociological analysis of data used here informs identification of potential and actual shifts and changes via consideration of discursive contexts through to realist positions. To suggest that sport and active recreation is potentially transformative evidently cannot be made via simplistic grand claims. In addition, given our references to emancipatory potential and a common theme of achieving greater social justice, we are mindful of the challenge of research evidence for scholars interested in this topic. Attention needs to be paid to the nature and type of activities being assessed; here it has been useful to draw on a 'dominant' theme such as football and to also include a focus on dance as commonly construed as a more 'female appropriate' activity. We thus emphasize the importance of the specific contexts of different activities for analysing elements of transformative potential. For the scope of this paper and in order to keep it manageable, we have had to omit methodological detail though arguably this can be the crux of transformative-based research. Indeed, emancipatory research agendas such as participatory action research are commonplace in seeking to effect (social) change and improve social justice, often on the premise that it is only through detailing the experiences of those affected by the 'power of sport' either oppressively and/or as potentially transformational that momentum for real change can be gained. Our previous reference to generating and maintaining a critical lens need not be limited by attempts to define and apply feminist standpoint, queer theory, intersectional analysis or a critical race theory perspective. The common underlying principle is to challenge sporting hegemonies. Our contribution is to highlight the value and significance of detailed empirical work for examining the complexities of marginalization and exclusionary practices that persist within sport and active recreation. We draw on these studies to add to conceptual debates that include theorizing on hegemony, discourse and normativities; the common theme is to address underlying messages that reproduce certain practices in sport, yet that also indicate change and some element of transformation.

Conclusion

This paper has sought to offer an outline of some of the different ways in which we can assess the transformative potential of sport and active recreation. This was done through the incorporation of three empirical studies, demonstrating how research on lived experience underpins our claims about the possibilities for challenging and changing prevalent social conditions. The first study on gay- and lesbian-identified football was used to highlight the macro heteronormative context of mainstream football, whereas the second study on local, recreational men's football team focused on the processes of dynamic leadership to bring about change in players' attitudes and behaviours. The third study on masculinity and dance emphasized how embodiment can more effectively inform our analysis of complex social relations. To some extent, all of the studies can be assessed as transformative, transformational and transforming, and all are significant in a quest to improve equity and social justice through sport in its broadest sense. The paper has argued that a critical lens on diversity should be sustained and, to some extent, reasserts claims about the dynamic relationship between structures and agents, however complex these may be in definition and practice.

> Structures, (. . .) are constituted by mutually sustaining cultural schemas and sets of resources that empower and constrain social action and tend to be reproduced by that action. (. . .) the same resourceful agency that sustains the reproduction of structures also makes possible their transformation.[51]

Notes

1. Mertens, 'Transformative Paradigm'.
2. Maguire, 'Challenging the Sports-Industrial Complex' and Jarvie, 'Sport, Social Change'.
3. Sugden, 'Critcial Left-Realism and Sport Interventions'.
4. Maguire, 'Challenging the Sports-Industrial Complex'.
5. Hargreaves, *Heroines of Sport.*
6. Caudwell, 'Queering the Field?'; Drury, 'It Seems Really Inclusive in Some Ways' and Pronger, 'Homosexuality in Sport'.
7. The Gay Footballers Supporters' Network.
8. Caudwell, 'Does Your Boyfriend Know You're Here?'.
9. Ibid. and Jones and MacCarthy, 'Mapping the Landscape of Gay Men's Football'.
10. Pronger, 'Homosexuality in Sport'.
11. Ibid.
12. Drury, 'It Seems Really Inclusive in Some Ways'.

13. Caudwell, 'Women Playing Football'; Drury, 'It Seems Really Inclusive in Some Ways' and Symons, *Gay Games.*
14. Drury, 'It Seems Really Inclusive in Some Ways'; Hargreaves, *Heroines of Sport*; and Wellard, *Sport, Masculinities and the Body.*
15. Messner, *Taking the Field* and Pronger, 'Homosexuality in Sport'.
16. Wellard, *Sport, Masculinities and the Body.*
17. Duggan, as cited in King, 'What's Queer About'.
18. Back, Crabbe, and Solomos, *Changing Face of Football.*
19. BBC, *Britain's Gay Footballers* and BBC, *Is Football Racist?*
20. Coghlan and Brannick, *Doing Action Research.*
21. Bhaskar, 'Societies', p. xvi.
22. Manicas, 'Realist Social Science'.
23. Bourdieu, *Sociology in Question*, 18.
24. Ledwith, *Community Development.*
25. Skeggs, 'Imagining Personhood Differently'.
26. Bass and Steidlmeier, 'Ethics, Character and Authentic'.
27. Wright Mills, *Sociological Imagination.*
28. Parker, 'Soccer, Servitude and Sub-Cultural Identity', 72.
29. Dempster, 'Having the Balls'.
30. Archer and Yamashita, 'Theorising Inner-City'; Hearn, 'Neglected Intersectionalities'; Anderson, *Inclusive Masculinities*; Bereswill and Neuber, 'Marginalised Masculinity, Precarisation'; and Connell and Messerschmidt, 'Hegemonic Masculinity'.
31. Alexander and Knowles, *Making Race Matter*; Carrington, *Race, Sport and Politics*; Back, 'The "White Negro": Revisited'; and Hooks, *We Real Cool.*
32. Bereswill and Neuber, 'Marginalised Masculinity, Precarisation', 83.
33. Anderson, *Inclusive Masculinities.*
34. Messerschmidt, 'Engendering Gendered Knowledge'.
35. Hearn, 'Neglected Intersectionalities' and Watson and Scraton, 'Leisure Studies and Intersectionality'.
36. Crossley, 'Researching Embodiment'.
37. Gard, 'When a Boy's Gotta Dance' and Risner, 'Rehearsing Masculinity'.
38. Anderson, *Inclusive Masculinities.*
39. Coalter, *Wider Social Role.*
40. Archer and Yamashita, 'Theorising Inner-City Masculinities' and Bereswill and Neuber, 'Marginalised Masculinity, Precarisation'.
41. Crossley, 'Researching Embodiment'.
42. Hooks, *We Real Cool.*
43. Anderson, *Inclusive Masculinities.*
44. Archer and Yamashita, 'Theorising Inner-City Masculinities' and Gard, 'When a Boy's Gotta Dance'.
45. Anderson, *Inclusive Masculinities.*
46. Carrington, *Race, Sport and Politics.*
47. Boog, 'Emancipatory Character of Action', 427.
48. Skeggs, 'Imagining Personhood Differently'.
49. Crossley, 'Researching Embodiment'; and Connell and Messerschmidt, 'Hegemonic Masculinity'.
50. Ibid.
51. Sewell, 'Theory of Structure', 27.

References

Alexander, Claire, and Caroline Knowles. *Making Race Matter: Bodies, Space and Identity*. Basingstoke: Palgrave Macmillan, 2005.

Anderson, Eric. *Inclusive Masculinities: The Changing Nature of Masculinities*. Oxon: Routledge, 2009.

Archer, Louise, and Hiromi Yamashita. 'Theorising Inner-City Masculinities: "Race", Class, Gender and Education'. *Gender and Education* 15, no. 2 (2003): 115–32.

Back, Les. 'The "White Negro" Revisited: Race and Masculinities in South London'. In *Dislocating Masculinity: Comparative Ethnographies*, ed. Andrea Cornwall and Nancy Lindisfarne, 172–83. London: Routledge, 1994.

Back, Les, Tim Crabbe, and John Solomos. *The Changing Face of Football: Racism, Identity and Multiculture in the English Game*. Oxford: Berg, 2001.

Bass, Bernard, and Paul Steidlmeier. 'Ethics, Character and Authentic Transformational Leadership', http://cls.binghamton.edu/BassSteid.html (accessed September 24, 1998).

BBC (British Broadcasting Corporation). *Britain's Gay Footballers*. VHS. London: BBC 3, 2012.

BBC (British Broadcasting Corporation). *Is Football Racist?* VHS. London: BBC 3, 2012.

Bereswill, Mechthild, and Anke Neuber. 'Marginalised Masculinity, Precarisation and the Gender Order'. In *Framing Intersectionality: Debates on a Multi-faceted Concept in Gender Studies*, ed. Helma Lutz, Maria Teresa Herrera Vivar, and Linda Supik, 69–88. Farnham: Ashgate, 2011.

Bhaskar, Roy. 'Societies'. In *Critical Realism: Essential Readings*, ed. Margaret Archer, Roy Bhaskar, Andrew Collier, Tony Lawson, and Alan Norrie, 206–57. London: Routledge, 1998.

Boog, Benn. 'The Emancipatory Character of Action Research in History and the Present State of the Art'. *Journal of Community & Applied Social Psychology* 13 (2003): 426–38.

Bourdieu, Pierre. *Sociology in Question*. London: Sage, 1993.

Carrington, Ben. *Race, Sport and Politics: The Sporting Black Diaspora*. London: Sage, 2010.

Caudwell, Jayne. 'Women Playing Football at Clubs in England with Socio-Political Associations'. *Soccer and Society* 7, no. 4 (2006): 423–38.

Caudwell, Jayne. 'Queering the Field? The Complexities of Sexuality within a Lesbian-Identified Football Team in England'. *Gender, Place and Culture* 14, no. 2 (2007): 183–96.

Caudwell, Jayne. 'Does Your Boyfriend Know You're Here? The Spatiality of Homophobia in Men's Football Culture in the UK'. *Leisure Studies* 30, no. 2 (2011): 123–38.

Coalter, Fred. *A Wider Social Role for Sport: Who's Keeping the Score?* London: Routledge, 2007.

Coghlan, David, and Teresa Brannick. *Doing Action Research in Your Own Organisation.*, 2nd ed. London: Sage, 2005.

Connell, Raewyn, and James W. Messerschmidt. 'Hegemonic Masculinity: Rethinking the Concept'. *Gender and Society* 19, no. 6 (2005): 829–59.

Crossley, Nick. 'Researching Embodiment by Way of "Body Techniques"'. *The Sociological Review* 55 (2007): 80–94.

Dempster, Steve. 'Having the Balls, Having it All? Sport and Constructions of Undergraduate Laddishness'. *Gender and Education* 21, no. 5 (2009): 481–500.

Drury, Scarlet. '"It Seems Really Inclusive in Some Ways, But…Inclusive Just for People Who Identify as Lesbian": Discourses of Gender and Sexuality in a Lesbian Identified Football Club'. *Soccer & Society* 12, no. 3 (2011): 421–42.

Gard, Michael. 'When a Boy's Gotta Dance: New Masculinities, Old Pleasures'. *Sport, Education and Society* 13, no. 2 (2008): 181–93.

Gay Footballer Supporters' Network. http://gfsn.org.uk

Hargreaves, Jennifer. *Heroines of Sport: The Politics of Difference and Identity*. London: Routledge, 2000.

Hearn, Jeff. 'Neglected Intersectionalities in Studying Men: Age(ing), Virtuality, Transnationality'. In *Framing Intersectionality: Debates on a Multi-Faceted Concept in Gender Studies*, ed. Helma Lutz, Maria Teresa Herrera Vivar, and Linda Supik, 89–104. Surrey: Ashgate Publishing, 2011.

Hooks, Bell. *We Real Cool: Black Men and Masculinity*. London: Routledge, 2004.

Jarvie, Grant. 'Sport, Social Change and the Public Intellectual'. *International Review for the Sociology of Sport* 42, no. 4 (2007): 411–24.

Jones, Louisa, and Mac McCarthy. 'Mapping the Landscape of Gay Men's Football'. *Leisure Studies* 29, no. 2 (2010): 161–73.

King, Samantha, J. 'What's Queer About (Queer) Sport Sociology Now? A Review Essay'. *Sociology of Sport Journal* 25 (2008): 419–42.

Ledwith, Margaret. *Community Development: A Critical Approach*. Bristol: The Policy Press, 2005.

Maguire, Joseph. 'Challenging the Sports-Industrial Complex: Human Sciences, Advocacy and Service'. *European Physical Education Review* 10 (2004): 299–322.

Manicas, Peter. 'A Realist Social Science'. In *Critical Realism: Essential Readings*, ed. Margaret Archer, Roy Bhaskar, Andrew Collier, Tony Lawson, and Alan Norrie. London: Routledge, 1988.

Mertens, Donna M. 'Transformative Paradigm: Mixed Methods and Social Justice'. *Journal of Mixed Methods Research* 1 (2007): 212–25.

Messerschmidt, James W. 'Engendering Gendered Knowledge: Assessing the Academic Appropriation of Hegemonic Masculinity'. *Men and Masculinities* 15, no. 1 (2012): 56–76.

Messner, Michael A. *Taking the Field: Women, Men and Sports*. Minneapolis: University of Minnesota Press, 2002.

Parker, Andrew. 'Soccer, Servitude and Sub-Cultural Identity: Football Traineeship and Masculine Construction'. *Soccer and Society* 2, no. 1 (2010): 59–80.

Pronger, Brian. 'Homosexuality in Sport: Who's Winning?' In *Masculinities, Gender Relations, and Sport*, ed. Jim McKay, Michael A. Messner, and Donald Sabo, 222–44. London: Sage, 2000.

Risner, Doug. 'Rehearsing Masculinity: Challenging the "Boy Code" in Dance Education'. *Research in Dance Education* 8, no. 2 (2007): 139–53.

Sewell, William H., Jr. 'A Theory of Structure: Duality, Agency, and Transformation'. *American Journal of Sociology* 98, no. 1 (1992): 1–29.

Skeggs, Bev. 'Imagining Personhood Differently: Person Value and Autonomist Working-Class Value Practices'. *The Sociological Review* 59 (2011): 496–513.

Sugden, John. 'Critcial Left-Realism and Sport Interventions in Divided Societies'. *International Review for the Sociology of Sport* 45, no. 3 (2010): 258–72.

Symons, Caroline. *The Gay Games: A History*. London: Routledge, 2012.

Watson, Rebecca, and Sheila Scraton. 'Leisure Studies and Intersectionality'. *Leisure Studies* 32, no. 1 (2013): 35–48.

Wellard, Ian. *Sport, Masculinities and the Body*. London: Routledge, 2009.

Wright Mills, C. *The Sociological Imagination*. 40th Anniversary ed. Oxford: Oxford University Press, 1959.

The civilized skateboarder and the sports funding hegemony: a case study of alternative sport

Daniel Turner

Department of Communication, Marketing and Media, Robert Gordon University, Aberdeen, UK

This paper critically investigates public funding of alternative and niche sports. Based on research examining the funding of skateboarding in Scotland, the paper demonstrates that sports funding and policy decisions are based upon a hegemonic conceptualization of sport and its benefits which clashes directly with the typically referenced motivation for participation in alternative sports. Subsequently, an environment is created in which such sports are the victims of funding discrimination, leading to fundamental problems for providers and causing social exclusion among participants. The paper draws upon the work of Norbert Elias to argue that funding methods for sport represent a 'civilizing process' which is directly at odds with emerging, alternative sporting forms such as skateboarding and other lifestyle sports and, that as such, greater consideration for alternative funding strategies and conceptualizations of sport is required in future.

Introduction

In the last 30 years, a range of new sporting forms which are best characterized as 'alternative' have emerged into the mainstream. Activities such as skateboarding, surfing, snowboarding and BMX, carrying labels such as 'lifestyle sports', 'extreme' or 'whiz sports', share a commonality in that they, as Rinehart highlights: 'either ideologically or practically provide alternatives to mainstream sports and to mainstream sport values'.[1] However, as these activities have grown in popularity and visibility, they have increasingly come into contact with the governance structures and funding mechanisms which typically manage and support the more traditional sports such as football, rugby or tennis.[2] Increasingly, public funds, via agencies such as SportScotland or the Big Lottery Fund, are being channelled into these lifestyle sports, despite there being a lack of understanding regarding the nature of such sports and their potential for contribution to achieving the goals of such organizations.[3] Drawing upon research examining the case of skateboarding provision in Scotland, this paper will develop an understanding of this issue, using an analysis centred around the figurational sociology of Nobert Elias, and in particular his theory of the civilizing process.[4] It will be demonstrated that, while lifestyle sports can make a contribution to achieving the goals of agencies interested in sports development objectives, the emergence of a hegemonic funding strategy which conflicts with the essence of such sports means the potency of this impact is restricted. The paper concludes that the result of this funding hegemony has been the forced advancement of a 'civilizing process' within the lifestyle sports terrain and, as a result, a reduction in the effectiveness of sports development initiatives within the area.

Understanding lifestyle sports

Historically, the UK has a long history and tradition of participation in what could be termed 'adventurous' activities. The development of organizations such as the Alpine Club and other groups developed in the nation's public schools, as Holt highlights, was linked to notions of quiet patriotism and quintessentially British Establishment values.[5] However, the contemporary lifestyle sports movement focuses less on such traditional values and, increasingly, around alternative notions of lifestyle and identity.[6] Indeed, Beal characterizes participation in such sports as offering opportunities for the rejection of such traditional values and standards, as well as representing a route to escape the constraints of modern life.[7] Iain Borden views skateboarding in particular, as a space in which the individual can reject dominant models of adulthood and normative values of family and work.[8] This is reflected in a number of skateboarding histories which emphasize the significance of groups such as the Z-Boys from Dogtown, Santa Monica, which were integral in linking skateboarding to alternative cultural lifestyle movements similar in attitude and outlook to the punk movement, and in the academic literature which highlights a dominant view of skaters as seemingly 'noisy, antisocial and reckless' in the eyes of mainstream society. Such activities, and by extension their participants, therefore, come to be viewed as anti-establishment and outside the pale of mainstream society. They can be considered to be focused upon the pursuit of individual freedom, escape and self-expression, an image which, as several researchers have suggested, is deliberately encouraged, pursued and cultivated by the skating community itself as part of a wider reflexive project of the self. By positioning themselves outside the mainstream and deliberately engaging in risky behaviours, designed to expose the participant into encounters with risk, danger and injury such sports enable participants to express resistance towards the 'dehumanizing nature of modernity' and the restrictions of contemporary social life.[9]

From an Eliasian perspective, such activities are, therefore, easily categorized as 'mimetic experiences'.[10] In his seminal work 'The Civilizing Process', Elias argued that everyday life had been characterized by the removal of actions and behaviours considered distasteful from public life.[11] At the core of this process is the notion that an individual's emotions 'have been gradually flattened out and instinctual desires and pleasures have been increasingly sublimated and channelled into civilized forms of cultural activity'.[12] This process leaves individuals searching for opportunities for escape and self-expression via the so-called mimetic experiences.[13] Sports, with their capacity to elicit excitement, offer a counter balancing arousal of the emotions and a chance to resist these wider civilizing processes.[14] However, as has routinely been shown in a range of traditional sports, such as football, cricket or rugby, such activities are themselves prone to civilizing processes, becoming stale and sanitized as a result of the introduction of complex governance controls, rules and regulations and etiquette systems controlling 'uncivilized' behaviours.[15]

In addition to renegotiating the relationship between the individual and society and redefining links with traditional values and standards, lifestyle sports such as skateboarding are often also seen as a route for participants to develop an alternative model of engagement with sport in general.[16] Brooke's history of skateboarding highlights failed attempts to set up tournament-style events in the USA in the 1960s and 1970s, whilst Beal's work notes the subversion of such events in the late 1990s and early twenty-first century.[17] Both suggest a rejection of the typical values which underpin traditional sports: individual skill accumulation, displays of dominance over other athletes and a clear definition of success and attainment through scoring. With Beatto describing the skateboard as an 'instrument for aggressive, irreverent, spontaneous self-expression', it is clear that, for participants, skateboarding offers opportunities for mimetic experience not just in opposition to everyday life, but also contemporary forms of sporting participation.[18] However, as the analysis conducted here will demonstrate, as skateboarding and other lifestyle sports become incorporated into sports development funding and provision models, this mimetic status causes issues for those involved in their provision and management.

Research process

The analysis presented here is based on research centred around a large indoor skatepark in Scotland. The facility, constructed in 2004, represents the first purpose-built indoor skatepark in Scotland. Construction of the 23,500 square feet facility cost £1.4 million and was made possible by contributions from a diverse range of funding bodies such as SportScotland, the Big Lottery Fund and a variety of charitable bodies, such as the Robertson Trust. In addition, a range of strategic relationships were developed with local agencies such as both the Communities Department and Education Department of the local city council in order to maximize the impact of the facility and ensure a sustainable income stream to protect its long-term future. The research process involved a series of in-depth interviews with representatives of key stakeholders involved in the operation and funding of the facility. A total of 13 such interviews were conducted. In addition, a comprehensive documentary analysis was completed, examining all reports published by the skatepark management team and any relevant reports published by funding or operational partners. Over 300 such reports ranging from national policy documents and annual reports within the facility, through to unpublished minutes and notes from meetings and funding committees, were examined to gain insight into funding priorities, decision-making processes and institutional policies and attitudes towards skateboarding in general, and the skatepark specifically across the entire stakeholder network surrounding the skatepark. Finally, in order to reach skateboarders themselves, an online discussion was hosted via the Skateboard Scotland web forum, enabling skateboarders to offer commentary on skateparks and formalized skating provision in general, and the skatepark itself specifically.

By conducting this research with the skating community outside of the confines of a facility, it became possible to reach both users of the park and non-users, enabling greater understanding of the reasons why skaters chose to use, or not use, the facility. In addition, carrying out research online enabled easier engagement with the skater community given the non-skating status of the researcher. As Mann and Stewart highlight, such online research reduces the barriers between 'closed' subcultural groups and researchers who may not share the same identity, enabling the collection of otherwise unavailable data.[19] In the context of this research, a wide range of skaters contributed to the discussion, offering opinions on a wide range of issues from the case study facility, to motivations for skating, and ideas relating to the funding and provision of skateboarding in general.

Over a two-week period, over a dozen participants engaged with the discussion. They regularly responded to both the initial questions and follow-up points raised, even challenging and correcting assumptions and summaries posited by the researcher, providing a large number of constructive comments to underpin the final analysis. Overall, this approach enabled a complete understanding of the 'figuration' surrounding the facility and allowed the researcher to fully understand the complex interactions between the facility management, the users and the agencies funding and supporting it.[20]

Understanding sports provision

Since the end of the Second World War, government agencies in the UK have taken an increasing level of interest in the provision and funding of sporting activities. In the last

60 years, a clear trend towards increasing interventionism and a focus upon sports development agendas, centred upon tackling social issues, can be identified. During this period, sport has increasingly been viewed as having the power to deliver wider policy agendas in areas such as health, education and crime with sports funding being closely tied to attainment in these areas.[21] This trend towards instrumentality and a focus on positive 'externalities'[22] are epitomized by a desire for 'Active Citizenship' and a sporting landscape in which participants both accrue social capital for themselves, but also feed this back into society through becoming community leaders, volunteers and activists, returning their skills to their community and passing the accrued benefits to increasing numbers.[23]

Simultaneously, a great focus has been placed on funding and supporting sports in which the UK has opportunity to reap success at an international level, particularly through events such as the Olympic Games.[24] Through documents such as 'Sport: Raising the Game', government funding, mirroring approaches taken in countries such as Australia, is increasingly centred around such sports in order to generate national pride and produce inspirational role models who will provide motivation for youngsters to enter sport at the grassroots level and accrue the benefits identified above.[25]

These twin agendas have formed the basis of the classic sport development model which has underpinned British sport policy in recent years. As Hylton et al. outline, this model can be seen as a four-stage pyramid, beginning with 'foundation', moving to 'participation' through 'performance' and finally reaching 'excellence' (Figure 1).[26]

At the bottom of the pyramid, the 'foundation' stage is broadly centred upon basic levels of engagement with sport in which individuals may participate broadly in a range of activities and spaces. Moving on from this, at the 'participation' stage, particular sports become the focus of individual participation with time and effort being dedicated to engagement, most typically in the form of regular access to clubs or competition structures. A smaller number of these participants will then progress to the 'performance' stage, actively seeking to improve and enhance their skills via purposive training and interaction with relevant coaching structures and development pathways. Finally, in the case of the talented elite athlete, the 'excellence' stage sees engagement in competitive activity at the highest levels relevant to their chosen sport. As the participant progresses from stage to stage, their level of engagement and involvement in the sport increases, thereby moving from casual engagement, through to a mode of participation mirroring Stebbins' concept of 'serious leisure', in which participation could be viewed in the context of a 'leisure career' through to, in the case of the Olympian or elite level performer, the cultivation of an actual career as a sportsperson.[28]

However, as Turner highlights, despite demonstrating a desire for sport to deliver increasing returns in the form of active citizenship or elite level success, the state has also

Figure 1. Sports development pyramid.[27]

increasingly shown a desire to play a less prominent role in the direct delivery and provision of such activity.[29] Increasingly, sports policy within the UK has been directed via an 'arm's length principle'.[30] Control over funding and strategy increasingly resides with Non-Departmental Public Bodies (NDPB), such as SportScotland, who co-ordinate actions and allocate financial resources in-line with government priorities, but which do not actively manage the delivery at grassroots level. This movement is typical of a policy trend, identifiable over the last 40 years, but which reached its zenith under the New Labour administration, which has seen a shift in the state's focus from 'directing and controlling' to 'empowering and enabling'.[31] Under such a strategy, grassroots agencies, community groups, private organizations and a host of other groups assume responsibility for the management and delivery of sporting provision, accessing a wide range of resources from public funds via relevant NDPBs, to contributions from voluntary and private sector sources in what is best described as a 'mixed economy' provision model.[32]

These trends are clearly articulated in the funding models employed by 'arm's length' agencies empowered by governments to deliver sports development policies and agendas. In the context of this research, SportScotland, the national body charged with delivering strategic leadership for Scottish sport, openly reflects these agendas in its vision for the nation as a country where:

(1) Sport is more widely available for all
(2) Sporting talent is recognized and nurtured.
(3) Achieving and sustaining world-class performances in sport.

And in its argument that:

> Sport makes a unique contribution to Scottish society. It significantly improves the nation's health, it supports employment for tens of thousands and it helps the economy to flourish. Sport is intrinsic to Scotland's culture and sense of pride, making a positive impact on communities across the country ... Sport can lift the spirit of the nation, it can provide direction and purpose. It can develop leaders and it can teach lessons of endeavour, of winning and losing. Sport can build confidence and self-esteem, it can challenge and inspire, it can entertain us. Most of all, sport has a limitless capacity to provide endless hours of enjoyment and fun.[33]

In keeping with this vision, the agency's organizational structure is similarly focused. SportScotland centres its work around three key areas, each reflecting an aspect of the vision: Widening Opportunities, Developing Potential and Achieving Excellence (Figure 2).[34]

As with the sports development model, the three elements of the vision are interlinked, organizations seeking funding for their projects must demonstrate how they will first enable more individuals to take part in sport, then in turn how those individuals can

Figure 2.   SportScotland strategic priorities.

maximize their ability via engagement with coaching pathways and training programmes before finally producing elite-level athletes.

In addition to the influence of the sports development pyramid structure, it is clear that funding is also dependent on working within a mixed economy model, with a heavy influence placed on the development of partnerships via the following requirement:

> an element of partnership funding and/or contributions in kind from other sources commensurate with the reasonable ability of different kinds of applicants to obtain such support.[35]

As the interview data collected highlighted, this requirement of partnership working is designed to ensure any project receiving funding does not become dependent upon the state for support in the longer term. By requiring a mixed economy approach, the expectation is that the project becomes self-sustaining:

> You'll have a feel for it, is the project going to be a drain on resources? Is there going to be enough money going to be coming in from every direction to fund it? (SportScotland, Project Manager)

On the basis of the information above, a clear picture for state-led sports development emerges. Sport increasingly focuses around both the attainment of social objectives and the development of participants through competition structures aimed at elite level attainment. Sports are funded in a manner which places the responsibility for management and delivery upon grassroots agencies which are expected to work in partnership with a range of other agencies to ensure sustainable delivery. However, this approach is one which has significant implications for the funding of sports in general and alternative recreation forms such as skateboarding specifically.

Hegemonic funding models

For lifestyle sports such as skateboarding, the model outlined above is inherently problematic. In the context of the case study facility, attempts to emulate the classic sports development model are clearly evident with the park claiming to have three over-arching purposes (Figure 3).

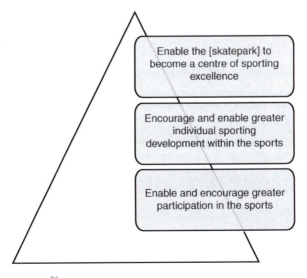

Enable the [skatepark] to become a centre of sporting excellence

Encourage and enable greater individual sporting development within the sports

Enable and encourage greater participation in the sports

Figure 3.   Skatepark aims.[36]

However, similar to the findings of L'Aoustet and Griffet in France, this vision, particularly attempts a widening access via specialist sessions aimed at beginners or special target groups, has been met with hostility from established skaters, who argue that the facility places: *far too much priority on suiting the younger skaters and beginners* (Participant 1,web forum data).[37]

In addition, the facility, in keeping with the aforementioned drive to use sport for social goals, has deliberately positioned itself as a community facility, targeting prominent social issues and attempting to bring at risk groups into the facility via social programming. The facility provides a range of diversionary activities including drop in clubs and graffiti classes, as well as acting as home to a range of community services including the office of the local Member of the Scottish Parliament (MSP) and local healthcare initiatives. However, once again, this clashes with the original user group, which adopts a territorial stance regarding the park and feels such activity is an invasion of its space:

> We have groups that are brought in, kids groups who are under observation and they're trouble and mouth and we've had the problem of them coming in and trying to take over ... the kids wonder what these "Neds' are doing in their skatepark and again you explain it's not just a skatepark and they're just as entitled to come in and get involved as you are ... that's been a challenge for the kids. 'What's these old folk doing in our skatepark? What's the Health Board doing here? Why's that MSP in our skatepark? Well it's not just a skatepark, it's a 21st century community facility. I have this fight with the skaters regularly". (Skatepark Operations Manager)

> why should skateparks have to accept the local scum because the council cant/wont provide activities for them? (Participant 2, web forum data)

Such clashes and conflicts appear inevitable given the typical view of lifestyle sports' participants, outlined at the outset of this paper, as being in opposition to such mainstream models of provision. As argued previously, skaters deliberately position themselves outside the typical structures and frames which govern social life.[38] As such, bringing the symbols and structures of those same frameworks into the facility, in the form of community officers and outreach programmes, will inevitably cause the difficulties outlined above. Furthermore, many of the skaters who participated in the online discussion underpinning this research indicated a desire to operate outside the structures which regulate the development and delivery of more traditional sports such as football:

> I used to play football for a team but the fact that I couldn't do my own thing wasn't for me so I sacked that. (Participant 3, web forum data)

> it's a lot more fun than just kicking a ball around all day, with football its really the same thing u do but with skateboarding you can learn something new everyday. (Participant 4, web forum data)

> skateboarding does offer experiences not found in team sports in that you basically do whatever you want to do with new rules, do what you want at your own pace. (Participant 5, web forum data)

As a result, this leads to conflict, as outlined above, in which skaters resist the introduction or targeted sports development initiatives such as beginner-only sessions or programmes aimed at reaching specified groups such as formal skaters.

However, facility management has little choice but to accept these conflicts within their facility if they wish to maintain sustainable funding schemes. As the facility's Operations Manager highlighted:

> We could trade to 65% but the 35% of our costs will always be dependent on grants and you can never be sure when your grant will finish, or be renewed, or be pulled. So it affects how you plan for the future ... we've had healthy eating, now we're on to physical activity. These

become key elements with the [Scottish] Exec and then they become key with funders and you're having to deal with their priorities.

This means that the facility is forced to live grant to grant, constantly trying to adapt to the requirements of funding bodies in order to ensure continued survival. In a mixed economy provision environment, such as the one outlined above, this should not necessarily cause concern for projects such as the case study facility. As Garrett's work highlights, one of the benefits of a mixed economy model is the plurality of funding options available to projects which can approach various public, private and third sector groups for support.[39] In addition, this plurality of provision should enable projects or participants who do not subscribe to a particular set of values or attitudes, in this case skateboarding, to ignore funding bodies which do subscribe to such approaches in favour of those that respond to their alternative approach.

However, as will now be examined, the reality of the mixed economy model is that it does not in fact enable a plurality of provision or opportunities to opt out of the types of funding priorities outlined above. Instead, as the data collected here highlight, a hegemonic model has emerged in which adherence to the priorities outlined above becomes the only way for projects such as the case study facility to survive.

When interviewed, the Project Manager allocated to the skatepark by SportScotland commented:

one of my perceptions is that once we fund, a lot more funders come on board. Now I have no evidence of that or proof of that, but it's the converse that is true. If we don't fund, then nobody else will fund.

This notion was supported by the other primary provider of public funding attached to the facility, the Big Lottery Fund. A Grant Officer argued that:

It tends to have a snowball effect as they can take the [funding] letter to others and say the Big Lottery is on board. We have lots of credibility, not just because we've got lots of money, but also because of how stringent we are and how closely we look at things... It's a bit like a standard tick that if the Lottery says it's good then it must have some credibility.

This line of thought was subsequently validated by one of the major charitable trusts supporting the skatepark which argued that public funding bodies such as the Big Lottery Fund legitimized projects in the eyes of other funding bodies. They argued that such partnerships would make it more likely that a project which aligned with those organizations would receive funding from other groups:

if we can't visit something and it's gone through, the Lottery put everyone through the wringer, so you know if they've been through that with the Lottery then it's a good project, they've passed every test. (Assessment Manager, Robertson Trust)

In addition to this, it was suggested that not only do charitable trusts and other funders look for the presence of these agencies before committing their own funding, but also they looked to these organizations for guidance as to *why* projects should be funded:

We would see them as the ones with the expertise. I mean we cover from the environment to animal welfare to drugs to education to care so we're not experts in sport by any means. So we would look to SportScotland and if they are there then we can see it is needed. (Assessment Manager, Robertson Trust)

Opinions such as this were found throughout the research process. The majority of the institutions contacted during the research process explicitly highlighted the importance of seeing major public funding bodies, such as SportScotland or the Big Lottery Fund, attached to projects when verifying its merits. In addition, almost all of the funding agencies demonstrated evidence that they too had assumed the priorities of those public bodies as their own, expecting recipients, such as the park examined here, to deliver the same outcomes in relation to sports development and social inclusion as those prioritized by publicly funded bodies, centred around, as Green suggests:

> a kind of checklist of preferences revolving around words and phrases like 'enjoyment', 'health', 'skills' and 'sport for all' ... commitments to particular ideologies, such as health promotion and sports performance.[40]

The sports funding *figuration*

From an Eliasian perspective, the situation outlined above and the conflicts it causes are both inevitable. Elias' theory of the 'civilizing process' argued that contemporary life is increasingly governed by an advanced threshold of repugnance which rendered distasteful behaviours and actions unacceptable within civilized society and led to their removal from everyday life.[41] Elias demonstrates this clearly in The Civilizing Process using accounts of court life in pre-revolutionary France and documents the courtization of the warrior classes within that society. This process draws the unruly warrior into dense 'figurations', interconnected networks of entwined individuals mutually dependent upon one another for success and advancement. As the warrior becomes ensnared in figurations, they become dependent on others to retain their position in the court and so transgression from the established rules of the figuration by engaging in uncivilized behaviours becomes impossible, due to the possibility of loss of position:

> The denser the web of interdependence becomes in which the individual is enmeshed with the advancing divisions of functions, the larger the social spaces over which this network extends and which become integrated into functional or institutional units – the more threatened is the social existence of the individual who gives way to spontaneous impulses and emotions, the greater is the social advantage of those able to moderate their affects and the more strongly is each individual constrained from an early age to take account of the effects of his or her own or other people's actions on a whole series of links in the social chain.[42]

In a sporting setting, these ideas have long been examined by academics, particularly colleagues and former students of Elias himself based at the Centre for the Sociology of Sport at Leicester University. As argued previously, numerous studies have identified civilizing processes within individual sports, charting the introduction of rules and development of codification systems, the growth of governing bodies and the introduction of affect controls, designed to remove unsavoury behaviours such as violent conduct. In each case, as Malcolm and Mennell's work highlights in particular, the individual sports became imbued with a bourgeois personality which reflected the middle- and upper-class values of the gentlemen patrons who possessed influence over governing bodies and similar institutions and, in turn, the development of the individual sports themselves.[43] Elias[44] argued that this was the inevitable result of a long-term civilizing process. The figuration surrounding a given point will, via what Elias termed a 'monopoly mechanism', inevitably start to resemble the world view of the more powerful and influential figures within the network:

> Within every large human network there are social hierarchies, some sectors which are more central than others. The functions of these central sections, for example, the higher co-ordinating functions, import steadier and stricter control not only because of their more central position and the large number of chains of action which cross in them; owing to the large number of actions in which depend on their incumbents, they carry greater social power.[45]

In the context examined here, the exact same processes can be seen, except rather than the codification of an individual sport to fit with a 'civilized' view of a particular group, it is evident that the funding mechanisms for sport have been standardized and imbued with the values of the dominant group (in this case, the state-funded agencies). As smaller funding agencies and community sports projects such as the case study examined here enter into the mixed economy funding figuration, it is inevitable that they will have to line up with the more dominant state-funded agencies, which possess both the majority of resources and influence within the figuration. For projects such as this skatepark, the choice is simple, accept the conflict which will inevitably exist between their user group and agencies such as SportScotland in return for securing funding or becomeing isolated from the broader funding network which has become imbued with the values of these dominant agencies. As Elias argued:

> if a noble ... lives at home in the provinces, he is free but without support, if he lives at Court, he is protected, but a slave.[46]

The result of this process, therefore, is a reified provision model which focuses broadly, across all agencies involved, in the funding of sport and upon the priorities and objectives of the state. Regardless of where funding originates, a hegemonic message of 'include, develop and achieve' is woven into the very fabric of sports provision as the 'civilized' truth, leaving projects with little choice but to adopt the same mantra even if it does not fit with their own operation or participants. For projects dealing with oppositional groups, such as participants in lifestyle sports, the choice is simple, accept the hegemonic position or wither on the vine without support. As will now be argued, this choice has significant implications for lifestyle sports such as skateboarding and those who participate in these activities.

The civilized skater

The primary implication of the emergence of the hegemonic funding environment (outlined above) for skateboarding has been to push the development of a 'civilizing process' within the sport, similar to that historically detailed in a range of other sporting forms. This can be noted when considering how participation in skateboarding differs within the formally managed environment of the skatepark in comparison with street skating in non-facilitized spaces. Typical accounts of motivations for involvement with extreme sports place an emphasis on 'edgework', deliberately encountering and navigating risks and danger as a key driver, underpinning the desire for participation.[47] In addition, as Haines et al highlight, participation is inherently linked to freedom of expression and experience.[48] Skaters are motivated by their ability to choose how to participate, when to participate and how that participation is structured. Being a skateboarder, for many, is not simply the act of being on the skateboard, actively participating, but also about being part of the culture surrounding the park, watching others and socializing.[49] As one interviewee explained, the culture is one of: *just come in and hang out and enjoy hanging out* (Skateboard Scotland Secretary).

However, as the data collected here evidence, participation in the formally managed skatepark is very different. The facilitization of skateboarding as a sporting activity has resulted in the development of 'civilized' behaviour patterns being imposed upon the users. The punk-styled participatory behaviours identified by a range of researchers exploring skateboarding, such as aggressive language and mannerisms, territorialism and a lack of interest, or indeed hostility, towards personal health and safety are, in the formal, managed skatepark, removed in order to satisfy other paying customers, insurance requirements and managerial imperatives related to maintaining a high-quality facility.[50] Skateboarders in the facilitized environment find themselves wearing helmets, queuing in line for a pay-per-use timed session and adopting a civilized behaviour code. Skateboarding as a sporting form has been brought in line with other sports and forced into the structure expected of other 'legitimate' sports, becoming 'civilized' in the process:

> by our very nature we have. to be fairly specific about what we ask for … we need to legitimate the sport. (Project Manager, SportScotland)

For the facility management, this is not necessarily a huge concern. The rules imposed upon the skaters are not considered to be hugely onerous. As the Operations Manager explained:

> you'll get it from, 'there's too many rules', which there aren't a lot of really, it's basically you wear your gear, pay to get in, don't abuse the place, each other and the staff.

However, while such opinions are understandable to most, within the culture of the park it is problematic:

> there were rules and regulations but no more than you would get in a community centre really, things about language and, no different really, nothing overtly in your face … and people may have issues with that because, particularly within skateboarding, you've got an anti-authority type of attitude that is strong within that … It comes down to anti-authority, free spirit thing that skateboarders have got, they don't like to be managed. (Skateboard Scotland Secretary)

This is then reflected in the complaints of the user group regarding the facility:

> there are always tons of rules to follow. Helmets suck. (Participant 6, web forum data)

> [the park] sucks for me cause the people its runned by and how its ran doesn't seem like its about skating. (Participant 7, web forum data)

> when you get there sure the people that work there were like "helmet, locker, go" and is a bit like a swimming pool. (Participant 8, web forum data)

All of these comments indicate a dislike for the 'civilized' form of skating taking place within the managed environment of the park with a final comment revealing a significant issue:

> the [skatepark] management should be more pro-active in finding out what people want from their facility, as it is surely in management's best interests to address the (apparently widespread) issues which are stopping people coming to the park. (Participant 9 web forum data)

As a result of the civilizing processes within skateboarding, driven by the need to fit in with the hegemonic funding environment detailed above, skaters are actually choosing to leave the facility rather than skate within its confines. In line with findings of similar studies elsewhere, some of the core target market of the facility are leaving the park and falling out of the reach of the facility management and its partners.[51]

As the Operations Manager admitted:

> There's always an issue though where you lose some of the older ones who don't want to be told what to do or what to wear. Don't want to wear safety gear, don't want to obey rules. You lose them … we're probably working with a younger age group now than before too. Our group is now aged six to eleven predominantly.

Instead of enabling participation, in many ways the provision of a skatepark has damaged the participation opportunities for skaters as a result of the practices and procedures forced onto the park by its partners. Or, as one interviewee acknowledged:

> So the very nature of the new build, all that has come with that, has ironically, had the effect of reducing the sustainability of the facility … there is a curious contradiction, the very anarchistic origins of some dangerous sports make them very attractive and yet we, to make

them sustainable, compromise some of these origins as we bring them into the mainstream. (Director of Leisure and Arts, Dundee City Council)

Concluding comments

From a basic analysis, facilities such as the chosen case study appear to be highly successful. It has a high rate of use and attracts a wide range of visitors. Funding and delivery partners report that they are happy with the work impact that the facility has upon the local area and the park has become a central part of its local community. Since its opening, the facility has grown to offer more services, facilities and events for its users. In many ways, the park is the very epitome of the type of successful project funding agencies, such as SportScotland, hope to encourage and the park goes a long way to validating the increasingly prevalent notion that activities such as skateboarding *can* contribute to the attainment of both 'sports development' and 'development through sport'.[52]

However, the evidence presented here suggests that great care must be taken to ensure that such projects are carefully managed to try and sidestep any negative consequences of a broad civilizing process. As such, it is argued that the reified structures for funding and provision detailed above must be continually unpacked, assessed and examined from a multitude of angles if the outcomes outlined in this paper are to be avoided in future and, moreover, the true potential of these projects is to be uncovered and realized. As part of this process, it is essential that consideration is given as to how to fund and support projects dealing with the emerging lifestyle sports terrain with an acceptance of the likelihood that such provision models may have to differ from that of traditional sports if they are to be successful. However, one final comment from a key interviewee for this study suggests this is unlikely:

> It's more likely though we'll say that "well, everyone else does it this way, why can't the skateboarding community follow the same path?" (Facility Development Project Management, SportScotland)

As such, it is the final conclusion of this study that whilst the current funding hegemony continues to exist without alternative, then lifestyle sports in general, and skateboarding in particular, are in danger of losing the mimetic properties which make them so attractive to participants in the first instance. While activities such as skateboarding and projects such as the case study examined here offer potential to deliver merit and offer social value, forcing conformity with a traditional conceptualization of sport and sporting provision upon these activities runs the risk of creating a form of what Putnam terms 'civic broccoli', an activity which is 'good for you but unappealing'.[53]

Notes

1. Tomlinson et al., *Lifestyle Sports and National Sports*; Wheaton, *Understanding Lifestyle Sports*; Guttmann, *Being Extreme*; Midol, *Cultural Dissents* and Rinehart, *Emerging Arriving Sport*, 506.
2. Gilchrist and Wheaton, 'Lifestyle Sports, Public Policy'.
3. Tomlinson et al., *Lifestyle Sports and National Sports*.
4. Elias, *The Civilizing Process*.
5. Holt, *Sport and the British*.
6. Wheaton, *Understanding Lifestyle Sports*.
7. Beal, 'Disqualifying the Official'.
8. Borden, 'Speaking the City' and Borden, Skateboarding.
9. Lewis, 'Climbing Body' and Holyfield, 'Manufacturing Adventure', 5.
10. Elias and Dunning, *Quest for Excitement*.

11. Elias, *Civilising Process*.
12. Haywood et al., *Understanding Leisure*, 228.
13. Elias and Dunning, *Quest for Excitement*.
14. Mennell, *Norbert Elias: An Introduction* and Dunning, *Sport Matters*.
15. Dunning and Curry, 'Public Schools'; Malcolm, 'Cricket and Civilising Processes'; Dunning and Sheard, 'Bifurication of Rugby'; White, 'Rugby Union Football' and Elias and Dunning, 'Folk Football'.
16. Beal, 'Disqualifying the Official'.
17. Brooke, *Concrete Wave* and Beal, 'Disqualifying the Official'.
18. G. Beatto, 'When Skateboarding Shook the World'. *The Guardian*, August 24, 2001.
19. Mann and Stewart, *Internet Communication and Qualitative Research*.
20. G. Beatto, 'When Skateboarding Shook the World'. *The Guardian*, August 24, 2001.
21. Garrett, 'Response of Voluntary Sports Clubs' and Green, 'From "Sport for All"'.
22. Ravenscroft, *Recreation Planning and Development*.
23. Coalter, 'Public and Commercial Leisure Provision' and Putnam, *Bowling Alone*.
24. Houlihan, 'Sport National identity'.
25. Department of National Heritage, *Sport Raising the Game* and Oakley and Green, 'Still Playing the Game'.
26. Hylton, Bramham, and Jackson, *Sports Development*, 5.
27. Adapted from ibid.
28. Stebbins, 'Serious Leisure'.
29. Turner, 'Skate Conform or Die'.
30. See Oakley and Green, 'Still Playing the Game'.
31. Garrett, 'Response of Voluntary Sports Clubs'.
32. Ibid.
33. Oakley and Green, 'Still Playing the Game'; Green, 'From "Sport for All"'; SportScotland, *Annual Report* and SportScotland, *Sport 21*, 4.
34. SportScotland, *Sport 21*.
35. SportScotland, *Annual Report*, 6.
36. Adapted from 2006 Annual Report for facility.
37. L'Aoustet and Griffet, 'Experience of Teenagers'.
38. Borden, 'Speaking the City' and Freeman and Riordan, 'Locating Skateparks'.
39. Garrett, 'Response of Voluntary Sports Clubs'.
40. Green, 'From "Sport for All"', 656.
41. Van Krieken, 'Norbert Elias and Process Sociology' and Elias, *Civilising Process*.
42. Elias, *The Civilising Process*, 370.
43. Malcolm, 'Cricket and Civilising Processes' and Mennell, 'Contribution of Eric Dunning'.
44. Elias, *Civilising Process*.
45. Ibid., 268, 381.
46. Ibid., 396.
47. Brymer, 'Risk Taking in Extreme Sports'; Allman, Mittelstaedt, and Goldenberg, 'Exploring Motivations of BASE Jumpers'; Haines, Smith, and Baxter, 'Participation in the Risk Taking' and Laurendeau, 2008 in Brymer, 'Risk Taking Occupation of Skateboard', 211.
48. Haines, Smith, and Baxter, 'Participation in the Risk Taking'.
49. Jenson, Swords, and Jeffries, 'Accidental Youth Club'.
50. Weyland, *Answer is Never* and Wooley and Johns, 'Skateboarding'.
51. L'Aoustet and Griffet, 'Experience of Teenagers'; Chiu, 'Street and Park Skateboarding' and Jenson, Swords, and Jeffries, 'Accidental Youth Club'.
52. Gilchrist and Wheaton, 'Lifestyle Sports, Public Policy'; Dumas and Laforest, 'Skateparks as a Health Resource' and Coalter, *Wider Social Role for Sport*.
53. Putnam, *Bowling Alone*, 406.

References

Allman, T., R. Mittelstaedt, and M. Goldenberg. 'Exploring the Motivations of BASE Jumpers: Extreme Sports Enthusiasts'. *Journal of Sport and Tourism* 14 (2009): 29–247.
Beal, B. 'Disqualifying the Official: An Exploration of Social Resistance Through the Subculture of Skateboarding'. In *Contemporary Issues in Sociology of Sport*, eds. A. Yiannakis and M. Melnick, 47–57. Champaign, IL: Human Kinetics, 2001.

Borden, I. *Skateboarding: Space and the City, Architecture and the Body*. Berg, 2001.
Borden, I. 'Speaking the City: Skateboarding, Subculture and Recompositions of the Urban Realm'. *Research in Urban Sociology* 5 (2000): 35–154.
Brooke, M. *The Concrete Wave: The History of Skateboarding*. Toronto, ON: Warwick Press, 2001.
Brymer, E. 'Risk Taking in Extreme Sports: A Phenomenological Perspective'. *Annals of Leisure Research* 13 (2011): 18–238.
Chiu, C. 'Street and Park Skateboarding in New York City Public Space'. *Space and Culture* 12 (2009): 25–42.
Coalter, F. 'Public and Commercial Leisure Provision: Active Citizens and Passive Consumers?' *Leisure Studies* 19 (2000): 163–81.
Coalter, F. *A Wider Social Role for Sport: Who's Keeping the Score*. London: Routledge, 2007.
Department of National Heritage. *Sport Raising the Game*. London: Department of National Heritage, 1995.
Dumas, A., and S. Laforest. 'Skateparks as a Health Resource: Are They as Dangerous as They Look?' *Leisure Studies* 28 (2009): 19–34.
Dunning, E. *Sport Matters: Sociological Studies of Sport, Violence and Civilisation*. London: Routledge, 1999.
Dunning, E., and G. Curry. 'Public Schools, Status Rivalry and the Development of Football'. In *Sport Histories: Figurational Studies of the Development of Modern Sports*, eds. E. Dunning, D. Malcolm, and I. Waddington, 31–52. London: Routledge, 2004.
Dunning, E., and K. Sheard. 'The Bifurcation of Rugby Union and Rugby League'. *International Review of Sport Sociology* 11 (1976): 31–72.
Elias, N. *The Civilising Process*. Oxford: Blackwell, 2000 [1939].
Elias, N., and E. Dunning. 'Folk Football in Medieval and Early Modern Britain'. In *The Sociology of Sport: A Selection of Readings*, ed. E. Dunning, 116–32. London: Frank Cass, 1971.
Elias, N., and E. Dunning. *The Quest for Excitement: Sport and Leisure in the Civilizing Process*. Oxford: Blackwell, 1986.
Freeman, C., and T. Riordan. 'Locating Skateparks: The Planner's Dilemma'. *Planning, Practice and Research* 17 (2002): 297–316.
Garrett, R. 'The Response of Voluntary Sports Clubs to SportEngland's Lottery Funding: Cases of Compliance, Change and Resistance'. *Managing Leisure* 9 (2004): 13–29.
Gilchrist, P., and B. Wheaton. 'Lifestyle Sports, Public Policy and Youth Engagement: Examining the Emergence of Parkour'. *International Journal of Sport Policy and Politics* 3 (2011): 109–31.
Green, M. 'From "Sport for All" to Not About "Sport" at All?: Interrogating Sport Policy Interventions in the United Kingdom'. *European Sport Management Quarterly* 6 (2006): 217–38.
Guttman, B. *Being Extreme: Thrills and Dangers in the World of High Risk Sports*. New York: Citadel Press, 2002.
Haines, C., T. Smith, and M. Baxter. 'Participation in the Risk Taking Occupation of Skateboard'. *Journal of Occupational Science* 17 (2010): 239–45.
Haywood, L., F. Kew, P. Bramham, J. Spink, J. Cappenhurst, and I. Henry. *Understanding Leisure*. Cheltenham: Stanley Thornes, 1995.
Holt, R. *Sport and the British: A Modern History*. Oxford: Clarendon Press, 1993.
Holyfield, L. 'Manufacturing Adventure: The Buying and Selling of Emotions'. *Journal of Contemporary Ethnography* 28 (1999): 3–32.
Houlihan, B. 'Sport, National Identity and Public Policy'. *Nations and Nationalism* 13 (1997): 113–37.
Hylton, K., P. Bramham, and D. Jackson. *Sports Development: Policy, Process and Practice*. London: Routledge, 2002.
Jenson, A., J. Swords, and M. Jeffries. 'The Accidental Youth Club: Skateboarding in Newcastle-Gateshead'. *Journal of Urban Design* 17 (2012): 371–88.
L'Aoustet, O., and J. Griffet. 'The Experience of Teenagers at Marseille's Skatepark: Emergence and Evaluation of an Urban Sports Site'. *Cities* 18 (2001): 413–8.
Lewis, N. 'The Climbing Body, Nature and the Experience of Modernity'. *Body and Society* 6 (2000): 58–80.
Malcolm, D. 'Cricket and Civilizing Processes'. *International Review for the Sociology of Sport* 37 (2002): 37–57.

Mann, C., and F. Stewart. *Internet Communication and Qualitative Research: A Handbook for Researching Online*. London: Sage, 2000.

Mennell, S. 'The Contribution of Eric Dunning to the Sociology of Sport: The Foundations'. *Sport in Society* 9 (2006): 514–32.

Mennell, S. *Norbert Elias: An Introduction*. Dublin: University College Dublin, 1989.

Midol, N. 'Cultural Dissents and Technical Innovations in the "Whiz" Sports'. *International Review for the Sociology of Sport* 28 (1993): 23–32.

Oakley, B., and M. Green. 'Still Playing the Game at Arm's Length? The Selective Re-investment in British Sport 1995–2000'. *Managing Leisure* 6 (2001): 74–94.

Putnam, R. *Bowling Alone: The Collapse and Revival of American Community*. New York: Simon and Schuster, 2000.

Ravenscroft, N. *Recreation Planning and Development*. Basingstoke: MacMillan, 1996.

Rinehart, R. 'Arriving Sport: Alternatives to Formal Sports'. In *Handbook of Sport Studies*, eds. J. Coakley and E. Dunning. London: Sage, 2000.

SportScotland. *Annual Report 1998/1999*. Edinburgh: SportScotland, 1999.

SportScotland. *Sport 21 2003–2007: The National Strategy for Sport*. Edinburgh: SportScotland, 2003.

Stebbins, R. 'Serious Leisure: A Conceptual Statement'. *The Pacific Sociological Review* 25 (1982): 251–72.

Tomlinson, A., N. Ravenscroft, B. Wheaton, and P. Gilchrist. *Lifestyle Sports and National Sports Policy: An Agenda for Research: Report to SportEngland*. Brighton: University of Brighton, 2005.

Turner, D. 'Skate Conform or Die'. In *The Role of Sports in the Formation of Personal Identities: Studies in Community Loyalties*, eds. J. Hughson, F. Skillen, and C. Palmer, 271–95. Lewiston: Edward Mellen Press, 2012.

Van Krieken, R. 'Norbert Elias and Process Sociology'. In *Handbook of Social Theory*, eds. G. Ritzer and B. Smart, 353–67. London: Sage, 2001.

Weyland, J. *The Answer is Never: A Skateboarder's History of the World*. London: Arrow Books, 2003.

Wheaton, B. *Understanding Lifestyle Sports: Consumption, Identity and Difference*. London: Routledge, 2004.

White, A. 'Rugby Union Football in England: Civilising Processes and the De-industrialisation of Amateurism'. In *Sport Histories: Figurational Studies of the Development of Modern Sport*, eds. E. Dunning, D. Malcolm, and I. Waddington. London: Routledge, 2004.

Wooley, H., and R. Johns. 'Skateboarding: The City as a Playground'. *Journal of Urban Design* 6 (2001): 211–30.

Sports clubs and civic inclusion: rethinking the poverty of association

Rod Dacombe

Department of Political Economy, King's College, London, UK

Most current scholarship agrees that low levels of civic participation in deprived neighbourhoods can, in part, be explained by the deficiencies of associational life in these areas. Significantly, most writers highlight the importance of neighbourhood effects – the characteristics of local areas – on participation in civic activity. Theoretically, this has been explained by the suggestion that deprived neighbourhoods lack the social structure to organize a vibrant associational life, suffering from high unemployment, an unstable population, poor community facilities and low levels of generalized trust. However, the role of sports clubs is neglected in much of the existing literature in this area. The position of sports clubs as a community resource, providing a hub for social networks, generating information and promoting trust, has long been acknowledged and yet this is rarely included in discussions about the dynamics of civic association in deprived areas. Instead, crude generalizations about the effects of poverty on social infrastructure, and the ability of people on low incomes to engage in group activity, abound in much of the existing research. This paper examines the relationship between theory and recent policy developments, raising three areas of uncertainty that need to be addressed if a coherent and effective programme for sports policy is to be implemented.

Introduction

Most recent writing on poverty tends to accept that it is a multidimensional problem.[1] In particular, a significant theme of contemporary theory emphasizes that material deficiencies, such as low incomes, educational attainment and long-term disengagement from the labour market, are reflected in the low levels of civic participation that occur in deprived areas.[2] In short, poverty can be understood, at least in part, through associational life. This is an insight that has gathered significant policy traction in recent years and has led to a reinvigoration of writing which follows the argument that the quality and density of social life maintained in deprived areas is a condition of poverty and contributes to the continued disadvantage of poor neighbourhoods.

Accordingly, discussion of the conditions of associational life in deprived areas tends to follow assumptions that highlight the importance of neighbourhood effects – the characteristics of local areas – on participation in civic life.[3] This line of thought holds that poor neighbourhoods are 'not only ecologically and economically different' from other areas but that they maintain unstable, weak social infrastructure and are ghettoized, their residents isolated from more stable and prosperous areas, with limited social connections outside of their locality.[4] This has the result of concentrating the effects of poverty within small, socially-isolated areas. These concentration effects compound the deprivation of the neighbourhood through obvious factors, such as the lack of connection

This paper was produced during an Early Career Fellowship funded by the Leverhulme Trust, award number ECF/2010/0393.

to sources of job information, but also by maintaining parochial social networks, which serve primarily to reinforce low expectations and disengagement with mainstream social life.

In the context of the UK, discussion of these developments in policy terms tends to be related to the understanding of poverty in terms of social exclusion.[5] Drawing on earlier conceptions of poverty as the inability to fully participate in society, this loose idea describes the processes of social disadvantage that can occur as a result of the multiple deprivations suffered by those in poverty.[6] Since the election of the first New Labour government in 1997, a wide variety of policy prescriptions have been produced which attempt to tackle the isolation of people in deprived areas from civic life in this context. Among these, attempts to promote participation in sport, both as a means of developing social efficacy and as part of a wider programme aimed at harnessing the benefits of volunteering, are among the most prominent.

Despite this, sports clubs have been largely neglected in scholarly discussion of civic participation and deprivation, and a number of critical issues remain in need of clarification. This paper focuses on this omission in the literature. It raises three related questions: (1) Can we assume there are particular benefits that participation in sport might provide people living in deprived areas? (2) How is participation in sports clubs supposed to encourage civic participation in poor neighbourhoods? (3) What are the particular features of participation in sports clubs which are distinct from other forms of voluntary activity? In raising these questions, the paper aims to highlight some of the key considerations that must be addressed in policy, if a coherent programme for the role played by sports clubs in tackling poverty and social exclusion is to be presented.

The paper begins with an outline of two theoretical perspectives on the relationship between civic participation and neighbourhood deprivation, highlighting the implications for sports clubs. The piece moves on to discuss the policy environment, establishing links between recent attempts to tackle social exclusion through sport and broader aspirations for social regeneration, which centre on promoting voluntary activity. From here, the paper provides an account of the relationship between theory and policy which raises a number of questions for policy-makers, highlighting the mismatch between the uncertainty over the mechanisms by which increased participation can alleviate poverty, and some of the assumptions underpinning recent policy. The primary focus of the discussion is on the UK, and the account of policy, in particular, is specific to this context. However, there are broader lessons to be drawn from the piece – in particular, it is hoped that the critical discussion of theory will have a wider resonance.

Understanding sport, poverty and civic participation

Scholarly discussion of the role of associations and social structure in determining the level of civic participation in a locality has undergone something of a theoretical renaissance since the 1990s. In his classic exploration of the structure of neighbourhood poverty, *The Truly Disadvantaged*, the sociologist William Julius Wilson influentially discussed poverty in terms of the associational life of the inhabitants of deprived neighbourhoods.[7] For Wilson, the disadvantage felt by the people who lived in poor areas could not be understood solely in monetary terms, but should be thought of in the context of the social connections maintained by those living in poverty, and their consequent effects on other aspects of social life.

This suggests that the kinds of social structure maintained in deprived neighbourhoods actually contribute to the disadvantage of the residents. In theoretical terms, in comparison with other areas, associational life in neighbourhoods exhibiting high levels of poverty is characterized as thin, with low levels of participation and a limited, uncoordinated infrastructure of voluntary organizations. Equally, where strong associations do exist, they tend to be parochial and inwardly-focused, providing few prospects for exit or the development of diverse social networks that reach outside the neighbourhood itself.

These insights are important because they tell us something about the *mechanisms* of poverty at a neighbourhood level. While there can be little doubt that when considering the organization of social life, deprived areas are qualitatively different from areas where people exist on higher incomes, numerous writers have claimed that the quality of civic participation in a particular area is closely connected with the broader functioning of social life.[8] Yet, it is precisely these dynamics of local participation which are little understood in both theoretical and policy terms. Critically, although considerable attention has been spent on examining the role that participation plays in shaping social life in deprived areas, independent of the structural conditions of poverty, there is surprisingly sparse consideration of the relationship between the two. One of the principal arguments made in this paper is that it is difficult to fully understand the effects of civic participation on poverty-stricken areas – and hence the efficacy of recent trends in government policy aimed at promoting participation – without an appreciation of these mechanisms.

Despite this, the structures of social life in deprived areas have been subject to sustained empirical and theoretical scrutiny. The particular structural features that characterize neighbourhood poverty – for example, transient populations, economic instability and poor community facilities – have long been identified and understood. From the middle of the last century, scholars have linked these features with the inability of local residents to exercise informal norms and sanctions over social life in their local areas.[9] More recent scholarship has refined these ideas, suggesting that the lack of social organization in deprived areas leaves residents struggling to arrive at solutions to collective action problems and providing a clearer focus on the strength and density of social networks maintained in the area as an important structural condition.[10]

Social disorganization and isolation

Theoretically, these insights into the social dynamics of neighbourhood poverty have crystallized into two related themes. Social disorganization theory suggests that the opportunities for civic participation in deprived localities are hampered by a weak social infrastructure, and a lack of stability and formal social structure (such as stable family units). This has been developed and extended in recent literature and now forms the starting point for the bulk of discussion about poverty and neighbourhood structure.[11] Social isolation, which is concerned with the reach of social networks maintained in a neighbourhood, has also grown in importance within the literature, and is present as a prominent theme in recent policy interventions. Together, these ideas provide an important conceptual tool kit, which helps to understand the many recent policy developments considered in this paper. This section considers these two ideas in turn, highlighting the implications for participation in sports clubs.

Social disorganization has become one of the most common theoretical positions to take in empirical exploration of the structural conditions of poverty and is certainly one of the most well established in the literature.[12] The idea assumes that deprived neighbourhoods not only maintain a limited social structure but also, significantly, suffer from deficiencies in the coordination of social activities. Put another way, although numerous studies have highlighted the presence of various forms of voluntary activity in areas experiencing high levels of poverty, social disorganization theory posits that this will make little difference to the civic lives of residents in practice – it is the differences in the organization of social structure, which can be detected between neighbourhoods that are responsible for the low levels of participation in deprived areas.[13] This means that neighbourhood poverty is characterized by weak local voluntary institutions, and people living in these areas tend to lack the skills and knowledge necessary for the generation of a vibrant social life. Opportunities to engage in civic action, such as participating in formal voluntary action, are hindered under these conditions, and the levels of civic participation are low.[14]

Logically, social disorganization theory suggests that any attempt to improve the civic lives of people in poverty should focus on developing the infrastructure which is maintained in deprived areas. Voluntary groups should be funded and provided with support, opportunities for participation should be publicized widely and the physical infrastructure of an area, such as community centres and playing fields, should be developed. Alongside this, the capacity of local people to undertake civic activity – their knowledge and skill in managing voluntary action – should also be developed. Essentially, the tenets of social disorganization theory suggest that associational life in deprived areas can be improved through investing in the capacity of civic organization.

Numerous critiques have been put forward that question some of the assumptions that underpin social disorganization theory.[15] Fundamentally, it is difficult to demonstrate a causal relationship between the differences in social structure and levels of civic participation that exist between localities. Although it would seem logical to assume that attempts to develop, say, a more formal means of recruiting volunteers in an area would result in higher levels of participation, it would take a careful analysis of the causal relationship between structural change, participation and the numerous other factors that might have an effect – such as residential stability, leisure time or income levels – to reach a solid conclusion. Furthermore, this kind of consideration happens only very rarely in policy terms. Although numerous attempts have been made to promote the development of infrastructure for sporting activities in deprived areas through capital building projects, funding for outreach programmes and sports provision in schools, there is little theoretical consideration given to the mechanisms by which these activities are supposed to develop civic participation more broadly.

Social isolation theory develops some of the main themes put forward as part of social disorganization theory, but it is less concerned with the order of social life than the density and extent of the social networks that are maintained in deprived areas. Here, the social connections maintained by people in deprived neighbourhoods serve to reinforce their disadvantage. There are two distinct elements to the literature on social isolation, each taking a different view of the nature of the problem. Conventionally, discussion of social isolation has been focused primarily at the individual level, highlighting the detrimental effects of minimal social connections on personal efficacy. Here, social isolation indicates an extreme condition of poverty characterized by the maintenance of very few, if any, social contacts (examples might include elderly people living alone), which are associated with long-term disengagement from the labour market, poor health and low incomes.[16]

However, ideas like this have also been applied at the neighbourhood or community level. Famously, the political scientist Robert Putnam examined the idea of social isolation through the use of a sporting metaphor when discussing the decline of civic participation in America.[17] For Putnam, the problems of declining civic participation were not to do with the level of activity (that is to say, the rate of participation in voluntary activity in a neighbourhood) or with the social infrastructure that supported it. Rather, the decline of civic life was to do with the character of social relations within and between communities. In his engaging metaphor, rather than bowling in leagues as part of a team, people spent their time isolated, pursuing the sport as an individual activity; although levels of participation remained high, it was a solitary pursuit.

Putnam's primary theoretical contribution, building on an extensive body of earlier literature, was to articulate an understanding of participation in terms of the social capital which was produced as a result of different forms of civic activity.[18] Social capital, a term that has now moved into mainstream usage in both policy and scholarly circles, remains a diffuse and much discussed idea. It rests on the assumption that there are external benefits produced from social relationships, which vary according to the timbre of the social connections maintained. In Putnam's terms, social capital refers to the 'features of social organisation, such as trust, norms, and networks, that can improve the efficiency of society by facilitating certain coordinated actions'.[19] Putnam distinguished between two main types of social capital: bridging social capital and bonding social capital. Bridging social capital was identified as being produced by social connections which are outward looking and encompass people from a broad social spectrum. Insofar as social capital is based in social networks, it fulfils useful functions in distributing information and providing links to social assets which lie outside of an individual's immediate social circle. Bonding social capital on the other hand, tends to be concentrated within homogeneous social groupings. Communities that display high levels of bonding social capital tend to be inward looking and parochial, with limited connections to the outside world.

Putnam notes that 'bonding social capital is good for undergirding specific reciprocity and mobilising solidarity' but is less useful in encouraging broader identities and reciprocity.[20] Although bonding social capital may create strong in-group loyalty, it may also create out-group antagonism and depress social aspirations.[21] In the context of discussing social capital and tolerance, Putnam notes that bonding social capital can reinforce social stratification.[22] Portes notes that group solidarity is at times fortified by a shared experience of hardship and opposition to mainstream society.[23] If an individual from a disenfranchised group experiences success in the broader community, group cohesion may be undermined because it is grounded on the belief that upward mobility is impossible or undesirable.[24] This may result in a downward levelling of norms across the downtrodden group that operates to keep its members in place.[25]

Both of these theoretical insights have significant implications for policy interventions aimed at tackling poverty. As Coalter points out, changes in the understanding of the nature of social problems have resulted in policy interventions taking 'an increased emphasis on social processes, relationships and the organisational capacities of communities'.[26] This policy focus on social structure as a condition of poverty has grown alongside an increasing realization that the connections people maintain are very closely related to their ability to participate fully in civic life. A broad consensus has formed around the notion that the promotion of association is an important policy goal because it can provide social resources and norms that facilitate beneficial social outcomes for those experiencing poverty. This assumption provides the backbone of the recent normative concern with participation as a prerequisite for a healthy social life and builds on the prescriptions of earlier theorists in prompting both institutional reform and changes in individual behaviour in order to harness social change.

Both social disorganization and social isolation theory provide potential avenues for critical thought about the success of sports policy in poverty alleviation. If policy-makers are determined to deal with low levels of civic participation through the promotion of sports clubs, then some appreciation of the relationship between the structural conditions of deprived neighbourhoods and participation is important if such initiatives are to be effective. In particular, the specific benefits for deprived communities of participation in sport (as opposed to other forms of voluntary activity) need to be articulated clearly, and an appreciation of the interplay between neighbourhood effects, participation and sports must be included in any analysis of these attempts to promote participation.

As it stands, it is clear that questions remain over the efficacy of recent policy. There has been little consideration of the specific merits of promoting participation in sport in spite of a general acceptance of the value of increasing levels of civic participation more generally. In particular, significant attention has been afforded over the past 15 years to the reconfiguration of sports infrastructure, with greater levels of national-level coordination and specific targets for the growth of participation. The following sections examine these trends in policy in more detail, highlighting the questions asked by the theory sketched previously in the text.

Sports and social exclusion

Increasingly, discussion of sports has been linked in scholarly literature and policy interventions with the now well-established discourse of social exclusion. This narrative has been adopted at the heart of government and informs much recent policy regarding participation in sport. The Social Exclusion Unit (based within the Home Office), created in 1997, took a remit to coordinate action on social exclusion across central government, with a particular focus on the role played by voluntary organizations, providing an institutional acceptance of the idea at the heart of government, and consideration of the issue is now a major concern of social policy.

As numerous commentators have noted, the idea of social exclusion is loose and difficult to pin down. Any attempt at definition serves to highlight the breadth of the term, but the implications for the theoretical discussion of neighbourhood poverty above are clear. For example, the Social Exclusion Unit suggests that the idea can be understood as deficiencies in 'social relationships; cultural and leisure activities; civic activities; basic services; financial circumstances and neighbourhood'.[27] Peter Mandelson, one of the most significant figures in government policy at the time, suggests that social exclusion 'is about more than poverty and unemployment. It is about being cut off from what the rest of us regard as normal life'.[28] Clearly, there is a concern with the relationship between place, social isolation and social structure.

Ruth Levitas identifies three distinct strands of social exclusionary discourse, in an attempt to explain the varied dynamics of thought regarding this issue.[29] The Redistributionist Discourse (RED) places importance on poverty as the primary cause of social exclusion and understands social exclusion as a multidimensional problem in contrast to more established understandings of poverty. The Moral Underclass Discourse (MUD) regards those experiencing social exclusion as an 'underclass', morally separate from mainstream society and dependent on state support. There is a further approach to understanding social exclusion, the Social Integrationist Discourse (SID), which holds exclusion as being related to disengagement from the labour market and paid employment.

Each of these understandings of social exclusion in some ways take oppositional views of the origins and symptoms of the problem. They all, however, place a premium on the social conditions surrounding poverty, and in each case, suggest that the effects of social exclusion are amplified by the local conditions that persist in areas exhibiting low levels of income. Graham Room suggests that viewing the problems of social exclusion in this way leads to a shift from policy interventions that are distributional, in the sense that they aim to tackle inequalities of income, towards relational policies, which focus on social participation and civic infrastructure.[30]

Policy prescriptions aimed at promoting participation in sport fit with narratives like this in a number of ways. The promotion of active participation in sports clubs is closely aligned with a realization of the value of voluntary action, which was first established as a policy goal under New Labour but which has continued under the coalition government elected in 2010 under the auspices of the 'Big Society'. This approach to understanding the role of voluntarism in policy has led to a devolution of responsibility for a wide range of public services away from the state and onto voluntary organizations, including sports clubs.

Sport, exclusion and social policy

As we have seen, sport has been largely neglected in theoretical discussion of the associational life of poor neighbourhoods, despite a growth of interest in issues related to civic participation and neighbourhood deprivation.[31] However, sport has been subject to a significant amount of *policy* attention in recent years. In particular, an emphasis on the potentially beneficial social effects of participation in sport on deprived areas has become prominent. Sport is an appealing prospect for policy interventions because it combines an emphasis on collective achievement with personal responsibility, echoing a broader ideological shift towards welfare conditionality which has characterized much of recent social policy in the UK.[32] It also provides a means of tackling the intractable problems of social exclusion in a way which cuts across established institutional boundaries between, say, different public agencies (such as health services and the police) or between central and local government. As Waring and Mason note, sport is being promoted in policy as not simply a means of encouraging healthy living, but as a pathway to full (active) citizenship.[33] This view of the transformative nature of sport has seen it placed prominently in attempts to tackle poverty and social exclusion, charged with a dual role of improving individual efficacy and wider social benefit.

This growth to prominence forms part of a broader attempt to reinvigorate voluntary action and needs to be understood in this context. The increasing attention on policy interventions based on participation in sport has come about alongside an ever-growing concern with promoting participation in voluntary activity more generally. This is important as sporting activities are held to have a distinct set of virtues, which mark them out as significant in tackling the problems of social exclusion, such as a lack of social connections and poor civic infrastructure.[34] Some of these are implicit within the reforms, but some have been outlined in detail as part of the significant institutional reconfigurations which have taken place over recent years.

Voluntary organizations have long been established as a significant presence in policy, but in recent years their position has grown, with successive governments viewing the voluntary sector as central to the success of their social programme. Indeed, various commentators have discussed both the emergence of the voluntary sector into the 'mainstream' of policy and as a core 'partner' in welfare delivery under New Labour, with continued attention under the coalition government.[35] Plans for the reform of the state's relationship with the voluntary sector had begun well before the election of the first New Labour government. A pre-election consultation document, 'Building the Future Together', outlined the new role of voluntary action within social policy.[36] This highlighted the social benefits of volunteering, suggesting that the voluntary sector was 'fundamental to a democratic, socially inclusive society' and emphasized the added value that independent voluntary action could bring to public service delivery. This is significant because it represents an early acceptance of the idea that voluntary organizations might have a wider value than simply acting as alternatives to state, or market-based service provision.

These ideas were carried through into policy, and it is possible to trace a number of high profile and influential policy reviews examining the state's relationship with the voluntary sector during this time which specifically articulated the value that voluntary action could bring to social policy. The Strategy Unit review, *Private Action, Public Benefit*, took in a wide range of issues related to voluntary action, including questions around the legal and regulatory framework, and governance within the voluntary sector.[37] Fundamentally though, it suggested that the aspiration for the state in its relations with the voluntary sector should be to enable 'the sector to become a more active partner with government'.[38] Likewise, the 2002 Cross-Cutting Review of relations with the voluntary sector (carried out by the Treasury) suggested that voluntary organizations can provide distinctive contributions to policy, thanks to their specialist skills/knowledge, ability to involve people directly in their work, independence, innovation, their lack of bureaucracy and flexibility and responsiveness.[39]

A later Treasury review, *Working Together, Better Together*, aimed to build on the 'significant steps [taken by the government] since 1997 to promote, enable and grow the third sector'.[40] It emphasized the virtues of voluntary organizations working in 'partnership' with the state, particularly at the local level, and outlined plans to strengthen the voluntary sector's role in local partnerships. This included funding of up to £90 million to promote the voluntary sector's role in public service partnerships along the themes of health and social care for older people; employment for people from ethnic minorities; correctional services; hostel provision for homeless people; support for parents and learning service for adults and integration for refugees and migrants.

Tied in with the Treasury review was the Home Office's adoption of two Public Service Agreements (PSAs), which were intended to provide concrete commitments to develop engagement in voluntary activity, with explicit reference to the role voluntary action could have in tackling social exclusion.[41] PSA 6 sought to increase participation in voluntary and community activities, particularly among those at risk of social exclusion. PSA 8 was more specific, referring to the government's commitment to increasing voluntary and community sector activity. It included a target to increase community participation by 5% over 5 years (2001–2006). The Home Office also adopted a broader aim around this time, articulated in Strategic Objective 5. Although not a firm commitment, this is intended to provide an overall guide to policy and working practices, including the aim that 'citizens, communities and the voluntary sector are more fully engaged in tackling social problems'.[42]

More recently, the 'Big Society' narrative articulated by the current coalition government has in many ways continued these themes, with Alcock identifying continuities in terms of the spirit and substance of policy.[43] For instance, the principle of an institutional presence at the heart of government with responsibility for voluntary action – introduced under New Labour as the Active Communities Directorate, and later the Office for the Third Sector – has continued (rebranded as the Office for Civil Society). In policy terms, the role of voluntary action has, if anything, been extended, with the potential for the transfer of public services to worker-owned cooperatives in recent policy underlining the emphasis on self-determination which characterizes recent reform.

Like wider engagement with the voluntary sector, the relationship between government and sport has also been subject to a significant period of 'modernization' over the past 20 years.[44] Previously, sport had been largely left alone by central government agencies, with leisure services remaining under local authority control and even governance of elite-level sport left to the voluntary sector. Fundamentally, sport was not a priority for policy-makers at the centre.[45] In recent years, however, central government has taken an increasing interest in sports policy, and since the election of the first New Labour government in 1997, it has taken a high profile on the policy agenda, and undergone wide-ranging reform.

A far-reaching reconfiguration of sports governance in 1997 led to the development of UK Sports Council (now UK Sport), a body whose primary function is the improvement of elite-level performance through the distribution of government funding and National Lottery grants. Alongside this, a Sports Council was created for each of the home nations, tasked with implementing government policy and, particularly, a mandate to tackle social exclusion through sport. In both cases, the centralization of policy responsibility resulted in a number of targets that explicitly outlined increases in participation as a policy aspiration. In 2004, for example, Sport England committed to an average minimum of '1% growth in participation annually with the objective of achieving at least 50% of the population playing sport by 2020'.[46] Contained within aims like this are aspirations for the involvement of sport in tackling social problems through greater levels of participation.[47]

Sport is seen as a valuable avenue for policy in this way because it has the ability to reinvigorate civic life in deprived areas.[48] By involving people in sport, deeper and more diverse reservoirs of social capital can be built, and the quality of social networks in poor areas improved. Fred Coalter frames this as a policy shift from 'developing sport in communities to developing communities *through* sport' [emphasis in original].[49] Similarly, Waring and Mason note the emergence of social capital in recent policy pronouncements, highlighting the presence of programmes specifically aimed at addressing sports in the government's neighbourhood renewal strategy.[50]

Particularly, Coalter highlights the expression of this theme in two, related, approaches to sports policy which are relevant, 'to seek to increase social/sports participation via geographically targeted programmes in socially deprived areas, and to emphasize the contribution which sports volunteering can make to "active citizenship"'.[51] In both cases, participation in sport is supposed to bring about a wide range of benefits to both individuals and communities.[52] Bloyce and Smith point out the centralizing tendencies in this agenda, noting that local agencies are 'expected to provide detailed data regarding the monitoring and evaluation of strategies to demonstrate the impact that their services are having on the achievement of desired *social* outcomes'.[53] Although much of the responsibility for the delivery of sports policy to tackle social exclusion was placed at the local level, an array of centralized targets coordinated the application of policy.

Sport England's 2008 report, *Shaping Places Through Sport*, perhaps represents this approach best, although it came soon after a number of other policy documents following similar principles. The notion that, locally, partnerships between the state, voluntary organizations and sports clubs can have a positive effect on deprived communities, as well as on individual health and efficacy, is clearly built on assumptions of the wider social value of participation in sport. These assumptions echo the earlier report of Policy Action Team 10 (PAT 10), which suggests that sports participation could have a beneficial effect on communities in four key areas: health, crime, employment and education.[54]

Clearly, we can see echoes of the wider reform of voluntary action in the discussion above. Although sport is a distinctive form of social activity, it is important not to view the changes in the way that sport is framed as a policy end in isolation. Alongside the specific refocusing of sport as a means of tackling social exclusion in deprived communities, successive governments have been concerned with a broader reform of community life, with a sustained and high-profile policy commitment to encourage participation in voluntary action. This raises a significant question: should the reform of sports policy be seen as just one aspect of this broader agenda or are there specific benefits to communities that can be gained through increasing sports participation which are distinct from other forms of voluntary participation? Just as importantly, can we assume that mechanisms through which participation in sport and social structure are related will function in a predictable way, given the uncertainty in theory?

This paper now explores these issues by raising three critical questions, each related to the mechanisms of participation which are exposed through the discussion of theory at the start of the piece and their implications for these trends in policy.

Can we assume there are particular benefits that participation in sport might provide people living in deprived areas?

In policy terms, the benefits that can be gained from promoting participation in sport are clear. There is an obvious logic in using sport as the vessel for a broader set of ambitions that are concerned with the framing of policy aspirations through the lens of social exclusion. Sport provides a relatively simple means for policy interventions that have clearly identifiable outcomes and provides a neat means of harnessing civic action in a way that promotes tangible benefits, such as health outcomes, alongside wider social goods. Sport also provides a popular setting for participation, with 12–14% of people in Britain being active members of sports clubs.[55]

This point is borne out through the literature. Scrambler highlights the social aspects of sport, providing opportunities to develop life skills.[56] In particular, this work highlights the idea that increased social skills can be derived from the lessons learned through playing sport and that these can translate into increased social participation and the engagement with new ideas and perspectives. This kind of assumption is echoed elsewhere, with the transformative nature of sports emphasized in empirical work and policy (see Watson et al., in this volume). Bloyce and Smith make this point well, suggesting that the recent policy understands sport as a malleable field of endeavour, which can have an effect on a wide range of 'non-sporting' activities.[57]

However, the dynamics of participation in sport are complex, and it is important to take any discussion of the benefits of participation critically. Most obviously, it cannot be guaranteed that a broad-based approach to encouraging participation in sport will actually reach people living in deprived neighbourhoods. There are significantly lower levels of regular participation in sport among people most at risk of social exclusion, and questions exist around the ability of sports clubs to engage the most disadvantaged social groups.[58] Equally, significant differences in the participation in sport also exist according to gender. Women, for example, are far less likely to take part in organized sporting activities than men. When they do, they tend to engage in more individualistic activities, rather than playing team sports.[59] Elsewhere, distinctions in the level and tone of participation have been detected according to ethnicity and sexuality, among other factors.[60]

This echoes the wider picture of participation in voluntary and civic activities.[61] In recent years, approximately 38% of adults in the UK have regularly taken part in voluntary activity, but this number is heavily weighted in favour of the well-to-do, with the most affluent groups of society far more likely to participate than the most disadvantaged.[62] Davis Smith identifies a strong correlation between socio-economic status and volunteering, with those in the highest income groups almost twice as likely to volunteer as those in the lowest.[63] Similarly, he finds that paid work seems to promote voluntary action, in that unemployed people are far less likely to volunteer. Data from the 2001 Census agree with these findings. In total, 57% of adults in England and Wales with annual household incomes of £75,000 or more participated in formal volunteering; nearly twice the proportion of those living in a household with an income of £10,000 or less.[64]

This final point raises significant questions for policy-makers regarding the benefits of sports policy. How can we be sure that the kinds of activity that are encouraged have a positive effect on social life in deprived areas? Particularly, policy design needs to have sympathy for the complexity and uncertainties of theory.

How is participation in sports clubs supposed to encourage civic participation in poor neighbourhoods?

Attempts at developing the sporting infrastructure of deprived areas are a clearly identifiable theme of recent policy in the UK. As we have seen, the success of attempts at encouraging participation in voluntary activity, and sports clubs in particular, is dependent on the wider social conditions of a neighbourhood. If, as theory suggests, deprived areas lack deep social structure, then an investment in the structures of voluntary activity makes sense as a policy aspiration. However, social disorganization theory also posits that a lack of infrastructure alone is not to blame for the low levels of participation in deprived areas. Rather, it is the lack of coordination of social life which is the issue here. Any attempt to promote social infrastructure without investing in the civic skill and capacity of an area would be uncertain. As Waring and Mason note, this is an area where little empirical work has been carried out, despite the assumptions of policy-makers.[65] Building on this theme, Coakley points to the lack of reliable evidence to support the assumption that investments in physical infrastructure would result in greater levels of participation.[66] Richardson and Mumford, in their account of the importance of social infrastructure in understanding social exclusion, highlight the importance of the wider dynamics of participation.[67]

All of this raises difficult questions over whether policy-makers can assume that social disorganization theory is correct in its assumptions of causality. Put another way, given the untidiness of theoretical assumptions over the mechanisms governing the relationship between social infrastructure and increased participation, there can be few guarantees that developing local sporting infrastructure will have the broader effects which are a desired policy outcome. A wide range of other factors might also be significant in determining the levels of local involvement in sport, and the coordination of social life, as well as the organization, should also be considered.

What are the particular features of participation in sports clubs which are distinct from other forms of voluntary activity?

If we are to accept that sport has a distinctive position within policy, which extends beyond the wider attempts to promote voluntary action, then it is important to think through some of the implications of the social isolation and disorganization which might be specifically applied to sport. Where these issues are considered in the existing literature, sports clubs tend to be treated much like other forms of voluntary association. In particular, the generation of social capital is widely assumed to be uniform, and few distinctions are made between the social externalities produced from sports participation and in volunteering more generally.

Participation in voluntary organizations enjoys a unique place in relation to social capital: they contribute to its generation and can also enjoy its benefits. According to David Wilson, 'the leading indicator – albeit not the only one – of social capital and civic engagement is membership of voluntary groups'.[68] Pattie et al. agree, identifying a statistical link between volunteering and civic participation. So we can see those who volunteer are likely to enjoy high levels of social capital.[69] Clearly then, consideration of the forms of social capital which might be developed through volunteering and through sport is needed in order to fully understand the potential benefits of sporting participation on the wider civic lives of people in deprived areas. At first glance, sport would appear to provide an ideal avenue for building greater reserves of social capital. The opportunities for coaching, playing, social activities and to engage in wider regional sports organization, all make grassroots sport a particularly 'clubbable' activity.

Once more, however, there is a complexity in the role that participating in sports can have in this context. Fred Coalter points out the propensity for sports to generate bonding social capital, referring to the historic role of sports clubs in providing a focus for group action for people who share similar backgrounds.[70] Essentially, the strong in-group bonding that can be generated by sports clubs can preclude social contact with people from outside the immediate group, as seen in other areas such as sexuality and ethnicity.[71] The lack of bridging social capital, in Putnam's conception, would be particularly troubling for theorists concerned with social exclusion. The downward levelling of norms that Putnam identified forms part of the construction of social life in deprived areas, according to social isolation theory. The lack of contact with diverse social resources and the parochial social networks maintained by deprived areas might, in this view, be reflected through participation in sports clubs.

The implications of this for understanding the effects of policy aimed at tackling social exclusion are clear. If the assumption that greater resources of social capital will have an effect on the levels of civic participation is to be believed, then policy-makers need to maintain a careful understanding of the kinds of social externalities which will be generated by participation in sport. Here, existing research is inconclusive, and significant questions over the outcomes of participation in sport remain unanswered. What forms of social capital might be accrued from participation in sport? Are all forms of sporting activity the same in this respect? Also, what are the mechanisms through which participation in sport affects other areas of social life? Without a full understanding of questions like these, the expectations of sport that have become prominent since the modernization of the sports policy agenda may not be met.

Conclusions: thinking through policy interventions

The questions I have raised in this paper are not intended to call into question the significance of participation in sport in improving the health and social life of many people. Despite some of the issues raised here, there is little doubt that sport can be vital in providing a focal point for community identity and in opening up opportunities to engage in voluntary participation. The questions I raise are to do with the uncertainty over the mechanisms through which participation and the broader conditions of neighbourhood poverty are related to one another. The distinct features of social structure which have been identified in the literature on neighbourhood poverty call some of the assumptions underpinning recent policy into question. Although there can be little argument with the aspiration of sports policy, the challenges raised by theory could provide an important means of focusing on the direction of policy interventions.

Just as significantly, the emergence of sport in a policy agenda concerned with tackling social exclusion needs to be understood within the context of a wider reframing of social policy. Of particular relevance has been the emergence of voluntary action in mainstream policy.[72] As has been noted elsewhere, the voluntary sector now provides a much fought-over territory between the main political parties and represents the current orthodoxy in social policy. Understanding the position of sports policy within this wider movement – and the changing landscape of state funding – is essential to gaining a full appreciation of the direction of recent policy. Too often, sport is marginalized from the discussion of policy, and political scientists in particular have displayed a tendency to treat the role of sport in the activities of government as something of an irrelevance.[73] The discussion in this paper provides a clear illustration that this kind of position is no longer tenable.

However, as much as theory has a role to play in questioning policy, a focus on the role of sports clubs in civic participation also has much to add to the ongoing discussion of associational life and its relationship to the dynamics of social exclusion. There are distinctive features about the role which sports clubs play which demand new ways of thinking about the theoretical underpinning to sports policy and which stretch established means of conceptualizing the social structure of deprived areas. The relationship between sport and social capital, usually assumed to be no different from other forms of voluntary activity, is in need of much greater exploration. The distinctive features of the kinds of social good generated through participation in sport are not well understood, and the particular relationship that exists between sports clubs, social infrastructure and the dynamics of neighbourhood poverty is absent in most theoretical discussion.

Policy-makers in the UK have demonstrated a keen commitment to the promotion of sport as a policy end, in great part on the basis of its ability to promote civic participation in deprived areas. As we have seen, however, this is a more complex picture that it may at first appear. This paper demonstrates that a close inspection of the existing theory related to participation and neighbourhood poverty raises a number of significant questions for policy, which remain unaddressed. In part, this is a function of the persistently difficult nature of social problems like these – empirical demonstration of neighbourhood effects remains a perennial problem for many social scientists. However, the benefits of this kind of discussion to the efficacy of policy interventions based on the promotion of sport, and the virtues of a theoretically grounded approach to policy, should make the value of a more forensic examination of these issues clearer.

Notes

1. Lister, *Poverty* and Alcock, *Understanding Poverty.*
2. Civic participation takes in a broad range of different activities. In the literature in this area, distinctions can be made between activities which are focused on affecting political decision-making, such as taking part in a protest, formally organized volunteering and informal associations. In each case, the benefits associated with participation are similar, and the theoretical conditions attached to deprived areas are the same.
3. Buck, 'Identifying Neighbourhood Effects on Social' and Small, *Villa Victoria.*
4. Wilson, *Truly Disadvantaged.*
5. Levitas, *Inclusive Society.*
6. See Townsend, *Poverty in the United Kingdom.*
7. Wilson, *Truly Disadvantaged.*
8. Richardson and Mumford, 'Community, Neighbourhood and Social Infrastructures'.
9. See, for example, Shaw and McKay, *Juvenile Delinquency in Urban Areas.*
10. Collins, *Sport and Social Inclusion.*

11. Small, *Villa Victoria.*
12. See ibid.
13. Examples include Whyte, *Street Corner Society* and Shaw and McKay, *Juvenile Delinquency in Urban Areas.*
14. See Patillo-McCoy, *Black Picket Fences* and Solt, 'Economic Inequality and Democratic Political'.
15. Small, *Villa Victoria.*
16. Shaw and McKay, *Juvenile Delinquency in Urban Areas.*
17. Putnam, *Bowling Alone.*
18. See Portes, 'Social Capital'.
19. Putnam, Leonardi and Nanetti, *Making Democracy Work.*
20. Putnam, *Bowling Alone*, 23.
21. Ibid.
22. Ibid., 358.
23. Portes, 'Social Capital', 17.
24. Ibid.
25. Ibid.
26. Coalter, 'Sports Clubs, Social Capital', 538.
27. Social Exclusion Unit, *Social Exclusion of Older People.*
28. Mandelson, *Labour's Next Steps.*
29. Levitas, *Inclusive Society.*
30. Room, *Beyond the Threshold.*
31. See Levitas, *Inclusive Society* and Alcock, 'Building the Big Society'.
32. Alcock, 'Building the Big Society'.
33. Waring and Mason, 'Opening Doors'.
34. Collins, *Sport and Social Inclusion.*
35. Kendall, 'Mainstreaming of the Voluntary Sector; Kendall, *Voluntary Sector*; Lewis, 'New Labour's Approach to the Voluntary' and Alcock, 'Building the Big Society'.
36. Labour Party, *Building the Future Together.*
37. Strategy Unit, *Public Action, Private Benefit.*
38. Ibid.
39. HM Treasury, *Cross-Cutting Review of the Voluntary.*
40. HM Treasury, *Working Together, Better Together.*
41. PSAs are undertakings by government agencies to reach specific targets in the nature and provision of public services. Each PSA target is underpinned by a *technical note*, which set out how the target is measured, how success is defined, the sources of the relevant data and any other relevant information such as geographic or demographic coverage.
42. Home Office, *Strategic Plan 2004–2008.*
43. Alcock, 'Building the Big Society'.
44. McDonald, 'Theorising Partnerships'.
45. Houlihan, *Sport, Policy and Politics.*
46. Sport England, *Framework for Sport in England*, 26.
47. Coalter, 'Sports Clubs, Social Capital'.
48. Ibid.
49. Ibid., 537.
50. Waring and Mason, 'Opening Doors'.
51. Coalter, *Wider Role for Sport*, 55.
52. See Jarvie, *Sport, Culture and Society.*
53. Bloyce and Smith, *Sport Policy and Development*, 52.
54. Policy Action Team 10, *Contribution of Sport and the Arts.*
55. Sport England, *Framework for Sport in England.*
56. Scrambler, *Sport and Society.*
57. Bloyce and Smith, *Sport Policy and Development.*
58. Waring and Mason, 'Opening Doors' and Jarvie, *Sport, Culture and Society.*
59. Sport England, *Shaping Places Through Sport.*
60. See Carrington and MacDonald, *'Race' Sport and British Society*; Drury, 'It Seems Really Inclusive'; Fletcher, 'All Yorkshiremen are from Yorkshire' and Fletcher, 'Aye, But It were Wasted on Thee'.

61. Wilson, 'Exploring the Limits of Public Participation' and Lowndes, Pratchett, and Stoker, 'Local Political Participation'.
62. Zimmeck, 'Government and Volunteering'.
63. Davis Smith, *National Survey of Volunteering*.
64. ONS, *General Report for the England*.
65. Waring and Mason, 'Opening Doors'.
66. Coakley, *Sport in Society*.
67. Richardson and Mumford, 'Community, Neighbourhood an Social Infrastructures'.
68. Wilson, 'Exploring the Limits of Public Participation', 255.
69. Pattie, Seyd, and Whiteley, 'Civic Attitudes and Engagement'.
70. Coalter, 'Sports Clubs, Social Capital'.
71. Carrington and MacDonald, *'Race', Sport and British Society*; Drury, 'It Seems Really Inclusive'; Fletcher, 'All Yorkshiremen are from Yorkshire' and Fletcher, 'Aye, But It were Wasted in Thee'.
72. Kendall, *Voluntary Sector*.
73. Jarvie, *Sport Culture and Society*.

References

Alcock, P. *Understanding Poverty*. London: Palgrave, 2006.
Alcock, P. 'Building the Big Society: A New Policy Environment for the Third Sector in England'. *Voluntary Sector Review* 1, no. 3 (2010): 379–89.
Bloyce, D., and A. Smith. *Sport Policy and Development*. London: Routledge, 2009.
Buck, N. 'Identifying Neighbourhood Effects on Social Exclusion'. *Urban Studies* 38, no. 12 (2001): 2251–75.
Carrington, B., and I. MacDonald. *'Race', Sport and British Society*. London: Routledge, 2001.
Coakley, J. *Sports in Society: Issues and Controversies*. Irwin: McGraw-Hill, 2006.
Coalter, F. 'Sports Clubs, Social Capital and Social Regeneration: "Ill-Defined Interventions with Hard to Follow Outcomes"'? *Sport in Society* 10, no. 4 (2007): 537–59.
Coalter, F. *A Wider Role for Sport: Who's Keeping the Score?* Abingdon: Routledge, 2007.
Collins, M. *Sport and Social Inclusion*. London: Routledge, 2002.
Davis Smith, J. *The 1997 National Survey of Volunteering*. London: Institute for Volunteering Research, 1998.
Drury, S. ''It Seems Really Inclusive in Some Ways, But … Inclusive Just for People Who Identify As Lesbian': Discourses of Gender and Sexuality in A Lesbian – Identified Football Club'. *Soccer and Society* 17, no. 3 (2011): 421–42.
Fletcher, T. '"All Yorkshiremen are from Yorkshire, But Some are More 'Yorkshire' than Others": British Asians and the Myths of Yorkshire Cricket'. *Sport in Society* 15, no. 2 (2012): 227–45.
Fletcher, T. '"Aye, But It were Wasted in Thee": Cricket, British Asians, Ethnic Identities, and the "Magical Recovery of Community"'. *Sociological Research Online* 16, no. 4 (2012). Also available online at http://www.socresonline.org.uk/16/4/5.html
HM Treasury. *Cross Cutting Review of the Voluntary Sector in Public Service Delivery*. London: HM Treasury, 2002.
HM Treasury. *Working Together, Better Together*. London: HM Treasury, 2004.
Home Office. *Strategic Plan 2004–2008*. London: Home Office, 2004.
Houlihan, B. *Sport, Policy and Politics: A Comparative Analysis*. London: Routledge, 1997.
Jarvie, G. *Sport, Culture and Society*, 2nd ed. London: Routledge, 2012.
Kendall, J. 'The Mainstreaming of the Voluntary Sector into Public Policy: Whys and Wherefores'. LSE, London: Centre for Civil Society Working Paper No. 2, 2000.
Kendall, J. *The Voluntary Sector*. London: Routledge, 2003.
Labour Party. *Building the Future Together: Labour's Policies for Partnership Between Government and the Voluntary Sector*. London: Labour Party, 1997.
Levitas, R. *The Inclusive Society?: Social Exclusion and New Labour*. London: Palgrave, 2005.
Lewis, J. 'New Labour's Approach to the Voluntary Sector: Independence and the Meaning of Partnership'. *Social Policy and Society* 4, no. 2 (2005): 121–31.
Lister, R. *Poverty*. Bristol: Policy Press, 2004.
Lowndes, V., L. Pratchett, and G. Stoker. 'Local Political Participation: The Impact of Rules-in-Use'. *Public Administration* 84, no. 3 (2006): 539–61.
Mandelson, P. *Labour's Next Steps: Tackling Social Exclusion*. London: Fabian Society, 1997.

McDonald, I. 'Theorising Partnerships: Governance, Communicative Action and Sport Policy'. *Journal of Social Policy* 34, no. 4 (2005): 579–600.

ONS. *General Report for eh England and Wales Census 2001*. London: ONS, 2004.

Patillo-McCoy, M. *Black Picket Fences: Privilege and Peril Among the Black Middle Class*. Chicago, IL: University of Chicago Press, 1999.

Pattie, C., P. Seyd, and P. Whiteley. 'Civic Attitudes and Engagement in Modern Britain'. *Parliamentary Affairs* 56, no. 4 (2003): 616–33.

Policy Action Team 10. *Report of the Policy Action Team 10: The Contribution of Sport and the Arts*. London: DCMS, 1999.

Portes, A. 'Social Capital: Its Origins and Applications in Modern Sociology'. *Annual Review of Sociology* 24 (1998): 1–24.

Putnam, R., R. Leonardi, and R. Nanetti. *Making Democracy Work: Civic Traditions in Modern Italy*. Princeton, NJ: Princeton University Press, 1994.

Putnam, R. *Bowling Alone: The Collapse and Revival of American Community*. London: Simon & Schuster Ltd, 2000.

Richardson, L., and K. Mumford. 'Community, Neighbourhood and Social Infrastructures'. In *Understanding Social Exclusion*, ed. J. Hills, J. Le Grand, and D. Piachaud. Oxford: Oxford University Press, 2002.

Room, G. *Beyond the Threshold: The Measurement and Analysis of Social Exclusion*. Bristol: The Policy Press, 1995.

Scrambler, G. *Sport and Society: History, Power and Culture*. Maidenhead: Open University Press, 2005.

Shaw, C., and H. McKay. *Juvenile Delinquency in Urban Areas*. Chicago, IL: University of Chicago Press, 1942.

Small, M. *Villa Victoria: The Transformation of Social Capital in a Boston Barrio*. Princeton, NJ: Princeton University Press, 2004.

Social Exclusion Unit. *Social Exclusion of Older People: Evidence from the First Wave of the English Longitudinal Study of Ageing*. London: ODPM, 2006.

Solt, F. 'Economic Inequality and Democratic Political Engagement'. *American Journal of Political Science* 52, no. 1 (2008): 48–60.

Sport England. *The Framework for Sport in England*. London: Sport England, 2004.

Sport England. *Shaping Places Through Sport*. London: Sport England, 2008.

Strategy Unit. *Public Action, Private Benefit: Charitable Statue*. London: HMSO, 2002.

Townsend, P. *Poverty in the United Kingdom*. Harmondsworth: Penguin, 1979.

Waring, A., and C. Mason. 'Opening Doors: Promoting Social Inclusion Through Increased Sports Opportunities'. *Sport in Society* 13, no. 3 (2010): 517–29.

Whyte, W. *Street Corner Society*. Chicago, IL: University of Chicago Press, 1946.

Wilson, D. 'Exploring the Limits of Public Participation in Local Government'. *Parliamentary Affairs* 52, no. 2 (1999): 246–59.

Wilson, W. *The Truly Disadvantaged: The Inner City, The Underclass and Public Policy*. Chicago, IL: University of Chicago Press, 1990.

Zimmeck, M. 'Government and Volunteering: Towards a History of Policy and Practice'. In *Volunteering and Society in the 21st Century*, ed. C. Rochester, A. E. Paine, and S. Howlett. Basingstoke: Palgrave Macmillan.

Sports-based intervention and the problem of youth offending: a diverse enough tool for a diverse society?

John Martyn Chamberlain

Department of Social Sciences, Loughborough University, Loughborough, UK

This paper discusses sports-based interventions (SBIs) and the problem of youth crime. It notes the positive role sport can play in changing to better the lives of young people. However, there is a lack of robust evidence to support the argument that participation in sporting activity can lead to a reduction in anti-social and offending behaviour. The paper discusses how through focusing on 'individual needs' and 'pathways to work', SBIs can become overly reductionist and mask broader structural class-, gender- and race-based inequalities that permeate through neoliberal nation-states and western criminal justice systems. It concludes that SBI advocates must seek to promote a less homogeneous idea of what an SBI is, as well as be more sensitive to the diverse needs of young people, particularly if they are to tackle the underlying structural inequalities that arguably create the social problem, that is youth crime in the first place.

Introduction

Over the last two decades, criminologists have noted that western youth justice systems increasingly seem to be emphasizing punishment over rehabilitation for even the most minor of first-time offence.[1] Against this background, this paper explores the use of sport-based intervention (SBI) from a critical criminological perspective to tackle the problem of youth crime and anti-social behaviour in the UK. There is a widespread support internationally from governments and key sporting bodies such as the International Olympics Committee for sporting programmes to tackle the problem of youth delinquency and crime.[2] SBIs for young offenders can involve a variety of sporting experiences, ranging from athletics and track and field to basketball, boxing, football and table tennis. In this paper, SBI is taken to cover sporting initiatives that are organized and run jointly by a mixture of criminal justice agencies, sporting professionals, charity organizations and community-based volunteers, and which share in common the aim of providing young people with a diversionary pathway away from an adult criminal career.

Critical criminology focuses attention on the role played by broader socio-structural factors, such as socio-economic and gender-based inequalities, rather than viewpoints which emphasize social bonds and socio-psychological developmental factors, in shaping how a person responds to being labelled a criminal and manages a 'spoiled identity'.[3] It is important to critically examine the available evidence in support of the argument that SBI can play a positive role in meeting the complex needs of young people and in doing so reduce or prevent offending behaviour. It is also necessary to examine whether SBIs sufficiently take into account that young people are not a homogeneous group, but rather come from a variety of differing social and cultural backgrounds. The critical criminological standpoint acknowledges the importance of paying attention to the class-, gender- and race-based inequalities which permeate through neoliberal nation-states and western criminal justice systems. Consequently, although focused on the UK context, the themes discussed in this paper are arguably common to many westernized criminal justice systems, a point that will be returned to as the following discussion of the problem of youth crime unfolds.

The problem of youth crime

Criminologists have long warned against treating young people as if they are an inherently deviant group responsible for many of the minor and not so minor day-to-day inconveniences and social ills that litter the everyday lives of the adult proportion of the population.[4] Self-report studies frequently show that a significant number of young people do engage in offending behaviour. One such study reported that:

> over half of males and almost a third of females aged between 14 and 25 admitted to committing criminal offences at some point in their lives.[5]

Offending behaviour amongst young people is arguably part and parcel of a normal and healthy transition into adulthood. A large number of young people engage in some sort of anti-social or criminal behaviour, albeit for a limited period of time and quite possibly without having any contact with criminal justice or youth services, before becoming law-abiding adults. This is because most commit non-violent, status-related crimes, such as underage smoking or drinking, and most do so once or only a few times. Nevertheless, a significant number of young people do commit serious offences, and what is more, repeat such behaviour on numerous occasions. Latest statistics from the UK released by the Youth Justice Board (YJB) show that there is a high level of criminal activity by young people that results in them coming into contact with the criminal justice system. The 2011/2012 YJB report figures reveal that there were 198,449 criminal offences committed by young people aged between 10 and 17 which resulted in conviction and disposal into either detention or a supervised community sentence. Sixty per cent of all offences were committed by young men aged between 15 and 17 years. The most common offence committed was theft and the handling of stolen goods (41,702). The other most common offences were violence against the person (38,744) and criminal damage (23,611).[6]

The reoffending rate for young offenders is officially measured by the Ministry of Justice as where someone who has received some form of criminal justice sanction (such as a conviction or a caution) subsequently goes on to commit another offence within a set time period. Worryingly, reoffending rates are high for young offenders. Known internationally as the recidivism rate, the reoffending rate after 1 year for youth offenders in the UK is 75% for offenders released from custody and 68% for young people on community sentences.[7] Given the statistics, it should come as no surprise to learn that it is conservatively estimated that youth crime and anti-social behaviour cost somewhere in the region of four billion pounds per year.[8]

The problem of youth crime and sport for social development

These statistics reinforce the point that there are a significant number of criminal offences being committed by young people which do warrant some form of formal punishment. No matter how much one would prefer to divert young people away from the criminal justice system, there will always be some individuals whose behaviour requires formal punishment, i.e. imprisonment. But it is equally important to introduce targeted rehabilitatory interventions to address offending behaviour and, in doing so, give young offenders the opportunity and support they need for positive change, as well as to introduce community-based programmes to try to divert young people away from anti-social and criminal activity before it starts. Some young people may well need to be imprisoned for a period of time, but the majority need to be diverted into community-based programmes which seek to provide essential skills, educational and work opportunities, positive role models and good peer relationships. Developing the self-esteem, life skills and support networks of the young people at risk of (re)offending, alongside promoting a sense of community belonging and social responsibility, must lie at the heart of youth work and youth criminal justice.[9]

Sport is often promoted as a gateway into a better life for young people who may otherwise have turned to a life of crime. Mutz and Baur argue that:

> sports activities are seen as a favourable, functional alternative to violent and aggressive behaviour. It is widely believed that physical activity allows a person to 'let off steam' without harming others. During sports, aggressive actions may only be displayed within a regulated context … the release of aggression can be achieved in a socially acceptable way.[10]

Faulkner and Taylor note that given that youth offenders often have few, if any, formal educational qualifications as well as poor self-esteem:

> sport provides an alternative to educational underachievement, blocked aspirations and low esteem.[11]

When young people have high self-esteem, they see themselves more positively and have more belief in their own abilities. For many young offenders, other areas of their life (school, home and work) may be difficult and limiting. Sport participation may allow them to demonstrate that they are talented and worthy of respect and support, not only to others but themselves too. Young offenders sometimes grow up in home environments where they have been the victim of psychological, physical and sexual abuse.[12] As a result, they frequently have no positive role models and authority figures to be able to look up to. In such circumstances, they often look to others for guidance and support. Unfortunately, for some the role models they look up to are not positive and law abiding. Some young people may feel that they have no choice but to turn to street gangs in order to satisfy their need for approval, belonging and self-worth.[13]

Professional sport can provide a range of positive role models and charismatic authority figures for young people, which can encourage participation and a sense of belonging. Indeed links have been made between the bonds of gang membership and the bonds that can be created in a sporting atmosphere:

> The key lies in the similarities of sport and gangs; both provide a sense of belonging, status and excitement. But, whilst sport also helps you develop control over your emotions and learn to respect certain boundaries, being in a gang can be much more destructive and sometimes even fatal.[14]

This brings to the foreground the possibility for using sport creatively as a 'hook' to encourage young people to get involved through designing sporting programmes which are attractive to them, in part, through replicating the sense of emotional belonging that gang membership can bring.

When dealing with anti-social and criminal behaviour amongst young people, SBIs are typically employed in one of two ways. First, they can be used as tools to aide offender rehabilitation, operating either in the prison environment prior to release, or as part of a community-based sentencing programme. Sport and physical activity play a big part in the lives of residents within youth secure units in the UK, which house some of the country's most serious young offenders.[15] The focus here is on using sport to develop young people's self-esteem and help them channel their energy constructively, while at the same time helping them to acquire team working, communication and life skills as part of a broader programme designed to tackle a range of underlying factors directly relevant to reoffending behaviour. Meek and Lewis discuss the use of sport in the UK youth justice system as a way of engaging young men in identifying and meeting their resettlement needs in the transition from prison custody to the community.[16] In doing so, they address a range of behavioural and mental health problems, drug and alcohol abuse issues, alongside poor education, training and communication skills. With sporting initiatives here being:

> designed to engage young offenders, improve their behaviour, achievement, skills and attitudes … a number of pathways were introduced offering offenders a variety of alternative opportunities on release from custody.[17]

Second, SBIs are also used pre-offence within communities through connecting young people to social- and job-skills training and educational programmes. Here, the aim is to help them find a pathway away from anti-social behaviour and a potential criminal career.[18] In essence, here SBIs are targeting young people from deprived areas which possess a high level of social disorganization indicators. These include high crime rates, long-term (often inter-generational) unemployment, poor public health and life expectancy indicators, as well as dependence on social welfare and voluntary services. In this context, diversionary sport programmes are used to establish relationships between young people and positive role models and authority figures, voluntary organizations and community groups, youth and social services, as well as training and educational providers. An example from the UK is the Tottenham boxing academy in London.[19] The academy describes their approach as using sport as the hook to get young people re-engaged with education and away from crime. Although focused on working with young people from at-risk areas before they become involved with the criminal justice system, some offenders on community-based sentences nevertheless also attend the academy. Similar programmes can be found internationally, including in the USA, Scotland, Australia, the Netherlands, Norway and Finland.[20]

Such initiatives do not just focus on sport training. Instead they use sport as a tool to help young people realize their potential, obtain training and recognize the importance of the shared community bonds. The individuals involved in these programmes often have been excluded from school, are known to social and welfare services and may well have been involved with criminal justice agencies. Here, sport is being combined with targeted support to engage hard-to-reach young people to try and divert them away from crime. For example, every student at the Tottenham boxing academy is required to attend lessons in Maths and English with the goal of obtaining GCSE qualifications in these subjects.

SBI and the problem of youth crime: do they really work?

Given such considerations, it is understandable why it is argued by some that SBIs can be

> effective in early intervention, preventing youth crime and acting as a diversion for those already caught up in the criminal justice system.[21]

Yet it is important not to accept at face value such claims, not least because the published research literature on the topic is not as extensive as might be presumed. Both Coakley and Donnelly and Kelly note that the assumption that sporting activity can act as a useful tool for preventing crime as well as helping to rehabilitate youth offenders has not been as rigorously tested as one might expect.[22] Furthermore, they argue that key social categories such as gender and race and ethnicity have been left largely unexplored in favour of rhetorically promoting the need for SBIs to pay attention to a young offender's 'individual needs'. The idea that young people have 'individual needs' is often taken to mean by SBI advocates and youth justice workers that they have psychological and/or social needs which must be met as part of a broader agenda to do with establishing 'pathways to work'. The value of sporting activity in this context is taken to be that it enables professionals and experts to identify and manage better the needs of young people who either are seen to be at risk of offending or who have offended in the past. This point is explored later in this paper when the role of sport as a mechanism for social control is examined. First, it is necessary to examine the empirical evidence that supports the argument that SBI can have a positive influence on the behaviour of young people.

There certainly is evidence available internationally from the USA, the UK, Australia and Europe, which suggests that sports participation by young people can be positively associated with reduced rates of anti-social behaviour and crime within local community areas.[23] For example, Cameron and MacDougall examined a wilderness camp in the USA which provides a varied SBI based around swimming, hiking and other outdoor activities.[24] It does this for young offenders aged between 12 and 17 who have been convicted of crimes ranging from petty theft and burglary to arson and murder. They found that 80% of participants from their programme did not reoffend in the first 6 months following completion.

Yet much of the data for the value of SBI is anecdotal in nature, consisting of relatively small sample sizes, as well as often omitting to track research participants beyond a relatively short period of time. Cameron and MacDougall themselves recognize that they were unable to identify the long-term effects of the programme they studied beyond the 6-month mark. Similarly Skille's study of the impact of SBI in Norway also concluded that it is difficult to establish the long-term impact of SBI on future offending behaviour.[25] While in the UK context, Agnew found that it was impossible to concretely identify impact of SBI programmes in communities in the east of England.[26] The key problem here noted by Cameron and MacDougall, Skille and Agnew is that the majority of studies are heavily reliant on qualitative research and/or questionnaire-based self-reports of behavioural change. These are typically obtained directly from research participants themselves and, therefore, are open to the accusation of subjective bias.

What is lacking in the current SBI literature is longitudinal statistical data pertaining to reoffending rates from which to measure change and so the impact of SBI on future offending behaviour.[27] For example, a study of the aforementioned Tottenham boxing academy in the UK argued that there was a 40% decrease in reconviction for the offenders who participated in the programme. It was also noted that this programme only needs to stop just over one in 400 young people a year from reoffending to break even, while:

if it stops two young people from reoffending the return on a £1 investment is £1.90.[28]

Such figures and claims appear impressive until it is noted that the size of offenders in the sample was very small ($n = 8$) and relied on qualitative self-reports from the individual offenders themselves, rather than the scrutiny of officially recorded reoffending data.

Furthermore, we are confronted with the fact that even when more statistically driven research exists, the evidence is inconclusive and in many ways serves to reinforce the problems which exist in seeking to link young people's participation in SBI with behavioural change through examining offending rates. For example, the swimming-based SBI Splash programme in the UK appears to present conclusive empirical evidence of the positive effect of SBI on youth offending behaviour.[29] It reported that in the 10 areas in which it operated between June and August 2002, total crime reduced by 7% and anti-social behaviour increased by 0.1% when there had been an increase of 13% for the previous June to August period in 2001 (a period that coincides with summer school holidays). Such figures point out that perhaps the most effective method to reduce youth crime is to divert young people away from negative social activities using SBI before they become involved in crime. But it is not possible to claim that there is a direct link between the Splash programme and a reduction in the crime rate and anti-social behaviour, due in part to the fact that it is not known, first, who exactly participated in the programme and, second, what other possible diversionary activities were occurring at the same time during the school holiday period, including local events and festivals, day trips and away days, family holidays and so on. Most importantly, it should be noted that the local police force had adapted their street-level policing and crime prevention strategies in targeted areas in the light of the recorded crime data of the previous year. This in itself may well account for much of the noted reduction in crime and anti-social behaviour.

Another informative example is the midnight basketball league from the USA. Its creator, Mr G. Van Standifer:

> had become convinced that one of the keys to the problems of poor, inner-city young men was the absence of safe, constructive activities during what he believed to be the high crime hours of 10:00 p.m. and 2:00 a.m.[30]

In response, he created a basketball league which would run during these high crime hours. This example of an SBI was both simple and inexpensive. It operated only during summer months and had three core components. First, that the target group was young men aged between 17 and 21. Second, games began at 10:00 pm sharply and not before. Third, two uniformed police officers attended each game. This project based its reasoning on the assumption that crime can occur because young people feel bored and that an organized activity like this could, therefore, steer potential offenders away from criminal behaviour. The results were remarkable – during the first 3 years of its operation, there was a 30% reduction in late-night crime in the communities it ran in. The Maryland County corrections chief, for example, told Chicago reporters:

> I haven't seen one single one of these basketball players back in my jail since the program began.[31]

Although such early indicators of success seemed to provide evidence for the value of midnight basketball in tackling crime, it was later established that crime rates dropped rapidly at a national level during this period, a point which made it difficult to accept the programme organizer's claims to success. This said, matching cities who adopted the midnight basketball programme with those that did not offer it did reveal that there was a reduction of property crimes running at around 5%.[32] Yet, it was not possible to say whether it was the young people playing basketball who were responsible for this isolated crime drop. Indeed, it is highly unlikely that all midnight basketball participants committed crime, let alone exclusively engaged in property crime. Hartmann and Depro argue that the extensive political and media interest generated by the midnight basketball programme brought positive attention to stigmatized and marginalized communities, which served to:

> send a more positive, proactive message to community members, one that puts a new emphasis on community outreach and builds trust, commitment and solidarity.[33]

This, it is claimed, had a knock on effect on property crime rates due to the closer social bonds created within the communities in question.

The Splash programme and the midnight basketball programme together remind us that sporting activity can influence the lives of community members at a broader level. But they also reinforce the point that problems exist in measuring the impact of SBIs on young people's behaviour. West and Compton draw a similar conclusion as a result of their meta-analysis of the effectiveness of SBI.[34] Drawing on over 20 studies from the USA they point out that although there is some supportive data for the benefit of SBI in tackling the problem of youth crime and anti-social behaviour, it is nevertheless difficult to claim that any reduction in crime is the direct result of sporting activity alone, not least because there is often a lack of consistency in the type of offence analysed as not all the studies they looked at included offenders who had committed more serious types of violent crime. There is also often a difference in the reoffending rate used by studies. Some studies analyse if reoffending occurs after 1 year and others look at a shorter or longer period of time. Furthermore, West and Compton note that a range of external factors are likely to intervene in any apparent relationship between SBI activity and a young person's offending or anti-social behaviour, including their personal circumstances, home environment, family relationships, alongside the nature of their peer networks. More recently, Kelley and Sokol-Katz have replicated West and Compton's findings in their large-scale longitudinal study of juvenile delinquency and sports participation across the USA.[35] Similar extensive studies from Australia, England, Scotland, Norway and Germany have concluded that when compared with powerful primary agents of socialization and social integration (notably family, school, peers and the media), participation in sporting activities seem to be of marginal influence on young people's behaviour.[36]

Finally, the limitations of SBIs in meeting the complex needs of offenders must be acknowledged. Andrews and Andrews argue in their study of the role played by SBI in secure youth offending units in the UK that a person-centred approach to the provision of sports opportunities is the key to its success in alleviating anti-social and criminal behaviour.[37] Activities must be purposeful for the individual and tailored to their individual needs, rather than being constructed for mass participation in a one-size-fits-all fashion, as is often the case. The most prolific young offenders often possess a range of problems and issues which make it difficult to prescribe a one-size-fits-all approach. Often the aggressive behaviour of these offenders is the result of their being a victim of childhood neglect or physical or sexual abuse. More often than not, they also have substance and alcohol abuse problems, distrust authority figures and have become disengaged from educational pathways, possess poor communication and life skills, have highly dysfunctional family and intimate relationships, as well as lack positive male and female role models.[38] For Andrews and Andrews, the complex needs possessed by young offenders' means that sporting activities can only ever be one small element of any programme of rehabilitation. They place significantly more emphasis on professionally led counselling, mentoring, life-skills training and educational programmes, for supporting young people to change their offending behaviour and connect with a pathway to work.

Sport for social control

So far this paper has discussed the potential for SBI to address the problem of youth crime. It has noted that although there is evidence for the positive impact of SBI on youth offending and anti-social behaviour, it is not conclusive. The evidence suggests that the relationship between sport participation and crime is too complex as to be reducible to a simple causal relationship. But there is also a broader issue here pertaining to how young people are viewed and treated within the criminal justice system in western nation-states. Underpinning much of the discussion of young people and crime is a particular set of somewhat familiar negative images. There is a tendency for the media, criminal justice agencies and political elites to propagate the well-worn caricature of the rebellious youth, with all its associated transgressive discursive imagery. Such imagery shapes much of the contemporary discourse surrounding the problem of youth crime and how to solve it. Indeed it has been argued that the last two decades in particular have witnessed the emergence of an actuarial-managerial penal policy for dealing with the problem of dangerous offenders and unruly youths. Here,

> the management of risks and resources has displaced rehabilitation as the central organisational aim of the criminal justice system.[39]

The aim now is for criminal behaviour to be increasingly profiled and predicted as the penal emphasis shifts from a focus on rehabilitation and towards containment and control. Evidence for this position can be found in the prison statistics. The prison population has dramatically risen in most western countries over the last two decades. For example, in the UK in 1984, there were 43,295 individuals in prison, but by 1994 it had risen slightly to 48,621, in 2004 it stood at 74,658 and by 2011 it stood at 84,812.[40] For critical criminologists, such a dramatic increase cannot be put down to routine fluxes in crime-rate patterns, it can only be the result of a deliberate shift in penal policy.[41]

This new actuarial-managerial penal policy is not solely concerned with containing crime through 'warehousing' a growing number of offenders, both young and old, in penal institutions. Its focus remains on managing instead of solving the problem of crime and this has led, in turn, to a widening of the surveillance net, in part, through the intensification in community-based surveillance and profiling of young people deemed to be at risk of offending.[42] This shift in emphasis towards managing the problem of crime through risk profiling and assessment means that the operation of diversionary and rehabilitative programmes intensifies. This is achieved through establishing a broader range of partnerships between criminal justice agencies and community stakeholders, i.e. community leaders, voluntary and charity groups, business leaders and so on. In the UK, criminologists have noted that the New Labour government of the mid-1990s onwards oversaw the rapid expansion of community-based interventions for youth offenders, with the 1998 Crime and Disorder Act establishing Youth Offending Teams (YOTs) in addition to YJBs to oversee them. The creation of YOTs extended the responsibility of youth intervention and supervision beyond probation and social workers alone. A wide range of criminal justice and welfare agencies were joined by local community voluntary groups and youth group organizations, including the police, the probation service, educational providers and benefit, housing and health agencies. Bound up with this was the introduction of Youth Inclusion and Support Panels to target young people under the age of 13 who were at risk of offending and introduce preventative strategies at a local level to tackle both offending and reoffending behaviour. This, in turn, led to an increase in the role of alternative programmes, involving a range of voluntary and statutory organizations with local community groups, to tackle the problem of anti-social behaviour and youth offending. The steady growth in the number of SBIs in the UK in the 1990s was a natural outcome of this state of affairs.[43]

The growing role of SBIs over the last two decades has arguably been the result of the shift towards a more surveillance heavy 'risk aware' punitive system of criminal justice in the UK. SBIs are undoubtedly attractive to young people and it is their ability to reach out to people and get them to agree to participate of their own accord which allows state crime control agencies to legitimately pursue a diversionary and rehabilitatory programme while at the same time extending their knowledge of the nature of the social problem that is youth offending and anti-social behaviour.[44] So they can (in theory) more effectively profile and risk-manage the phenomena at both the local and national levels. Furthermore, the current Conservative and Liberal-Democratic coalition government, in announcing their future plans for youth justice in 2010, signalled their intention to continue to promote alternative crime prevention strategies, such as SBI.[45] Critical of their New Labour predecessors in many ways, the coalition nevertheless is continuing to pursue an actuarial-managerial penal policy. Hence, the increasing emphasis placed on restorative justice with youth offenders being required to participate in

> community payback programmes that promote the tough discipline of regular work, tougher curfews [and] paying back the debt they owe society.[46]

This development is underpinned by a series of payment by results 'pathfinding' projects. These are designed and run by a mixture of private and publically funded bodies tasked with reducing the number of youth offenders in custody by diverting them into less costly community-based alternatives. Governmental bonuses are awarded to private bodies and their profits ensured through a reduction in reoffending behaviour. Whether this strategy works or not is a matter for long-term analysis and debate as such programmes continue to be piloted and rolled out across the country over the next few years. There is even the possibility that SBIs may become an integral part of these pathfinder initiatives, not least of all because of their synergy with the 2012 Olympic legacy.[47]

The ties that exist between the emergence of SBI to tackle the problem of youth crime and broader shifts in criminal justice policy and practice should not come as too much of a surprise, given the assumptions about the nature of youth offending they share in common. I am not just talking here about the academic position, often shared by the SBI advocate, that youth offending and anti-social behaviour are likely to occur when young people are inadequately socialized into commonly held norms for appropriate and inappropriate behaviour, with sporting activity being held to offer a solution to such issues by providing a mechanism through which these norms can be both taught and learned.[48] Rather, to the mind of the critical criminologist, this ignores or underplays the importance of the structural inequalities that arguably shape the very social landscape that young people are born into and grow up in.

Coakley, Coakley and Donnelly and Kelly all point out that the use of recreational sporting activity by governments to monitor and control what are held to be problem behaviours, such as violence and aggression, is tied up with broader exclusionary social categories and processes that tend to operate in neoliberal western societies.[49] They note how SBIs internationally can often be divided into two types: sport for 'social opportunity' and sport for 'social control'. Furthermore, they argue that the former is by and large targeted at the socially mobile white middle classes and the latter the less mobile working class, poor and socially excluded. For SBI advocates such as Coalter, Sport as social opportunity emphasizes sport as an opportunity for the personal development, growth and social mobility.[50] In contrast, sport as social control focuses on young people from inner-city areas and 'at-risk' housing estates. It views them somewhat homogeneously as a potentially dangerous group who are likely to get into trouble if they are not placed in structured settings and made to participate in activities controlled by responsible adults (teachers, social workers, youth justice workers, etc.), not least of all because their parents are (allegedly) uninvolved and/or seemingly unable to control them. Here, particular types of groups of young people are seen as being more inclined towards anti-social and criminal behaviour. Hence, they are in need of protection, from both their environment and themselves, because the community will be safer if they are controlled and socialized through leisure and sporting activity.[51]

Coakley and Coakley and Donnelly note the class-, gender- and race-based inequalities which permeate through the sport as social control model.[52] Undoubtedly, a significant number of young people involved in SBIs come from inner-city areas where young people from middle-class white backgrounds tend not to 'hang-out'. Kelly discovered the same in her analysis of SBI as a mechanism to promote social inclusion in the UK.[53] She notes that SBIs often serve to conceal or obscure broader social inequalities through individualizing the problem of youth offending and anti-social behaviour. In part, they do this through their incorporation of a 'pathways to work' discourse, such as those promoted by Andrews and Andrews, where individualized counselling, mentoring, life-skills training and educational programmes are bound up with organized sporting activity to support young people to change their anti-social and offending behaviour.[54] For Kelly, such initiatives, no matter how beneficial they are for some of their participants, by and large do not work because they de-emphasize the very structural inequalities that she argues bring about the behaviour they are seeking to change in the first place. The core problem, from the perspective of young people themselves, is that SBI programmes often fail to fully account for their lived experience and so the overarching structural inequalities which confront them everyday, i.e. blocked social opportunity, poverty, stigmatization, racial and class tension, gender-based violence and so on.[55]

Criminological research has repeatedly shown that, firstly, ethnic minority groups and individuals from working class backgrounds are disproportionately overrepresented in the criminal justice system; secondly, that Black, South Asian and mixed-race youths are more often subject to formal criminal justice processes and frequently get higher penal tariffs than their white counterparts and thirdly, that young female offenders are similarly often treated more punitively than their male counterparts (white or otherwise) while at the same time often being the victims of gender-based violence.[56] If such research is not engaged with by SBI promoters and advocates, then SBIs run the risk of serving to further exclude the already excluded as the young people involved disengage with programme activities which they instinctively feel are not 'in-tune' with their everyday lived experience. This is why Kelly concludes that the impact of SBI on changing behaviour

> is inevitably limited. Moreover, sports-based interventions risk legitimating a reductive analysis of these complex processes, highlighting individual deficits and de-emphasizing structural inequalities.[57]

Conclusion

This paper began by noting that the transformative power of sport to change lives for the better should not be underestimated. It has discussed how SBIs are used internationally to successfully connect 'at-risk' young people to youth services, community networks and job-skills training and education programmes. SBIs can bring criminal justice agencies, social services, youth workers, voluntary organizations and community groups together to address anti-social and offending behaviour among young people. Indeed it was noted that research evidence exists which reinforces the positive role that sport can play in changing the lives of some young people for the better.[58] But the limitations of the available literature to conclusively support SBIs claims to success were also noted. There is a lack of methodologically robust evidence to support the argument that participation in sporting activity can directly lead to a reduction in antisocial and offending behaviour. In addition, it was noted how SBI's can act as a social control mechanism and in doing so may serve to mask the broader structural inequalities, which often shape a young person's lived experience of growing up in marginalized and stigmatized communities. This point is particularly important given the race-, gender- and class-based inequalities that permeate through neoliberal nation-states, western criminal justice systems and official recorded crime statistics.

But what does this all mean for SBI advocates and sport and leisure managers seeking to promote a critical re-evaluation of existing practices? Clearly, many young people do benefit in one way or another from participating in sport. Yet, it is nevertheless necessary to acknowledge the limitations of SBIs alone in addressing offending and antisocial behaviour. SBI programmes work best when they form part of a broader targeted strategy for dealing with the problem of youth crime. It is also necessary to enlarge the definition of what is meant by diversity in SBI and as part of this perhaps move beyond the more traditional choices of athletics, football, swimming and basketball. This will help to connect SBI with a broader range of role models, community leaders and coaching volunteers who are sensitive to the diverse needs of minority groups as well as the broader social forces and structural inequalities that can impact on their lives. There is an urgent need for SBI advocates to pursue a 'bottom-up' rather than 'top-down' view of how SBIs can and should operate. Here, governmental agencies, including its crime control elements, must take a back seat and allow local people to decide for themselves how SBIs can be best used as a crime prevention strategy within their communities.

Only time will tell whether notions of inclusion and diversity, rather than a neoliberal concern with cost and efficiency, will emerge to dominate the contemporary youth justice agenda. The UK coalition government wishes to give power back to local communities and authorities so they can have a bigger say in issues which affect them, including crime.[59] As this paper has discussed, a more inclusive approach to partnership development is essential to the long-term success of any 'bottom-up' approach to promoting SBI as a crime prevention and rehabilitation tool. Community representatives and cultural leaders from minority groups who may feel their needs are not currently being catered for must be placed at the centre of SBI activity. All too often SBIs seem to be focused primarily on the interests and needs of young people from white or black working class backgrounds. In doing so, they run the risk of not paying enough attention to the diverse interests and needs of other minority groups; including South Asian, Middle Eastern and Eastern European groups. The South Asian male prison population grew by 261% between 1985 and 2009, while the last 10 years have seen a gradual increase in the number of Middle Eastern and Eastern European offenders entering the UK criminal justice system.[60] It is important that SBIs be more sensitive to such trends. Yet perhaps the most under-represented group, certainly in terms of targeted research, remains teenage girls. The majority of published literature details the outcomes of SBIs interventions that primarily cater for the interests and needs of teenage boys, who are by and large positioned as dangerous and inherently 'risky subjects', often on the grounds of nothing more than where they live or who they associate with.[61] There is an urgent need to challenge such stereotypes by enlarging the concept of diversity currently employed within the SBI discourse. Only by doing this, SBIs will be made more relevant to the lived experiences of the young people whose behaviour they are seeking to influence as well as the local communities they come from.

Notes

1. Goldson and Muncie, *Youth Crime and Justice*.
2. Kidd, 'New Social Movement'.
3. Chamberlain, *Understanding Criminological Research*.
4. Goldson and Muncie, *Youth Crime and Justice*.
5. Maguire, Morgan, and Reiner, *Oxford Handbook of Criminology*, 496.
6. Youth Justice Board, *Annual Report and Accounts 2011/12*.
7. Ministry of Justice, *Breaking the Cycle*.

8. Laureus Sport for Good Foundation, *Teenage Kicks.*
9. Goldson and Muncie, *Youth Crime and Justice.*
10. Mutz and Baur, 'Role of Sports', 308.
11. Faulkner and Taylor, *Exercise, Health and Mental Health*, 195.
12. Millie et al., *Anti-Social Behaviour Strategies.*
13. Carmichael, *Youth Sport vs. Youth Crime.*
14. Laureus Sport for Good Foundation, *Teenage Kicks*, 4.
15. Coakley, 'Youth Sports'.
16. Meek and Lewis, 'Role of Sport in Prisoner Health'.
17. Mapstone, *2nd Chance Project*, 12.
18. Alonso and O'Shea, 'You Only Get Back'.
19. Laureus Sport for Good Foundation, *Teenage Kicks.*
20. West and Crompton, 'Review of the Impact of Adventure'; Hartmann and Depro, 'Rethinking Sports-Based Community Crime Prevention'; Kelley and Sokol-Katz, 'Examining Participation in School Sports'; Coalter, *Social Benefits of Sport*; Morris et al., *Sport, Physical Activity*; Sherry and Strybosch, 'Kick in the Right Direction'; Rutten et al., 'Contribution of Organized Youth Sport'; Skille, 'State Sport Policy'; and Theeboom, 'The Social-Psychological Outcomes'.
21. Sport for Change, *Sport for Change Project*, 1.
22. Coakley and Donnelly, *Sports in Society*; Kelly, 'Social Inclusion Through Sports-Based Interventions'; and Kelly, 'Representing and Preventing Youth Crime'.
23. Cameron and MacDougall, *Crime Prevention*; West and Crompton, 'Review of the Impact of Adventure'; Morris et al., *Sport, Physical Activity*; Laureus Sport for Good Foundation, *Teenage Kicks*; and Sherry and Strybosch, 'Kick in the Right Direction'.
24. Cameron and MacDougall, *Crime Prevention.*
25. Skille, 'State Sport Policy'.
26. Agnew, 'Providers to Enablers'.
27. Seefeldt and Ewing, 'Youth Sports in America'.
28. Laureus Sport for Good Foundation, *Teenage Kicks*, 43.
29. Splash Extra National Support Team, *Splash Cymru Final Report.*
30. Hartmann, 'Notes on Midnight Basketball', 342.
31. Ibid.
32. Ibid.
33. Hartmann and Depro, 'Rethinking Sports-Based Community Crime Prevention', 192.
34. West and Crompton, 'Review of the Impact of Adventure'.
35. Kelley and Sokol-Katz, 'Examining Participation in School Sports'.
36. Morris et al., *Sport, Physical Activity*; Agnew, 'Providers to Enablers'; Coalter, *Social Benefits of Sport*; Skille, 'State Sport Policy'; and Mutz and Baur, 'Role of Sports'.
37. Andrews and Andrews, 'Life in a Secure Unit'.
38. Millie et al., *Anti-Social Behaviour Strategies.*
39. Garland, *Mass Imprisonment.*
40. Ministry of Justice, *Proven Re-Offending Statistics.*
41. Chamberlain, *Understanding Criminological Research.*
42. Garland, *Mass Imprisonment.*
43. Carmichael, *Youth Sport vs. Youth Crime.*
44. Coakley, 'Using Sport to Control Deviance'.
45. Independent Commission, *Time for a Fresh Start.*
46. Ministry of Justice, *Breaking the Cycle.*
47. Olympic Delivery Authority, *Investing in the Future.*
48. Coalter, *Social Benefits of Sport.*
49. Coakley, 'Using Sport to Control Deviance'; Coakley and Donnelly, *Sports in Society*; and Kelly, 'Representing and Preventing Youth Crime'.
50. Coalter, *Social Benefits of Sport.*
51. Sherry and Strybosch, 'Kick in the Right Direction'.
52. Coakley, 'Using Sport to Control Deviance' and Coakley and Donnelly, *Sports in Society.*
53. Kelly, 'Social Inclusion Through Sports-Based Interventions' and Kelly, 'Representing and Preventing Youth Crime'.
54. Andrews and Andrews, 'Life in a Secure Unit'.

55. Goldson and Muncie, *Youth Crime and Justice.*
56. Bell, *Statistics on Race*; Feilzer and Hood, *Difference in Discrimination?*; and Kelly, 'Social Inclusion Through Sports-Based Interventions', 126.
57. Alonso and O'Shea, 'You Only Get Back'.
58. Ministry of Justice, *Breaking the Cycle.*
59. Ibid.
60. Maguire, Morgan and Reiner, *Oxford Handbook of Criminology.*
61. Coakley and Donnelly, *Sports in Society.*

References

Agnew, Stuart. 'Providers to Enablers: Reflections on the Provision of Positive Activities Targeting Criminal and Anti-Social Behaviour of Young People'. *Contemporary Social Science* 1 (2013): 1–15.

Alonso, Abel D., and Michelle O'Shea. 'You Only Get Back What You Put In: Perceptions of Professional Sport Organizations as Community Anchors'. *Community Development* 43 (2012): 656–76.

Andrews, Justin, and Gavin Andrews. 'Life in a Secure Unit: The Rehabilitation of Young People Through the Use of Sport'. *Social Science and Medicine* 56 (2003): 531–50.

Bell, Iain. *Statistics on Race and the Criminal Justice System.* London: Ministry of Justice, 2010.

Cameron, Margaret, and Colin MacDougall. *Crime Prevention Through Sport and Physical Activity.* Canberra: Australian Institute of Criminology, 2000.

Carmichael, David. *Youth Sport vs. Youth Crime: Evidence that Youth Engaged in Organized Sport Are Not Likely to Participate in Criminal Activities.* Ontario: Active Healthy Links Ltd, 2008.

Chamberlain, John M. *Understanding Criminological Research: A Guide to Data Analysis.* London: Sage Publications, 2013.

Coakley, Jay. 'Using Sport to Control Deviance and Violence Among Youth: Let's Be Critical and Cautious'. In *Paradoxes of Youth and Sport*, eds. Margaret Gatz, Michael Messner, and Sandra Ball-Rokeach, 13–30. Albany, NY: State University of New York Press, 2002.

Coakley, Jay. 'Youth Sports: What Counts as "Positive Development?"'. *Journal of Sport and Social Issues* 35 (2011): 306–24.

Coakley, Jay, and Peter Donnelly. *Sports in Society: Issues and Controversies.* Toronto: McGraw-Hill Ryersen, 2004.

Coalter, Fred. *The Social Benefits of Sport: An Overview to Inform the Community Planning Process.* Edinburgh: Sport Scotland, 2005.

Faulkner, Guy, and Adrian Taylor. *Exercise, Health and Mental Health – Emerging Relationships.* Abingdon: Routledge, 2005.

Feilzer, Martina, and Rodger Hood. *Difference in Discrimination?* London: Youth Justice Board, 2004.

Garland, David. *Mass Imprisonment: Social Causes and Consequences.* London: Sage Publications, 2011.

Goldson, Barry, and John Muncie. *Youth Crime and Justice.* London: Sage Publications, 2006.

Hartmann, Douglas. 'Notes on Midnight Basketball and the Cultural Politics of Recreation, Race and At-Risk Urban Youth'. *Journal of Sport and Social Issues* 25 (2001): 339–72.

Hartmann, Douglas, and Brooks Depro. 'Rethinking Sports-Based Community Crime Prevention: A Preliminary Analysis of the Relationship Between Midnight Basketball and urban Crime Rates'. *Journal of Sport and Social Issues* 30 (2006): 110–7.

Independent Commission. *Time for a Fresh Start: The Report of the Independent Commission on Both Youth Crime and Antisocial Behaviour.* London: Police Foundation and Nuffield Foundation, 2010.

Kelley, Margaret, and Jan Sokol-Katz. 'Examining Participation in School Sports and Patterns of Delinquency Using the National Longitudinal Study of Adolescent Health'. *Sociological Focus* 44 (2011): 81–101.

Kelly, Laura. 'Social Inclusion Through Sports-Based Interventions?' *Critical Social Policy* 31 (2011): 126–50.

Kelly, Laura. 'Representing and Preventing Youth Crime and Disorder: Intended and Unintended Consequences of Targeted Youth Programmes in England'. *Youth Justice* 12 (2012): 101–17.

Kidd, Bruce A. 'New Social Movement: Sport for Development and Peace'. *Sport in Society* 11 (2008): 370–80.

Laureus Sport for Good Foundation. *Teenage Kicks – The Value of Sport in Tackling Crime*. London: Laureus Sport for Good Foundation, 2011.

Maguire, Mike, Rod Morgan, and Robert Reiner. *The Oxford Handbook of Criminology*. 5th ed. Oxford: Oxford University Press, 2012.

Mapstone, James. *2nd Chance Project: How It Started*. London: Second Chance Project, 2011.

Meek, Rosie, and Gwen Lewis. 'The Role of Sport in Prisoner Health'. *International Journal of Prisoner Health* 8 (2012): 117–30.

Millie, Andrew, Jessica Jacobson, Eraina McDonald, and Mike Hough. *Anti-Social Behaviour Strategies: Finding a Balance*. London: The Policy Press, 2005.

Ministry of Justice. *Breaking the Cycle: Effective Punishment, Rehabilitation and Sentencing of Offenders*. London: HMSO, 2010.

Ministry of Justice. *Proven Re-Offending Statistics: Definitions and Measurements*. London: HMSO, 2011.

Morris, Lessa, Jo Sallybanks, Katie Willis, and Toni Makkai. *Sport, Physical Activity and Antisocial Behaviour in Youth*. Canberra: Australian Institute of Criminology, 2003.

Mutz, Michael, and Jurgen Baur. 'The Role of Sports for Violence Prevention: Sport Club Participation and Violent Behaviour Among Adolescents'. *International Journal of Sport Policy* 1 (2009): 305–21.

Olympic Delivery Authority. *Investing in the Future*. London: Olympic Delivery Authority, 2008.

Rutten, Esther, Gert Stams, Gert Biesta, Carlo Schuengel, Evelien Dirks, and Jan Hoeksma. 'The Contribution of Organized Youth Sport to Antisocial and Prosocial Behaviour in Adolescent Athletes'. *Journal of Youth Adolescence* 36 (2007): 255–64.

Seefeldt, Vern, and Martha Ewing. 'Youth Sports in America: An Overview'. *President's Council on Physical Fitness and Sport Research Digest* 2 (2002): 1–10.

Sherry, Emma, and Virgina Strybosch. 'A Kick in the Right Direction: Longitudinal Outcomes of the Australian Community Street Soccer Program'. *Soccer and Society* 13 (2012): 495–509.

Skille, Eivind. 'State Sport Policy and Voluntary Sport Clubs: The Case of the Norwegian Sports City Program as Social Policy'. *European Sport Management Quarterly* 9 (2009): 63–79.

Splash Extra National Support Team. *Splash Cymru Final Report*. Woking: CapGemini Ernst and Young, 2003.

Sport for Change. *Sport for Change Project*. London: Sport for Change Project, 2011.

Theeboom, Marc. 'The Social-Psychological Outcomes of Martial Arts Practise Among Youth: A Review'. *Journal of Sports Science and Medicine* 9 (2010): 528–37.

West, Stephanie T., and John L. Crompton. 'A Review of the Impact of Adventure Programs on At-Risk Youth'. *Journal of Park and Recreation Administration* 19 (2001): 113–40.

Youth Justice Board. *Annual Report and Accounts 2011/12*. London: Youth Justice Board, 2012.

Enter the discourse: exploring the discursive roots of inclusivity in mixed-sex martial arts

Alex Guy Channon

School of Education, University of Greenwich, London, UK

In this paper, I explore the discursive roots of inclusivity in mixed-sex martial arts training in the UK. On the basis of data from two qualitative studies conducted in the East Midlands, I briefly account for the level of integration among several martial arts schools, before focusing on the unique meanings of martial arts that appeared to facilitate the normalization of this integration among participants. Drawing on insights from queer feminist theory, I argue that the discursive framing of martial arts in contemporary Western culture is significant in the generation and normalization of mixed-sex inclusivity in these settings. As such, I suggest that scholars interested in the potential of sex-integrated sports for challenging dominant sexual hierarchies should be attentive to the unique discursive meanings of specific sports cultures, which may be generative of possibilities for radical forms of embodiment and practice.

Introduction

Issues pertaining to the restriction of women's and girls' access to sports, along with the concurrent meanings of male-dominated and male-centred sport, have previously been central to the efforts of feminist research and writing in the field of sports studies. Broadly concerned with challenging inequity while redefining the meanings of sport and the athletic woman, such work has also forwarded the promise of sport as a potentially profound site for women's liberation and empowerment.[1] Within this framework, feminist researchers have begun to explore the phenomenon of mixed-sex participation in sport. While this is currently an emerging field of interest within the broader feminist sociology of sport, a small number of studies of specific sports, including softball, soccer, cheerleading and judo, as well as more generalized investigations, have appeared across a variety of academic journals in recent years.[2] McDonagh and Pappano's book, *Playing with the Boys*, forwarded an argument common among such works: that mixed-sex sports can provide unique, transformative experiences to participants, posing clear challenges to the discourses of male superiority otherwise embedded in many aspects of contemporary sports culture.[3] This is principally achieved through the implications of *physical equality* between the sexes, which integrated sports represent, articulated via their unique relationship to the sexed body and showcasing of its evident potentials.

In contemporary feminist theory, such understanding of the sexed body takes a place of prominence as a key aspect of debates concerning the socially constructed character of gender, itself an important element of the legitimation of patriarchy. Institutions that emphasize differences between male and female bodies – such as differently 'gendered' sports cultures – are seen as important sites for the *naturalization* of inequitable sexual difference, particularly when they cause men and women to *embody* those differences, making them appear biological and thus 'natural'.[4] As such, 'queer' feminist theorists, such as Judith Butler, Donna Haraway and Elizabeth Grosz, have suggested that gender, as a culturally mandated set of performances, causes individuals' bodies to be shaped according to the discursive limits and imperatives that it sets out for them.[5] By 'doing' their socially legitimated gender, male bodies accrue 'masculine' traits, while female bodies become 'feminine', overemphasizing and distorting whatever biologically predestined differences may exist between differently sexed bodies. In this regard, the very idea of there being two 'natural', totally distinctive sexual groups is suspect, as the effect of culturally constructed, performatively embodied gender discourse effectively obscures similarities between bodies in the process of constructing this binary, and hierarchal, system of difference. And because segregated sport is largely predicated upon discursive constructions of essential sex difference, as well as upon emphasizing and showcasing men's positioning as superior to women within this system, it has been argued that 'gender divisions and men's superiority are more naturalized in sport than perhaps any other institution' in contemporary society.[6]

Such theory, however, suggests that physical practices that do away with sex as an organizing category, which 'fall outside' of typical gender discourse, hold out the possibility to subvert this hierarchal system.[7] For when men and women are not bound by the limits of a discourse emphasizing such essential and predestined differences, and thus act in ways that stand outside of its typical dictates, they are able to realize the potentials of each other's sexed bodies in new ways. This then opens opportunities for the construction of a diversity of alternative gendered practices, shaped by novel experiences of male and female bodies that do not conform to the essentialist categories productive of an immutable sexual hierarchy. It is in this regard that mixed-sex sports might be seen as important for feminist understandings of physical culture. Doing away with sex as an organizing principle, they can afford participants with embodied experiences predicated more or less on physical equality between groups of men and women, the likes of which sex-segregated sports cannot, by definition, provide. And while it is true that such sporting experiences may potentially reaffirm essentialist beliefs about male physical superiority – for instance, when men beat women at various sports or when integrated contests feature different rules concerning men's and women's performances[8] – evidence from recent studies suggests that this potential has, to a point, begun to be realized.[9]

In this paper, I offer an exploration of the underpinnings of mixed-sex participation in martial arts, detailing the particular discourses that surround such activities and help to legitimize their break from normative models of segregation. I begin by briefly detailing the ways in which this form of inclusivity exists in martial arts training cultures, discussing the limited extent to which this promise of integration has been realized. I then focus on attempting to outline how this is made possible, exploring the specific, somewhat unique meanings of these physical cultural settings with regard to media representations, 'female-appropriate' adaptations and pedagogical focuses among various styles of martial arts.

Method

The body of data informing this paper is drawn from two qualitative studies of mixed-sex martial arts conducted in the East Midlands during the years 2007–2011. The first of these studies was conducted within a single kung fu club, involving combined participant observation and interviewing of club members and instructors. The second was a wider study of several different martial arts clubs across the region, based on interviews with a series of long-term practitioners. In addition to these research methods, the studies were informed by my personal experiences of martial arts participation, having practised freestyle kick-boxing and shaolin kung fu for over a combined period of seven years.[10]

Interviewee selection was based on observations of club training in the first study, within which my situated position as a regular member of the training group helped to facilitate easy access to a range of participants. Meanwhile, 'snowball' sampling was used in the second study, beginning with personal contacts and enquiries at a few local training centres, eventually leading through a range of martial artists at a number of different clubs. Interviewees were prioritized on the grounds of experience, with three years' continuous training as a minimum requirement. Topical, semi-structured and one-to-one interviews were used in both studies, which were then transcribed and thematically coded before being analysed, with follow-up interviews held in order to clarify findings. To ensure privacy and prevent potential bias, interviews were held either away from interviewees' training centres or within them at times when no other club members were present. Following transcription, interviewees' names were changed, using self-selected pseudonyms to protect their anonymity.

In total, 37 interviewees took part across both studies, including 17 men and 20 women. With an age range of 18–43 for the men and 18–32 for the women, the mean ages of both groups were 26 and 24, respectively. It is possible to describe the sample as being predominantly 'middle-class'; 32 interviewees had gained an academic or vocational degree, or were currently studying for one, and many worked in knowledge-based or specialist skilled jobs (e.g. accountant, school teacher). Most of the interviewees self-identified as being White British, although two of the men identified themselves as Black British, while three men and three women identified themselves as British Chinese, one man British Asian and one woman mixed-race (British/Japanese). Finally, all of the interviewees identified themselves as being heterosexual.

Of further note is that these interviewees represented 15 different martial arts clubs and 11 distinctive martial arts disciplines between them, including choi kwang do, judo, jujitsu, karate, kick-boxing, kung fu, mixed martial arts (MMA), muay thai, taekwondo and taijiquan. Furthermore, almost all of the interviewees had trained at other clubs previously, and often in other martial arts disciplines.[11] As such, the sample of interviewees from these two studies is considered to consist of martial arts *aficionados*, whose collective experiences represent a diverse range of knowledge about training at various different types of martial arts, including more 'traditionalist' Eastern styles as well as ostensibly more 'Westernized' variants.[12] Thus, the research data discussed here are largely concerned with practitioner experiences and discursive constructions of martial arts in a general sense, rather than within any specific (sub)cultural setting.

Integrated training environments in martial arts

Previous discussions of mixed-sex sport have tended to claim that sex segregation is virtually ubiquitous across all forms of (Western) sports, so much so that even feminist scholars have failed to adequately recognize or criticize it.[13] Despite 'Western history (being) replete with examples of women competing against men in sport', the examples of the past are thought to be often forgotten, as segregating the sexes from an early age is such a normalized practice that it has become one of sport's most taken-for-granted principles.[14] However, having spent several years training, and subsequently researching various martial arts, such segregation was far from normal in my experience of contemporary martial arts training cultures in the UK. Indeed, the majority of interviewees taking part in my research noted that 'coercive sex segregation' was rarely, if ever, seen in their own training environments.[15] Rather, it was sex *integration* that was seen as 'normal', even if this appeared odd to practitioners at first:

> When you first walk in … you don't expect women to be there, but after a while when you've done it enough, it's normal … (I wonder) why aren't there more people doing it, more women doing it? (Ed, muay thai competitor)

> All of the clubs I've trained in have been mixed-sex, it's quite normal I think … Yeah, all of them, training together, it's normal. (Steve, kung fu instructor)

Indeed, the 'normality' of women's involvement in martial arts, and their participation alongside men in particular, has been reported in other recent studies, notably in the relatively new (and highly 'masculinized') combat sport of MMA.[16] Even in boxing, a sport historically considered synonymous with orthodox expressions of masculinity and the concurrent exclusion of women, there is evidence that women and men are sharing training spaces and, in some cases, training together.[17]

The extent of this integration is not always 'complete' though, as practical or symbolic differentiations between men and women persist in many cases, such as in Lafferty and McKay's and Mennesson's accounts of gendered discriminatory practices in Australian and French boxing gyms.[18] For many of those interviewed in the course of my research, practices that most directly foregrounded practitioners' physicality, such as 'conditioning' exercises and competitive sparring, were thought to be more likely segregated – although this was often qualified not simply in terms of sexual difference, but relative to a noted correlation between sex and size.[19] However, practices that involved direct hitting could become particularly problematic, as conceptions of essential female weakness, along with the requirements of masculine honour, made 'men hitting women' a distinctly difficult prospect for some men to manage.[20]

Nevertheless, in some cases, even such practices as these were integrated. For instance, several interviewees told me how women, particularly when preparing for competitions, would spar at high intensity with male opponents, while mixed sparring in training, at lighter intensities, was a typical element of all of my interviewees' experiences.[21] In addition, many told of women taking coaching and other leadership roles in their clubs, being widely accepted by male and female practitioners alike, which stands in contrast to other instances of women's coaching of men in sport.[22] Many interviewees also described their clubs having made deliberate efforts to market themselves to women and of generally welcoming the atmosphere of mixed-sex environments, seen as broadly beneficial for training.[23] Finally, some even described instances of mixed-sex sparring competition at tournaments, with many of those who had such experiences being eager to see them become more common. 'Brazilian' jujitsu competitor and part-time MMA coach Rachel described her feelings after having won second place in the 'men's' division of her weight category at a grappling competition:

> I want women to be allowed to fight with men … If anything what I've done so far shows you how putting us in different divisions is like, well it's stupid to begin with.

Thus, not only are women involved at multiple levels of participation in martial arts, but also they are commonly training alongside men, frequently attaining coaching positions in mixed-sex clubs and in some cases, even competing against men at tournaments. Having asked a range of experienced male and female martial artists to explain this, the most typical response by far was that sex integration in training was simply 'normal'. Some even went further, stating that it was also justified as being true to the central meanings of martial arts. According to kung fu instructor Evelyn:

> It's all the same, men and women together, yeah, and it should be like that. We don't want to make things different and make it look like women need to do a softer or weaker thing because that would really go against a lot of what kung fu is about.

It may seem surprising that this level of inclusivity exists within a set of practices that are largely concerned with enhancing and measuring practitioners' ability to fight, as fighting is often considered a classically 'masculine' occupation in orthodox Western gender discourse.[24] Relative to the normalization of segregation seen elsewhere in Western physical culture, this discursive framing of sex integration in martial arts as 'normal' is, therefore, quite *ab*normal. How is it then, that when sex segregation is thought to be so widespread and normalized elsewhere, that it is considered to 'go against' what martial arts is 'really all about'? What shapes the normative parameters of martial arts training cultures in ways that legitimate or promote this form of inclusivity? In the following sections, I discuss how the unique cultural location of martial arts in the UK provides the discursive underpinnings for justifying the normalization of this integrated practice.

Martial arts mythologies: kung fu movies and orientalist legend

Arguably, the popularity of Eastern martial arts in many Western countries today owes much to the success of 'kung fu' movies, a notable sub-genre of action cinema popular since the latter half of the twentieth century.[25] Iconic Asian actors including Bruce Lee, Jackie Chan and Jet Li, along with Westerners such as Jean-Claude Van Damme, Steven Seagal and Chuck Norris, brought disciplines including aikido, karate and wushu, and derivative styles such as kick-boxing, to the cultural mainstream. Importantly, though, on-screen martial artistry has not been limited to male action heroes; movies depicting women's use of martial arts, often against men, have also proliferated over the past half-century, including in 1960s exploitation films (e.g. *Faster Pussycat! Kill! Kill!*, 1963), Hong Kong action dramas (*Yes, Madam*, 1985), historical *wuxia* epics (*Crouching Tiger, Hidden Dragon*, 2000) and Hollywood blockbusters (*Kill Bill*, 2003–2004). In addition, television shows from as early as the 1960s and 1970s (*The Avengers*; *Charlie's Angels*), through to the 2000s and beyond (*Buffy the Vampire Slayer*; *Nikita*), have featured female protagonists whose highly stylized proficiency in martial arts is a central dynamic of their roles, more often than not used to subdue larger, stronger and better armed male assailants. Finally, martial arts videogames have also extensively featured female fighters, beginning with *Street Fighter II* (1991) but now seen in all major fighting game franchises (*Mortal Kombat, Soul Calibur, Tekken*, etc.), with their inclusion premised upon the fact that they are an even match for the games' male characters.

For lack of space, I cannot here attempt to unpack the multiple gendered meanings of women in action media, which often involve (hetero)sexualization, racial stereotyping or reactionary patriarchal narratives; compelling analyses of such things have been offered elsewhere.[26] However, what all these depictions of (specifically female) martial artistry have in common is an emphasis on the superiority of technical fighting mastery – the somewhat hidden, internal capabilities of the body – over physical size or strength – its most outwardly visible, and almost always sexed, characteristics. Here, the typical association between (male) sex and (superior) physical power is rendered meaningless, as the discursive construction of martial arts as a technical system that transcends other elements of physicality takes precedence in determining one's combative ability. Such depictions are very often divorced from reality, such as with explosive 'special moves' in videogames and computer-generated imagery/'wirework' in film.[27] Yet, the exaggerations of martial arts media speak to the underlying discourse permeating much martial arts practice: anybody, regardless of size or strength – and thus by extension, sex – can become an accomplished fighter provided they dedicate themselves to mastering their body's latent combative potentials. In this regard, many interviewees described how their consumption of martial arts media helped to inspire participation or make sense of men's and women's abilities:

> I always thought (martial arts were) quite cool actually, exciting ... like *The Karate Kid*, I love it ... When I was growing up these movies made me feel like anyone could do it. (Andrea, choi kwang do practitioner)

> In the (martial arts) games, the women have different fighting styles, like they're always smaller and faster, and in a way it's quite accurate because martial arts training is based on what you can do with your own body type ... Games and films (featuring women) are more accurate because they show you how martial arts isn't just for like, big, strong men. (Bob, kung fu practitioner)

Often an important element of 'kung fu' media, the 'Asian' roots of many popular martial arts systems also represent a unique discursive resource for breaking with typical Western assumptions about sex, physicality and fighting ability – and thus making sense of sex integration in training. 'Orientalist' understandings of Asia pervade contemporary discourse about cultural practices imported to the West from this region, such that 'orientalism remains an important backdrop to the collective social meaning of Eastern movement forms in the West today, and to the experiences and behaviours of its practitioners'.[28] Broadly conceiving of 'the East' as an exotic place shrouded in mystery, the status of the 'other' conferred by this popular cultural mythology partly legitimizes the otherwise peculiar practice of sex-integrated martial arts in particularly Eastern disciplines, as practitioners recognize an incompatibility between Eastern traditions and modernist, Western conceptions of a clearly demarcated gender order. According to kung fu and MMA practitioner Gavin:

> When it comes to kung fu, in the East anyway, there's a lot of female activity in it ... you got a lot of females doing it. It's like in the East (martial arts) is ok for females, they don't think it's just a male thing ... It's a different culture, different traditions, I guess they don't think about (sex) like (Westerners) do so they bring it over here and carry on offering it to females.

For some, this cultural difference was explained as an effect of a historical legacy of women warriors who, in the legendary history of Eastern martial arts, had played pivotal roles in their development. Kung fu and jujitsu practitioner David described his perception of the normative status of women in martial arts with reference to the legendary history of wing chun kung fu, which helped to make sense of, in particular, the role of women as coaches or instructors of male practitioners:[29]

> I think there is a history of (women teachers), because traditionally in Chinese kung fu, there are some styles like wing chun for example, it was created by a woman, designed for women, and they obviously taught men how to do it too ... So women have always been in martial arts, and especially wing chun, well it is really popular in lots of countries and it was invented by a woman so I guess (women teaching men) is quite normal.

In these regards, the mythologized meanings of martial arts are quite different from other sporting activities, in that they are regularly depicted in various mediated forms as being somewhat 'sex-neutral' (although rarely *gender* neutral, given the often feminized or masculinized aesthetics of videogame and film characters, for instance). They are also often described with recourse to orientalist discourses stressing the exotic 'otherness' of the East, removing them from the historical/cultural milieu out of which masculinist, modern Western sport arose. This sets the various martial arts disciplines in a somewhat unique position, as the major discursive structures that define the practices in the media (technical mastery trumps size and strength; Eastern mysticism defies supposedly rationalized, Western cultural norms) create possibilities to imagine the body, and thus invitations to physically perform, in relatively unique ways, marking out integrated training as a more acceptable proposition. However, women's presence in martial arts has also been framed by meanings less foreign to Western gender typologies, which also have some bearing here.

Female versions: non-combative arts and feminine fighters

'Female-appropriate' sports are those that are culturally valued for being predicated upon the enhancement or measurement of typically 'feminine' (bodily) characteristics.[30] Variously differentiated from 'men's sports', they have historically served as sites where women can participate in sporting recreation without posing an overt challenge to the assumed 'natural' hierarchy between the sexes, which sports are otherwise implicated in supporting. In this regard, the gender-troubling phenomenon of women's desire to be involved in sport is diffused, as their participation in activities that emphasize, measure or enhance 'femininity', and thus difference from men, becomes a means of further entrenching the patriarchal norm of binary and hierarchal sex difference, rather than challenging it.[31] Some forms of martial arts practice have developed into such female-appropriate activities, principally via their adaptation into non-combative fitness programmes designed at enhancing women's heterosexual attractiveness.

Women's participation for the purposes of 'fitness' in fact represents a typical form of entry into the wider cultural space of martial arts. Hargreaves notes that since the 1980s, non-combative forms of boxing – such as 'boxercise' aerobics – have become a popular form of workout for women, as the training was seen to help produce a desirably firm, shapely, yet 'feminine' body.[32] Coupled with popular media representations of 'feisty', (hetero)sexy female martial artists, this generates an appeal among young women who may otherwise not have been interested in such ostensibly 'masculine' activities. Indeed, for many of the female interviewees in my research, the attraction of martial arts as a comprehensive workout system, good for 'toning up' the muscles and 'losing weight', was a compelling factor that initially drew them to clubs, also forming a key marketing tool for coaches wishing to expand their female clientele:

> It's all these celebrity workout videos isn't it, they think (martial arts exercise) is gonna make them fit, and it's got that (fitness) image now, for women anyway ... it's a good way to sell it to them. (Travis, kung fu instructor)

> I definitely wanted to lose weight, that was important to me, it's helped a lot and I do feel a lot more confident with my body ... And you see it in the films don't you, the *Charlie's Angels* thing, girls fighting and looking hot, I like that sort of thing, yeah, it's cool. (Keeley, kickboxing practitioner)

However, rather than confining such 'feminine' forms of participation within a female-only space, the existence of this fitness-oriented version of martial arts could, in turn, become a gateway for women to go on to participate in more combative forms of training. Commonly, this was explained as a function of enjoying the activity to the extent that women wanted to experience it in its fullest form and meet their own greater potentials as martial artists. Kick-boxing instructor Amir described how:

> Women come here for the fitness really, and then when they realise how good they are they might want to take the next step (and become competitive fighters). Some of them get the bug, and that's all they wanna do then, fight.

For such women, transitioning from 'fitness' to 'fighting' did not mean leaving behind the feminine aesthetics for which they initially entered the training environment. Rather than seeing themselves as adopting a form of 'female masculinity', they continued to emphasize (heterosexual) femininity through their appearance, clothing/kit or other interests while also remaining 'serious' about their training. Thus, for these women, combative martial arts and femininity could be effectively reconciled:

> I don't know anything that's as close to how much I love (martial arts), like, I just love it, I love being able to do this ... (but) I still love to have a sense and a feel of being a girl. I'm not embarrassed about fighting ... but at the same time I still like to have some sort of girliness into it, so I have my hot pink gloves, it's quite cool, things like that ... People definitely still see me as a girl, yeah. (Sylvia, muay thai and MMA competitor)

> I teach pole dancing too, that's another part of me really. It's two extremes, isn't it! ... So I think through doing that I really explored my sexuality and everything, because I'm now teaching girls how to be feminine, and yet I'm a serious kickboxer ... It's all a part of who I am. (Helen, kickboxing competitor)

Furthermore, the achievements of these visibly 'feminine' women were important in shaping others' attitudes towards inclusion and sex integration, as they would often prepare for competitive fights by training with male fighters. This was a product of another iteration of the gendered patterning of participation, as while the 'female-appropriate', fitness-oriented lessons offered by clubs primarily appealed to women, their more combative, competitive martial arts training sessions, which resonated more closely with socially idealized forms of masculinity, were disproportionately populated by men.[33] Thus, because there were relatively few women involved in competitive martial arts, and training partners within one's weight category were therefore hard to come by within any given club, women who 'crossed over' this divide would often do their competition training – which typically involved high-intensity sparring – with men. In addition to this, several interviewees also told of women competing in men's divisions at tournaments when too few female competitors entered, showing the degree to which combative participation alongside men could be opened to women.[34]

However, rather than being treated as 'honorary males', the increasingly visible example of successful, yet 'feminine' female martial artists who were capable of holding their own against men held significance by laying down a precedent of 'normal' women taking part in otherwise 'masculinized' training practices. This perception was shared among male and female club members, as these 'feminine' fighters were seen to break with social stereotypes of 'butch' female athletes typically constitutive of heterosexist discourse:[35]

> I'd say that nine out of ten of (the women I train with) I'd see at the weekend in a nice dress, looking quite attractive actually. Even the better girls, like the ones who might compete, they're not really like any kind of textbook hard woman. They're quite womanly, feminine I guess ... Just goes to show you that this is a sport for everyone. (Claude, kickboxing coach)

> (We are) showing that normal everyday women are capable of doing something which a lot of people say we're not. I think it's a good thing what we're doing. (Rachel)

While this process may draw criticism from some quarters for implying that a 'compulsory heterosexuality' restricted such women's performances of gender, this was not how the women reported the experience, as feelings of personal agency in choosing to 'do' femininity simply for the enjoyment of 'being girly' were an important element in all of those interviewees' accounts. More pertinently, however, their enduring femininity heralded a potent shake-up of essentialist sex discourse stressing the transgressive nature of women's embodiment of 'male' characteristics, such as fighting ability. Often interpreted as 'a pathological sign of (women's) misidentification and maladjustment', female masculinity risks the discursive annihilation of 'butch' girls as aberrant, probably homosexual, and thus not representative of 'real' women.[36] Instead, combative martial arts participation among otherwise 'feminine' women revealed 'the power of being in a feminine-gendered body', troubling normative and exclusive conceptions of feminine heterosexuality.[37]

While no doubt dependent upon the heterosexist frames of reference through which they were initially attracted to non-combative, 'female-appropriate' versions of participation, this gendered dynamic nevertheless provided a route for women to cross over into mixed-sex/combative participation in ways that destabilized this heterosexism, revealing just what so-called 'normal', feminine women were capable of relative to their male counterparts. However, not all women initially took up martial arts as a 'female-appropriate' workout programme. For some, the attraction was based more on the self-defence application of martial artistry, which was also important for many men, being significant for both groups in structuring ideas about the inclusivity and integration of training.

Alternative physical culture: self-defence and the rejection of 'masculinity'

In many respects, martial arts are not sports. While many martial arts disciplines have become 'sportized' in both meanings and practice, a great variety of disciplines and schools continue to represent an alternative form of physical culture to the sporting mainstream in various Western contexts.[38] Their diverse meanings and purposes leave open many different possibilities for making sense of martial artistry and by extension, the gendered significance of participation. While much can be said about the possible philosophical, pedagogical and cultural uniqueness of martial arts practice, two notable differences from mainstream sports cultures bear mention here for their role in helping to legitimize mixed-sex inclusivity. These include self-defence readiness as a key outcome of (particularly women's) training, and the critical comparisons made between male practitioners' identities and supposedly 'mainstream', sporting masculinities.

The practice of martial arts for self-defence is widely popular today for both men and women. Much has been written by feminist sociologists about women's self-defence martial arts, broadly celebrating and advocating the practice as a form of liberation, empowerment and self-realization.[39] However, while previous scholars have generally not directly highlighted the significance of mixed-sex training for helping to reach such ends, and more often than not have advocated single-sex environments for their more woman-centred or explicitly feminist pedagogies, the martial artists I interviewed unanimously suggested that effective women's self-defence training was largely dependent upon sex integration. This principally reduced to a perceived necessity for women to practise with men in order for the training to be 'realistically' effective, based on conceptions of sex and violence that resonate with typical constructions of sex difference and the patriarchal norms of 'rape culture', which self-defence is meant to oppose.[40]

First, women's self-defence training was considered more effective when they trained with men because of perceived size and strength differences, meaning that learning to escape from holds or take hits from men was necessary to push the boundaries of women's abilities:

> If a guy grabs hold of you it's different to a girl grabbing hold of you, they can hold you tighter. So when you practice with the big guys that's more useful, more realistic to what a real situation would be like. I wouldn't expect a ten year old girl to grab my wrist on the street! (Andrea)

Similarly, and more commonly, the second reason for supporting integrated training also drew on this idea of 'realism', given that men were considered the most likely perpetrators of violence against women and that such violence was thought common. This cast women's self-defence training as important within a social context where the risk of being (sexually) assaulted by a man was high and wherein men's power to physically coerce women was more or less taken for granted. Therefore, training with men was psychologically important in preparing women to fight back, as most women would not believe themselves capable otherwise:

> It's good for (women) to work with guys to get an idea of what it might be like to be attacked, because men are the most likely attackers. (David)

> I think it's so important for us to learn how to stand up to a man physically … I'm not scared of that any more, since I've been sparring against men for years and I know what it's like to be hit (by them), I'm used to the confrontation. (Marie, kickboxing instructor)

Such practicalities as these were made all the more urgent given that self-defence confers serious connotations on martial arts training, crediting it with enhancing one's personal safety ahead of potentially life-or-death situations. And unlike similar safety-enhancing physical activities, such as swimming, mixed-sex participation was required if this training was to be of any practical use for women. Legitimized as appropriate and necessary by a popular cultural discourse of women's vulnerability to male violence, such integrated training can also become a pathway to potentially subvert such discourse by revealing women's ability to resist men's violence and thus rejecting the role of women as men's inevitable victims. In this regard, self-defence is a practice that is not only embedded within the typical discursive parameters of patriarchy, but also aimed at overcoming the effects of such structures by transforming the ways in which women think about and perform within their bodies.[41] The popularity of martial arts as self-defence for women thereby contributes significantly to the transformative potential of normalized, integrated training, as it is explicitly concerned with enhancing women's fighting abilities relative to men's, and is thereby far removed from the typical constructions of sex difference common among segregated sports cultures more generally.

Further differentiation from other sporting activities revolved around the tendency for martial arts disciplines to have broader, more holistic pedagogical outcomes than the typically competitive focus of most Western sports.[42] With reference to this distinction, particularly male participants in my research were critical of a form of masculinity that they believed to be commonplace among men involved in highly competitive, pedagogically narrow and philosophically empty 'mainstream' sport.[43] Distancing themselves from a confrontational, violent and crude masculine style that they believed to be common in such other sports, and in particular the practice of sport as a means of 'proving' one's masculinity to others, they valorized an approach to training that was based on humility, introspection and a dedication to self-improvement in various ways.[44] This ultimately contributed to a broad rejection of a specific and supposedly widespread articulation of masculinity, and a male egotism seen by some as being harmful to the outcomes of training:

> (Men) who do martial arts … they don't go around wearing it on their sleeves, 'I do kung fu', that sort of thing. They're more subdued about it … Yeah, I think a real man isn't into superficial things … I guess a real man is someone who's respectful of everyone around him, accepting other people, not really into all that masculinity stuff. (Steve)

> Guys with something to prove don't fit in here, it isn't right for (martial arts), isn't the right mentality … A lot of guys come in here with that ego, the big man ego … most of them drop out within a week. (Amir)

Such criticisms of other men's *machismo*, and broad rejection of 'masculinity' as an organizing principle of participation, contributed to the men's readiness to accept women as training partners. Unanimously agreeing that martial arts was not a 'manly' activity, or a 'man's sport', being valued as a fellow martial artist was thus based on sharing a set of idealized characteristics grounded in a focus on personal development and growth, which had nothing to do with one's sex:[45]

> If your partner is more experienced, then whether they are a man or woman isn't important, because you can learn from anyone who's like, above you in skill level … It's all about how good they are at technique, movement, that kind of thing, and how much discipline they bring to their training, that's what makes a (training) partner useful. (Simon, karate practitioner)

Such a rationalization as this compares strikingly with the kinds of reactions to integrated sport suggested in previous studies, where the politics of gender within various other sports cultures rarely problematizes the masculinity of the male athlete.[46] Here, though, sex integration was considered logically compatible with the goals of martial arts training, regarding both the high-stakes, practical realities of self-defence and the importance of focusing on personal development as the central purpose of the activity, rather than becoming fixated upon enhancing or proving one's masculinity. Thus, the focus of training philosophies stressing either the singular importance of developing martial competency or the holistic approaches to broader self-improvement provided further discursive legitimacy for the normalization of sex integration.

Discussion and concluding thoughts

This paper has explored the discursive underpinnings of inclusion in mixed-sex martial arts, examining several features of martial arts cultures that legitimize the otherwise socially problematic practice of integrated training. These have included broader representations of martial arts, the pathways for crossover opened by sex-differentiated forms of training and the practical and ideological separation of martial arts activities from mainstream sporting cultures. The meanings of these phenomena were sometimes connected to conservative constructions of sex difference, which otherwise might make integrated training difficult to imagine, yet through participants' simultaneous performance of other, martial-arts-specific discourses, and within the practical necessities and realities of training, new and contradictory possibilities for action emerged. In this regard, and while I have not discussed this in great detail here, the reciprocal effect of practitioners' experiences of performatively *embodying* the possibilities represented by these discourses further normalizes integrated practice. Here, men's and women's joint performance of a discourse of equity and inclusion, through the shared, physical experiences of training, then becomes its own 'dramatic symbolic proof', just as segregated sport has long done for sexist ideals of exclusion.[47]

Yet, it is important to recognize that this inclusivity is not something that has simply sprung from the ground, paving the way for the performance of an altogether radical bodily practice through which otherwise entrenched ideals of fixed, binary and hierarchal sex difference might be challenged and potentially undone. While the effects of men's and women's performances are vital in helping to shape out new discourses concerning sex, gender and the body, understanding what first enables such performances is an important step in grasping how the transformative phenomenon of inclusive, mixed-sex sports participation can come about; thus, I have focused here on the discourses and practices underlying this integration.

In helping to understand the importance of this perspective, queer feminist theory emphasizes the post-structuralist tenet that language is just as much a means of *constructing* social realities as of describing them. In this way, the physical reality of sex difference is something that individuals bring about, following their gendered performances of specific cultural scripts or discourses. According to Butler, this perspective holds that 'there is no possibility of agency or reality outside of the discursive practices that give those terms the intelligibility that they have'.[48] If this be the case, then determining the underlying discursive parameters of integrated inclusivity in sports cultures is a vital first step in understanding how the radical social action represented by such practices is initially made possible. Without being able to draw on alternative schemes of intelligibility, the cyclical relationship between discourse and performance – in this case meaning conservative constructions of gender and segregated, hierarchal and patriarchal forms of sport – would repeat itself *ad infinitum*. In the context of martial arts cultures, several important discursive structures exist that enable participants to perceive the world in ways that 'fall outside' of the otherwise widely normalized, taken-for-granted system of binary, hierarchal sexual difference. As these are put into practice, they provide alternative means for imagining, and then performing, the reality of living in a sexed body, such that following their logics can lead practitioners to accept the normalization of mixed-sex training as appropriate and even useful in a number of ways. Such performance can then help to realize the transformative promise of integrated sport, as discussed at the outset.

As such, I would suggest that efforts to understand sex integration in sports cultures should be attentive to the sources of this particular form of inclusivity in various contemporary settings. While previous studies have explored the role of legal and policy interventions in imposing such inclusion 'from above', here I have outlined how normalized, integrated inclusion has emerged more or less 'from the ground up', by exploring the relatively unique features of contemporary martial arts training cultures in the UK, which are supportive of this inclusion.[49] My analysis here is somewhat limited, in terms of its demographic bias (i.e. predominantly 'middle-class', heterosexual, young adult Britons), present-centredness and focus on martial-arts-specific discourses rather than wider, contemporary social attitudes towards sex and gender. While further research efforts could help to better locate such findings as these within their broader sociocultural and historical contexts, the apparent importance of the unique meanings of martial arts in participants' constructions of mixed training as 'normal' (and even appropriate) nevertheless reveals the importance of examining the roots of such practices within their specific social locations. I would suggest, therefore, that future endeavours in exploring sex-integrated sport would do well to look not only to the effects of such phenomena on practitioners' embodiment, identities and beliefs, but also to the underlying discursive structures that facilitate their existence and acceptance in the first place. In so doing, a knowledge base will emerge from which future efforts at transforming the widely entrenched norms of default, sex-segregated sport may be able to draw potentially useful insights.

Notes

1. Hargreaves, *Sporting Females*; Roth and Basow, 'Femininity, Sports, and Feminism'; Theberge, 'Sport and Women's Empowerment'.
2. Wachs, 'Levelling the Playing Field'; Henry and Comeaux, 'Gender Egalitarianism'; Anderson, 'I Used to Think'; Guérandel and Mennesson, 'Gender Construction'; Love and Kelly, 'Equity or Essentialism'; Travers, 'The Sport Nexus'.
3. McDonagh and Pappano, *Playing with the Boys*; see also Anderson, 'I Used to Think'; Fields, *Female Gladiators*; Messner, *Power at Play*; Messner, *Taking the Field*.

4. Bryson, 'Challenges to Male Hegemony', 175.
5. Butler, *Gender Trouble*; Haraway, *Simians, Cyborgs and Women*; Grosz, *Volatile Bodies*.
6. Messner, 'Sports and Male Domination'; Love and Kelly, 'Equity or Essentialism', 228.
7. Butler, *Gender Trouble*, 32.
8. Wachs, 'Levelling the Playing Field'.
9. Anderson, 'I Used to Think'; Channon, 'Hit Me!'; McDonagh and Pappano, *Playing with the Boys*, 58–63.
10. See Channon, 'Do You Hit Girls?'
11. In the following sections, interviewees are identified as practitioners of whichever discipline(s) they were involved in at the time of interview, along with their level of participation, categorized here as (non-competitive) practitioner, competitor or instructor.
12. Theeboom and De Knop, 'Asian Martial Arts'; Theeboom, De Knop and Vertonghen, 'Experiences of Children', 20.
13. Love and Kelly, 'Equity or Essentialism'; McDonagh and Pappano, *Playing with the Boys*.
14. Travers, 'The Sport Nexus', 89.
15. That being when women are not allowed to participate in 'men's' sporting spaces – or vice versa – rather than voluntary segregation, wherein women/men elect to be separated. McDonagh and Pappano, *Playing with the Boys*, 7–8.
16. Abramson and Modzelewski, 'Caged Morality', 156–8.
17. Mennesson, '"Hard" Women'.
18. Lafferty and McKay, 'Suffragettes in Satin Shorts'; Mennesson, '"Hard" Women'; see also McCaughey, *Real Knockouts*, 79.
19. 'Conditioning' typically involves partnered drills wherein participants strike one another's limbs, head or torso repeatedly to toughen up the tissue and become familiarized with the pain of combat; see Spencer, 'Habit(us), Body Techniques'.
20. Channon, 'Do You Hit Girls?'; Guérandel and Mennesson, 'Gender Construction'.
21. In the course of regular training, martial artists rarely use their full force to strike or throw, in order to minimize injury risk. In fact, being 'controlled' was considered an important attribute when working with partners, regardless of sex differences; the use of greater force was typically only legitimized in preparation for competitive fights. See Channon, 'Way of the Discourse', for a fuller discussion of these themes.
22. See Norman, 'Feeling Second Best'.
23. Channon, 'Way of the Discourse', 134–5.
24. For example, Hirose and Pih, 'Men Who Strike'; McCaughey, *Real Knockouts*; Messner, 'When Bodies Are Weapons'.
25. Krug, 'At the Feet'.
26. For example, Inness, *Action Chicks*; McCaughey and King, *Reel Knockouts*; Mikula, 'Gender and Videogames'.
27. Brown, Jennings and Leledaki, 'Changing Charismatic Status', 184–5.
28. Brown and Leledaki, 'Eastern Movement Forms', 128.
29. The legend of Wing Chun was depicted in the 1994 movie of the same name, starring Michelle Yeoh; see Gomes, 'Doing it (Un)like a Lady'.
30. Caudwell, 'Sporting Gender'; Lenskyj, 'Power and Play'.
31. Roth and Basow, 'Femininity, Sports, and Feminism'.
32. Hargreaves, 'Women's Boxing'.
33. Even though male martial artists are often quick to deny that 'masculinity' is an important element of their practice (see below); also see Mayeda and Ching, *Fighting for Acceptance*; Spencer, *Ultimate Fighting and Embodiment*.
34. See Rachel's quote above.
35. See Caudwell, 'Femme-Fatale'.
36. Halberstam, *Female Masculinity*, 9.
37. De Welde, 'Getting Physical', 273.
38. Brown and Johnson, 'The Social Practice'; Villamón et al., 'Reflexive Modernization'.
39. De Welde, 'Getting Physical'; Guthrie, 'Liberating the Amazon'; Hollander, 'I Can Take'; McCaughey, *Real Knockouts*.
40. McCaughey, *Real Knockouts*.
41. Ibid.
42. See Brown and Johnson, 'The Social Practice'.

43. See Channon, 'Western Men', for a more detailed empirical analysis.
44. Ibid.
45. Abramson and Modzelewski, 'Caged Morality', 156.
46. For example, Bryson, 'Challenges to Male Hegemony'; McDonagh and Pappano, *Playing with the Boys*; Messner, *Power at Play*; Messner, *Taking the Field.*
47. Messner, 'Sports and Male Domination', 200; for a more comprehensive discussion of the transformative outcomes of integrated martial arts training, see Channon, 'Way of the Discourse'.
48. Butler, *Gender Trouble*, 202.
49. Fields, *Female Gladiators*; Love and Kelly, 'Equity or Essentialism'.

References

Abramson, Corey M., and Darren Modzelewski. 'Caged Morality: Moral Worlds, Subculture, and Stratification among Middle-Class Cage-Fighters'. *Qualitative Sociology* 34, no. 1 (2011): 143–75.

Anderson, Eric. '"I Used to Think Women Were Weak": Orthodox Masculinity, Gender Segregation, and Sport'. *Sociological Forum* 23, no. 2 (2008): 257–80.

Brown, David, and Alan Johnson. 'The Social Practice of Self-Defense Martial Arts: Applications for Physical Education'. *Quest* 52, no. 3 (2000): 246–59.

Brown, David, and Aspasia Leledaki. 'Eastern Movement Forms as Body-Self Transforming Cultural Practices in the West: Towards a Sociological Perspective'. *Cultural Sociology* 4, no. 1 (2010): 123–54.

Brown, David, George Jennings, and Aspasia Leledaki. 'The Changing Charismatic Status of the Performing Male Body in Asian Martial Arts Films'. *Sport in Society* 11, no. 2–3 (2008): 174–94.

Bryson, Lois. 'Challenges to Male Hegemony in Sport'. In *Sport, Men, and the Gender Order: Critical Feminist Perspectives*, ed. M. Messner and D. Sabo, 173–84. Champaign, IL: Human Kinetics, 1990.

Butler, Judith. *Gender Trouble*. Abingdon: Routledge, 1990.

Caudwell, Jayne. 'Femme-Fatale: Re-thinking the Femme-Inine'. In *Sport, Sexualities and Queer/Theory*, ed. J. Caudwell, 145–58. Oxon: Routledge, 2006.

Caudwell, Jayne. 'Sporting Gender: Women's Football Bodies as Sites/Sights for the (Re)Articulation of Sex, Gender, and Desire'. *Sociology of Sport Journal* 20, no. 4 (2003): 371–86.

Channon, Alex. '"Do You Hit Girls?" Striking Moments in the Career of a Male Martial Artist'. In *Fighting Scholars: Habitus and Ethnographies of Martial Arts and Combat Sports*, ed. R. Sánchez García and D. Spencer. London: Anthem, Forthcoming.

Channon, Alex. '"Hit Me!" Mixed-Sex Martial Arts and the Subversion of Gender'. Paper presented at the 6th meeting of the Transnational Working Group for the Study of Gender and Sport, Bath, UK November 26–27, 2010.

Channon, Alex. 'Way of the Discourse: Mixed-Sex Martial Arts and the Subversion of Gender'. PhD diss., Loughborough University 2012.

Channon, Alex. 'Western Men and Eastern Arts: The Significance of Eastern Martial Arts Disciplines in British Men's Narratives of Masculinity'. *Asia Pacific Journal of Sport and Social Science* 1, no. 2–3 (2012): 1–17.

De Welde, Kristine. 'Getting Physical: Subverting Gender through Self-Defense'. *Journal of Contemporary Ethnography* 32, no. 3 (2003): 247–78.

Fields, Sarah K. *Female Gladiators: Gender, Law, and Contact Sport in America*. Chicago: University of Illinois Press, 2005.

Gomes, Catherine J. 'Doing it (Un)like a Lady: Rethinking Gender in Martial Arts Cinema'. *Graduate Journal of Asia-Pacific Studies* 2, no. 1 (2004): 11–20.

Grosz, Elizabeth. *Volatile Bodies: Towards a Corporeal Feminism*. Bloomington: Indiana University Press, 1994.

Guérandel, Carine, and Christine Mennesson. 'Gender Construction in Judo Interactions'. *International Review for the Sociology of Sport* 42, no. 2 (2007): 167–86.

Guthrie, Sharon. 'Liberating the Amazon: Feminism and the Martial Arts'. In *Women's Spirituality, Women's Lives*, ed. Judith Ochshorn and Ellen Cole, 107–20. New York: The Haworth Press, 1995.

Halberstam, Judith. *Female Masculinity*. London: Duke University Press, 1998.

Haraway, Donna. *Simians, Cyborgs and Women: The Reinvention of Nature*. New York: Routledge, 1991.

Hargreaves, Jennifer. *Sporting Females: Critical Issues in the History and Sociology of Women's Sports*. London: Routledge, 1994.

Hargreaves, Jennifer. 'Women's Boxing and Related Activities: Introducing Images and Meanings'. *Body & Society* 3, no. 4 (1997): 33–49.

Henry, Jacques M., and Howard P. Comeaux. 'Gender Egalitarianism in Coed Sport: A Case Study of American Soccer'. *International Review for the Sociology of Sport* 34, no. 3 (1999): 277–90.

Hirose, Akihiko, and Kay Kei-ho Pih. 'Men Who Strike and Men Who Submit: Hegemonic and Marginalized Masculinities in Mixed Martial Arts'. *Men and Masculinities* 13, no. 2 (2010): 190–209.

Hollander, Jocelyn A. '"I Can Take Care of Myself": The Impact of Self-Defense Training on Women's Lives'. *Violence Against Women* 10, no. 3 (2004): 205–35.

Inness, Sherrie A., ed. *Action Chicks: New Images of Tough Women in Popular Culture*. New York: Palgrave Macmillan, 2004.

Krug, Gary J. 'At the Feet of the Master: Three Stages in the Appropriation of Okinawan Karate into Anglo-American Culture'. *Cultural Studies: Critical Methodologies* 1, no. 4 (2001): 395–410.

Lafferty, Yvonne, and Jim McKay. '"Suffragettes in Satin Shorts"? Gender and Competitive Boxing'. *Qualitative Sociology* 27, no. 3 (2004): 249–76.

Lenskyj, Helen. 'Power and Play: Gender and Sexuality Issues in Sport and Physical Activity'. *International Review for the Sociology of Sport* 25, no. 3 (1990): 235–45.

Love, Adam, and Kimberly Kelly. 'Equity or Essentialism? US Courts and the Legitimation of Girls' Teams in High School Sport'. *Gender & Society* 25, no. 2 (2011): 227–49.

Mayeda, David T., and David E. Ching. *Fighting for Acceptance: Mixed Martial Artists and Violence in American Society*. Lincoln, NE: iUniverse, 2008.

McCaughey, Martha. *Real Knockouts: The Physical Feminism of Women's Self-Defense*. London: New York University Press, 1997.

McCaughey, Martha and King, Neil, eds. *Reel Knockouts: Violent Women in the Movies*. Austin: University of Texas Press, 2001.

McDonagh, Eileen, and Laura Pappano. *Playing with the Boys: Why Separate is Not Equal in Sports*. Oxford: Oxford University Press, 2008.

Mennesson, Christine. '"Hard" Women and "Soft" Women: The Social Construction of Identities among Female Boxers'. *International Review for the Sociology of Sport* 35, no. 1 (2000): 21–33.

Messner, Michael. *Power at Play: Sports and the Problem of Masculinity*. Boston, MA: Beacon Press, 1992.

Messner, Michael. 'Sports and Male Domination: The Female Athlete as Contested Ideological Terrain'. *Sociology of Sport Journal* 5, no. 3 (1988): 197–211.

Messner, Michael. *Taking the Field: Women, Men, and Sports*. Minneapolis: University of Minnesota Press, 2002.

Messner, Michael. 'When Bodies Are Weapons: Masculinity and Violence in Sport'. *International Review for the Sociology of Sport* 25, no. 3 (1990): 203–20.

Mikula, Maja. 'Gender and Videogames: The Political Valency of Lara Croft'. *Continuum* 17, no. 1 (2003): 79–87.

Norman, Leanne. 'Feeling Second Best: Elite Women Coaches' Experiences'. *Sociology of Sport Journal* 27, no. 1 (2010): 89–104.

Roth, Amanda, and Susan A. Basow. 'Femininity, Sports, and Feminism: Developing a Theory of Physical Liberation'. *Journal of Sport and Social Issues* 28, no. 3 (2004): 245–65.

Spencer, Dale C. 'Habit(us), Body Techniques and Body Callusing: An Ethnography of Mixed Martial Arts'. *Body & Society* 15, no. 4 (2009): 119–43.

Spencer, Dale C. *Ultimate Fighting and Embodiment: Violence, Gender and Mixed Martial Arts*. London: Routledge, 2011.

Theberge, Nancy. 'Sport and Women's Empowerment'. *Women's Studies International Forum* 10, no. 4 (1987): 387–93.

Theeboom, Marc, and Paul De Knop. 'Asian Martial Arts and Approaches of Instruction in Physical Education'. *European Journal of Physical Education* 4, no. 2 (1999): 146–61.

Theeboom, Marc, Paul De Knop, and Jikkemien Vertonghen. 'Experiences of Children in Martial Arts'. *European Journal for Sport and Society* 6, no. 1 (2009): 19–35.

Travers, Ann. 'The Sport Nexus and Gender Injustice'. *Studies in Social Justice* 2, no. 1 (2008): 79–101.

Villamón, Miguel, David Brown, Julián Espartero, and Carlos Gutiérrez. 'Reflexive Modernization and the Disembedding of Judo from 1946 to the 2000 Sydney Olympics'. *International Review for the Sociology of Sport* 39, no. 2 (2004): 139–56.

Wachs, Faye Linda. 'Leveling the Playing Field: Negotiating Gendered Rules in Coed Softball'. *Journal of Sport and Social Issues* 26, no. 3 (2002): 300–16.

Not a job for 'girly-girls': horseracing, gender and work identities

Deborah Butler

Department of Geography, Environment and Earth Sciences, University of Hull, Hull, UK

Women began to work in the British horseracing industry in the late 1960s, early 1970s. In order to be accepted they had to be as strong, tough and able as the 'lads'. Drawing upon historical accounts and an ethnographic study of work relations in British horseracing, including semi-structured interviews with female stable 'lads', this paper analyzes how class and gender shape the way these women negotiate masculinity. Bourdieu's concepts of habitus, capital and field provide the tools to help explore the masculine work identities that are embodied by those working in the racing industry, and whether women working in the racing industry can in any sense be regarded as embodying masculinity in a 'field' of power that can be characterized as patriarchal and masculinized.

Introduction

... racing is traditionally a man's job; although the lads have had to accept the arrival of women, they feel that their domain is being poached upon ....as far as the lads are concerned, girls are only good for one thing and they get no respect if they are foolish enough to oblige in that direction, either.[1]

This quote is from Susan Gallier's semi-autobiographical account of life as a stable 'lad' as stable staff are referred to, in response to a labour shortage in the late 1960s.[2] Gallier's quotation can be compared to that of footballer Trevor Ford who said that football 'is not a woman's game, it's not a pastime for milksops or sissies, it's a man's game'.[3] Within the motor racing field Sir Stirling Moss took a different yet still denigrating view of women; whilst he thought women had the physical strength to drive Formula 1 cars, they lacked the necessary mental aptitude to race hard when wheel-to-wheel with male drivers.[4] Sport, whether horseracing, motor racing or football, is a patriarchal and sexist institution and one of the last bastions of masculine domination.[5] Since the 1960s, however, women have been employed in increasing numbers in horseracing in the UK and in this paper I explore the ways in which female stable 'lads' describe the work they do as not suitable for 'girly-girls' and how they develop a masculine work identity.

I begin by providing an overview of the contradictory attitudes that women must negotiate when working in male-dominated occupations, as well as in the sporting field, before using the work of Bourdieu[6] – especially his concepts of habitus, capital and field – to explore how class and gender intersect within the racing field. I then describe the setting for the research, Conborough[7] racing yard, where most of the empirical data were collected. Drawing on historical accounts,[8] the next section provides a contextual background for my empirical analysis in which I set out the ways in which habitus, economic, social and cultural capital(s) help shape the way in which women learn to negotiate masculinity and develop a working identity.

Negotiating masculinity in male-dominated occupations

Much research has explored women's negotiation of masculinity in male-dominated occupations. The racing field is both a sport and an industry and so, in order to situate this paper, I consider first the experiences of women who work in male-dominated occupations and second, the sporting field showing that women have to embody certain aspects of masculinity while, at the same time, retaining their femininity.[9] I particularly focus on manual occupations as the work of a stable lad is manual work.

Women's perceived lack of muscularity and lack of innate ability are seen as potential barriers to women performing manual work, for example, as a carpenter or a bricklayer.[10] It has been estimated that in the construction industry where manual occupations dominate the workforce, only about 1% of manual workers are women.[11] Research into gender roles in the Scottish construction industry illustrates men's perceptions in explaining women's lack of participation; women are seen as lacking in strength and in the ability to use tools and therefore unsuited to working in some trades.[12] Some of the problems that women operatives working in construction have to contend with on a regular basis are sexual harassment, crude language and having their tools stolen by male colleagues who then claimed the women were incompetent. Women found the best way to negotiate their place was by 'being able to take a joke, being broad-minded and giving back as good as they get'[13]; they also had to be very good at their work and to 'prove' themselves.[14]

There is also evidence that women underestimate their skills and equate technical competence with masculinity and men.[15] Engineering as a profession is often viewed as a masculine one and has reproduced the perception that it is unsuitable for women. Historically its image is one that is tough, dirty and heavy, dominated by men with the prevailing culture and ethos of the industry extremely masculine.[16] As in the construction industry different strategies have been used to try and increase the number of women entering engineering, but their success has been limited.[17] Women engineering students had to utilize various coping strategies in order to gain male acceptance, such as acting as one of the boys, accepting gender discrimination and adopting an 'anti-woman' approach.[18] As in the sporting field, women had to 'undo' their gender and uphold an environment which was hostile to women whilst perpetuating the gendered culture of engineering which is masculinist and male-dominated.[19] However, if they do this too successfully their sexuality and their gender identities are questioned.[20]

Within the sporting field women have to display certain features of masculinity in order to be accepted but, at the same time, efforts are made to preserve their 'femininity'.[21] Consider, for example, the 2012 London Olympics and the debate as to whether women boxers and female badminton players should wear skirts rather than shorts to help the viewing public distinguish between male and female competitors. Women boxers were competing for the first time in their own competition, part of a highly masculinized field where strength, violence and control are important attributes and are associated with hegemonic masculinity.[22] Attempts to distinguish the women visually through dress when compared to male boxers highlight gendered notions of sexual differentiation, showing how processes of sexual differentiation persist even though gendered regimes are being challenged and reconstituted. Research into women's wrestling shows that wrestling – a male-dominated sport in terms of participation, with the requirement of muscular strength, courage, fighting spirit and combat – is perceived as a masculine sport.[23] Women wrestlers, like women footballers, displayed a compliant femininity, engaging in feminizing strategies and exaggerating their femininity whilst at the same time transgressing traditional social norms by entering a typically male sporting field. Similarly women entering the male-dominated world of football have to challenge dominant notions of young female behaviour, defining themselves in opposition to femininity and performing as self-defined 'tomboys'.[24] This act of self-definition does not help to transform gender relations and by perceiving themselves as 'honorary boys' they reproduce and reinforce perceptions of masculinity, the binary between men's/women's sports and the power relations between male and female.

This discussion illustrates how women who succeed in male-dominated occupations learn to embody a particular style of working that reproduces 'male norms' but that is contradictory. Thus women conform to the 'norms' of femininity away from the field of play at the same time taking part in male-dominated sports where, in order to be able to progress their careers, they have to challenge dominant notions of femininity and adopt 'male' ways of behaving. They must embody 'masculine' attributes in order to be taken seriously yet if they are seen to be over emphasizing this, their femininity and sexuality may be called into question. Their options are limited in that if they challenge 'traditional' notions of femininity they are called lesbian and butch, but if they do nothing and accept the doxic values of the field their roles will be limited to those that fit men's sexualization of women and their place in society. The practices that are found in racing, in sport, in the army and at work are the result of resources and dispositions which, when they come together and are structured by power relations, cause the individual to learn a certain way of acting and reacting which in time becomes second nature, an almost unconscious action. These ideologies and values are institutionalized through the dominant ruling sporting organizations which define and reinforce a masculinist ideology, which includes tough-ness, competition and aggression.[25] In a similar way, the racing field is masculine, and it is difficult for women to achieve recognition within it.[26]

Historically, the equestrian field is masculine; horses played an integral part in the army, in agriculture and as visible bodies of class, status and position.[27] However, horseracing, like other equestrian sports, is unusual in that women and men work and ride against each other on equal terms.[28] Despite this formal equality and common rules, a gendered order exists where women occupy subordinate positions within the different occupational sub-cultures, of stable 'lad' and jockey where attitudes, dispositions and tastes are rooted in a male perspective.[29] It has been suggested that women face discrimination on account of a number of factors, one of which is the deeply rooted culture of sexism maintained by fashion, tradition and history embedded within the industry.[30] Other factors include women's alleged lack of physical strength and their body shape, reasons that were given for limiting the career trajectories of women jockeys.[31]

This research begins to address the classed and gendered nature of the horseracing industry by focusing on the work of female stable staff. There is a lack of research on the training of stable staff, who are the potential jockeys for the racing industry. A few anthropological studies investigate 'racing society', while Gallier produced a semi-autobiographical account of her life as a stable 'lad'; as did Philip Welsh who describes the daily life of a 'stable "rat"' as stable "lads" were sneeringly referred to'.[32] Contemporary studies on racing provide social historical analyses, analyses of the labour market and gender relations.[33] Although the effects on women participants of a masculinized sporting field have been considered for many sports, such as boxing, motor racing, ice hockey, wrestling, rugby and football, what has been missing from the literature is a consideration of class and how it distinguishes different groups of women and their ability to participate.

This paper draws on Bourdieu's conceptual armoury to understand the intersections of class and gender in the racing field. It uses Bourdieu's work to highlight a model of class that is not exclusively linked to employment inequalities but to the interaction between economic, social and cultural capital.[34] It draws upon habitus, capital and field to show how working-class women develop a masculine work identity. This results in their embodiment of a contradictorily gendered habitus and the physical strength needed to engage in manual labour.

Habitus, capital and the racing field

To Bourdieu, the relationship between subjectivity and society can be understood through the concepts of habitus and field.[35] Field refers to a set of positions in social space defined through the social relations of the field, structured by the distribution of capitals and producing relations of power, including those of class, gender and 'race'.[36] Relational social fields map the differential distribution of economic, social, cultural and symbolic capital.[37] Symbolic capital is the form which different types of capital take when they are recognized as legitimate. The value of the various capitals in the social field is assessed by the extent to which they can be converted into symbolic capital.[38] As Bourdieu points out, the capitals held by those who are 'unequally armed in the fight to impose their truth'are not valued or acknowledged as legitimate.[39] This is evident, for instance, in the naturalization of female occupational skills when women first started to work in racing in the late 1960s, when assumptions were made about their 'natural love of horses'.[40] In so doing, these conceptualizations disallowed any recognition of women as skilled workers.[41]

Habitus is a system of dispositions acquired experientially through childhood socialization and is shaped by the social circumstances of its production; it differs by class, gender and ethnic positioning.[42] It is a concept which explains how individuals engage in practices and how, through the dispositions of the habitus, people perceive, categorize, understand, evaluate and act upon the social fields to which they belong.[43] The distinctions in entitlement based on class, 'race' and gender become embedded in both the dispositions of the habitus and as attributes of the field.[44] To exemplify this, Moi highlights how the military is a powerful arena, in which the embodied cultural capital of masculinity can be invested and legitimated because it 'fits' and is recognized by the 'nomos', or rules of the field.[45] Masculinity is more than simply an attribute of a masculine habitus but also relates to the field; thus the military, like the racing field, is gendered masculine as a field of power. Thus, legitimacy and entitlement are embedded in both the habitus and the field.

Using these concepts it can be argued that a racing habitus is classed, 'raced' and gendered and develops in the context of the social practices and values that predominate within the racing field. Individuals make decisions about whether and on what terms they wish to enter other fields, or feel themselves to be disqualified from entering. The gender dimension of habitus can be used to analyze women's individual behaviour in a given sporting field.[46] How a racing habitus is formed and embodied and how women embody a racing habitus which is gendered masculine are the central concerns of this paper. Bourdieu's concepts will be used to understand how women were positioned within the racing field and how the struggle to achieve 'equality of opportunity' resembles a handicap race that has lasted for generations.[47]

The study

This research forms part of a larger study investigating apprenticeships and gender in the horseracing industry. The focus of this paper is on how women negotiate masculinity in the racing field, which is predicated on a doxa where women have to (and want to) be 'one of the lads' in order to be accepted. In other words, they adopt a 'doxic attitude' which involves unconscious and bodily submission to a set of deep-founded universal principles and conditions which form the fundamental core values and discourses articulated by the racing field and are seen as necessary and true but are quite contingent and arbitrary. Thus in a doxic state, the social world in which an individual is located is perceived as natural and is taken-for-granted.[48] In this paper, I draw on semi-structured interviews with one male and seven female stable staff, who had worked or were still working in racing, four female apprentice jockeys, one of whom was still riding, and a 12 month ethnographic study carried out at Conborough racing yard. The ethnographic study involved participant observation and detailed field notes (hoof notes) recorded whilst riding out and working in the yard as a 'lad'. Pseudonyms have been used for names and places to preserve anonymity.

The research and the wider study are informed by my autobiography, growing up as part of a family that was and is still involved in racing, as race goers, stable 'lads', trainers and jockeys.[49] My status as 'native' was such that I considered myself one of the racing 'tribe'.[50] Having worked in racing as a 'lad' I was particularly interested in how the racing field is gendered and classed and how this appears invisible to those within it. I do not define the study as an auto-ethnography; rather than a self-narrative it was a reflexive ethnographic study where the researcher was an insider, 'situated in relation' to those being studied.[51] As I knew or worked with some of my interviewees, I shared their assumptions, experiences and values and as a result, it was difficult to ensure that I asked them to make explicit what was implicit in what they were saying. As I was part of the racing 'tribe', it was almost too easy at times to become totally immersed in the work; sometimes the daily working routine became the pilot, with myself, the would–be researcher being piloted, rather than the opposite and where 'the comfortable sense of being "at home" was a danger signal'.[52] I also found it difficult to reveal the 'secrets' of the racing field to the 'outsider'; I felt I was questioning the doxic values I had once unconditionally accepted, as well as being disloyal to my former work colleagues. I tempered my anxiety about not being able to see the wood for the trees by remembering the words of C. Wright Mills that 'you must learn to use your life experience in your intellectual work, continually to examine and interpret it' and so I tried to approach my fieldwork akin to looking in a mirror, and seeing myself as well as others, with the researcher as both subject and object.[53]

Entering a male-dominated field

Women, whatever their class location, face opposition from men within the racing field. In the mid 1960s racing was administered and governed by The Jockey Club, a self-selected, self-perpetuating private gentlemen's club for male aristocratic racehorse owners and those of their class.[54] It was a man's social position, not his administrative ability and financial acumen, that determined election to the Jockey Club. Members of the Jockey Club developed their entitlement to power and their collective identity by exclusion, based on class and gender and being part of a cultural field whose core values and discourses were embedded in their habitus and were seen as being legitimate and taken for granted as the natural order of things. Very few working-class women (or 'girls' as they are known within the industry) were employed in racing around the turn of the twentieth century; a situation that persisted to at least the 1970s, and it has been estimated that women constituted only 10% of the existing work force during this period.[55] It was during the late 1960s, early 1970s that more working-class women began to be employed in racing, due to an inability to attract and retain suitable male stable staff due in part due to poor employment relations, very low wages and the introduction of equalities legislation at the beginning of the 1970s.[56] Working-class women had virtually no access to any cultural, economic and social capital apart from the physical capital they developed through the manual labour of working in a yard. The entrance of women into the ranks of the 'lads' initially caused some resentment. At that time, young men were taken on as apprentices but women were not able to 'serve their time' as indentured apprentices because apprenticeships were only open to men; this meant that women stable staff were not permitted to race ride. They were, however, often employed under the same terms and conditions as a 'boardwage man'[57] who, by definition, had 'served his time' as an apprentice. This changed with the abolition of indentured apprenticeship in 1976 and women were finally employed under the same terms and conditions as men. Nevertheless, they faced considerable hostilities and had to show they could be as good if not better than the men.

In what follows I explore the experiences of working-class women working in racing, drawing on interviews conducted with women who have entered the racing field at different times since 1970. My concern is to highlight how these women learnt to accept as normal the classed and gendered structure of the racing field as they developed masculine work identities and how, in turn, these practices become embodied in their habitus and within their working lives.

A 'natural love of horses'

In the 1970s, working class women were entering a male-dominated field where hitherto entry had been controlled by trainers themselves through male-only indentured apprenticeships.[58] Overall this period represents an important shift in the gendering of the racing field, as women gained the right to race ride as amateur and professional jockeys and were being employed as stable 'lads' to bolster the ranks of the work force. Indeed, a Jockey Club committee saw women as ideal employees because of their implicit,[59]

> natural love of horses . . . it is clear that for them working with horses is frequently a more attractive proposition than secretarial and shop work.[60]

Women were thus seen as a useful resource, not because of their equestrian knowledge and riding ability, but because of their perceived gendered aptitude, their 'feminine' disposition, an orthodoxy that constituted the received wisdom and the status quo of the racing field. It is also quite dismissive and patronizing. Women are seen to be doing work they are naturally suited to and as such are using skills which are not valued or rewarded in women as opposed to men.[61] Attitudes such as this still exist and, as will be shown later, are contradictory. Women were encouraged into racing through having a 'natural' feminine nurturing disposition yet needed to embody a masculine work identity if they were to be accepted within the male-dominated racing field.

There is evidence from my interviews that women entered the racing field because of their love of horses and the relationship they were able to develop with them. Many interviewees found it hard to articulate exactly what it was that first attracted them to racing. Ruth was drawn to working in the racing industry by the involvement and close working relationship a 'lad' can have with 'their' horse and did not mention wanting or expecting to race ride. She thereby accepted the doxic values of the Jockey Club and those in the wider racing field, that women were there to make sure the horses made it to the race track.

> I loved show jumping, I thought there was too many people involved with racehorses, you know, the owner, trainer, the lad, the jockey and I thought you didn't get to do as much with the horse . . . but it's totally the opposite way round isn't it? Because when you're the lad you can do all the work, right up to the day he runs. (Ruth, 40, stable 'lad')

Women entering the racing field accepted their subordinate position within it. If they did not, they left. For example, Mary had noticed how quite a few of the young women she had worked with, and who had not long been in the industry, disappeared,

> I think some of the ones that came to Bullers are still there but, where have the others gone . . . some get put off, yeah they do, they get frightened, the lads are horrible to them, bullied almost, and kids won't stand it, being sort of, harassed, or sexually harassed these days, you know why should they, and they leave and do other things and it seems such a waste, but it is like everything though, if you think like with, with the yards with schooling 'Oh we don't let girls school', like at Bullers. It was always the lads, and the girls would take the horses backwards and forwards . . . and given the chance we can do it as well as they can . . . (Mary, 30, stable 'lad')

This quote shows that women are marginalized and made to feel out of place in two ways: they are subjected to harassment and not permitted to school a horse. Mary's comments indicate that the women who were 'still there' were able to take the harassment, they stood up for themselves and were learning how to become 'lads', developing a disposition, a gendered habitus that suited a male-dominated environment. Women were also not permitted to school a horse as this is something that is done by someone who race rides, a jockey. 'Schooling' is the process whereby horses are taught to jump over fences and as such requires a certain level of expertise, knowledge and experience. It also indicates that the person is brave and willing to take risks by jumping the horse. Racing yards tend to have 'schooling' mornings when jockeys will come in specifically to jump the horses. Other staff, amongst them the women, ride the racehorses to and from the 'schooling' area, but are not permitted to school them. This happens to men as well as women, but the women accept it while the men feel they are entitled to school and expect to be given the opportunity at a later date.

Dawn, 19, a young apprentice jockey, reiterated what Mary said, although her view of racing was tempered by the fact that it 'was the buzz although I want to get a job [outside racing] as how many jockeys make it'. Dawn's attitude was different from Mary's in that, although she had already been given race rides, she saw the racing industry as having little to offer by way of a career unless she became a travelling head lad who is responsible for horses at race meetings or head lad who is in charge of the other staff in the yard. Dawn accepts that very few women are successful in the racing industry and in light of this she did not see it as a long-term career. It did not hold much by way of employment although it was an exciting industry to work in when riding out, or in her case, race-riding. She is from a different generation from the other interviewees quoted here, being born in 1990 and having done 'A' levels; she had other opportunities within the world of work and would be prepared to go to college or study if she felt she was not getting anywhere in racing. In addition, she thought racing was male-dominated and sexist. Her view was that the 'lads' she worked with were 'chauvinist pigs', especially the older men who thought women 'had wrecked it' [racing]. A male-dominated environment is still clearly prevalent in some yards, but what is different now is that some young women are not prepared to work in a field that they find hostile and challenging and where their roles are limited by their gender. The two points raised here are linked because trainers control access to who becomes an apprentice jockey and the perceptions still exist whereby men are more competent as race-riders at the top level.[62]

Inequality, opportunity and capital

Many of the interviewees wanted to race ride, 'just one, say I've done it' (Mary, stable 'lad') but most of them, as recorded earlier, were not given the opportunity. The trajectory from stable 'lad' to jockey is dependent on the patronage of the racehorse trainer who employs the individual. It is the trainer who decides whether the 'lad' has the potential to become a jockey through their riding ability and through displaying the correct attitude; they need to have a racing habitus which reproduces and embodies the values, attitudes and practices of the racing field. In other words a 'lad' must demonstrate that they can work physically hard, they are strong, tough, deferential, respectful of authority and polite. Access to cultural and social capital helps, especially for women who want to have the opportunity to race-ride. For instance, Lucy Alexander, who was the first woman jockey to win the champion conditional jockey's title in April 2013, had the backing of her father, a racehorse trainer who has supported her throughout the 2012–2013 National Hunt (NH) racing season. It is not only patronage that is important but also access to the right cultural and social capital.

> Unless you were the trainer's daughter, trainer's wife or you were going out with somebody, or a well connected background, you did not get to school [a horse]. And when I was at Wrigleys [trainer], the only girls who were ever allowed to do any schooling of any type were his daughters, and you weren't even considered and at that time that's when I was, I wanted to be able to prove that, I could, I was up for it then, 'cause you are when you're that age. I would have loved to have been able to school and as time goes on you just think, what am I following this 'cause, you're not going to get anywhere [here] but when I went racing and you talked to people, then you realise, well, actually, it's not just me, it's racing. I think that's why I work hard because that's the only way I could prove I could do anything. (Ruth, 40, stable 'lad')

Ruth's observation exemplifies how access to capital, through having a 'well-connected' background, distinguishes between different groups of women and acts as a class divide. This does not operate in the same way for male jockeys and male 'lads' who because of their gendered capital are at an advantage compared to female stable staff. As highlighted earlier, there is an expectation on the part of the male lads that it only a matter of time before they get the chance to race; women tend to have lower expectations than men with regard to race-riding. This has similarities found in other equestrian sports where male riders suggested that there was a 'male advantage' inherent within equestrianism with men being more ambitious, and pushing themselves forward thereby making themselves more visible.[63] The lack of 'participatory parity'[64] or 'equality of opportunity'[65] is exemplified by Mary, who did not have enough economic capital herself and lacked the cultural, social and symbolic capitals that might have given her the chance of a ride:

> Yeah, I did, yeah, I would have loved to [race ride] when I was sixteen, seventeen there's nothing I wanted more than to, you know, get on, and ride, but for one I never really had a horse, never had the money. At that age you get paid next to nothing and that's when you want to do it the most … when you're sixteen, seventeen, a lot of people are lucky, they've got the family, family background or friends of the family that give them a spin[a race-ride]. (Mary, 30, stable 'lad')

Mary was subjected to the symbolic violence of the racing field, that is, she was limited in her social mobility and aspirations through her lack of resources which denied her the opportunity to have a ride, but this is something she accepted as the way the racing field was structured.

The gendered contradictions inherent within the racing field are reproduced through a process of symbolic violence which denies women for some of the opportunities available to men. Ruth only became aware of the inequalities that existed when she left racing for a while to work at the Royal Mail, where attitudes were in sharp contrast to those she had previously encountered. By leaving, she became conscious of the misrecognition which made her accept the working environment in which she was situated.[66] She had been comfortable in what she had been doing and had 'misrecognized,' forgotten, taken for granted that her masculine work identity had been produced within a male-dominated field. She was thus surprised at the way she was treated when at Royal Mail and it was only when she returned to work in racing, having been away from it, that she realised how unequal it was. Working outside racing enabled her to recognize the doxa of the racing field and the symbolic violence to which she had been subjected.

> [In racing] you've been expected to hold your own just like anybody else, so that's the way I look at it really. You [all] do the hay, you [all] do the bale carting and you're [all] doing it … and I can see like in Royal Mail, 'you're not lifting that, are you alright with that? and I, [think], why not? … in racing you're just kind of expected to. See that's where you're alright being equals … when you're not? Riding ability. They can't, they can't pick and choose where you're equal and where you're not. You're alright for your strength, take your barrows out, but why aren't you strong enough to ride that horse? I think it's been a very male dominated [job], [that's] why it's been so male dominated and it's just taken so long to change, it was a male dominated area for such a long time. (Ruth, 40, stable 'lad')

Whilst Ruth was aware of these inequalities and the double standards in operation, her situation provides a good example of the relation between misrecognition and symbolic violence.[67] Her daily routine was predicated on the fact that she carried out the same hard physical labour as a man, she embodied a masculine work identity yet, concomitantly, the gender relations which structure the racing field meant she was trapped by her gender. She was able to display a masculine work identity so was accepted within the field as part of the work force, but her gender rendered her not suitable for race-riding.

Working-class women as stable 'lads' did not have access to the same capitals as upper and middle-class women, neither did they have masculine gender capital. Moreover they had to develop the physical capital that goes along with hard, manual labour and a racing habitus that embodies a masculine work identity. A racing habitus disposes the 'lad' to display behaviours such as deference, subservience and obedience, and to develop bodily qualities, such as toughness, strength, stoicism and stamina, all of which express the historically and culturally constituted values of the racing field.[68] This is true for both women and men; however, women's work identity was predicated on the notion of being hard working, strong, tough and in addition, not acting like a 'girly-girl'. Young women working in a racing yard have to learn to behave in ways which are acceptable to the men in the yard. This involves embodying certain aspects of working class masculinities such as physical strength, toughness and an ability to withstand pain. Women had to demonstrate that they were able to perform, as well as the 'lads', if they are to survive and be accepted in the racing field. The work is heavy, involving mucking out, pulling heavy barrows and lifting bales of bedding and forage. Mary explained her longevity in racing due to her attitude and as she put it,

> … you think, well if they can do that, I can do that and that's the thing, if they can get on that and ride that, I can ride that, … lift that bale of straw, I can lift that bale of straw … I've always been a bit like that, at a young age as well, just … trying to keep up with them. I think … if you're a girly-girl in the racing industry I don't think – well it's not for you anyway if you're a girly-girl … it's a man's world isn't it? And it's a pretty tough life isn't it? (Mary, 30, stable 'lad')

Women are also subject to sexual banter and harassment and, in order to be accepted, they have to respond to this appropriately, that is by shrugging it off and retaliating in the same vein. In this way women are negotiating masculinities in so far as they perform and embody certain aspects of masculinity while accepting their second-class status in the yard. Their status is reinforced by sexual banter and harassment which re-inscribes gendered boundaries and sexual difference. Tina, a former apprentice jockey and former lad, remembers how the men would call her 'split arse' and 'if you can't ride that, come and ride me' when riding out and when working in the yard. Working in a masculine racing field she learnt that to survive in racing you had to be tough, resilient, hard working and think,

> ... I'm not going to let you bastards beat me down, I'm gonna do it. You know, you've got to, not swear and curse ... but stand your corner, say, if they start ribbing into you, say, excuse me ... I'm paid to do my job, you're paid to do yours' ... you have got to stand your ground more and you just got to get on with it, but yeah, I think, even now, girls have just got to be a bit more oomphie. (Tina, 42, former apprentice jockey and 'lad').

A gendered habitus

The racing field is informed by understandings of 'masculinity' as associated with physical strength and stamina, where those with such a habitus feel comfortable. For the stable 'lad' this involves being strong, fit, light in weight, stoical and showing an ability to work hard. The habitus is shaped by practices within the racing field but is also dependent on the actions and dispositions of individuals for its existence. Each individual's habitus will be partly similar but they are 'strands in a collective history'.[69] For example, the habitus acquired in the racing field, by the racing workforce and the racing establishment working in it, incorporated particular views of women. Women were assumed to occupy a subordinate position, being physically weaker and not as tough or strong as men, and they were resented for taking up positions that could have been given to 'lads'. At Conborough, the female staff all recognized this, but accepted that in racing such attitudes are hard to overcome. As a result, they became resigned to comments from some of the male 'rider outers' whose role was simply to exercise the horses. One of them, Neil, found his entrenched attitudes challenged when a 'bird,'[70] as women are condescendingly referred to, rode a horse he thought only he would be able to ride on the basis of its strength. He was therefore quite taken aback and 'surprised that Brenda had ridden Chippy' who was 'strong' and hence, difficult to ride. I questioned Ruth about Neil's attitude as she had worked outside of racing and knew that some attitudes had changed. She said, with a resigned look on her face,

> in this day and age, you would have thought that male chauvinist pigs like Neil would have learnt their lesson that things don't work like that anymore. (Ruth, 40, stable 'lad')

In the context of attitudes such as these which are widespread amongst men and many women within the field, women develop a habitus that is subjected to symbolic violence, whereby they are treated as inferior and limited in their social mobility and aspirations. Within the racing field female bodies are 'imprisoned' to a degree by the workings of the habitus. This is accepted as 'the natural order of things' as Ruth explains,

> ... all I ever wanted to do was to be able to do every aspect of my job and do it well, I knew that I'd, I don't know where I got it from but I just knew that if you were a girl you weren't gonna go far. (Ruth, 40, stable 'lad')

Although attitudes towards women race riding are gradually changing and women are now an accepted, though subordinate, part of the workforce, they have developed a work identity that is predicated on the notion of being hard working, strong, tough and, as

Mary explained, not acting 'like a girl'. Shelley found that being a woman working in a busy point to point yard (amateur jump racing) was not,

> particularly a problem because I was always one of the lads, if that makes sense.... I was always happy to get on anything, and get on with it. (Shelley, 32, former 'lad')

Her acceptance of the orthodoxy of the field was unquestioned as she had formed and embodied a habitus and disposition which engaged with the way in which the racing field was structured. Her use of the word 'lad' in describing herself is an implicit part of her linguistic habitus and is part of the discourse that characterizes the racing field and which contributes to masculine hegemony within it as it renders women invisible.

Risk and physical strength

One of the reasons advanced for women not being exposed to the rigours of race riding echoes Ruth's experiences at the Royal Mail and is in contradiction with women's ability to work as 'lads', undertaking hard, physical labour. It relates to the idea that women may be more at risk of physical injury than men, especially in (NH, jump) racing where the chances of being hurt are greater than in racing on the flat.

One of the women told me about a trainer who will only have male 'lads' riding out; the 'girls' this trainer employs are ground staff, caring for the horses in the yard. She said,

> And it's a male trainer, and he has a wife and he's got girls that do pony racing and things like that... so I'm not sure if it's 'cause he doesn't wanna be picking broken girls up ... or, 'cause, there are some men that worry about injuring females and, it's a Welsh yard and it's a hard yard, as well ... and so I'm not sure of his reasons for it, whether he thinks we can't do the job or are a bit softer... (Shelley, 32, former 'lad')

Her comments suggest that injuries to women are viewed differently from those to men, as something to be avoided at all costs. Historically, men's discomfort with women riding and the paternalistic nature of the racing field became evident as women began to challenge dominant ideas of what was appropriate for them and what women's bodies were capable of doing. This was particularly the case when women were first allowed to ride as professional NH jockeys.[71] The horses in NH racing tend to be bigger than in other types of racing and there is more risk of injury and accident with horses falling and bodies being broken. When women first began to ride as professional jump jockeys, the accepted view of many in racing was that women needed protecting from these dangers and that they therefore should not be riding as their bodies were not strong enough to withstand any falls they might have, thus legitimating women's exclusion from various sports and other occupations.[72]

The historically and culturally informed values that structure the racing field are that women should be employed for their 'natural love of horses', which, as we have seen, was one of the reasons given for encouraging women to enter the racing industry as stable 'lads' in the late 1960s, early 1970s. There were some trainers then who had a reputation for not employing women on the grounds that they were simply not strong and tough enough to cope with physical work. Strength and stamina were seen as mandatory attributes for stable staff, but were qualities which women were seen to lack. In the 1970s, the introduction of equalities legislation speeded up the process whereby the Jockey Club had to grant professional licences to women, but herein lies the contradiction. Although women who work as 'lads' are expected to 'get some balls about them' (Tina, 41, ex-apprentice jockey), that is embody masculinity, be strong, tough and not act like a 'girly-girl' (Mary, 30, stable 'lad') they are not seen as strong and tough enough by many women and men in the racing field when it comes to race riding. Thus, the habitus underlies the structuring of all subsequent experiences such as the assimilation of the messages regarding women in the racing industry and so continues, structuring and restructuring, and although attitudes to women are changing, their physical 'weakness' is still assumed.

The contradictions that underpin such attitudes are illustrated by Sarah, a 'lad',

> Yeah, what really gets to me is the fact that we, us girls, are expected to do all the hard jobs, pull heavy barrows, move bales, muck out, you name it, we do it yet when it comes to race riding we are not considered. Not strong enough. (Sarah, 32, stable 'lad')

Discussion

Throughout the paper, I have used habitus as a concept to explain how an individual or organization develops dispositions and attitudes and how, for instance, the 'lad' becomes part of the field. Thus, a racing habitus disposes the 'lad' to develop bodily qualities, such as toughness, strength, stoicism and stamina, all of which express the historically and culturally constituted values of the racing field. These qualities are taken in through practice, which brings the concepts of capital, in the form of resources, and field, in the form of individual and institutional power, into the picture. The habitus is 'the social made body'.[73] Whilst the habitus expresses itself through posture, movements and the way the body is used, the body is also a repository for social experience, and as such, constitutes an essential part of the habitus. Bodily experience is profoundly influenced by gender although, as a process, this bodily experience is completely hidden from consciousness.[74]

The women who become stable 'lads' are entering a field that is gendered masculine. They have to develop a 'feel for the game' through a practical sense which leads to them embodying the attitudes and dispositions needed to work in a male-dominated field, for instance, learning how to cope with sexual harassment. As mentioned earlier, the habitus is a 'structure' defined as a system of dispositions.[75] Dispositions are described as a predisposition, tendency, propensity, inclination and as a way of being as an organizing action and a habitual state (especially of the body).[76] Taking each of these ideas in turn I argue that these women could partly embody a masculine habitus.

From a gender perspective, I would suggest that the women I spoke to had an unconscious relationship between their habitus and the racing field as illustrated by Ruth who 'knew she was not going to go far' in racing. What she means relates to the doxa of the field which defines women as weaker than men and as unsuitable bodily material to be jockeys unless they have the economic, social and cultural capital that meant they could ride as amateurs. The symbolic violence of the racing field that denied some women the opportunities open to men meant that she unconsciously knew, in her 'social body', that she needed another way to prove herself, to show that whilst she never would, in her eyes, be a jockey, she had other qualities of equivalent value. These could be achieved by replicating a bodily hexis similar to that of her male co-workers. This habitual state of the body was expressed by a physical attitude that was tough, hard working, gave as good as it got, was stoical and was impervious to pain. Women could embody a certain type of masculinity in this way and by so doing could develop their 'feel for the game'. Through 'practice' and responding to the masculine racing field, working-class women worked like men, they undertook the hard physical labour involved in being a 'lad', the men gave them no quarter; women were expected to do the same work as men if they wanted to be accepted and this involved developing a masculine work identity. At the same time, they are subject to sexual harassment which emphasizes their difference from the men they work with. This points to the complexity of gendered embodiment and suggests that women in the racing field embody elements of both masculinity and femininity; rather than embodying a completely 'masculine' habitus, their habitus can be seen as contradictorily gendered.

Acknowledgements

I would like to thank Professor Nickie Charles for her advice, support and encouragement in the production of this paper. Kate Dashper and Tom Fletcher provided very useful editorial advice as well as the comments from an anonymous reviewer which were spot on.

Notes

1. Gallier, *One of the Lads*, 44.
2. Toner, 'Survival and Decline'.
3. Ford, cited in Polley, *Moving the Goalposts*, 89.
4. Barretto, 'Sir Stirling Moss Says Women Lack Mental Aptitude for Formula 1' *BBC Sport*. http://www.bbc.co.uk/sport/0/formula1/22083547?print=true (accessed May 2, 2013)
5. Anderson, *Snowboarding*; Cohen, *Women in Sport*; Duke and Crolley, *Football*; Messner, 'Studying up on Sex'; Messner, *Taking the Field*; and Sparkes, Partington and Brown, 'Bodies as Bearers'.
6. Bourdieu, *Outline of a Theory* and Bourdieu, *Logic of Practice*.
7. All names and places in this paper are pseudonyms.
8. Within the racing industry the term 'lad' has been used traditionally to refer to male stable staff; it is now used to refer to both men and women and is an aspect of the hierarchical relations within which stable staff are located. It is a term which is sometimes used to refer to women as well as men.
9. Cassidy, *Sport of Kings*, 54; Harkness, 'Out of Bounds'; and Sisjord and Kristiansen, 'Elite Women Wrestlers'.
10. Fielden et al., 'Women, Equality and Construction'.
11. Briscoe, 'Women and Minority Groups'.
12. Agapiou, 'Perceptions of Gender Roles', 701.
13. Ibid., 703.
14. Ibid.
15. Henwood, 'From the Women Question in Technology to the Technology Question in Feminism'.
16. Evetts, 'Women and Management and Engineering'.
17. Powell et al., 'How Women Engineers Do and Undo Gender' and Watts, 'Allowed into a Man's World'.
18. Powell et al., 'How Women Engineers Do and Undo Gender'.
19. Butler, *Undoing Gender*.
20. Cockburn, *Brothers* and Butler, Indentured and Modern Apprenticeship.
21. Harkness, 'Out of Bounds'; Sisjord and Kristiansen, 'Elite Women Wrestlers'; and Slater and Tiggemann, 'Gender differences in Adolescent Sport Participation'.
22. Connell, *Iron Man*.
23. Sisjord and Kristiansen, 'Elite Women Wrestlers'.
24. Scraton et al., 'It's Still a Man's Game?'; Cox and Thompson, 'Multiple Bodies'; and Sisjord and Kristiansen, 'Elite Women Wrestlers'.
25. Connell, *Gender and Power*; Marvin, *Bullfight*; Sabo, 'Sport, Patriarchy and Male Identity'; and Wellard, 'Men, Sport, Body Performance'.
26. Gallier, *One of the Lads*.
27. Dashper, 'Together, Yet Still Not Equal?'; Plymoth, 'Gender in Equestrian'; and Hedenborg and Hedenborg White, 'Changes and Variations'.
28. Dashper, 'Together, Yet Still Not Equal?'; Adelman and Moraes, 'Breaking Their Way In'; Butler and Charles, 'Exaggerated Femininity'; Hedenborg, 'Female Jockeys in Swedish Horseracing'; and Ray and Grimes, 'Jockeying for Position'.
29. Plymoth, 'Gender in Equestrian Sports'.
30. Roberts and Maclean, 'Women in the Weighing Room'.
31. Velija and Flynn, 'Their Bottoms Are the Wrong Shape'.

32. Cassidy, *Sport of Kings*; Fox, *Racing Tribe*; Gallier, *One of the Lads*; and Welsh, *Stable Rat*.
33. Huggins, *Flat Racing and British Society*; Huggins, *Horse-Racing and British Society*; Vamplew, *Turf*; Vamplew and Kay, *Encyclopaedia of British Horseracing*; Winters, 'We Don't Want to Frighten the Horses'; also see Ray and Grimes, 'Jockeying for Position'; Tolich and Bell, 'Commodification of Jockey's Working Bodies'; Greiff, 'Presumably I am Like a Mother'; Hedenborg, 'Female Jockeys'; Hedenborg and Hedenborg White, 'Changes and Variations'; Butler, 'Indentured and Modern Apprenticeship'; Butler and Charles, 'Exaggerated Femininity'; and Velija and Flynn, 'Their Bottoms Are the Wrong Shape'.
34. Savage, *Identities and Social Change*.
35. Bourdieu, *Outline of a Theory* and Bourdieu, *Logic of Practice*.
36. Moi, 'Appropriating Bourdieu'.
37. Bourdieu, *Distinction*.
38. Ibid.
39. Bourdieu, 'What Makes a Social Class'.
40. Joint Racing Board, *Report of the Committee*, 25.
41. See for example, Butler and Charles, 'Exaggerated Femininity' and Liddle and Michielsens, 'NQOC'.
42. Bourdieu, *Outline of a Theory*; Bourdieu, *Distinction*; Thompson, *Making of the English Working Class*; and Moi, 'Appropriating Bourdieu'.
43. Bourdieu, *Outline of a Theory*.
44. Moi, 'Appropriating Bourdieu'.
45. Ibid.
46. Krais, 'Gender and Symbolic Violence' and McCall, 'Does Gender Fit'.
47. Bourdieu, *Pascalian Meditations*.
48. Webb, Schirato, and Danaher, *Understanding Bourdieu*.
49. See for example, Butler and Charles, 'Exaggerated Femininity'.
50. Zaman, 'Native Amongst the Natives' and Fox, *Racing Tribe*.
51. Narayan, 'How Native Is a Native Anthropologist'.
52. Hammersley and Atkinson, *Ethnography*, 115.
53. Wright Mills, *Sociological Imagination*, 196.
54. Huggins, *Flat Racing and British Society*; Huggins, *Horse-Racing and British Society*; and Vamplew, *Turf*.
55. Joint Racing Board, *Report of the Committee*, 25.
56. Ibid.
57. A boardwage man was an ex indentured apprentice who had served his indentured apprenticeship but continued to work in the yard for his board and wages. He was no longer eligible to race ride.
58. See for example, Cockburn, *Brothers and Indentured Apprenticeships*.
59. Joint Racing Board, *Report of the Committee*, 25.
60. Ibid.
61. See for example, Tyler and Taylor, 'Exchange of Aesthetics'.
62. Dashper, 'Together, Yet Still Not Equal?'.
63. Ibid.
64. Fraser, 'Feminist Politics in an Age of Reconstruction'.
65. Bourdieu, *Pascalian Meditations*.
66. Bourdieu, *In Other Words: Essays Towards a Reflexive Sociology*.
67. Bourdieu, *Logic of Practice*.
68. Ibid.
69. Crossley, 'Phenomenological Habitus'.
70. 'Bird' is a derogatory term commonly used in racing to refer to women.
71. Alcock, *They're Off*.
72. Caudwell, 'Football in the UK'; Marvin, *Bullfight*; Kidder, 'Parkour, Masculinity, and the City' and Pink, 'Breasts in the Bullring'.
73. Bourdieu and Wacquant, 'Purpose of Reflexive Sociology'.
74. Krais, 'Gender and Symbolic Violence'.
75. Bourdieu, *In Other Words*.
76. Bourdieu, *Outline of a Theory*, 214n.

References

Adelman, Miriam, and Fernanda Moraes. 'Breaking Their Way in: Women Jockeys at the Racetrack in Brazil'. *Advances in Gender Research* 12 (2008): 99–123.

Alcock, A. *They're Off. The Story of the First Girl Jump Jockeys*. London: J.A. Allen.

Anderson, Kristen. 'Snowboarding: The Construction of Gender in an Emerging Sport'. *Journal of Sport and Social Issues* 23 (1999): 55–79.

Agapiou, Andrew. 'Perceptions of Gender Roles and Attitudes Toward Work Among Male and Female Operatives in the Scottish Construction Industry'. *Construction Management and Economics* 20 (2002): 697–705.

Bourdieu, Pierre. *Distinction*. London: Routledge, 1984.

Bourdieu, Pierre. *In Other Words; Essays towards a Reflexive Sociology*. Cambridge: Polity Press.

Bourdieu, Pierre. *The Logic of Practice*. Cambridge: Polity, 1990.

Bourdieu, Pierre. *Outline of a Theory of Practice*. Cambridge: Polity Press, 1977.

Bourdieu, Pierre. *Pascalian Meditations*. Cambridge: Polity Press, 2000.

Bourdieu, Pierre. 'What Makes a Social Class? On the Theoretical and Practical Existence of Groups'. *Berkeley Journal of Sociology: A Critical Review* XXXII (1987): 1–17.

Bourdieu, Pierre, and Lois Wacquant. 'The Purpose of Reflexive Sociology'. In *An Invitation to Reflexive Sociology*, ed. Pierre Bourdieu and Lois Wacquant, 61–215. Cambridge: Polity Press, 1992.

Briscoe, Geoff. 'Women and Minority Groups in UK Construction'. *Construction Management and Economics* 23 (2005): 1001–1005.

Butler, Judith. *Undoing Gender*. London: Routledge, 2004.

Butler, Deborah. 'Indentured and Modern Apprenticeship in the Horseracing Industry: A Gendered Analysis'. Unpublished PhD Thesis, University of Warwick, 2011.

Butler, Deborah, and Nickie Charles. 'Exaggerated Femininity and Tortured Masculinity: Embodying Gender in the Horseracing Industry'. *Sociological Review* 60 (2012): 676–95.

Cassidy, Rebecca. *The Sport of Kings: Kinship, Class and Thoroughbred Breeding in Newmarket*. Cambridge: University Press, 2002.

Caudwell, Jane. 'Football in the UK: Women, Tomboys, Butches and Lesbians'. In *Sport Leisure Identities and Gendered Spaces*, ed. Sheila Scraton and Becky Watson, 95–110. Eastbourne: LSA Publications, 1999.

Cockburn, Cynthia. *Brothers. Male Domination and Technical Change*. London: Pluto Press, 1991.

Cohen, Greta. *Women in Sport: Issues and Controversies*. Thousand Oaks, CA: Sage, 1993.

Connell, Robert. *Gender and Power*. Stanford, CA: Stanford University Press, 1987.

Connell, Robert. 'An Iron Man: The Body and Some Contradictions of Hegemonic Masculinity'. In *Sport, Men, and the Gender Order: Critical Feminist Perspectives*, ed. Michael Messner and Don Sabo. Champaign, IL: Human Kinetics, 1990.

Crossley, Nick. 'The Phenomenological Habitus and its Construction'. *Theory and Society* 30 (2001): 81–120.

Dashper, Katherine. 'Together, Yet Still Not Equal? Sex Integration in Equestrian Sport'. *Asia-Pacific Journal of Health, Sport and Physical Education* 3 (2012): 213–25.

Duke, Victor, and Elizabeth Crolley. *Football, Nationality and the State*. Harlow: Longman, 1996.

Evetts, Julia. 'Women and Management and Engineering: The Glass Ceiling for Women's Careers'. *Work, Employment and Society* 8 (1993): 19–25.

Fielden, Sandra, Marilyn Davidson, Andrew Gale, and Caroline Davey. 'Women, Equality and Construction'. *Journal of Management Development* 20 (2001): 293–304.

Fox, Kate. *The Racing Tribe*. London: Metro, 2002.

Fraser, Nancy. 'Feminist Politics in the Age of Reconstruction; A Two-Dimensional Approach to Gender Justice'. *Studies in Social Justice* 1 (2007): 23–35.

Gallier, Susan. *One of the Lads. Racing on the Inside*. London: Stanley Paul, 1988.

Greiff, Mats. 'Presumably I Am Like a Mother to the Horses I Tend: Gender Relations Within Harness Racing in Sweden, 1930–2005'. In *The Global Racecourse: Work, Culture and Horse Sports*, ed. Chris McConville, 49–64. Melbourne: Australian Society for Sports History, 2008.

Hammersley, Martyn, and Paul Atkinson. *Ethnography: Principles in Practice*. London: Routledge, 1995.

Harkness, Geoff. 'Out of Bounds: Cultural Barriers to Female Sports Participation in Qatar'. *The International Journal of the History of Sport* 9 (2012): 2162–83.

Hedenborg, Susanna. 'Female Jockeys in Swedish Horse Racing 1890–2000: From Minority to Majority – Complex Causes'. *International Journal of the History of Sport* 24 (2007): 501–19.

Hedenborg, Susanna, and Manon Hedenborg White. 'Changes and Variations in Patterns of Gender Relations in Equestrian Sports During the Second Half of the Twentieth Century'. *Sport in Society: Cultures, Commerce, Media, Politics* 15 (2012): 302–19.

Henwood, Flis. 'From the Women Question in Technology to the Technology Question in Feminism: Rethinking Gender Equality in IT Education'. *European Journal of Women's Studies* 7 (2000): 209–227.

Huggins, Mike. *Flat Racing and British Society 1790–1914. A Social and Economic History*. London: Frank Cass, 2000.

Huggins, Mike. *Horse-Racing and British Society 1919–39*. Manchester: Manchester University Press, 2003.

Joint Racing Board. *Report of the Committee of Enquiry into the Manpower of the Racing Industry*. London: The Jockey Club, 1974.

Kidder, Jeffrey. 'Parkour, Masculinity, and the City'. *Sociology of Sport Journal* 30 (2013): 1–23.

Krais, Beatte. 'Gender and Symbolic Violence: Female Suppression in the Light of Pierre Bourdieu's Theory of Social Practice'. In *Bourdieu: Critical Perspectives*, ed. Craig Calhoun, Edward Li Pouma, and Moishe Postone, 156–77. Chicago, IL: University of Chicago Press, 1993.

Liddle, Joanna, and Elisabeth Michielsens. 'NQOC: Social Identity and Representation in British Politics'. *British Journal for Politics and International Relations* 9 (2007): 670–95.

Marvin, Garry. *Bullfight*. Urbana: University of Illinois Press.

McCall, Leslie. 'Does Gender Fit? Bourdieu, Feminism and the Concept of Social Order'. *Theory and Society* 26 (1992): 837–67.

Messner, Michael. 'Studying Up on Sex'. *Sociology of Sport Journal* 13 (1997): 221–37.

Messner, Michael. *Taking the Field: Women, Men, and Sports*. Minneapolis, MN: University of Minnesota Press, 2002.

Moi, Toril. 'Appropriating Bourdieu: Feminist Theory and Pierre Bourdieu's Sociology of Culture'. In *Feminist Cultural Studies*, ed. Terry Lovell. vol. 2. Cambridge: Cambridge University Press, 1991.

Narayan, Kirin. 'How Native is a Native Anthropologist'. *American Anthropologist* 95 (1993): 671–686.

Pink, Sarah. 'Breasts in the Bullring: Female Physiology, Female Bullfighters and Competing Femininities'. *Body and Society* 2 (1996): 45–65.

Plymoth, Birgitta. 'Gender in Equestrian Sports: An Issue of Difference and Equality'. *Sport in Society: Cultures, Commerce, Media, Politics* 15 (2012): 335–48.

Polley, Martin. *Moving the Goalposts*. London: Routledge, 1998.

Powell, Abigail, Barbara Bagilhole, and Andrew Dainty. 'How Women Engineers Do and Undo Gender: Consequences for Gender Equality'. *Gender, Work and Organisation* 16 (2008): 411–427.

Ray, Margaret, and Paul Grimes. 'Jockeying for Position: Winnings and Gender Discrimination on the Thoroughbred Racetrack'. *Social Science Quarterly* 74 (1993): 46–61.

Roberts, Laura-Jayne, and Malcolm MacLean. 'Women in the Weighing Room: Gendered Discourses of Exclusion in English Flat Racing'. *Sport in Society: Cultures, Commerce, Media, Politics* 15 (2012): 320–34.

Sabo, Don. 'Sport, Patriarchy, and Male Identity: New Questions About Men and Sport'. *Arena Review* 9 (1985): 1–30.

Savage, Mike. *Identities and Social Change in Britain since 1940. The Politics of Method*. Oxford: Oxford University Press, 2010.

Scraton, Shiela, Kirsten Fasting, Gertrud Pfister, and Anna Bunuel. 'It's Still a Man's Game? The Experiences of Top-Level European Women Footballers'. *International Review for the Sociology of Sport* 34 (1999): 99–111.

Sisjord, Mari, and Elsa Kristiansen. 'Elite Women Wrestlers' Muscles: Physical Strength and a Social Burden'. *International Review for the Sociology of Sport* 44 (2009): 231–46.

Slater, Anthony, and Marika Tiggemann. 'Gender Differences in Adolescent Sport Participation, Teasing, Self-Objectification and Body Image Concerns'. *Journal of Adolescence* 34 (2011): 455–63.

Sparkes, Andrew, Elizabeth Partington, and David Brown. 'Bodies as Bearers of Value: The Transmission of Jock Culture Via the "Twelve Commandments."' *Sport, Education and Society* 12 (2007): 295–316.

Thompson, Edward. *The Making of the English Working Class*. Harmondsworth: Penguin, 1980.

Tolich, Martin, and Martha Bell. 'The Commodification of Jockey's Working Bodies: Anorexia or Work Discipline?' In *The Global Racecourse: Work, Culture and Horse Sports*, ed. Chris McConville, 101–13. Melbourne: Australian Society for Sports History, 2008.

Toner, Phillip. 'Survival and Decline of the Apprenticeship System in the Australian and UK Construction Industries'. *British Journal of Industrial Relations* 46 (2008): 431–8.

Tyler, Melissa, and Steve Taylor. 'The Exchange of Aesthetics: Women's Work and the "Gift"'. *Gender, Work and Organization* 5 (1998): 165–71.

Vamplew, Wray. *The Turf: A Social and Economic History of Racing*. London: Allen Lane, 1976.

Vamplew, Wray, and Joyce Kay. *Encyclopaedia of British Horseracing*. London: Routledge, 2005.

Velija, Philippa, and Leah Flynn. 'Their Bottoms are the Wrong Shape. Female Jockeys and the Theory of Established Outsider Relations'. *Sociology of Sport Journal* 27 (2010): 301–15.

Webb, Jan, Tony Schirato, and Geoff Danaher. *Understanding Bourdieu*. London: Sage, 2002.

Wellard, Ian. 'Men, Sport, Body Performance and the Maintenance of "Exclusive Masculinity"'. *Leisure Studies* 21 (2002): 235–48.

Welsh, Phillip. *Stable Rat: Life in the Racing Stables*. London: Eyre Methuen, 1979.

Winters, Janet. 'We Don't Want to Frighten the Horses: The 1975 Stable Lads' Strike'. Paper presented at the British Society of Sports History Annual Conference, Eastbourne, September 6, 2008.

Wright Mills, Charles. *The Sociological Imagination*. New York: Oxford University Press, 1959.

Zaman, Shahaduz. 'Native Amongst the Natives. Physician Anthropologist Doing Hospital Ethnography at Home'. *Journal of Contemporary Ethnography* 37 (2008): 135–154.

The concepts underpinning everyday gendered homophobia based upon the experiences of lesbian coaches

Leanne Norman

School of Sport, Leeds Metropolitan University, Leeds, UK

This study focuses upon conceptualizing everyday gendered homophobia based upon the narratives of 10 lesbian coaches in the UK, connecting their stories of everyday inferiorizations to wider structural practices. This theory highlights that lesbians in sport and coaching continue to encounter marginalization through their gendered sexual identity. The participants recounted experiences such as being treated as paedophiles or predators, constructed as less able leaders and less knowledgeable than male coaches. Oppressive structural practices that influenced such experiences included inflexible or gendered professional development opportunities, apathetic stances towards welfare issues, inadequate sociocultural coach education and a culture of 'unspoken truths' that suppressed discussions of sexuality. The gender-blindness and sexuality-blindness cultures of governing bodies for how these ideologies allow organizations to ignore the construction of male privilege, heterosexism and homophobia and the impact on everyday lives of lesbian coaches are highlighted.

Introduction

While writing this paper, I took a break during a Saturday afternoon to watch my nephew play soccer for our local youth boys' team in a league match. When I arrived at the match, and watched the first half of the game, a group of parents gathered at the sidelines to cheer on our team, most of whom were mothers of the boys playing. At half time, the male referee came over to the group of us to ask if a parent could stand in for the linesman who had picked up an injury during the first half and was unable to continue. With my knowledge and understanding of the game as both an avid fan and a qualified coach, I volunteered for the role. The referee responded with silence and so thinking that he had not heard me, I continued to voice my availability until the referee asked one of the fathers, who reluctantly took the linesperson's flag and proceeded to the side of the pitch. Bemused by this, I approached the referee and enquired into why he did not consider me for the job, given that I was willing and experienced in the sport. To this, he replied 'you're a woman, what do you know?' On hearing this, some of the mothers enquired into why this referee, a regular official for the team, never asked one of them to be linesperson for any of the matches. Laughing, the referee turned to the group and remarked, 'unless it's netball, you lot wouldn't have a clue ... '.

My experience of this referee and how he views women is evidence of the wider, cultural beliefs that exist within a sports context surrounding women's abilities and 'limits'. Although women participate in sport more than ever and women's sport in the UK has never been more visible or marketable, those of us who do compete in or coach a sport still remain ideologically controlled by what is deemed 'proper' and normal for athletic women.[1] Sport continues to be constructed as a sex-segregated activity, erroneously based upon what is deemed to be 'natural' and on biological differences between males and females.[2] However, what is deemed to be 'natural' is socially constructed and is the thread that runs through ideologies that prize particular masculinities over others and relegates women to 'athletic intruders'.[3] Kolnes added that the social construction of men and women in sport takes place within a heterosexual paradigm, privileging certain images of masculinity and femininity as well as men's dominance and women's oppression.[4] Thus, not only is sport organized around gender differences but heterosexuality is also a key organizing principle. Research shows that within sport, institutionalized heterosexuality is the *status quo* and that the sporting world is a homonegative space.[5] This is because sport continues to be governed by the tenets of idealized heterosexual masculinity that reinforce men's superiority and women's inferiority.[6] Within this, white, heterosexual men comprise the privileged social groups and to gain acceptance in this sexist, patriarchal culture, individuals often have to conform to a system that surveys and scrutinizes collective and individual behaviours and appearances.[7] Women who play or coach a sport are at risk to this patriarchal ownership of sport and so the consequence is that women often face hostility and prejudices.[8] One strong pervasive cultural ideology that surrounds women in sport is the connection between their participation and questions surrounding their sexual identity.[9]

Review of literature

Sport has long been documented as an extremely homophobic institution for all participants, whether athletes or coaches, for men as well as women.[10] Adams and Anderson contend that this has been accomplished through cultural narratives that emphasize the rejection of homosexuality and the suppression of gay identity through homophobic discourse.[11] The sporting context has been depicted as a site of discrimination, personal struggles and even harassment.[12] For men, it has even been argued that homophobia has been the most significant social factor influencing constructions of ideal heteromasculinity. Nevertheless, scholars researching homophobia within the sporting contexts have begun to argue that, while the number of openly lesbian, gay, bisexual or transgendered (LGBT) athletes is still very low, there is a discernible sense of decreasing cultural homophobia, greater acceptance of homosexuality and improved social attitudes within sporting settings.[13] But as Adams and Anderson observe, examining homophobia is contextually specific and homophobia in sport can no longer be discussed as a global construct.[14] Thus, while this research notes the improved social attitudes towards sexual orientation that have permeated into sport settings from wider society, three aspects of this work mean that transferability to other contexts is difficult. First, much of the work that has found a growing climate of inclusivity has based a research upon educationally based sports settings, such as universities. Comparisons with other contexts, such as club sport or high performance sport, are difficult. Second, this study has only examined the views of athletes, not other individuals within the sporting system, such as coaches or those in significant positions within the governing bodies. This is odd because these are, after all, the main holders of power within sport. Finally, and most crucially, the majority of the research into decreasing homophobia has only focused upon men and masculinity. Homophobia has been viewed from the perspective that it is a tool to differentiate men in accordance with the hegemonic notions of masculinity.[15] Therefore, the processes and effects of homophobia as described in this research may not be applicable to women, including lesbians.

It is not just within the literature examining decreasing homophobia in sport that the subject of lesbian experiences is rare. As identified within the recent UK review of sexual orientation in sport, there is only a small body of research that centres upon lesbians in sport and this tends to focus primarily upon the connection between participation in sport, sexuality and femininities.[16] Literature specifically focusing on lesbianism in sport accounted for just 7% of the sources found in the extensive literature search.[17] Within this, the research is concentrated in the area of understanding lesbian experiences as athletes.[18] An outstanding knowledge gap, as identified by the review, is understanding the experiences of lesbian coaches.[19] While the coaching context has been the subject of a few research studies dealing with sexual orientation, this work has predominantly involved collecting the attitudes *towards* sexual minorities as coaches or the attitudes *of* coaches towards homophobia or coaching LGB athletes.[20]

According to the review, only three studies have specifically centred upon the experiences of lesbian coaches from the perspective of the coaches themselves. Within the groundbreaking book, *Strong Women, Deep Closets*, Griffin presented the accounts of the strategies that US collegiate lesbian coaches utilized to manage their sexual identity.[21] While some coaches were open as to their sexual identity within their work place, all of the women went through a process of continual decision-making regarding to whom they disclosed their sexuality, weighing this up against potential consequences to their image and professional identity.[22] The second study specifically focusing upon the experiences of lesbian coaches was Iannotta and Kane's examination of the 'sexual stories' of intercollegiate coaches.[23] Exploring the plurality of strategies used by the participants to reveal and be open about their sexual identity, as well as to actively resist the homophobic culture of the sporting environment, Iannotta and Kane found that how the participants conceptualized their sexual identity performance did not 'fit' with the categories outlined in Griffin's identity management continuum.[24] Through the study, it was also demonstrated that there is a plurality of strategies to challenge homophobia within sport, not only on linguistic terms. Finally, the most recent research with lesbian coaches was Krane and Barber's study into the identity tensions felt by 13 American college lesbian coaches.[25] Krane and Barber presented the decisions, actions and negotiations that the participants experience between identifying as a coach and as a lesbian in a context that is grounded within strongly homophobic and heterosexist social norms.[26] The findings revealed the stress and frustration that such minority groups experience as a result of being outside of the dominant social groups.

In this paper, I explore the underpinning concepts of everyday gendered homophobia to discuss the everyday inferiorizations experienced by UK-based professional women coaches who self-identify as lesbian, related to their gendered and sexual identity. First, I outline my methodology to study the participants' experiences, and second, I present the findings from this research, connecting their narratives of the everyday to the structure in which these experiences occur. Following the findings, I conclude with important messages for coaching sociology and sporting organizations regarding the importance of understanding the everyday, and some solutions offered by my research participants to support minority groups within coaching. For this study, the two research questions that underpinned the research were (i) how do the participants experience their gendered, sexual identity within their profession? and (ii) what are the structural practices that shape these personal experiences?

Methodology

Participants

It is currently not known how many lesbian (or any other sexual orientation) coaches there are in the UK because such figures are not monitored by the governing bodies or coaching agencies. Ten women coaches based in the UK who self-identified as lesbian came forward to be included in this study following a process of snowballing, and through adverts detailing the study and requesting participants distributed to governing bodies, gay and lesbian literature and to coaching agencies to include in their newsletters and websites.

The participants represented a variety of individual and team sports, including cricket, tennis, athletics, football, hockey and basketball. The participants included coaches from a variety of performance levels, including club head coach or specialist coaches, county-level coaches and head coaches of national junior and senior squads. The national junior and senior coaches were also club coaches on a day-to-day or weekly basis. All of the coaches had at least 5 years experience in coaching. While this was not a pre-requisite for inclusion in the study, it was requested that participants coached on at least a part-time, paid basis; all of them did. This was so that the participants had been immersed within the coaching system for a prolonged period. Given the focus of the research (to discuss how gender and sexual orientation was experienced in the UK coaching profession) and the anticipated difficulty in recruiting participants, no other requirements for the study were provided. Four of the coaches were current coaches of women's teams or women athletes. One participant was a current coach of a women's team but also had previous experience of coaching men's and women's teams within her sport. The five remaining participants were currently coaching either both men's and women's teams/athletes or head coaches of men's teams within their sport. While all of the coaches were based within the UK, eight of the participants were British, one coach was from South Africa and another was Spanish. A significant limitation of the study is that all of the participants identified themselves as white and able-bodied; thus, the representativeness of the sample was low.

Data collection and analysis

The findings of this study are based upon one-to-one in-depth interviews with the participants with the aim to understand the participants' experiences in greater depth, to consider the women's stories as legitimate sources of knowledge and to privilege the participants as experts on their own lives.[27] Within the notion of studying the everyday, experiences (including personal, meditated, vicarious and cognitive) form the central focus of enquiry. It is in these experiences that individuals come to form their understanding of injustices. Discussing personal experiences can yield important knowledge as to the nature and effect of practices that support injustices because these incidents can often appear insignificant, trivial or even invisible 'from the outside'. In this way, personal experiences are legitimate sources of knowledge because of the subtlety of prejudices.[28] The work of Essed that examined everyday experiences of racism has been criticized on the grounds that individuals may be incorrectly interpreting and misreading incidents of inferioriza-tions, as well as reporting false motives of the perpetrators.[29] Nevertheless, the purpose of collecting participants' stories and experiences is not for 'verification', rather these interpretations are reflections of social reality and everyday life in themselves.[30]

Interviews with the participants lasted between 60 and 120 min and were digitally recorded. The recordings were then transcribed verbatim. An interview guide approach was employed to provide focus for the interviews. The interview guide, created for the purpose of this study, centred upon the following areas: (1) background in coaching/early experiences, (2) intersectionality of identity, (3) perceptions of gendered and sexuality ideologies surrounding sport and coaching, (4) everyday relations within coaching and (5) ways in which the participant challenged inequalities within their everyday coaching practices, and their understanding of governing bodies' attempts to challenge gendered and sexual inequalities. Participants were also asked to elaborate on any further information they deemed relevant during the course of the interview.

To improve the trustworthiness of the data and to provide the participants the opportunity to volunteer additional information, a member check of the interview transcripts was employed with all the participants before data analysis. None of the participants requested any changes to their transcript. Analysis of the data was carried out using the software Atlas Ti to code the interview data, to locate recurrent themes across the transcripts and to group these themes together to form an understanding of how and why the coaches experienced their gendered and sexual identities.

Understanding the experiences of lesbian coaches: a theory of everyday gendered homophobia

The notion of everyday gendered homophobia has four evident components similar to that of everyday racism: (a) one part describes that it is about the everyday, (b) the understanding of gender within the everyday, (c) another part describes that it is related to gendered homophobia and (d) the notion of everyday gendered homophobia.[31] To reveal discriminations such as homophobia, we must question meanings, illuminate underlying practices and problematize what is taken for 'common-sense' or acceptable.[32] This is not such a well-researched area within the sport science family of disciplines.[33] Instead, the coaching literature contains a significant knowledge gap with regard to exploring the subjective lives of coaches.[34] These accounts of coaches' everyday lives are not just collections of 'off the cuff' stories. They are interpretations based upon reflections of reality.[35] In the following sections, I discuss the four central components of everyday gendered homophobia, along with excerpts from the interviews with the participants who illustrate these concepts.

The concept of everyday

The first component of a theory of everyday gendered homophobia is the concept of the everyday. The term 'everyday' refers to the familiar world of an individual and in Essed's words, 'a world of practices with which we are socialised in order to manage the system'.[36] It is a world in which individuals understand and use knowledge of cultural values, norms, rules and languages to live in societies.[37]

It is in the everyday that public and private spheres of social life amalgamate to create social relations and conditions.[38] The analysis of everyday experiences link micro-experiences to the structural context in which they are moulded. In the case of coaching, the everyday lives of the professionals within this system are significantly influenced by the norms and values of their organizations and governing bodies. Specifically, for the participants, their understanding of their gendered, sexual identities was sculpted in part by organizational approaches to equity, equality and diversity issues. They felt, on a daily basis, that there was a culture of 'ignorance' surrounding difference. This 'definition of reality' that shapes the everyday constructed the values of non-recognition of difference and reluctance to take action against inequality within the sporting and coaching context.[39] In turn, this meant that on a day-to-day level, the participants experienced marginalization and exclusion. The most significant evidence of this, according to the participants, was in the failure to provide broader coach educational programmes that were grounded in a day-to-day coaching practice. The absence of a formal programme of equity education for coaches was noted by all the 10 participants. For three of the participants, there was no social justice training for coaches available at all within their governing bodies. For the other seven coaches, existing education for coaches related to social issues was ad hoc, narrow in focus, poorly led and lacked meaning and impact. This was the case for Kelly, a part-time specialist coach who worked within a club from a culturally visible and popular UK sport. She found that the one-off training workshop she attended only dealt with a small number of issues:

> Gender was not mentioned, age wasn't mentioned, working with minorities wasn't mentioned.[40]

Maggie is a part-time coach within a men's academy at a professional club, in a sport that is one of the most popular in the UK. Alongside this role, she is also a paid part-time coach for the regional branch of her national governing body. She shared a similar experience regarding the narrow focus of her equity training course. She was critical of the lack of relevance for her day-to-day coaching practice:

> It was extremes, so it was kind of "these are the right words to use, these are the wrong words to use" and I think a lot of it focused around disability and race, instead of sexual orientation and gender. It was very much about people's ability. A lot of it was about the extremes of language ... extreme cases but not cases that would confront you every day. Sitting in on them, you sort of looked and thought "I'm not sure I've ever come across cases like that". Everyday cases ... they never got dealt with, the grey issues never got dealt with.[41]

For Lucy, a coach from an individual sport at a high performance level in an environment that is male dominated, she found the one workshop she attended felt like a 'gimmick' by the governing body and contained little substance:

> I had to do [the course] because we've had to be "club marked". I just see them as Mickey Mouse courses [because] you turn up for three hours, get there, get your tick, sit in a room, read your thing and off you go.[42]

These social justice training workshops for coaches took place within organizational cultures that placed little value upon challenging inequalities in sport that occur on an everyday basis. Such lip service was further evidenced by the lack of any tangible strategic plan and action within any of the national governing bodies. Tanya, who is the head coach of a well-known women's club within her sport and had been national senior head coach prior to this, illustrated the approach of her organization towards equity issues and the impact at a micro-level, for those individuals who are not from a hegemonic group:

> Sexual orientation, we have work to do. We monitor, but we do not publish ... That is symptomatic of the culture. Publishing the stats is not going to change me but it does tell me that [my organisation] is thinking differently ... If you don't publish all we are doing is invisibility. We have visible differences and then you have invisible difference. Invisible differences stay invisible if you don't publish.[43]

For Tanya, this invisibility linked to an organizational failure to acknowledge difference and meant that she did not disclose her sexual orientation in her relationship with others on a day-to-day basis. In these everyday narratives such as Tanya's, the connection between structural practices and personal experiences is made evident:

> I wouldn't say it's overtly encouraged, as in, "please tell us". My experience of things that have been said, not overtly ... but in the sense that here there are still plenty of people who think its private, keep it to yourself. There are members of staff that still say, "it's nothing to do with us". We still have to get over that ... it's the perception that it's nobody's business.[44]

Instead, the coaches want a drive within the governing bodies and coach system builders towards improving this education. This is in order for coaches to pass on to their athletes the need to understand and embrace diversity within their everyday practices, the importance of an inclusive team and work environment and so that the participants themselves feel valued by others. This belief was shared by Gemma, a national junior squad head coach and club coach. She had struggled in her daily interactions with others for disclosing her gendered, sexual identity in a sport that is male dominated and where she works alongside heterosexual women who embraced hegemonic femininity:

> As a coach, I think a definite underlying philosophy of appreciation of diversity would help me be out. I think there is a tendency to make your [players] all look the same in terms of skills, technical skills. For me, what would drive my coaching philosophy would be that culture of appreciation of differences, so that all different players would be a better side, so differences make a better team, including that in appreciation of differences in a wider perspective, race, sexuality, age. Just laying down that culture of openness. [Coach education should play a role in promoting women and sexual orientation], I think definitely. It's about raising the level of awareness. For me, it's really about opening up the dialogues and having the conversations. In terms of coach education, that kind of diversity training would be huge.[45]

Tanya shared this view:

> I would like to see existing coaches, whoever they are, given a better understanding of what diversity really means, some evidence so that they understand the difference of coaching athlete A and athlete B because of who they are, so greater depth in coaches coaching athletes. When it comes to coaches themselves, some of that is marketing, promotion and accessibility of coach education. So the image you see is a real image [of coaches], not an aspirational image if you like from the national governing body point of view. [The effect is] "coaching is for a particular group, not for me".[46]

With the absence of any strategic direction, action or guidance from the governing bodies at a national level, or adequate sociocultural education for coaches, existing oppressive ideologies of gender and sexuality continue to thrive at a micro-level. Hegemonic ideologies remain the norm, difference is not valued and for minority groups, their everyday lives are stories of negotiation, marginalization or invisibility. In the case of the participants in this study, these women worked in a patriarchal, heterosexist culture. This leads me to discuss the second constituent part of everyday gendered homophobia, that is gender, within the everyday.

The concept of gender

Gender refers to the culturally defined ways of being a man or woman, which becomes part of an individual's sense of self.[47] As discussed previously, the themes of lesbian and women/femininities has been well represented in the sporting literature. The questioning of women's sexuality for their participation in sport has been extensively critiqued in the literature. What this research tells us then is that ideologies underpinning sexual orientation are also connected to other relations of power, such as gender. Therefore, in discussing lesbian experiences of sport, we must explore the gendered nature of these narratives.

In the case of my research, the lives of the lesbian coaches are experiences of their sexual identity intersected by gendered ideologies. Being a woman and thus 'other' in a context that has long been historically male dominated meant that the lesbian coaches had to endure the ontological anxiety that their presence caused men. The women felt that they carried a burden of representation within their professional lives which meant their day-to-day role involved more just than coaching their athletes and planning performances. Instead, they become representative of all women coaches. The negative cultural connotations that male coaches, male officials (such as umpires and referees) and governing body representatives attached to women's abilities as leaders were regularly communicated and projected onto the participants. Women were constructed as less able leaders than men as a result of the combination of the idea that women were less physically able as athletes, that women were conceived as unknowledgeable about sport and coaching, and thus less intellectually able. For the participants, this meant their role as coaches involved constant daily battles against feeling trivialized, marginalized and undervalued. In their relations with male coaches, seven of the participants described being made to feel invisible and patronized. Tanya referred to these social constructions of what it meant to be a woman in sport when discussing her experience of being made to feel invisible by the opposition's male coach:

> There is something of an attitude that says, we still have to get over the simple barriers that women (a) understand the game and (b) can play it. But I had to work really hard to get beyond the alpha males. It's just assumed I'm not a coach. One of the best stories is when I was head coach at [my club side] and one opposition team came to the club ... another coach came up, I was standing next to the assistant [male] coach and of course, the other coach walks straight up and shakes hands with [my male assistant], saying "good to see you, are you ready for the game today?" I felt like a spare part! So I said "hi, I'm the head coach" and he said "ahhh". So it's just these assumptions ... I was in the kit so I must have been a physio or a Mum or a supporter or I don't know. So now I make a point with the opposition ... I make sure they know who I am and what my role is. So from an identity point of view, I learnt very quickly that they [male coach] aren't going to know [I'm the head coach], even if they have done their background work on the team.[48]

Hayley is an experienced national junior squad head coach within a globally popular team sport. She believed that being made to feel invisible by male coaches was because they disliked the possibility of being 'bettered' by a woman:

> Two of these [other] coaches, one of them was my England coach, the other was my team manager when I was England under-16, and those guys barely acknowledge my existence [now] yet have known me since I was a kid. Because they can't stand the fact that I have grown into somebody who is a better coach than they are ... I don't think anything is going to change their opinion as to female coaches.[49]

Feeling undervalued and marginalized as women also extended to the participants' experiences with male officials at games and competitions. The negative assumptions regarding women's ability to coach were demonstrated by referees and umpires presuming that the participants were at the game in another capacity, such as physios, or ignoring the participants altogether. These officials, the participants asserted, could not consider women in powerful leadership roles and failed to take them seriously. Janet, who at the time of the research, was the head coach of one of the national junior squads in her sport as well as a head club coach, described the experiences she had with umpires in her capacity as the current head coach of a men's club in her sport:

> So [I experience discrimination] ranging from abuse from opposition players to[wards] my own players about being coached by a "bird" or a girl, to opposition players being abusive to me and umpires not taking me seriously, "oh, you're just some player's dolly bird". That's quite difficult. It's just simple things like you go across with your captain to introduce yourself [to the umpire] and hear how they want the game to be run, they might not look at me or [they] say "Oh you're a posh club; you've got your own physio". My captain is fantastic and he'll go "No this is coach". Things like, any other coach has to stay within a specific area [on the touchline], [but] I can normally get a couple of laps in before they [the umpire] even contemplate I might be doing something wrong or I might be the coach. At the end of the game, you are entitled to go and speak to an umpire and I will often to go and talk to them, some of them are like "is there any point in us having this conversation?" "Well, you're quite happy to sit and chat with the guys over a beer".[50]

As Janet implies, such discrimination often appears trivial or minor. However, these subtle gendered relations occur so frequently that, coupled with other incidents that also happen on a daily basis, they create feelings of being 'second best' and marginalized for minority groups.

The construction of gender was also revealed within the coaching system in terms of the educational pathways available for professionals. Six of the participants described a male privilege for coaching jobs and education courses. Women coaches were 'marked' as different and gendered by the governing bodies in comparison with men's coaching experiences and male standards that were considered the 'norm'. In our interviews, Maggie discussed how her achievements were gendered by the men in her organization:

> For men, it's a lot more, not expected, but "it's well done" whereas "here's a girl, hasn't she done REALLY well to get here!" It's that sort of, you still feel like you're battling against the tide a little bit, whereas men, it's almost expected that they'll be there [in coaching positions]. When I found myself in circumstances where I am the only female there's been jokes in the staffroom and little comments. You can take it for so long but after a while, you start to think "hold on, this isn't right" and it can be getting a little bit personal. It's the little comments in the staffroom and the little jokes ... if you get anything wrong it's picked up on the female side. Its little things like, "oh were you washing your hair?" and if you forget something, it's picked up on, on the gender side. Whereas, with the men, [gender is] never mentioned, it's just accepted.[51]

Maggie believed that men in positions of power within her governing body normalized male-coaching experiences because they had such low expectations for women as leaders:

> I often get the impression that it's like, "there's so many other things you could have done but you've chosen to do [coaching] and we'll support you, that's really good, well done". Whereas, for the men I know, they just get on with it. It's low expectations of females, and female coaches. Often you surpass people's expectations and there can be a little bit of shock there and surprise that you've done something or you've achieved something. When I got the job at [the regional governing body] it was a big thing because they've never employed a female coach before. So it was like "here's a female coach!" It wasn't "here's a coach"; it was "here's a female coach". They wouldn't have made a song and a dance if it had been a man. It felt a little bit patronising to me, I'm a coach so why does it make any difference? [52]

The participants also described fewer opportunities to undertake professional development than male coaches and that the opportunities that were available were inflexible and restricted. Janet spoke critically of the limited chances to advance her coaching career compared with the greater and more flexible opportunities her male colleagues experienced:

> In terms of my [governing body], I think they're quite derogatory towards their women coaches and they pay them lip service. One of the biggest things was I knew I would like to do my level 4, I was working at an international level and to stay coaching at that level, there was going to be a time when I had to do the level 4. They seemed to be keen to have women involved but when it came to that, there seemed to be no energy. I became part of that "women in high performance programme" and it was supposed to help identify pathways but it just never worked. I was told, under no circumstances could you dip in and out of the course, you had to do all the modules. Yet I know they had some of the [high profile] England male players who wanted to do some work with some international [players], had a week and then they could dip in and out of it. So why couldn't I dip in and out?![53]

Hayley too discussed the gendered coach education system in her sport and the impact on her willingness to remain in coaching:

> My aspirations, three years ago, were to be part of the 2012 [Olympic] set up. There is no way I want a piece of it now and I don't even think I would be even looked at to be a piece of it. They identified me two years ago as a prospect for the future for women's coaching as a female... But it's to no avail because the people higher up aren't interested ... the GB governing body weren't interested and I think that's because they're male dominated. The guy

who took my level three advanced coaching [course], he said [to me] "you're a rarity, honestly, and the [governing body] will kill you off in the next four years and make you not want to coach anymore. They won't support you, they won't do anything to advance you, they won't do anything to identify you to make you more known around the country and the league". And he's right. Two years on and another two years of this and I'll be done because I can't deal with it anymore. It's volunteering your time to get no reward whatsoever and not even be appreciated.[54]

These stories illustrate that these coaches experience sexism within the coaching system because of the social constructions of gender. Nevertheless, the participants' narratives also reveal that gender is intertwined with other relations of power, and in the following section, one salient concept is sexual orientation. Therefore, our understanding of the gendered conditions of the everyday lives of these participants must also be read in conjunction with sexual orientation as an evident source of oppression. The participants' experienced sexism but these negative connotations were connected with negative perceptions of their sexual identity as lesbians. This leads me to discuss the third constituent part of everyday gendered homophobia, that is gendered homophobia.

The concept of gendered homophobia

Everyday injustices or inferiorizations are founded upon similar grounds, that is social constructions of biological differences.[55] Within this, heterosexuality is an essentialist concept of sex differences. The belief that biological differences in men and women determine sexuality creates the ideology that heterosexuality is 'normal' and any other sexual identity is deviant.[56] Homophobia could then be conceived, in a similar way to which Essed defined racism, in terms of thoughts, actions and processes that contribute and maintain a system in which heterosexism is the dominant ideology.[57] But to reiterate my point in the previous section, in discussing lesbian experiences of sport we cannot separate the connected concepts of being a 'woman' and sexuality. It is therefore appropriate to speak of gendered homophobia and this will form the focus of this section. Gendered homophobia shapes an individual's sporting experiences through understanding of masculinity and femininity as well as ascribed meanings of sexual orientation. In the case of my research, it relates to actions against the lesbian coaches. One particularly frequent and harmful assumption concerned their relationships with their young women and girl athletes. Many parents of the girls that my participants coached regularly questioned and had issues with the participants, as head coaches of their daughters' team, because of the coach's gendered sexuality. These parents made (erroneous) assumptions that the women coaches could be paedophiles or sexual predators towards their female athletes. Yet, according to the participants, heterosexual male coaches were not subject to the same assumptions. This was the experience that Hayley suffered when she returned to the UK from working in the USA:

So when I came back, I was now gay. I came back with a partner. I wasn't going to hide it ... but the junior parents had a few issues. When the parents started discovering I was gay, issues arose that I was coaching the girls. As a coach [in my sport], sometimes I'm physical, I put the girls in place to show them how to do things and it was the fact that I was touching their daughters. I've never experienced anything like that in my life so it was shocking to me. What's the difference between a male coach doing it and me doing it? That was the only thing that hurt me, that I was disappointed in, that all of a sudden because I'm gay, I'm a paedophile, I'm interested in their daughter who's 13 years old.[58]

Lucy also frequently experienced discrimination based on assumptions made by her male colleagues and men from her governing body about her sexual orientation and their expectations of femininity:

> I think part of it depends upon what you look like. I think if you have the right figure, wearing the right clothes, you have a certain image and then you will never get labeled as the "dykey coach". If you are short-haired and in a different way, than the label automatically comes with it.[59]

A heterosexist coaching system was not just maintained through unequal social relations as evidenced here. For Hayley, she never wanted to be out to members of her governing body. She felt as if she, as a woman, had and continued to negotiate and battle strong patriarchal power relations in order to be recognized as a legitimate elite coach. She believed that to reveal herself to be a gay woman would make her power struggles even greater to overcome:

> It's the "don't ask, don't tell"; it's almost like the Army. You don't talk about it [being gay]. Nobody talks about it, of influence; even other national coaches don't talk about it. The male coaches won't approach it at all… [For example] The Europeans [Championships] [are coming up] and [the other woman head coach who is gay] and me are the only two coaches that have never taken our partners to the European Championships. There would be talk if we did and we don't want to deal with that. Coaches take their wives or husbands to the Europeans but heaven forbid I take my partner. It would take away from me as a coach, I can't be a professional. That's how we feel and that's why we don't take our partners.[60]

All the participants agreed that their governing bodies did not seek to be deliberately discriminatory towards their gendered sexual identity. In this way, sporting organizations did not have homophobic ideas but rather their ideas about gender and sexuality were (perhaps unintentionally) oppressive, and thus had the same effect. The approach of these governing bodies was a policy of 'gender-blindness' and 'sexuality-blindness'; as long as a coach was competent, their gender or sexual orientation was irrelevant. While governing bodies may not be deliberating seeking to oppress sexual diversity, the effect of such blindness is a form of homophobia in itself. Individuals, like the coaches interviewed, do not feel as if they can be open, or that who they are is valued by their governing bodies. The practices and processes within Janet's governing body towards sexual orientation, in the case of a transgendered woman athlete, also revealed a gendered homophobic attitude towards Janet's club, as a team with a lesbian head coach:

> [My governing body] had to re-write a lot of their books when the Disability Act came in and also [they had to] put in gender. Possibly to a degree, initially, it was just token issues. It became more prevalent when we had a gender change person want to start to play [my sport] two years ago and she was directed towards the club that I play at because [according to the governing body] "they're a gay club". We've worked really hard to change that perception but to the head of the [governing body], leopards don't change their spots. No recognition that this is a male who's turned into a female, [that] has absolutely nothing to do with whether you are gay or not. It's a gender change. And I know the [governing body] had a great deal of difficulty because they weren't sure if she was allowed to play. So she was hidden away in our club. There has been no guidance from our governing body even though they should set the benchmark and the standard.[61]

Homophobia is a process that is manifested in multiple relations and situations.[62] Due to this, and the complexity of recognizing homophobia, governing bodies within sport perhaps ignore the existence of homophobia or that it is a significant factor in the lives of its members. Yet, as discussed in the earlier section concerning understanding the importance of the 'everyday' in the lives of these coaches, experiencing prejudices day-to-day is a challenge that often proves to be the most niggling, tiring, frustrating and often the most trivialized. Putting together the concepts of the everyday, gender and homophobia leads me to discuss the notion of everyday gendered homophobia.

The concept of everyday gendered homophobia

What distinguishes everyday gendered homophobia from other forms of homophobia is not only that it is specific to women, in this case, but also the involvement of taken-for-granted, frequent, familiar practices (which include relations, acts and attitudes) that occur in a given system.[63] In this way, everyday gendered homophobia is neither an institutional nor an individual issue. Everyday gendered homophobia is the integration of gendered homophobia into daily situations through practices that initiate and sustain unequal power relations between lesbians and dominant social groups. These practices then become normalized by these dominant groups.[64] The concept of everyday gendered homophobia in this way links the narratives of day-to-day experiences of discrimination and prejudice towards lesbians, as documented within this study, to the wider structural context in which these inferiorizations take place.

As discussed in an earlier section, within the lives of the participants the coaching system they work in places little value on minority groups and fails to appreciate the difference. This culture of ignorance and blindness is a form of homophobia and means that, for the participants, each day involves an element of 'negotiation' and decision-making about whether to disclose their sexual identity. All 10 of the lesbian coaches experienced difficulty in disclosing their sexual identity in their interactions with their governing bodies and at organizational events because of the covert 'don't ask, don't tell' culture, and subsequently, all felt as if they were holding back a part of themselves. While 9 of the 10 coaches were confidently 'out' to select people within their clubs, they did not openly express their sexual orientation to the members of their governing body. One participant was not out in any context. In this way, the participants talked about their sexuality as an 'unspoken truth'. This is how Maggie experiences day-to-day life within the workplace as a coach for a regional governing body:

> It became evident when I was working for the [governing body] simply because my partner found a lump and we had to go to the hospital and things like that. Obviously I spoke to my supervisor and asked for the time off . . . but he just didn't know how to handle it. That's really the only situation when [my sexuality] has been mentioned . . . It's more the unspoken truths rather than anything said. I think people often get so worried that they're going to offend you they just say nothing. Like when I was at [the regional governing body], and everybody found out I was the "lesbian in the office", nothing was really said but it was people's attitudes that changed . . . it's the unspoken truth and it's never really mentioned.[65]

For Gemma, her everyday life as a sports coach involves more than making decisions about tactics, player selection and development or training, for example. It is a process of negotiating her sexual identity. Her status as a gay woman has meant that she finds it more difficult to feel comfortable in male-dominated sporting environments, something that her heterosexual female colleague did not experience:

> I have been chatting to the lady who is recruiting for [a coaching position I am going for] and I have been thinking, at what point do you want to drop in that your partner's a woman and you're gay? In club coaching, you can get away without socialising with people at the club so it's not really a big deal. [My girlfriend] did use to come down and watch the games. So it's not like we hid that we were in some kind of relationship. [No one ever asked who she was] it was that silent, unwritten rule like, "you know and I know, everyone knows so let's not talk about it!" You do feel that undercurrent. Like the undercurrent I felt, when I was seeing a guy [to hide my sexuality] and how excited people were about it, you know? It's ridiculous. I remember when [I was a coach at one school] one of [my colleagues] came over and said "we're so glad you have finally found the way". That kind of comment. For me now . . . to go into a male-dominated environment is quite intimidating. We are doing this work with the [governing body of the sport] and they are all polite on the surface because of the old traditions

of the old English [sport] and sometimes you wonder, would you ever get in there? I saw one of my [colleagues] who was blatantly using her sexuality to get in. I just thought, "I'm not going to do that". Well obviously I'm not going to do [as a lesbian].[66]

These everyday experiences demonstrate that for the participants, negotiation and suppression of their sexual identities can lead to invisibility. In a profession that is already mostly made up of white, heterosexual men, women coaches have reported feeling marginalized regardless of their sexuality. For lesbian coaches, they may experience even further trivialization.

The coaches in this study also described feeling isolated because they could not always disclose their sexual orientation. If they chose to be 'out' to particular people within their national governing body and it was known to others as a form of 'unspoken truth', little support was offered in their daily coaching practices. For example, coaching younger athletes often provided sources of anxiety for Kelly because of the frequent questioning of and challenges to her femininity:

So they automatically assume because I am coaching them ... and I have short hair and look and act like me that I'm [a lesbian]. I do get asked filthy questions [about my sexuality by my athletes], but I just have to say "not appropriate questions, not appropriate time, if you want to come and chat to me about sexual preference, we can chat about that after the coaching". It's interesting because people automatically presume I'm a raving dyke because of my image. As soon as people twig I'm female, they're not going to assume I'm straight. A lot of kids will think I'm a guy to begin with, find out my name and then be like "you didn't tell us you were a girl?" Why should I? Should I have to come out as female?! I try and go at it from an educational perspective but to be honest, I've had stick for looking like me.[67]

For Janet, her daily life as a coach was not just problematized by being a woman in a male-dominated sport. Her identity as a gay woman, and a woman in a position of responsibility and authority, meant a struggle against homophobic associations between sexual orientation and possible sexual abuse in the case of coaching young players. As Janet explains, this is a situation unique to lesbian coaches:

It has an been issue to a few parents and I was informed by the governing body that I had to be more particular over the children's code of conduct because I was gay ... male coaches seem to put themselves in [risky] situations and they don't get it ... It's almost laughed off, I mean the last child protection course I did at [a ground which is considered the home of my sport] and a very senior ex-England player who runs [a high profile club] said "well this is ridiculous, I don't know why we're here, I know all my coaches and none of them would [do anything]". It's this bury-your-head-in-the-sand thing about blokes. Yet I'm constantly warned and I know other [lesbian] coaches have been warned about, like taking kids home [after training]. There's a kid who plays at my club and lives in my village, I know the Mum doesn't have a car, and I'm sitting there going "no [I can't take you home]". It's ludicrous ... I would prefer them [my governing body] not to say to me as a coach, "here's your child protection policy and oh and don't forget because you're 'that way' make sure you're not on your own with any of the girls". I don't think there needs to be that add-on; we adhere to the child protection policy.[68]

These experiences demonstrate that Janet is working in an environment with little support. For her, the lack of support from her sporting organization was of particular concern because Janet also experienced a serious mental health issue: clinical depression. The lack of interest from her governing body towards supporting the person behind the professional led to her losing her job as national coach of the women's senior team in her sport. It was whilst she was national head coach that her partner experienced a serious accident and as a result became permanently paralysed. Consequently, Janet suffered a nervous breakdown and depression, and was unable to meet the requirements of being a national head coach. However, on disclosing this to her governing body, an organization shown earlier to privilege men coaches, they failed to support her absence or provide help for her illness and disabled partner. Instead, they terminated her contract as national coach:

> My partner had a massive stroke playing [sport], got hit in the neck and tore the carotid artery so is quite profoundly disabled. Obviously that had an impact on me and I couldn't turn up to the next training camp I was supposed to be running ... From a governing body level, I was told I couldn't let it affect my job, and they're really sorry for me but if it was going to affect my job or if I wasn't going to show up, there were always other coaches that were available to take my place. So it was a really difficult time and they were really not interested in me as a person as long as I did my job. I really got that feeling that they weren't interested, "I needed to do my job, I needed to take these girls [certain places], I needed to make sure I turned up to this tournament, I needed to behave, why was my face like thunder"? Well, it was because I was quietly falling apart and I hadn't had the energy left to hide it ... I asked not to do a junior tournament ... I said "well actually I'm going into a mental health facility", [in reply, they said] "well we don't think it's appropriate you work with the players". So that was how I lost my job, in an email, "it's not appropriate you work with players if you are going into a mental health facility". [So that's] the reason why I've given up coaching [this sport altogether] because [my other sport] was much more supportive of my mental health problems and my [partner's] disability.[69]

All the interviewed coaches expressed awareness that they were subject to unfair treatment connected to their status as a lesbian coach. Narratives such as these provide evidence of what it means to be an individual living facing daily insidious forms of discrimination as a consequence of, in this case, their gendered, sexual identity. These experiences are located within sport's culturalized homophobia. Collecting everyday experiences such as these, of gendered homophobia or other prejudices, means that we are able to construct a more detailed, complex analysis of the processes that create or maintain inequality.

Discussion and conclusion

These findings highlight the structural practices that are shown to be limiting to the participants' ability to fully be themselves within their profession and to their opportunities to undertake professional development. This makes them feel invisible, unsupported and unchampioned by their organizations. At first, observers of sport and coaching may ask: 'what is the issue?' The participants are actively coaching in paid positions; they have never been sacked or verbally or physically threatened and all have the choice to progress through the coaching ranks. Some have even reached the pinnacle of the coaching ladder in becoming national head coaches. However, these accounts highlight what everyday injustices are all about, what Essed refers to as, 'the invisibility of oppression'.[70] The participants' day-to-day lives are stories of negotiation, of feeling underestimated, trivialized and marginalized and of having their sexuality suppressed or problematized through structural practices that appear 'normal' and are difficult to detect. These participants are not just individuals with 'chips on their shoulders' who have personal grievances with their governing bodies.[71] These experiences are shared amongst the coaches, all working within different organizations. These stories are also reflective of the wider sporting culture; the women interviewed have experienced these feelings and practices over a number of years and have taken the time to consider the impact on their sense of self and professional practices.

In highlighting some of the inequalities that these women coaches experienced, the findings reveal in turn some of the male privileges within the UK coaching system. These include greater cultural value attached to male leadership and ability to coach, their gendered identity and ability to go without scrutiny and a greater quality in professional development opportunities. These privileges serve to maintain the profession as male dominated. Yet, while male privilege has been discussed elsewhere in the sporting literature in relation to male athletes, such as violence, bonding or in the locker room, the topic of male privilege within coaching remains an under-researched area and warrants further investigation.[72] This is an additional focus to women's inequality as coaches and offers another lens through which to understand women's under-representation in such leadership positions. This research has demonstrated that male privilege is protected from recognition or termination through denials of (female) homosexuality that amount to taboos surrounding these participants' sexuality, the failure to implement a clear plan of action to understand and challenge gender and sexual inequality, the absence of a comprehensive, in-depth and broad programme of coach education related to social issues and a lack of personal support for minority groups.[73]

The findings demonstrate a failure by national governing bodies to understand, appreciate and in turn promote women's qualities as coaches. The participants also described a culture of 'unspoken truths' in which individuals within their governing bodies and their coaching colleagues around them were aware of their sexual orientation but made a point of not acknowledging or discussing it. As mentioned earlier, this is not to state that governing bodies are intentionally discriminatory. Rather, organizations champion the view that 'sport is for all' and a meritocracy, and that, as part of the Equality Standard, we should 'treat everyone the same'.[74] However, this act of disregarding difference, such as the refusal by sporting bodies to publish statistics related to the sexual orientation of its employees as mentioned by one participant, is a form of gender-blindness and sexuality-blindness, which could be deemed discriminatory ideologies.[75] Rhetoric such as 'equal opportunities' that is promoted by sporting organizations allows these bodies to ignore the construction of (white) male privilege, heterosexism and sexism, and supports the continuation of these dominant norms and values. Future research should be directed towards exploring the notion of what 'equal opportunities' in sport really means and whether this is a symbolic gesture in the absence of any real action or change. Within this, research should seek to understand the impact of cultures of 'blindness', such as gender and sexual orientation, on organizational practices and on the individuals within these bodies.

While some of these findings highlight that for lesbian coaches at least, the sporting arena and coaching context are often homophobic spaces, there were some positive elements to the participants' stories. They all agreed that wider, improved social attitudes towards sexual minorities have permeated sport and within their club settings, homophobic views by other coaches and athletes are becoming the minority. This finding is congruent with the body of literature examining homophobia and gay men's sporting experiences.[76] However, at the same time, the participants also believed that whilst attitudes may have become more inclusive, there still remains strong gendered, homophobic ideologies within the coaching profession towards lesbians and cultures of ignorance underpinning the structural practices of their governing bodies. The leadership of sporting organizations and coaching agencies is vital to implementing strategies to create a more inclusive and respectful treatment of social minority groups within the coaching profession.[77] When leaders of governing bodies become public champions for the values of equity and diversity, then these values are more likely to be integrated into the organization and filter through to the staff, coaches and athletes.[78] The first step towards making the coaching profession more inclusive is that sporting organizations need to learn more about issues to do with diversity, in this case, sexual orientation and gender. There needs to be the recognition that LGBT individuals are in the workforce and that they need to be supported and championed, like any other person, even if they have not identified themselves.[79] Once there is an increase in knowledge and awareness, there then needs to be a change in coaching practices and organizational expectations towards ethical professional standards and behaviours. These standards could be evidenced in a clear code of ethics for the entire workforce. This is in addition to revised organizational policies and responsibilities towards non-discrimination. More positive methods for recruitment of coaches also need to be implemented to encourage a more diverse workforce. However, the most important initiative, according to the participants, was a broader educational programme for coaches that included mandatory and frequent professional development workshops for coaches on inclusion and respect. These workshops could also be extended to governing body staff. Within these training workshops, there needs to be a more comprehensive discussion of all forms of differences. These programmes should 'include information about sexual orientation and gender identity as well as specific strategies for creating inclusive environments'.[80] At present, the content of coach education curricula is over-occupied with enhancing performance.[81] Instead, this programme should be balanced with enabling coaches and staff to instil and maintain inclusive and non-discriminatory teams and organizational cultures.[82] These educational workshops could also provide coaches and governing body staff with a code of ethics and organizational handbook that includes staff expectations and a reminder of the responsibilities and policies towards non-discrimination. To supplement these workshops, sporting organizations need to support their staff, and the participants in this study would have liked to see specific support groups for LGBT coaches and staff, possibly in partnership with diversity organizations such as Stonewall. In conclusion, it is worthwhile to note that these are not naïve strategies that ignore that the focus of most teams, athletes, coaches and governing bodies is winning. Rather, the idea is to enable everyone to strive to win through creating a culture of inclusion that allows every person to contribute their skills towards this goal and in doing so, to feel valued.[83]

Notes

1. Griffin, 'Changing the Game'.
2. Brackenridge et al., *Review of Sexual Orientation*.
3. Brackenridge et al., *Review of Sexual Orientation*.
4. Kolnes, 'Sexuality as an Organising Principle'.
5. Clarke, 'Queering the Pitch and Coming Out'; Fink, Pastore, and Riemer, 'Do Differences Make a Difference?'; Griffin, *Strong Women, Deep Closets*; Krane and Barber, 'Lesbian Experiences in Sport'; Messner, *Taking the Field*; and Wellman and Blinde, 'Homophobia in Women's Intercollegiate Basketball'.
6. Griffin, *Strong Women, Deep Closets* and Messner, *Taking the Field*.
7. Krane, 'One Lesbian Feminist Epistemology'.
8. Burton-Nelson, *Stronger Women Get, the More*.
9. Griffin, *Strong Women, Deep Closets* and Messner, *Taking the Field*.
10. Messner, *Power at Play* and Pronger, *Arena of Masculinity*.
11. Adams and Anderson, 'Exploring the Relationship Between Homosexuality and Sport'.
12. Griffin, *Strong Women, Deep Closets*.
13. Adams and Anderson, 'Exploring the Relationship Between Homosexuality and Sport'; Anderson, *Inclusive Masculinity*; Anderson, ' "Being Masculine" '; Anderson, 'Updating the Outcome'; Harris and Clayton, 'First Metrosexual Rugby Star'; McCormack and Anderson, 'Re-Production of Homosexually-Themed Discourse'; and Southall et al., 'Investigation of Male College'.
14. Adams and Anderson, 'Exploring the Relationship Between Homosexuality and Sport'.
15. Pharr, 'Homophobia'.
16. Brackenridge et al., *Review of Sexual Orientation*.

17. Brackenridge et al., *Review of Sexual Orientation*.
18. Caudwell, 'Hackney Women's Football Club'; Caudwell, 'Football in the UK'; Hart, 'Lesbian Professional Athletes,'; Krane, 'Homonegativism Experienced by Lesbian'; Krane and Barber, 'Lesbian Experiences in Sport'; and Ravel and Rail, 'On the Limits of "Gaie" Spaces'.
19. Brackenridge et al., *Review of Sexual Orientation*.
20. Barber and Krane, 'Creating a Positive Climate for Lesbian'; Cunningham and Melton, 'Prejudice Against Lesbian, Gay'; Oswalt and Vargas, 'How Safe is the Playing Field?'; Wellman and Blinde, 'Homophobia in Women's Intercollegiate'; Vargas-Tonsing and Oswalt, 'Coaches' Efficacy Beliefs Towards Working'; and Wolf-Wendel, Douglas, and Morphew, 'How Much Difference is Too Much Difference?'.
21. Griffin, *Strong Women, Deep Closets*.
22. Griffin, *Strong Women, Deep Closets*.
23. Iannotta and Kane, 'Sexual Stories as Resistance Narratives'.
24. Iannotta and Kane, 'Sexual Stories as Resistance Narratives' and Griffin, *Strong Women, Deep Closets*.
25. Krane and Barber, 'Lesbian Experiences in Sport'.
26. Krane and Barber, 'Lesbian Experiences in Sport'.
27. Campbell and Bunting, 'Voices and Paradigms'.
28. Essed, 'Everyday Racisms'.
29. Essed, *Understanding Everyday Racism* and Riggins, 'Gendered Racism'.
30. Berger and Luckman, *Social Construction of Knowledge*.
31. Essed, *Understanding Everyday Racism*.
32. Essed, *Understanding Everyday Racism*.
33. Denison, 'Social Theory for Coaches' and Jones, 'Coaching as Caring'.
34. Jones, Armour, and Potrac, *Sports Coaching Cultures*.
35. Essed, *Understanding Everyday Racism* and Riggins, 'Gendered Racism'.
36. Essed, *Understanding Everyday Racism* and Riggins, 'Gendered Racism', 205.
37. Heller, *Everyday Life*.
38. Smith, *Everyday World as Problematic*.
39. Essed, *Understanding Everyday Racism*, 279.
40. Interview, May 12, 2009.
41. Interview, June 4, 2009.
42. Interview, May 1, 2009.
43. Interview, April 10, 2009.
44. Interview, April 10, 2009.
45. Interview, May 14, 2009.
46. Interview, April 10, 2009.
47. Schlegel, 'Gender Meanings'.
48. Interview, April 10, 2009.
49. Interview, July 25, 2009.
50. Interview, June 20, 2009.
51. Interview, June 4, 2009.
52. Interview, June 4, 2009.
53. Interview, June 20, 2009.
54. Interview, July 25, 2009.
55. Essed, *Everyday Racisms*.
56. Robinson, 'Everyday [Hetero]Sexism'.
57. Essed, *Understanding Everyday Racism*.
58. Interview, July 25, 2009.
59. Interview, May 1, 2009.
60. Interview, July 25, 2009.
61. Interview, June 20, 2009.
62. Essed, 'Everyday Racisms'.
63. Essed, *Understanding everyday Racism*.
64. Essed, 'Everyday Racisms'.
65. Interview, June 4, 2009.
66. Interview, May 14, 2009.
67. Interview, May 12, 2009.

68. Interview, June 20, 2009.
69. Interview, June 20, 2009.
70. Essed, *Understanding Everyday Racism*, 146.
71. Essed, *Understanding Everyday Racism*, 146.
72. Messner, *Power at Play*; Curry, 'Fraternal Bonding in the Locker Room'; Kane and Disch, 'Sexual Violence and the Reproduction'; and McDonald, 'Unnecessary Roughness'.
73. McIntosh, 'White Privilege and Male Privilege'.
74. Hylton, 'Talk the Talk, Walk the Walk' and Sport England, *Equality Standard.*
75. Bonilla-Silva, 'Linguistics of Color Blind Racism'.
76. Adams and Anderson, 'Exploring the Relationship Between Homosexuality and Sport'; Anderson, *Inclusive Masculinity*; Anderson, ' "Being Masculine" '; Anderson, 'Updating the Outcome'; Harris and Clayton, 'First Metrosexual Rugby Star'; McCormack and Anderson, 'Re-production of Homosexually-Themed Discourse'; and Southall et al., 'Investigation of Male College'.
77. NCAA, *Champions of Respect*.
78. NCAA, *Champions of Respect*.
79. NCAA, *Champions of Respect*.
80. Barber and Krane, 'Creating a Positive Climate', 54.
81. C. J. Cushion, 'Coaching Research and Coach Education: Do the Sum of the Parts Equal the Whole?' *SportaPolis*, September 2001. http://www.sportsmedia.org/Sportapolisnewsletter4.htm (accessed October 1, 2012).
82. NCAA, *Champions of Respect*.
83. NCAA, *Champions of Respect*.

References

Adams, A., and E. Anderson. 'Exploring the Relationship Between Homosexuality and Sport Among the Teammates of a Small, Midwestern Catholic College Soccer Team'. *Sport, Education & Society* 17, no. 3 (2012): 347–63.

Anderson, E. ' "Being Masculine is not About Who You Sleep With…": Heterosexual Athletes Contesting Masculinity and the One-Time Rule of Homosexuality'. *Sex Roles* 58, no. 1–2 (2008): 104–15.

Anderson, E. *Inclusive Masculinity: The Changing Nature of Masculinities*. New York: Routledge, 2009.

Anderson, E. 'Updating the Outcome: Gay Athletes, Straight teams, and Coming Out in Educationally Based Sports Teams'. *Gender & Society* 25, no. 2 (2011): 250–68.

Barber, H., and V. Krane. 'Creating a Positive Climate for Lesbian, Gay, Bisexual, and Transgender Youths'. *The Journal of Physical Education, Recreation & Dance* 78, no. 7 (2007): 6–52.

Berger, P., and T. Luckman. *The Social Construction of Knowledge*. New York: New American Library, 1967.

Bonilla-Silva, E. 'The Linguistics of Color Blind Racism: How to Talk Nasty about Blacks without Sounding "Racist" '. *Critical Sociology* 28, no. 1–2 (2002): 41–64.

Brackenridge, C., P. Alldred, A. Jarvis, K. Maddocks, and I. Rivers. *A Review of Sexual Orientation in Sport: Sportscotland Research Report no. 114*. Edinburgh: Sport Scotland, 2008.

Burton-Nelson, M. *The Stronger Women Get, the More Men Love Football: Sexism and the Culture of Sport*. San Diego, CA: Harcourt Brace & Company, 1994.

Campbell, J., and S. Bunting. 'Voices and Paradigms: Perspectives on Critical and Feminist Theory in Nursing'. *Advances in Nursing Science* 13 (1991): 1–15.

Caudwell, J. 'Football in the UK: Women, Tomboys, Butches and Lesbians'. In *Sport, Leisure and Gendered Spaces*, ed. S. Scraton and B. Watson, 95–110. Eastbourne: LSA, 2000.

Caudwell, J. 'Hackney Women's Football Club: Lesbian United?' In *Women, Football and Europe: Histories, Equity and Experience*, ed. J. Magee, J. Caudwell, K. Liston, and S. Scraton, 64–84. Aachen: Meyer & Meyer, 2007.

Clarke, G. 'Queering the Pitch and Coming Out to Play: Lesbians in Physical Education and Sport'. *Sport, Education & Society* 3 (1998): 145–60.

Cunningham, G. B., and N. Melton. 'Prejudice Against Lesbian, Gay, and Bisexual Coaches: The Influence of Race, Religious Fundamentalism, Modern Sexism, and Contact with Sexual Minorities'. *Sociology of Sport Journal* 29, no. 3 (2012): 283–305.

Curry, T. J. 'Fraternal Bonding in the Locker Room: A Profeminist Analysis of Talk About Competition and Women'. *Sociology of Sport Journal* 8, no. 2 (1991): 119–35.

Denison, J. 'Social Theory for Coaches: A Foucauldian Reading of One Athlete's Poor Performance'. *International Journal of Sports Science & Coaching* 2, no. 4 (2007): 369–83.

Essed, P. 'Everyday Racisms'. In *A Companion to Racial and Ethnic Studies*, ed. D. T. Goldberg and J. Solomos, 202–16. Malden, MA: Blackwell, 2002.

Essed, P. *Understanding Everyday Racism: An Interdisciplinary Theory*. Newbury Park, CA: Sage, 1991.

Fink, J. S., D. L. Pastore, and H. A. Riemer. 'Do Differences Make a Difference? Managing Diversity in Division IA Intercollegiate Athletics'. *Journal of Sport Management* 15 (2001): 10–50.

Griffin, P. 'Changing the Game: Homophobia, Sexism and Lesbians in Sport'. *Quest* 44 (1992): 251–65.

Griffin, P. *Strong Women, Deep Closets: Lesbians and Homophobia in Sport*. Champaign, IL: Human Kinetics, 1998.

Harris, J., and B. Clayton. 'The First Metrosexual Rugby Star: Rugby Union, Masculinity, and Celebrity in Contemporary Wales'. *Sociology of Sport Journal* 24 (2007): 45–164.

Hart, K. L. 'Lesbian Professional Athletes: What was the Cost of Coming Out?' PhD diss., University of Oregon, 2001.

Heller, A. *Everyday Life*. London: Routledge & Kegan Paul, 1984.

Hylton, K. 'Talk the Talk, Walk the Walk: Defining Critical Race Theory in Research'. *Race Ethnicity and Education* 15, no. 1 (2012): 23–41.

Iannotta, J. G., and M. J. Kane. 'Sexual Stories as Resistance Narratives in Women's Sports: Reconceptualizing Identity Performance'. *Sociology of Sport Journal* 19 (2002): 347–69.

Jones, R. L. 'Coaching as Caring (the Smiling Gallery): Accessing Hidden Knowledge'. *Physical Education and Sport Pedagogy* 14 (2009): 377–90.

Jones, R. L., K. M. Armour, and P. Potrac. *Sports Coaching Cultures: From Practice to Theory*. London: Routledge, 2004.

Kane, M. J., and L. J. Disch. 'Sexual Violence and the Reproduction of Male Power in the Locker Room: The "Lisa Olson Incident"'. *Sociology of Sport Journal* 10, no. 4 (1993): 331–52.

Kolnes, L. 'Sexuality as an Organising Principle in Sport'. *International Review for the Sociology of Sport* 30 (1995): 61–77.

Krane, V. 'Homonegativism Experienced by Lesbian Collegiate Athletes'. *Women in Sport & Physical Activity Journal* 6, no. 2 (1997): 141–64.

Krane, V. 'One Lesbian Feminist Epistemology: Integrating Feminist Standpoint, Queer Theory and Feminist Cultural Studies'. *The Sport Psychologist* 15 (2001): 401–11.

Krane, V., and H. Barber. 'Lesbian Experiences in Sport: A Social Identity Perspective'. *Quest* 55 (2003): 328–46.

McCormack, M., and E. Anderson. 'The Re-production of Homosexually-Themed Discourse in Educationally-Based Organized Sport'. *Culture, Health & Sexuality* 12 (2010): 913–27.

McDonald, M. G. 'Unnecessary Roughness: Gender and Racial Politics in Domestic Violence Media Events'. *Sociology of Sport Journal* 16, no. 2 (1999): 111–33.

McIntosh, P. 'White Privilege and Male Privilege'. In *Privilege*, ed. M. S. Kimmel and A. L. Ferber, 147–60. Boulder, CO: Westview Press, 2003.

Messner, M. A. *Power at Play: Sports and the Problem of Masculinity*. Boston, MA: Beacon Press, 1992.

Messner, M. A. *Taking the Field: Women, Men, and Sports*. Minneapolis, MN: University of Minnesota Press, 2002.

NCAA. *Champions of Respect: Inclusion of LGBTQ Student-Athletes and Staff in NCAA Programs*. Indianapolis, IN: NCAA, 2012.

Oswalt, S. B., and T. M. Vargas. 'How Safe is the Playing Field? Collegiate Coaches' Attitudes Towards Gay, Lesbian, and Bisexual Individuals'. *Sport in Society* 16, no. 1 (2013): 120–32.

Pharr, S. 'Homophobia: A Weapon of Sexism'. In *Making Sense of Women's Lives: An Introduction to Women's Studies*, ed. L. Umansky and M. Plott, 424–38. New York: Rowman & Littlefield, 2000.

Pronger, B. *The Arena of Masculinity: Sports, Homosexuality, and the Meaning of Sex*. New York: St. Martin's Press, 1990.

Ravel, B., and G. Rail. 'On the Limits of "Gaie" Spaces: Discursive Constructions of Women's Sport in Quebec'. *Sociology of Sport Journal* 24, no. 4 (2007): 402–20.

Riggins, S. H. 'Gendered Racism'. *The Semiotic Review of Books* 4, no. 3 (1993): 9–10.

Robinson, C. M. 'Everyday [Hetero]Sexism: Strategies of Resistance and Lesbian Couples'. In *Everyday Sexism in the Third Millennium*, ed. C. R. Ronai, B. A. Zsembik, and J. R. Feagin, 33–50. New York: Routledge, 1997.

Schlegel, A. 'Gender Meanings: General and Specific'. In *Beyond the Second Sex: New Directions in the Anthropology of Gender*, ed. P. R. Sanday and R. G. Goodenough, 21–42. Philadelphia, PA: University of Philadelphia Press, 1990.

Smith, D. E. *The Everyday World as Problematic*. Toronto, ON: Toronto University Press, 1987.

Southall, R. M., M. S. Nagel, E. Anderson, F. G. Polite, and C. Southall. 'An Investigation of Male College Athletes' Attitudes Towards Sexual-Orientation'. *Journal of Issues in Intercollegiate Athletics* 2 (2009): 62–77.

Sport England. *The Equality Standard: A Framework for Sport*. London: Sport England, 2004.

Vargas-Tonsing, T. M., and S. B. Oswalt. 'Coaches' Efficacy Beliefs Towards Working with Gay, Lesbian, and Bisexual Athletes'. *International Journal of Coaching Science* 3, no. 2 (2009): 29–42.

Wellman, S., and E. Blinde. 'Homophobia in Women's Intercollegiate Basketball: Views of Women Coaches Regarding Coaching Careers and Recruitment of Athletes'. *Women in Sport & Physical Activity Journal* 6, no. 2 (1997): 63–82.

Wolf-Wendel, L. E., T. J. Douglas, and C. C. Morphew. 'How Much Difference is Too Much Difference? Perceptions of Gay Men and Lesbians in Intercollegiate Athletics'. *Journal of College Student Development* 42, no. 5 (2001): 465–79.

Marketing strategies within an African-Brazilian martial art

Marcelo Almeida[a], Janelle Joseph[b], Alexandre Palma[c] and Antonio Jorge Soares[d]

[a]Curso de Educação Física, Universidade Gama Filho, Rio de Janeiro, Brazil; [b]Faculty of Education, University of Ontario Institute of Technology, Oshawa, ON, Canada; [c]Escola de educação física e desporto, Universidade do Estado do Rio de Janeiro, Rio de Janeiro, Brazil; [d]Faculdade de Educação, Universidade do Estado do Rio de Janeiro, Rio de Janeiro, Brazil

This paper analyzes the marketing strategies of groups that practise *capoeira*, a martial art of African-Brazilian origins. Group leaders seek financial and symbolic success in competitive Brazilian and international markets. Leaders use several marketing strategies to augment their prestige, student base and remuneration. They present their martial art classes as authentic African-descendant culture, a venue to maintain Brazilian traditions, and as an art of resistance against racial discrimination. We show that the marketing of capoeira, which includes the (un)intentional disguising of its product dimensions and the celebration of a lineage of 'authentic' *mestres* (masters), has its roots in the first half of the twentieth century, when the first two capoeira schools emerged in the physical culture scene of Bahia, Brazil. We interrogate the ways in which the reification of African-Brazilian culture through capoeira relies on students' psychic distance from Brazilian culture and cosmopolitan desires for cross-cultural consumption.

Introduction

Compared with other issues examined in the sport marketing literature, cross-cultural marketing strategy has received little attention. In addition, there has been little empirical research on 'alternative sports', including a martial art that originated in Brazil, called capoeira.[1] To address this issue, this paper analyzes the marketing strategies practised by capoeira *mestres* (masters of the art) and their student–teachers and group administrators (hereafter collectively referred to as 'leaders') in selling their product: classes, shows and merchandise. It is no secret that over the past century many leaders in Brazil operated within the spectre of poverty.[2] To avoid a life of privation, our multi-sited ethnographic research has shown that leaders today, especially outside of Brazil, use capoeira's African and Brazilian traditions to market the martial art as a valuable product to sell. With near religious fervour, Brazilian leaders in locations as widespread as New Zealand, Canada, Portugal and Brazil promote their distinct styles as 'authentically Brazilian' and increase the value of their product by demonstrating proximity to a history of struggles for class and racial inequality and celebrations of multiculturalism in Brazil.

We also posit that selling capoeira as a product is nothing new. The branding of capoeira has its roots in the first half of the twentieth century with the advent of two distinct styles. *Mestres* Bimba and Pastinha fought to establish which of their respective styles, *Regional* or *Angola*, would come to represent the 'true' capoeira, bequeathed by African slaves.[3] Today, with the transnational expansion of the capoeira market, groups have intensified disputes initiated by *Mestres* Bimba and Pastinha even more. The marketing of capoeira is complex. As each group espouses old traditions and exclusive links to a mythical past and singular nation, it must also demonstrate its inclusivity, ability to revel in diversity and capacity to incorporate multicultural ideologies in Brazil and around the world.

It is our contention that the symbols of capoeira and African-Brazilian culture that are marketed worldwide are based on the legends of the physical activity's origins and that links to this socio-history translate to profits for group leaders. Although the attempt to document any history necessarily leaves out certain perspectives, narratives and political views – and this is especially so for a phenomenon that survived with an oral history for much of its existence – in the following section, we attempt to capture a brief history of the two styles of this martial art. We then review the cultural marketing literatures, present our methods of data collection and our findings of three of the marketing strategies currently being used by leaders to legitimate their capoeira groups and thus augment their social status and financial earnings.

A history of *'Regional'* and *'Angola'* capoeira

Capoeira is widely accepted as the embodiment of slave resistance and anti-racism struggles. Although there is no written history of the art prior to the late nineteenth century, today's leaders rely on legends and folk tales to explain that African slaves in the 1500s disguised their fight as a dance in order to practise their martial skills in a clandestine fashion. There is little evidence to support the myth that it was used on plantations or escaped slave villages in contest with slave masters or the army.[4] In contrast, there is much evidence, including criminal records, that capoeira was performed against police officers by violent *maltas* (gangs) in the late 1800s and early 1900s, particularly in Rio de Janeiro.[5] Criminal records show that rather than operating as anti-colonialism or anti-racism freedom fighters, some players of capoeira were found guilty of assaulting any type of person including Whites, Blacks and Mulattos, whether they were government agents or ordinary citizens.[6] Nevertheless, a distorted and romantic view of capoeira's origins remains, despite the clear similarity between capoeira groups in the nineteenth century and drug gangs of contemporary Rio de Janeiro.[7]

The older bibliographical records use only the term *'capoeiragem'* to designate the activity prior to the 1930s.[8] *Capoeiragem* was learned exclusively by *oitiva,* a form of teaching in which a more experienced practitioner confers skills to a beginner in an unsystematic manner. *Oitiva* teachings often took place near cheap liquor shops in return for small favours, such as paying for a drink.[9] Arguably, the most famous person to learn capoeira in this manner was Manoel dos Reis Machado (*Mestre* Bimba). A native of the state of Bahia, born in 1900, he learned the art from an Angolan ex-slave named Bentinho.[10] After becoming a *mestre,* he decided to bring capoeira from the street into a school building and in 1932 his *Centro de Cultura Física Regional* (Regional Center for Physical Culture) received an official seal of approval from the Ministry of Education.[11] With the creation of what he called *Regional* capoeira and the regimentation of instruction methods, the social stigma associated with capoeira began to dissipate. *Mestre* Bimba took a playful pastime, a spontaneous activity of men who were idle on streets and beaches and therefore, maligned by mainstream society, and altered it into a more respectable sport and martial art; critical for physical education, self-defense and significantly, national identity.[12] Because his students paid for classes, he became a service renderer and transformed capoeira into a product for consumers. *Mestre* Bimba fought to incorporate elements of Asian martial arts such as karate and jiu-jitsu, and distinguish his *Regional* style from the African rituals and mock fighting elements of the traditional form.

Vieira postulates that, according to the old *mestres* from Bahia, the traditional form of capoeira came to be known as *Angola* only after *Regional* was created.[13] *Angola* featured Vicente Ferreira Pastinha, known as *Mestre* Pastinha, as its icon. Pastinha was born in 1889 and, while still a child, was initiated in capoeira through *oitiva* by an Angolan called Benedito. Perturbed by the changes he saw occurring in capoeira, with the promotion of *Regional*, he set out to preserve traditional ways of playing and established the *Centro Esportivo de Capoeira Angola* (Sport Centre for Capoeira Angola) in 1941 for the practice of a 'pure and original' capoeira.[14] *Angola* leaders today continue to follow the teachings of *Mestre* Pastinha and tout the African heritage of the art.[15] In all periods, capoeira satisfied a sense of belonging and inclusion; however, after the creation of the first Capoeira Centres, the practitioner was socially acknowledged for the first time as a 'client' or 'customer', making the marketing strategies an important dimension in selling the product.[16] In this paper, we show that current capoeira leaders draw from Mestre Bimba and Pastinha's exclusionary, tradition and lineage-focused marketing strategies.

Cultural marketing strategies

With the globalization of markets, cross-cultural and international marketing research has assumed great importance in the academic, business and sports worlds.[17] It is widely accepted that the product and its associated meanings are the most critical element of business for any company, because they dictate the pricing, promotion and distribution strategies to be applied in domestic and international marketing environments.[18] In particular, the ways a product's meanings are advertised and consumed must change in order to be sold to a foreign market, and the extent of the modifications is dictated by the marketplace.[19] Capoeira is a sport product that is sold in foreign markets with distinct meanings attached.

We draw from the marketing concept of 'psychic distance', that is, the individual consumer's perception of the differences between the home country and the foreign country (or city), to explain how a product is marketed in its country of origin and outwith.[20] Sousa and Bradley indicate that psychic distance is personal and 'cannot be measured with factual indicators, such as publicly available statistics on economic development, level of education, language, etc. Accordingly, the psychic distance concept should be applied at the individual level'.[21] On the basis of our conversations with and observations of them, we therefore demonstrate that individual leaders aim to shape and take advantage of capoeira consumers' perceptions of the past and of a particular place: Bahia, Brazil.

The specific meanings of a product are created based on its socio-history, which is often tied to nationalist rhetoric; yet, we know that discourses associated with a time or place brought back by memory are usually an assortment of verifiable facts amalgamated with fabricated myths.[22] In the production of discourses about the origin of nations, for example, Hobsbawm points out that identity is anchored in the past by means of myth disguised as history.[23] Nations espouse versions of their history that consist of anachronism, omission and decontextualization and, in some cases, fabrication. It is clear that the meanings associated with selling national products are constantly changing with changing national identities.[24] Using the example of the Yoruba revivalist kingdom of Oyotunji, SC, USA, Lorand Matory explains that an identity results from 'a deft blend of symbolic practices by Cuban priests of Ocha, Africanist anthropologists, African-American political nationalists, and tourists of all colors'.[25] He explains that their 'canonization of tradition' generates 'pride, as well as profit'.[26] A central marketing strategy is to sell meaningful products that allow tourists to feel a sense of belonging and attachment to a place.

Sport marketing research is replete with studies on a range of topics, including the relationship between sponsors, fan identities and event/team promoters, and the role of traditional media and the Internet in sales, viewership and advertising.[27] Yet, even within research that examines international contexts, little attention has been paid to cross-cultural sports marketing.[28] In this paper, we show that sports leaders intentionally link national culture and rhetoric to their product to augment social and economic capital.

Research settings and methods

This paper is based on the research and writing of four investigators, two of which conducted multi-sited ethnographic investigations in disparate capoeira settings. While none of us set out to discover 'what marketing strategies do leaders use?', we each found this to be a salient research question in our various fieldwork environments.

Marcelo Almeida, a Brazilian male, practised capoeira for 27 years with established Brazilian *mestres* and worked as a capoeira instructor for 20 years. He completed an ethnographic research project from 2004 to 2007 where he made observations and conducted 20 interviews and questionnaires with 50 capoeira participants in Brazil, Portugal and Uruguay, with particular attention to the *Roda de Caxias* which takes place in Caxias, approximately 30 km from the city of Rio de Janeiro.[29] He initiated the writing of this paper. Born in Canada, Janelle Joseph began studying capoeira physically in 2001 and academically in 2004. She attended open *rodas* (capoeira games performed in a circle), classes and group events such as social gatherings and graduation ceremonies in Canada from 2004 to 2007, and in New Zealand and Canada between 2010 and 2011. She interviewed 37 participants including *mestres*, student–teachers and students with three groups who performed *Angola* and/or *Regional* styles.[30] For this paper, she contributed to its conception, structuring, translation and writing. Alexandre Palma and Antonio Jorge Soares, both Brazilian males, conducted participant observation research on capoeira throughout the state of Rio de Janeiro since the mid-1990s. Their specific input here is in the design and writing of the paper.

Each of the authors recorded participant observation notes about the marketing discourses used by teachers to sell their particular version of capoeira. We each recorded two types of notes: (1) 'expanded notes' about the events that took place including 'description of the physical context, the people involved, as much of their behavior and non-verbal communication as possible, and in words that are as close as possible to the words used by the participants' and (2) 'meta-notes' that 'include comments on notes, summary of the evidence for a particular argument collected to that point, preliminary interpretations, hypotheses and questions for further research'.[31] These were recorded as brief jot notes during classes and events whenever feasible, and expanded on in rich detail as soon as possible afterwards. Although we all practised capoeira before we researched the martial art and, therefore, were able to use emic (from within the culture) viewpoints, we also used etic perspectives (examining the phenomena from outside the culture) when we travelled and conducted research with capoeira groups other than our own. Data were analyzed manually (i.e., without the use of data management software) using inductive coding, meaning, we 'allow[ed] research findings to emerge from the frequent, dominant or significant themes inherent in raw data, without the restraints imposed by structured methodologies'.[32] In contrast to marketing research that suggests different strategies must be used in different cultural contexts, our discussions revealed that similar strategies were used in multiple locations, including various cities across Brazil and internationally, which prompted this joint writing venture.[33] We draw from our observations and secondary sources to explain the 'psychic distance' from Brazil and Bahia that is exploited in the marketing strategies we have witnessed and in some cases participated in over the past 27 years in five countries: Brazil, Canada, New Zealand, Portugal and Uruguay. All names used below are pseudonyms.

Findings: capoeira marketing strategies

The following sections deal with the proliferation of capoeira in the past century, and specifically, the last three decades. Capoeira had to adapt to new social reconfigurations in President Vargas' era (1930–1945). During this time, it began to be practised in private centres, in which, as previously indicated, it became a product as the teachers began to be paid service providers. In this context, offering the most 'authentic,' 'traditional' or 'pure' capoeira made it more profitable; a strategy that, based on our research, appears to continue to be used today by capoeira groups in Brazilian and international settings. Below we outline the strategies that different group leaders use to market their capoeira product. Their objective is to expand their groups, secure and maintain students, and increase their profits. Three ways they accomplish this are presenting (1) 'true' capoeira, (2) a capoeira lineage and (3) Brazilian/Bahian capoeira.

Marketing strategy one: presenting 'true' capoeira

As a result of its decriminalization, capoeira became a product in the leisure, physical education, sport and fitness service markets, advertised through discourses that intended to inform and convince consumers about the qualities of a certain style. This section discusses the use of phrases such as '*Angola* is the mother capoeira' or '*Regional* is the most efficient as a martial art,' which are often repeated to differentiate various products in the capoeira market, denoting some products as 'true' and valuable and others as 'fake' and therefore worthless.

To substantiate the hypothesis that the dispute between capoeira styles and marketing of 'authentic' capoeira began with *Mestres* Pastinha and Bimba, we offer an excerpt from a short film called Dança da Guerra, produced and directed by Jair Moura, a former student of *Mestre* Bimba, in 1968.[34] In the film, *Mestre* Bimba teaches how to make a *berimbau* [instrument] and suggests that the process of making 'true' *berimbaus* was different from what the '*Angolas*' practised:

> I will explain how true *berimbaus* are made. Wood from the forest is left fifteen days to dry... Then you place a piece of leather [on the end]; insert a piece of wire, then a layer (...) of varnish. That's it. It isn't like the Angolas' *berimbau*, that they take when the wood is still green, paint it and sell it to the tourists as a good *berimbau*. However, for an authentic, true berimbau, there's only this here, the one I make.[35]

The '*Angolas*', in contrast, proclaim that theirs is 'true' capoeira because it was brought from Africa, specifically by enslaved Angolans. In *Mestre* Pastinha's posthumously published book, he writes as follows:

> It is obvious to refer to Capoeira Angola as the legitimate capoeira, brought by the Africans, and not the mixture of capoeira and boxing, American wrestling, judo, jiu-jitsu etc., which removes its characteristics, being no more than a mixed martial art or self defense modality.[36]

Pastinha does not specify any particular martial arts 'mixture'; however, when he refers to a 'self-defense modality' he is clearly criticizing *Regional* created by *Mestre* Bimba and foreshadows, or rather, is the instigator of, subsequent generations of *Angoleiros'* disdain for *Regional.*

Although there have been significant changes in capoeira since the times when *Mestres* Bimba and Pastinha were alive, the discourses of current leaders and their respective groups have changed little. The competition between these two legendary *capoeiristas* is replicated in the current international capoeira market, as each group vies to authenticate itself based on discourses of tradition and history. One informant, at the *Roda de Caxias* in 2006 explained to Marcelo: 'Here, we are part of a lineage of a popular culture that *mestre*s who have dedicated themselves to this art brought to us. We are not mutts, our capoeira has pedigree! Tradition is tradition and that has to be valued'.[37] This participant rebuffs an ideology of mixing styles and claims to practise 'true' capoeira with 'pedigree', the way his *mestre* and his *mestre's mestre* learned.

Similarly, in New Zealand at the *roda* held in a university campus dance studio every Friday, one participant told Janelle: 'I did kung fu and whatnot but capoeira is the only martial art I've found that stays true to its original traditions. At least in this group [our leader] teaches us the true Bimba-style capoeira'.[38] Talmon-Chvaicer explains that 'The conflict between the need to attract more students and the desire to maintain the purity of capoeira and its traditional values' is a significant hurdle teachers have to overcome.[39] In fact, there was embodied evidence that this group practised certain movements in a different style than Bimba's (e.g., a *quexada* kick using the front leg instead of the back leg as Mestre Bimba did). Nevertheless, it is clear that the discourse of a cultural heritage associated with capoeira adds value to the product. Leaders are expert salesmen, in some cases, convinced by their own rhetoric, in others, intentionally misleading students to increase their profits. In either case, if they can convince students that the style of capoeira they offer is more 'original', 'true' or has more 'pedigree', they can attract and maintain more students, sell more group uniforms and win the battle for profits in the competitive capoeira market.

Marketing strategy two: presenting a capoeira lineage

Competition in today's *Regional* and *Angola* market leads to temporal and spatial legitimation strategies. This section discusses the strategies many current leaders use as they try to show their possession of an original capoeira linked to a mythical past. They attempt to demonstrate a connection with capoeira *mestres* who worked in the first half of the twentieth century in the city of Salvador, Bahia and to the city itself in order to build the identity of their respective groups. Although there is usually no biological connection between teachers and students, being a disciple of a particular *mestre* is akin to a genealogical link.[40] Being able to trace a lineage to a *mestre* of great renown in the past provides a 'certificate of nobility' among the practitioners of this cultural manifestation and converts to greater symbolic and, consequently, economic capital in the market.

To consolidate their brand, it is common for leaders to sell an image of tradition or a genealogical connection to certain *mestre*s when in reality they possess but a few years of existence or no such ancestry. Upon visiting a group in Christchurch, New Zealand in September 2011, Janelle heard stories about capoeira games that had occurred only three years prior, narrated as if they belonged to a remote past. One student was in the process of writing a song about a putatively 'famous' game to document and honour his teacher's legacy. Evidently, tradition does not depend solely on longevity, but above all on the efficiency of the narrative used to communicate it.

Capoeira groups often form when a student decides – amicably or under duress – to leave his or her own *mestre* to form a new group. The most famous example of this is the formidable capoeira group, *Senzala*, created in Rio de Janeiro at the end of the 1960s by a group of young men who did not belong to any group, but who were endorsed by *Mestre* Bimba.[41] The group Senzala developed a new capoeira style designated *Regional Senzala*, the techniques of which strongly influenced the history of capoeira. Despite their tangential association with Bimba's *Regional*, and their intentional transformation of some of the techniques of the art, Senzala and its subsequent offshoots, *Grupo Capoeira Brasil* (Brazil Capoeira Group) and *ABADÁ-Capoeira* (Brazilian Association for the Support and Development of the Art of Capoeira) continue to highlight that they are part of this 'original' lineage of *Regional* capoeira. In an interview with Marcelo, one informant explained that some teachers act tough and aggressive: 'Maybe they [other teachers] act this way because they don't have a true *mestre*, like I had. We [members of our group] have an obligation to be good. We owe it to Bimba and to Capoeira Regional'.[42] Another member of the same group stated: 'To be a Bamba [capoeira expert], you have to be the son of Bimba. Those who are created by Bambas are also the sons of Bimba. That's us!'[43] They did not need to posture and act tough because they had exceptional skills. They believed that they owed their skills to *Mestre* Bimba, a man they had never met, but with whom they had a connection through their leaders.

To become renowned and financially successful in capoeira takes more than just superlative martial arts skills. Beyond artistry and fighting techniques, it is important for leaders to represent the traditions of an honourable lineage and demonstrate a long apprenticeship with a formally instituted group and specific mestre. The importance of possessing a lineage was made clear when Janelle realized a leader in Toronto had invented his past. This leader, called Moreno, is infamous for claiming an instructor's status and association with a famous *mestre*. One participant Janelle interviewed clarified:

> Years ago [Moreno] said he had some *mestre* in Brazil, then I heard from someone his *mestre* was supposed to be in Spain, but you can't find this guy anywhere online. And it's obvious [Moreno's] skills are nowhere . . . [Now] you see he's tryin' to join our group 'cus he know he needs one to be taken seriously . . . but he doesn't want to do the . . . hard work to actually train under a *mestre*. In a word, he is fraudulent.[44]

Moreno, posing as an instructor, attended a public capoeira event in Toronto with one of his students in May 2007. The event was hosted by a *mestre* with a verifiable genealogy and three decades of experience. Janelle captured his introduction to the group in her field notes:

> When Moreno first entered the *roda* with [*mestre*] he was promptly delivered with a *benção* (blessing kick) – a subversive way to 'welcome' him to the event. He stumbled backwards and fell out of the *roda*. He tried to shake hands and end the game, but was summoned back into the *roda* for several more games with [*mestre*] and his senior students. Once they were finished with him, a bruised and battered Moreno slunk into the background, stood on the periphery, clapped and played instruments, never to enter the *roda* again. After witnessing her teacher being dominated by every capoeira player he encountered, I overheard Moreno's exasperated student: 'What have I been doing all these months?' She asked no one in particular.[45]

Moreno's student realized that she had been duped by his marketing strategies that included claims to authentic lineage, and quickly defected.

According to Eric Hobsbawn, in reference to national identities, 'If a satisfactory past does not exist, one can always invent it'.[46] Moreno had invented a past, which he knew was important to attract students; however, with the diasporization of *mestres*, proliferation of groups and appearance of new digital technologies, capoeira players around the world have become more knowledgeable and interconnected and can distinguish between the myths teachers share and reality.[47] It is both the claims leaders make and their embodied performances that are used to market their groups. Because most of what a *mestre* says about the art, his particular group or lineage can now be verified on the internet, through academic texts, or in his style of play and skill, it has become more difficult to manipulate students. Therefore, *mestres* must create more subtle ways of making students' believe in their traditions and gaining students' devotion.

Marketing strategy three: presenting Brazilian/Bahian capoeira

As Bahia – especially the city of Salvador – was the cradle of many famous *mestres* and the scene for several legendary capoeira *rodas* in the twentieth century, it came to be as important to some capoeira devotees as Mecca is for Muslims. This section discusses the fact that *mestres* born there accrue a certain status, which has produced a 'Bahia-centric' discourse among many leaders. In this discourse, the codes, rituals, music and techniques of Bahian capoeira are considered by many practitioners throughout Brazil and internationally to be superior to capoeira practised elsewhere.[48]

We observed the popularity of certain capoeira songs that transcended geography. Surely these songs became popular in Lisbon, Portugal, Christchurch, New Zealand and Rio de Janeiro, Brazil for many reasons (melody, timbre and distribution) in addition to lyrics.[49] However, a cursory examination of passages of many popular songs reveals the importance of Bahia:

> *Todo baiano tem no sangue a capoeira* (Everyone from Bahia has capoeira in their blood)
> *Jogo desde pequeno vou jogar a vida inteira* (Been playing since I was little, I will play it my whole life).[50]

> *Hoje me leva o coração pra Bahia,* (Today I take my heart to Bahia)
> *Hoje me leva o coração pra Bahia,* (Today I take my heart to Bahia)
> *Lembra dos mestres que agora estão com Deus,* (Remember the mestres who now are with God)
> *Minha Bahia* (My Bahia).[51]

The image of Bahian capoeira as the unique, original and main locus of authentic (African-) Brazilian culture had its propagation facilitated through the works of some writers (Jorge Amado), artists (Hector Julio Páride Bernabó, known as Carybé) and photographers (Pierre Verger) who lived in Bahia. They documented, portrayed and projected Bahian popular culture including Candomblé, carnival and capoeira as Brazilian culture. Being born in Bahia, playing capoeira in Bahia, or being a student of a famous Bahian *mestre* confers cultural capital in a flourishing (inter)national, capoeira-as-a-product market. Many leaders who cannot boast a direct link to a Bahian *mestre*, strategically incorporate elements of Bahian culture into their curriculum, behaviour, style and songs. Through lyrics that weave a tapestry of experiences in Bahia, they can use the music of capoeira to communicate a message of their authenticity. To sing of Bahia conjures images of a homeland to which the teacher may or may not have a direct affiliation. With this market expansion to more economically developed nations, the possible financial gains are even higher, and a prestigious Bahian capoeira lineage is even more important as it may translate to greater remuneration for the teacher.

Some capoeira teachers create a link to a Bahian *mestre*, becoming a student for a short period, whereas others may simply invent a connection between their trajectories as players and a renowned and often deceased *mestre*. Marcelo heard many capoeira participants in Rio de Janeiro claim that they, their father or some other close relative trained with a Bahian as a child in order to convert their alleged connections into prestige and financial advantages. Legitimately joining a capoeira association that works as a franchise is the fastest way to become part of a Bahian capoeira aristocracy. In this way, a foreign capoeira player can capitalize on Bahian traditions in the market without ever training there.

In Toronto, 'authentic' Bahian culture comes in the form of specifically African-Brazilian martial dances, such as *maculelê*, circle dances such as *samba de roda*, street dances such as *samba-reggae* and the fisherman's dance such as *puxada de rede,* which were a regular feature of classes of one capoeira group Janelle practised with in 2006 and again in 2010. Dance and other elements of African-Brazilian culture such as altars to honor orixas, or leather hats to signify the cattle raising roots of many enslaved African-Brazilians, are used as effective tools to capture a Bahian essence and communicate the values of 'racial democracy' – the ongoing myth of racial equality in Brazil.[52] One leader in Toronto emphasized that 'dance is for everyone, irregardless [sic] of race or culture or sex' as he encouraged students to 'shake that booty'.[53] He also noted that multiculturalism is a cornerstone of both Bahian and Torontonian cultures. If capoeira leaders can keep students focused on their capacity to celebrate diversity through the movements of their bodies and the cross-cultural friendships they can create within the capoeira class, they are guaranteed to augment their income among students with cosmopolitan desires for cross-cultural consumption. In Canada, the marketing strategies utilized to obtain economic success involve the presentation of capoeira classes and products 'as authentic Brazilian sport and culture [which] transforms this commodity into a more valuable object of desire...allow[ing] *mestre*s (masters) and graduados (student teachers) to garner more income from their practice'.[54]

It has been argued that, on the one hand, teaching students other cultural formations alongside capoeira allows them to develop a 'kinaesthetic citizenship', that is, an embodied connection to another nation/culture.[55] This is key to celebrations of diversity where intercultural learning helps to break down perceived differences among people, and thereby decreases discrimination.[56] On the other hand, limiting understandings of culture to the musical, physical and sartorial, or locating cultures elsewhere without critical attention to contemporary transnational politics, ongoing discrimination and white privilege in Brazil and elsewhere serves to reinforce racist understandings of others.[57] It is possible that this tension is circumvented when the 'other culture' presented is one of political awareness.

Marcelo witnessed one leader who had lived in the north of Rio de Janeiro for 25 years adopting a Bahian accent and style of dress. Invited to teach capoeira classes in the USA, Baleiro returned one year later with a strong accent, not from California where he had lived, but from Bahia Brazil. In addition, he wore clothing that made him look like an activist of *O Movimento Negro,* an organization in Bahia that affirms African cultural expressions as beautiful and political, rejects White (European) cultural modes and raises awareness of socio-economic oppressions.[58] Baleiro wore a smock, bracelets, necklaces and braided hair to signal his newfound Black consciousness. When asked about his sartorial transformation, he claimed he had always wanted the clothes and ornaments, but had never possessed the financial means to buy them. We suspect that, in addition to this reason, he had (perhaps subconsciously) adopted a Bahian, and specifically a political Bahian style, because it afforded him greater social capital in the capoeira market of the USA. In addition to offering his martial arts acumen, he 'sold' a Bahian activist identity to his US students. His authority was legitimated through his capacity to capitalize on the psychic distance of his US students to the politics of the *Movimento* and Bahia more generally. He ostensibly preserved and presented a cultural practice that bore the mark of African-descendant resistance and Brazilian nationality, potentially decreasing the uncritical cross-cultural consumption that promotes racist understandings of difference.

An 'authentic' capoeira product in the UK market has also been shown to gain and maintain new followers.[59] The majority of UK students have 'no direct experience of *capoeira* in Brazil: they 'experience' Brazilian *capoeira* vicariously through their teachers ... [who] emphasize that *they* are Brazilian, and have authentic knowledge and experience'.[60] Those who pay for capoeira classes are not merely students; rather, they are consumers who purchase knowledge of a physical culture and exposure to a national and regional culture as well. There are a great variety of versions of capoeira in Brazil, from the street *rodas* of indigent Blacks to the fitness classes of elite Whites and everything in between. Yet the marketing strategies delivered by the leaders we studied rely on an African-Brazilian model, and perfectly match the narratives espoused by *Mestres* Bimba and Pastinha nearly a century ago. In competition for a share of the market in capoeira, in international settings and saturated Brazilian cities, leaders emphasize their authenticity, lineage and connections to Brazil, specifically Bahia.

Final considerations

As martial artists and researchers, over the past three decades, we have witnessed a number of leaders who struggle in the competitive capoeira market. To gain and maintain students, leaders sell their capoeira groups based on discourses of inter-cultural learning, ethnic harmony and cohesion, martial efficiency, artistic and historical dance, and soulful music. Their group management procedures, uniform sales and fees for enrolment, tuition and graduation ceremonies are often negotiated under the guise of maintenance of tradition or guardianship of capoeira lineage, without interest in financial profit. But make no mistake, capoeira groups are businesses in a competitive sport and culture market. Encouraging students to participate in exclusive rituals and be devoted to a single teacher obscures the existence of the business relationship among teachers and students, and thus hides the formation of what Machado calls a 'market identity'.[61]

The process of creating a capoeira group 'market identity' was initiated by *Mestres* Bimba and Pastinha in the early twentieth century when they created the first Capoeira Centres. The strategies contemporary leaders use to create a valuable (and profitable) group identity include discursively linking their form to the history and culture of Brazil. They refer to what they do as the 'true' style of capoeira, a 'traditional' style, traced directly to Bahia, Brazil through a lineage of *mestres*. Capoeira group leaders emphasize differences in their respective styles, especially the alleged inauthenticity of their competition.

Long-term participant observation of capoeira classes and events in five different nations revealed cultural meanings emerge through capoeira when it is attached to recognizable symbols and stereotypes of authentic Brazilianness. We find it interesting that leaders who repeatedly tout capoeira as the embodiment of freedom for African slaves and central to the struggle for economic and racial equality for all peoples in Brazil also engage in performances of racist stereotypes. The capoeira player who presents himself as the epitome of African-Brazilianness, always happy, musical, proficient at a number of styles of dance, and concerned with social equity, especially fights for racial equality, may or may not be fully aware of his role in the selling of a cultural commodity. For example, although many leaders are aware of historical research that demonstrates the legend of capoeira's origins as a disguised fight used to liberate slaves, or anti-racist gang warfare to be misleading, others are not, but both continue to perpetuate such myths, with the objective of increasing their profits.[62] The forefathers of 'capoeira-as-product', *Mestres* Bimba and Pastinha, created a capoeira market that relied on notions of selling authentic culture. Nearly 100 years later, capoeira leaders in Brazil and around the world continue the custom of promoting their 'true', 'traditional', 'Bahian' capoeira to attract more participants and garner more financial success.

Acknowledgements

The authors would like to thank the capoeira participants, two anonymous reviewers and Dr. Mark Falcous. Janelle Joseph would like to thank the generous support of a Social Sciences and Humanities Research Council Canada Graduate Scholarship, and a Postdoctoral Fellowship from the School of Physical Education, University of Otago.

Notes

1. We use the term martial art with acknowledgement of capoeira's dance, ritual, music and game dimensions. For more on how capoeira is played see Downey, *Learning Capoeira.*
2. Assunção, *Afro-Brazilian Martial Art* and Rosenthal, 'Capoeira and Globalization'.
3. Vieira and Assunção, 'Mitos, controvérsias e fatos'.
4. Assunção, *Afro-Brazilian Martial Art*; Talmon-Chvaicer, *Hidden History*; Soares, *Negregada Instituição*; and Vieira and Assunção, 'Mitos, controvérsias e fatos.' Soares explains that the narrative of the origins of capoeira, widely accepted by scholars and practitioners of the twentieth century, was the one presented by Antônio Joaquim Macedo Soares in his *Dicionário Brasileiro da Língua Portuguesa* of 1889. The hypothesis is that 'capoeira' – the martial art – derived from the indigenous word 'capueira', a place of creeping vegetation, a region where the Black slave ran to escape and develop the martial art and dance for retaliation against the slave masters. Thus, capoeira developed a connotation of slave resistance.
5. Soares, *Negregada Instituição.*
6. Soares, *Negregada Instituição*; Soares, *Capoeira Escrava*; Dias, *Quem tem medo*; and Holloway, *Policing Rio.*
7. Almeida, 'Roda de Caxias'.
8. Vieira, *Jogo da capoeira* and Assunção, *Afro-Brazilian Martial Art.*
9. Abreu, *Barracão.*
10. Talmon-Chvaicer, 'Vicente Ferreira Pastinha', 152.
11. Sodré, *Mestre Bimba* and Capinussú, *Administração e Marketing.*
12. Rosenthal, 'Scholarly and Popular Works'; Teles dos Santos, 'Mixed-Race Nation'; and Talmon-Chvaicer, 'Capoeira', 177.
13. Vieira, *Jogo da Capoeira.*
14. Talmon-Chvaicer, *Hidden History.*
15. Joseph, 'Practice of Capoeira'.
16. Pesavento, *História Cultural.*
17. Malhotra, *Marketing Research*; Malhotra, Agarwal, and Peterson, 'Methodological Issues'; and Ratten and Ratten, 'International Sport Marketing'.
18. Elliott and Acharya 'Cross-Cultural Product Strategy'.
19. Elliott and Acharya 'Cross-Cultural Product Strategy'; Jain 'Standardization'; and Shoham, 'Marketing-Mix Standardization'.
20. Sousa and Bradley, 'Global Markets' and Sousa and Bradley, 'Cultural Distance'.
21. Sousa and Bradley, 'Cultural Distance', 51–2.
22. Wilson, *Nostalgia.*
23. Hobsbawn, *Sobre história.*
24. Lorand Matory, 'Illusion of Isolation'.
25. Lorand Matory, 'Illusion of Isolation', 949.
26. Lorand Matory, 'Illusion of Isolation', 950.
27. Bee and Kahle, 'Relationship Marketing'; Dionísio, Leal, and Moutinho, 'Fandom Affiliation'; Burnett, Menon, and Smart, 'Sports Marketing'; and Wenner, 'MediaSport'.
28. Ratten and Ratten, 'International Sport Marketing'.

29. Almeida, 'Roda de Caxias'; and Almeida, Bartholo, and Soares, 'Memories of the Caxias'; Almeida, Bartholo, and Soares, 'Uma roda'.
30. Joseph, 'Logical Paradox'; Joseph 'Going to Brazil'; Joseph, 'Cultural Transformation'; and Joseph, 'Intersectional Analysis'; Joseph, 'Practice of Capoeira'. Two groups were defined as *Contemporanea* (Contemporary) and performed a mixture of Angola and Regional styles.
31. DeWalt and DeWalt, *Participant Observation*, 165, 170.
32. Thomas, 'General Inductive Approach', 238.
33. Malhotra, *Marketing Research*.
34. Moura, *Dança da guerra*.
35. Moura, *Dança da guerra*.
36. Pastinha, *Capoeira Angola*, 31.
37. 28 May 2006.
38. 19 February 2011.
39. Talmon-Chvaicer, *Hidden History*, 159.
40. Assunção, *Afro-Brazilian Martial Art*, 182.
41. Taylor, *Jogo de Angola* and Assunção, *Afro-Brazilian Martial Art*.
42. 17 September 2006.
43. 5 November 2006.
44. 15 June 2007.
45. 15 May 2007.
46. Hobsbawn, *Sobre história*, 285.
47. Joseph, 'Logical Paradox'.
48. Interestingly, even in Rio de Janeiro, which has had a flourishing capoeira industry for over a century, Bahian capoeira is also valued.
49. Assunção, 'History and Memory', recognizes the significance of lyrics to the capoeira games played and identity of players.
50. *Mestre* Camisa, 'ABADÁ-Capoeira'.
51. Voador, 'Hoje Me Leva'.
52. Joseph, 'Practice of Capoeira' and Twine, *Racism in a Racial Democracy*.
53. 18 August 2010.
54. Joseph, 'Logical Paradox', 512.
55. Joseph, 'Going to Brazil, 197.
56. Schwartz, 'Multicultural Dance Education'.
57. Bissondath, *Selling Illusions*; and Hage, *White Nation*.
58. Covin, 'Brazil's Unified Black Movement'.
59. Delamont, 'Authority and Authenticity'; de Campos Rosario, Stephens, and Delamont, 'Authenticity and Authority'; and Delamont and Stephens, 'Embodied Habitus'.
60. Delamont and Stephens, 'Embodied Habitus', 65, original emphasis.
61. Machado, 'Identidade-Para-o-Mercado'.
62. Assunção, *Afro-Brazilian Martial Art* and Dias, *Quem tem medo*.

References

Abreu, Frederico. *O Barracão do Mestre Valdemar*. Salvador: Zarabatana, 2003.
Almeida, Marcelo. 'Roda de Caxias: Memórias e Etnografia de uma Roda de Capoeira' (master's thesis, Gama Filho University, 2007).
Almeida, Marcelo, Tiago Bartholo, and Antonio Soares. 'Memories of the Caxias "Roda de Capoiera"'. *Federation Internationale D'Education Physique Bulletin* 76 (2006): 245–8.
Almeida, Marcelo, Tiago Bartholo, and Antonio Soares. 'Uma roda de rua: Notas ethnográficas da roda de capoeiira de Caxias'. *Revista Portuguesa de Ciências do Desporto* 7 (2007): 124–33.
Assunção, Matthias. *Capoeira: The History of an Afro-Brazilian Martial Art*. London: Routledge, 2005.
Assunção, Matthias. 'History and Memory in Capoeira Lyrics from Bahia Brazil'. In *Cultures of the Lusophone Black Atlantic*, ed. Nancy Naro, Roger Sansi-Roca, and David Treece, 199–217. New York: Palgrave Macmillan, 2007.
Bee, Colleen, and Lynn Kahle. 'Relationship Marketing in Sports: A Functional Approach'. *Sport Marketing Quarterly* 15 (2006): 102–10.

Bissondath, Neil. *Selling Illusions: The Cult of Multiculturalism in Canada.*, 2nd ed. Toronto: Penguin, 2002.

Burnett, John, Anil Menon, and Denise Smart. 'Sports Marketing: A New Ball Game with New Rules'. *Journal of Advertising Research* 33 (1993): 21–35.

Camisa, *Mestre.* 'Bate o Machado'. *Moda de Viola ABADÁ-Capoeira.* CD, 1997.

Capinussú, José. *Administração e Marketing nas Academias de Ginástica.* São Paulo: Ibrasa, 1989.

Covin, David. 'The Role of Culture in Brazil's Unified Black Movement, Bahia in 1992'. *Journal of Black Studies* 27 (1996): 39–55.

Dança de guerra. Produced and Directed by Jair Moura. Brazil: Motion Picture IJM, 1968.

de Campos Rosario, Claudio, Neil Stephens, and Sara Delamont. '"I'm Your Teacher, I'm Brazilian!": Authenticity and Authority in European Capoeira'. *Sport, Education and Society* 15 (2010): 103–20.

Delamont, Sara. 'The Smell of Sweat and Rum: Authority and Authenticity Among Capoeira Teachers'. *Ethnography and Education* 1 (2006): 161–75.

Delamont, Sara, and Neil Stephens. 'Up on the Roof: The Embodied Habitus of Diasporic Capoeira'. *Cultural Sociology* 6 (2008): 57–74.

DeWalt, Kathleen, and Billie DeWalt. *Participant Observation: A Guide for Fieldworkers.* Lanham, MD: AltaMira Press, 2011.

Dias, Luiz. *Quem tem medo da capoeira? Rio de Janeiro, 1890–1904: Report of Secretaria Municipal das Culturas.* Rio de Janeiro: Arquivo Geral da cidade do Rio de Janeiro, 2001.

Dionísio, Pedro, Carmo Leal, and Luiz Moutinho. 'Fandom Affiliation and Tribal Behaviour: A Sports Marketing Application'. *Qualitative Market Research: An International Journal* 11 (2008): 17–39.

Downey, Greg. *Learning Capoeira: Lessons in Cunning from an Afro-Brazilian Art.* Oxford, England: Oxford University Press, 2005.

Elliott, Greg, and Chandrama Acharya. 'Cross-Cultural Product Strategy'. In *Cross-Cultural Marketing*, ed. Robert Rugimbana and Sonny Nwankwo, 108–16. London, England: Thomson, 2003.

Hage, Ghassan. *White Nation: Fantasies of White Supremacy in a Multicultural Society.* New York: Routledge, 2000.

Hobsbawn, Eric. *Sobre história.* São Paulo: Companhia das Letras, 1998.

Holloway, Thomas. *Policing Rio de Janeiro: Repression and Resistance in a Nineteenth Century City.* Stanford, CA: Stanford University Press, 1993.

Jain, Subhash. 'Standardization of International Marketing Strategy: Some Research Hypotheses'. *Journal of Marketing* 53 (1989): 70–9.

Joseph, Janelle. 'Cultural Transformation of Capoeira: Brazilian, Canadian and Caribbean Interpretations'. In *Latin American Identities After 1980*, ed. Amy Huras, 197–216. Waterloo, ON: Wilfred Laurier University Press, 2010.

Joseph, Janelle. '"Going to Brazil": Transnational and Corporeal Movements of a Canadian-Brazilian Martial Arts Community'. *Global Networks* 8 (2008): 194–213.

Joseph, Janelle. 'An Intersectional Analysis of Black Sporting Masculinities'. In *Race and Sport in Canada: Intersecting Inequalities*, ed. Janelle Joseph, Simon Darnell, and Yuka Nakamura, 237–63. Toronto: Canadian Scholars Press, 2012.

Joseph, Janelle. 'The Logical Paradox of the Cultural Commodity: Selling an "Authentic" Afro-Brazilian Martial Art in Canada'. *Sociology of Sport Journal* 25 (2008): 498–515.

Joseph, Janelle. 'The Practice of Capoeira: African And Black Diaspora Discourses in an Afro-Brazilian-Canadian Martial Art'. *Ethnic and Racial Studies* 35 (2012): 1078–95.

Lorand Matory, James. 'The Illusion of Isolation: The Gullah/Geechees and the Political Economy of African Culture in the Americas'. *Comparative Studies in Society and History* 50 (2008): 949–80.

Machado, Igor. 'Estado-nação, Identidade-Para-o-Mercado e Representações de Nação'. *Revista de Antropologia* 47 (2004): 207–33.

Malhotra, Naresh. *Marketing Research: An Applied Orientation.*, 2nd ed. Saddle River, NJ: Prentice-Hall, 1996.

Malhotra, Naresh, James Agarwal, and Mark Peterson. 'Methodological Issues in Cross-Cultural Marketing Research'. *International Marketing Review* 13 (1996): 7–43.

Pastinha, *Mestre.* *Capoeira Angola.* Salvador: Fundação Cultural do Estado da Bahia, 1988.

Pesavento, Sandra. *História e História Cultural.* Belo Horizonte: Autêntica, 2004.

Ratten, Hamish, and Vanessa Ratten. 'International Sport Marketing: Practical and Future Research Implications'. *Journal of Business of Industrial Marketing* 26 (2011): 614–20.

Rosenthal, Joshua. 'Capoeira and Globalization'. In *Imagining Globalization: Language, Identities and Boundaries*, ed. Ho Leung, Matthew Hendley, Robert Compton, and Brian Haley, 145–64. New York: Palgrave Macmillan, 2009.

Rosenthal, Joshua. 'Recent Scholarly and Popular Works on Capoeira'. *Latin American Research Review* 42 (2007): 262–72.

Schwartz, Peggy. 'Multicultural Dance Education in Today's Curriculum'. *Journal of Physical Education, Recreation and Dance* 62 (1991): 45–8.

Shoham, Aviv. 'Marketing-Mix Standardization: Determinants of Export Performance'. *Journal of Global Marketing* 10 (1996): 53–73.

Soares, Carlos. *A Capoeira Escrava e Outras Tradições Rebeldes no Rio de Janeiro (1808–1850)*. Campinas: Editora da Unicamp, 2001.

Soares, Carlos. *A Negregada Instituição: Os Capoeiras no Rio de Janeiro: Report of Secretaria Municipal das Culturas*. Rio de Janeiro, Brazil: Departamento Geral de Documentação e Informação Cultural, 1994.

Sodré, Muniz. *Mestre Bimba: Corpo de Mandinga*. Rio de Janeiro, Brazil: Manati, 2002.

Sousa, Carlos, and Frank Bradley. 'Cultural Distance and Psychic Distance: Two Peas in a Pod?' *Journal of International Marketing* 14 (2006): 49–70.

Sousa, Carlos, and Frank Bradley. 'Global Markets: Does Psychic Distance Matter?' *Journal of Strategic Marketing* 13 (2005): 43–59.

Talmon-Chvaicer, Maya. 'Capoeira'. In *Encyclopedia of Black Studies*, ed. Molefi Asante and Ama Mazama, 175–8. Thousand Oaks, CA: Sage, 2005.

Talmon-Chvaicer, Maya. *The Hidden History of Capoeira: A Collision of Cultures in the Brazilian Battle Dance*. Austin: University of Texas Press, 2008.

Talmon-Chvaicer, Maya. 'Vicente Ferreira Pastinha (1889–1981): The "Angolan" Tradition of Capoeira'. In *The Human Tradition in the Black Atlantic 1500–2000*, ed. Beatriz Mamigonian and Karen Racine, 147–62. Lanham, MA: Rowman & Littelfield, 2010.

Taylor, Gerard. *Capoeira: The Jogo de Angola: From Luanda to Cyberspace*. Vol. 2. Berkeley, CA: North Atlantic Books, 2007.

Teles dos Santos, Jocélio. 'A Mixed-Race Nation: Afro-Brazilians and Cultural Policy in Bahia, 1970–1990'. In *Afro-Brazilian Culture and Politics: Bahia, 1790–1990*, ed. Henrik Kraay, 117–33. London: M.E. Sharpe, 1998.

Thomas, David. 'A General Inductive Approach for Analyzing Qualitative Evaluation Data'. *American Journal of Evaluation* 27 (2006): 237–46.

Twine, France. *Racism in a Racial Democracy: The Maintenance of White Supremacy in Brazil*. New Brunswick, NJ: Rutgers University Press, 1998.

Vieira, Luiz. *O jogo da capoeira*. Rio de Janeiro, Brazil: Sprint, 1988.

Vieira, Luiz, and Matthias Assunção. 'Mitos, controvérsias e fatos: construindo a história da capoeira'. *Estudos Afro-Asiáticos* 34 (1999): 81–120.

Voador, Graduado. 'Hoje Me Leva Coração'. *Capoeria Nagô*. vol. 2. CD, 2005.

Wenner, Lawrence. 'Playing the Mediasport Game'. In *MediaSport*, ed. Lawrence Wenner, 3–13. New York: Routledge, 1998.

Wilson, Janelle. *Nostalgia: Sanctuary of Meaning*. Cranbury, NJ: Rosemont, 2005.

The making of an ethnically diverse management: contested cultural meanings in a Dutch amateur football club

Michel van Slobbe, Jeroen Vermeulen and Martijn Koster

Utrecht School of Governance, Utrecht University, Utrecht, The Netherlands

This paper discusses ethnographic research on the planned transition from an all-white Dutch management towards an ethnically diverse management of an amateur football club. This study is based on a 3-year period of ethnographic fieldwork in a football club, located in an ethnically diverse neighbourhood in the Netherlands. We argue that the transition led to contested understandings of cultural practices and artefacts within the club. The meaning-making processes of the club's organizational culture reinforced us–them divisions between the two groups. What is at stake is the symbolic ownership of the club that comes from a deep-rooted desire among members of the club to be 'among themselves'. Findings suggest that apparent equity in terms of shared participation in the club's management does not necessarily lead to bridging of ethnic differences on the level of the club's culture.

Introduction

This paper presents ethnographic research that studied the transition of an all-white Dutch to an ethnically mixed committee of an amateur football club in one of the large cities in the Netherlands. The football club, situated in an ethnically diverse neighbourhood, had seen a change in membership that reflected the changing demography of the neighbourhood. White Dutch members left the club and were replaced by young Moroccan Dutch players.[1] Despite these changes, the club's committee membership was white Dutch only. The club suffered from financial deficits, which made it largely dependent on the local municipality (government/council). The municipality supported the club financially on the condition that Moroccan Dutch members would be allowed to participate in its management. The underlying idea was to reorganize the club into an organization that was embedded in the local community as well as a representative of its ethnic diversity.

The case of this local football club represents broader issues that deal with the real and alleged meanings of sport for social integration in the Netherlands (and elsewhere). In recent years, Dutch policy-makers embraced the idea that sport is both means and site for the social integration of ethnic minorities.[2] This corresponds to wider held views about sport as 'the great social leveler'.[3] Expectations are high concerning sport's potential for bridging social differences and removing inequality(ies).[4] Ethnic minorities in the Netherlands, including the Moroccan Dutch, have established their own football clubs since the 1960s. However, current public opinion and policy emphasize the need to create so-called ethnically *mixed* clubs. Ethnically 'separate' or ethnic-specific clubs are considered undesirable as they allegedly hinder the social integration of ethnic minority groups into wider Dutch society.[5] Comparable discussions about ethnic minority clubs are found in England about British Asian amateur football clubs.[6] In the Netherlands, many individuals from ethnic minority groups opt for membership of what we would describe as 'established' Dutch football clubs. These clubs are becoming increasingly ethnically 'mixed'. However, for the most part, the management of these clubs remains in the hands of white Dutch men. Our study analyses the processes involved in a transition from a white Dutch to an ethnically diverse club management structure.

The purpose of this paper was to examine how members of two different ethnic groups in the football club perceived and experienced this transition. We are concerned with a number of questions: How did they interact during the period of the planned transition? How did they perceive each other? Were they able to share the management of the club? Did the process of mixing – the explicit aim of local policies – succeed? Based on our findings, we argue that the transition towards a mixed management led to a conflict over understandings about the symbolic practices and artefacts within the club's organizational culture. The meaning-making processes of organizational culture intensify us–them divisions that impede the process of establishing an ethnically mixed club committee. Therefore, when an ethnically diverse management was eventually installed, the us–them divisions continued to exist. We conclude that apparent equity in terms of shared participation in the club's management does not necessarily lead to bridging of ethnic differences on the level of the club's culture.

Methodology

Ethnography, both as an epistemology and as a method, is appropriate for trying to grasp interpretations and understanding of complex processes and actions that are characteristic of local settings.[7] In recent years, ethnographic studies have been carried out in sports clubs, such as cricket, golf and football.[8] These studies show how norms, values, ideologies and power relations are either critically challenged or reinforced by members in their local setting. Lake argues that the relatively autonomous nature and established hierarchical structure of voluntary sports clubs 'provide excellent locations for analyzing power relations between members, and how social status and cohesion are emphasized'.[9]

One of the authors conducted research in the football club from October 2008 to December 2011. In this period, he collected data through participant observation of naturally occurring events, informal talks and interviews. His role is best described as 'participant-as-observer'.[10] That is, during his research he was functioning as a member of the social setting at the football club. He participated as a member of a task force that was assigned to create an ethnically mixed club committee. Members of both the task force and the football club were informed about his research. This situation provided opportunities to 'discover aspects which interviewees may be unaware of or which, for other reasons, they find difficult to articulate'.[11] For example, directly after task force meetings, the researcher would ask individual informants to reflect in detail on what had been said and done during the meeting they had both participated in. The data were obtained during weekly task force meetings, meetings with municipal officials, training sessions, as well as matches involving junior and senior teams, social activities and club celebrations. Field notes were written after each event. For deeper understanding of the meanings and motives behind the social interactions of the informants, interviews were conducted with the task force members, senior club members, parents of youth members, municipal officials and senior players. Most of the interviews were informal, occurring as part of the natural flow of events, addressing specific topics in no particular sequence. In addition to the data collected from observations, informal talks and interviews, the researcher analysed emails between club members and the task force, policy documents and membership figures.[12]

During his immersion in the field, the researcher developed theoretical propositions. Four 'key incidents' from the collected data were selected that function as illustrations of our arguments.[13] Before presenting findings of our fieldwork, we will provide a description of the football club studied, its background and context.

The amateur football club *Among Ourselves*

The football club we studied is named *Onder Ons*, Dutch for *Among Ourselves*. The club was founded in 1948 by employees of the then state-owned Postal and Telephone Company. Originally, the club used a farmer's grassland, adjoining the city borders. In the 1960s, due to urban development, the club had to move. The municipality offered a residence in a new municipal sport complex at the other side of the city, in Overvecht. The district had been built as a solution to the housing shortage of the fast-growing city of Utrecht, the fourth largest city in the Netherlands. At its new home, *Among Ourselves* developed into a club with 300 members. The club also became a popular community centre for the district's working-class residents. On Saturdays, members and their friends/ neighbours gathered at the club, where, besides football, weekly dance nights with live music, card games and billiards were organized. In the 1990s, Overvecht's demography changed in terms of ethnicity. Due to ill-maintenance, the neighbourhood offered relatively cheap social housing which attracted many families from lower income brackets, of which many were of Moroccan descent.[14] With the demographic change many members left the club. In 1998, only 60 members were left. Unable to survive financially, the municipality suggested a merger with another club that was experiencing similar difficulties. However, the members of *Among Ourselves* refused the proposal and the club's management negotiated with the municipality about moving to a new location and owning their own playing facilities. The municipality agreed on the condition that *Among Ourselves* would develop towards a club of mixed ethnicity with a membership that would mirror the neighbourhood's increasingly diverse population.

In 2000, *Among Ourselves* moved to its current location in the centre of the district. The district's population comprises 21% Moroccan Dutch people.[15] In the neighbourhood surrounding the club, over 50% of the residents are of Moroccan descent.[16] The Moroccan Dutch form the second largest migrant group with 'non-western origins' in the Netherlands; they are second only to the Turkish Dutch. There are approximately 360,000 Moroccan Dutch people in the Netherlands. This number equates to 2.2% of the total Dutch population of 16.7 million people.[17] The first immigrants from Morocco came to the Netherlands as guest workers in the 1960s.[18] Many of them settled permanently in the Netherlands, making use of 'a rather generous programme of settlement and family reunion'.[19] Most of the Moroccan Dutch live in one of the four large cities (Amsterdam, The Hague, Rotterdam and Utrecht). They are doing significantly less well than white Dutch, in terms of employment and average income. The unemployment rate among Moroccan Dutch youths is about three times higher than among native Dutch youths.[20]

In order to meet its financial needs and to comply with the municipality's conditions, *Among Ourselves* admitted 40 Moroccan Dutch youth players and a youth committee from another local club that had recently had to close. After this, the number of youth members increased substantially and the youth committee coordinated their training and participation in the league. In 2006, due to a clash between the youth committee and the general committee of the club, the organizing of youth football ceased. As a result, the club experienced decreasing membership, shortage of volunteers and negative food and beverage turnover. In 2008 *Among Ourselves* had 155 members, of which 140 were playing members (94 senior and 46 junior). Approximately 60% of its members were migrants – mainly of Moroccan descent.

The sports club as community and culture

Notwithstanding inclusionary policy rhetoric about sport's supposedly integrative powers, the entrance of increasing numbers of ethnic minorities in amateur sports clubs does not necessarily lead to higher participation of these 'new' members in the management of sports clubs. Endorsing this observation Fletcher argues that, despite the political claims to characterize sport as meritocratic and 'colour blind', numerical representation of ethnic minorities in sport is not equivalent to acceptance and integration.[21] In this section, we aim to better understand this contradictory observation, exploring the concept of 'culture' with regard to amateur sports clubs. We take Long, Robinson and Spracklen as our point of departure. In discussing the situation of sport and equity at management level in the UK, they argue that 'what are at stake are the cultures within sport and the communities of sport ... that establish their own boundaries of belonging and exclusion'.[22]

In this paper, we focus on cultures within amateur sports clubs. Sports clubs are voluntary associations characterized by bonding relationships between like-minded people.[23] Studies point to sport's potential to enhance a sense of identity and of community.[24] Burdsey contends that minority ethnic clubs, for example, British Asian amateur football clubs in England, functioned as sites where minorities are able to balance between 'retaining their identities with becoming more inclusive institutions'.[25] Studies into ethnic minority clubs in the Netherlands seem to underscore Burdsey's findings.[26] Sports clubs, in Cohen's terms, are symbolically constructed communities of people who share common understandings.[27] Those who belong to the community share the ability to use, interpret and understand the communal symbols.[28] In that sense, they form 'communities of meaning'.[29] As Cohen argues, people become 'most sensitive' to their own shared meanings and symbols when they encounter 'others'. When people feel that the base of their community is undermined as a result of the interactions with 'others', people tend to reinforce the symbolic boundaries of their community.[30] These encounters reaffirm one's own cultural values and, at the same time, reinforce boundaries between communities and groups. Intergroup interactions thus tend to 'define differences, not similarities'.[31] Inclusion and exclusion are ongoing processes that take place in day-to-day interactions between people. In sport literature, the practices of inclusion and exclusion – in terms of gender, sexuality, ethnicity, class and age – have been well examined.[32]

Sports clubs often reflect the social stratification of society at large. Historically, people organized themselves into sports clubs according to social class and, at least in the Netherlands, according to religious affiliations.[33] Stokvis points out: 'Social intercourse, in the form of membership in these clubs, was restricted to people who conformed to the same lifestyle'.[34] From this, it follows that sports clubs are very much internally oriented and focused on socializing their members into established symbolic understandings. Newcomers need to learn the cultural codes and meanings of the dominant groups in the sports club.[35] From that perspective, sports clubs are sites for identity formation.[36] As is well established in cultural studies, the formation of identity goes hand in hand with the production of difference, for each act of inclusion and identification is based on exclusion and the making of boundaries.[37] Hence, the production of differences, based on hegemonic understandings of what counts as accepted behaviour and of what it means to belong, is characteristic of cultures in sports clubs. In sport, organizational cultures have developed which tend to operate in an exclusionary fashion towards homosexuals, women and particular ethnic groups.[38] However, we must be cautious not to overstate the case. No culture, whether sports in general, or sports clubs in particular, are fixed entities with unmovable boundaries. On the contrary, the symbolic understandings and the identities these produce are always contested.[39]

We argue that the concept of organizational culture, as it is studied in the interpretive and critical branches of organizational studies, is useful for grasping the dynamic processes of inclusion and exclusion in sports clubs.[40] First, the concept of organizational culture allows us to take a broad view on meaning-making processes in sports clubs. Meanings are embodied in symbolic language, objects and acts.[41] One finds cultural meanings expressed in stories that people tell and in the ways the buildings are arranged, used and decorated. Moreover, cultures are shaped in the relationships between members and in the relationships with newcomers and 'outsiders'. Second, through these meaning-making processes, people organize their activities, relationships and settings. They create a symbolic order in the sense of agreed upon arrangements among members about 'how things are done around here'.[42] Third, organizational cultures are characterized not only by means of their *shared* understandings but also by the *contestation* which takes place over these understandings.[43] In so doing, the meaning-making processes of organizational cultures produce symbolic boundaries between groups of individuals within organizations.[44] Following Parker, we conceptualize organizational culture as a 'process of making claims about difference and similarity between individuals in an organization, making divisions between "us" and "them"'.[45]

The established and the outsiders

In the Netherlands, we see that ethnic minorities increasingly participate in sport organizations, notably in voluntary amateur sports clubs. These minorities are often considered as 'space invaders', in the terms used by Puwar.[46] Puwar argues that ethnic minorities 'as racialized bodies are, unlike white bodies, visible carriers of their ethnic identity, and perceived to be marked and bounded by their ethnic identities'.[47] Dutch anthropologist Arie de Ruijter describes sports clubs as arenas in which different, and by definition non-equivalent, partners clash. The nature and structure of the contest is more or less formalized as a 'negotiated order'.[48]

The organizational cultures of sports clubs encounter new contestations from 'outsiders' invading the club's space and from policies aimed at social integration through sports. For our analysis, we turn to the concept of 'established and outsiders', as presented by Norbert Elias and John Scotson in their study of local relationships between resident groups of a small suburb in a large and wealthy British industrial city.[49] In their 'established–outsiders' theory, the concepts of 'mutual dependency' and 'power balance' play a central role. According to Elias, people are to be understood in their mutual dependency; what he terms, a 'figuration'.[50] Interdependences are related to power, which Elias sees as relational and reciprocal, i.e. the more powerful group is dependent on the less powerful group and vice versa. For Elias, the existing power balance is a result of the search for the order in which both groups are mutually dependent.[51] In their study of the power relationships between 'established' and 'outsiders' among resident groups, Elias and Scotson found that the (longer) duration of residence in the neighbourhood – what they call oldness of association – enabled the 'established' to develop greater cohesion relative to the outsiders and this, in turn, enabled them to monopolize key positions in local associations.[52] Consequently, the 'established' were able to define the local rules of the game and reproduce a historically grown position of power. In such a 'figuration', the established group aims at maintaining its position and the 'outsiders' strive for improvement of their position in the power balance.[53] According to Elias and Scotson, 'stigmatizing' and 'the possession of key positions' appeared the main sources of power in the contest between the two resident groups.[54] Our study aims to offer insight into the ways the 'established' (white Dutch) and the 'outsiders' (Moroccan Dutch) interact in the space(s) of an amateur football club during the transition towards an ethnically mixed management structure.

Contested cultural meanings in the football club *Among Ourselves*

We will present four key incidents that illustrate how the club's externally imposed transition towards an ethnically mixed management led to a contestation over cultural meanings in the club and how this reinforced us–them divisions between the two ethnic groups. The first incident refers to an institutional intervention by the municipality which initiated the transition. The second incident was marked by a struggle over understandings of cultural practices in the club. It concerns the seemingly trivial symbolic meanings of drinking tea in the club's canteen. The resistance by task force members towards the candidacy of a Moroccan Dutch member for the new committee is the focus of the third incident. Eventually, at a membership meeting, two Moroccan Dutch candidates were elected by the majority of the members. It appears, therefore, that the intervention was successful as the transition towards an ethnically mixed club had been made. However, the club's power balance changed as a result, which led to further contestation. This becomes clear in the last incident, which is concerned with the exclusion of the last remaining 'established' white Dutch team.

'This club is needed there'

In this first key incident, we describe a 'club saving' meeting with white Dutch club members, municipal officials and external professionals. The meeting followed a cry of distress by club members towards the municipality and resulted in the installation of a task force. In 2008, the club developed serious debts as a consequence of unpaid energy bills and inadequate canteen management. The club was close to folding, but was given a lifeline when a substantial part of these debts was paid off by the municipality. The simple reason for this intervention was that local politicians and policy-makers attached social value to the club; in particular its role for the local youth. In the meeting, a municipal official declared:

> Among Ourselves is having some troublesome years, for both management and finance and also in organizing the youth department. With the social problems in that specific area of Overvecht, with its young dropouts, we see this club as one of the most important clubs. In that part of Utrecht, the need for organized football is enormous....This club is needed there. But at the moment it is organized and managed poorly. Eventually, the club and its management should also represent the population of the neighborhood.

Furthermore, the municipality made it clear that this was the last time it would help the club financially. With the financial assistance, it imposed a condition on the club. The municipality installed two external professionals who, together with two key club members, would form a task force. One of the professionals is Frank, who would later become the task force's Chair.[55] He is white Dutch, then 50 years old, working as a government official and Chairman of a successful amateur football club in Utrecht. The other is Mimoum, a 38-year-old Moroccan Dutch economist and club consultant for the Dutch Football Association (KNVB). The task force assignment involved:

> ... stabilizing the club financially; organizing volunteers and voluntary management, making a policy plan and nominate a new representative committee. (at least a Chairman, Secretary and Treasurer)[56]

Both the municipal official and the task force assignment speak of 'representation'. This fits within a municipal policy aimed at voluntary sports clubs becoming more open, removing membership restrictions, recruiting youth members with subsidized coaching and developing connections between sports clubs and schools. Thus, 'representative' here implies an ethnically mixed committee, consisting of both 'established' members and the more recently arrived residents of the neighbourhood, the Moroccan Dutch. The official emphasizes the importance of the club in that area when he says 'this club is needed there'. His statement is illustrative for Dutch policy discourse in which sports clubs are presented as meeting points in deprived neighbourhoods. The municipality's expectations were high regarding the club's potential for bridging social differences and removing inequality. The task force stands for an institutional intervention in the club's 'arena'. However, as we will see, it initiated contestations among members and acted as a catalyst for generating a clear us–them division. Before long, this division became articulated in the seemingly trivial activity of selling tea in the canteen.

Selling tea in the canteen

This key incident shows the contestation of meanings between the 'established' and the 'outsiders', attached to particular practices and artefacts in the club's organizational culture. It relates specifically to the selling of food and drinks in the club's canteen. In the canteen, a prominent place was reserved for the bar with two beer taps and lightened signboards with beer brands. On one of the walls was a painting of a life-sized white male football player in club uniform. The other walls were covered with team photos from the 1970s and showed only white players.

Shortly after the task force had started its work, the professionals encountered the 'symbolic boundaries' and 'us–them divisions' of everyday club life. The task force organized a membership meeting to present itself, learn about the club's daily challenges and listen to members. Fatima, a Moroccan Dutch mother of one of the youth players, raised the issue of selling tea in the club's canteen. At the crowded meeting, attended by both Moroccan Dutch and white Dutch, following a discussion about the canteen's finances, she stood up and asked the taskforce: 'Can't we buy a cup of tea here?'

At that time, tea was not served in the canteen. Most of the Moroccan Dutch members were Muslim and did not drink alcohol. Instead, they had coffee or soft drinks. They welcomed the idea of serving tea. Frank, the Chair of the task force, promised to talk to the canteen manager, Ari, to arrange for the sale of tea. Two weeks later, after a task force meeting, Frank went to Ari, an active and appreciated volunteer, who fiercely countered the idea and shouted to Frank:

> We will not sell tea or halal food in our canteen. Over my dead body!

Despite Ari's objections, shortly after this confrontation, a tea box appeared in the bar and 'Moroccan' tea was served. Furthermore, a Moroccan Dutch canteen volunteer started to sell halal meat. However, these actions were not without resistance. Although several white Dutch members started to appreciate the Moroccan tea, several others questioned the 'unnecessary' investment in an extra halal deep fryer and explicitly doubted whether this would benefit the club financially. A municipal official, when informed about the development, acknowledged the resistance to selling Moroccan tea in the canteen. In an interview, he argued that he and his colleagues were worried about the club's financial situation:

> Here [at the club] parents only drink Moroccan tea and that … does not generate enough turnover. You just need members who drink beer.

However, it is arguable whether the profit on tea is lower than on beer, knowing that herbs and water for Moroccan tea are very inexpensive. When this was brought into discussion, the official reinforced the notion that selling and drinking beer is an essential component of football culture – the 'third half of the match' – and would therefore be an unquestionable source of income for *Among Ourselves*. At the club, the issues of alcohol and halal food did not articulate religious differences, but it marked the Moroccan Dutch members as outsiders.[57] Afterwards, in an interview with Johan, one of the 'established' canteen volunteers, the issue about halal food was trivialized. Johan recalls:

> Halal is the same meat as what we purchased before. Simply the way of slaughter differs. If we had decided to switch to halal food at once, there would have been less of a fuss, I think. But with the selling of both halal and non-halal it caused confusion and arousal among members. We did not know much about halal and no one explained anything about it.

By standing up publicly and asking about the tea, Fatima gave voice to a feeling of social inequality and uneven power relations, shared by other Moroccan Dutch members at the club. Through her act, she explicitly claimed a part of the canteen's space, which is clearly not neutral with regard to the consumption of particular food and beverages. The beer taps, the painting on the wall, the photos of white Dutch teams and the possession of key positions in the canteen symbolize the 'oldness of association' of the white Dutch members.[58] The historically grown position of power gave them the opportunity to decide about the food and drinks in the canteen. In line with Cohen's arguments, the white Dutch members became 'most sensitive' to their own shared meanings of drinking beer when they encountered Moroccan Dutch who abstained from drinking alcohol and preferred to drink tea.[59] The white Dutch members, feeling that their community was undermined, started to symbolically reinforce the (exclusionary) boundaries of their community. The attendance of many Moroccan Dutch members and the Chairman's promise to arrange the selling of tea symbolized a change at the club; arguably, they represented a shift in power. Both Fatima's question and Ari's fierce reaction articulated an us–them division, between the tea drinking 'outsiders' and the beer drinking 'established' members. Moreover, in his statement about the importance of selling beer, the municipal official reinforced this division.

The candidacy of Fatima for a committee position

The third key incident concerns the resistance by task force members towards the candidacy of Fatima. As we mentioned, the numerical representation of ethnic minority groups in sport does not necessarily mean the acceptance and integration of outsiders, especially when committee positions are concerned.[60]

In the second half of the season (2008–2009), Fatima presented herself as a candidate for Treasurer in the new 'representative' committee that was to be installed as part of the task force's mission.[61] She had financial experience as a member of the youth committee, worked as a financial assistant for a bank and studied Financial Management. Fatima, 43 years old, raised and educated in the Netherlands and recently divorced, lived with her only son of 9 years old, in an apartment facing the club. In an informal conversation, she complained about the way some white Dutch club members would drink excessively and be generally antisocial at club events. On this basis, she said to the rest of the committee that she seriously doubted whether the club was good for her son's development. However, she also told that her son was proud to be a member of an 'official' football club and that he was happy playing with his school friends. Later, Fatima said:

> You should know that Among Ourselves has a bad name here in the neighbourhood. We suffer
> from the noise, nuisance and harassment by senior members in the surroundings of the club,
> especially on Saturday evenings when they have drunk and smoked too much. That is not the
> place I prefer for my son, you can imagine. But he [her son] insists on playing for that club.
> I hope the new committee can make a difference and I am willing to contribute.

However, two task force members resisted her candidacy. They argued that Fatima was
unable to commit herself to the club in the long term. They portrayed Fatima as an
opportunistic person who would leave as soon as her son was able to move to another club.
Task force member Henk, for instance, argued:

> Fatima will certainly leave the club when her son is accepted by another club. Besides, she is
> not willing to commit herself for three years.

Fatima's candidacy stimulated other Moroccan Dutch members and parents to become
more involved with the club. More parents entered the canteen, they became members and
players in senior teams and they took on voluntary work. One of the parents, for instance,
became a canteen volunteer and started to organize daily tea sessions. The involvement of
Moroccan Dutch volunteers also led to the refurbishment of the canteen. Even a few of the
old team photos were replaced by photos of the present mixed youth teams. Actions such
as these suggest that the 'culture' of the club was changing.

However, task force member Henk wrote an email in which he expressed his unease
about the developments at the club (i.e. the changing power relations). He accused Fatima of
being part of a 'coup', in which she tried to convince Aziz, another Moroccan Dutch
member, to stand as a candidate for the committee as well. Henk's insinuations can be read
in the email fragment below, part of an exchange between Henk and the task force members:

> … a secret talk between Aziz and Fatima … looks like a conspiracy to take over the club,
> from which I would like to distance myself.[62]

At a subsequent meeting, Henk insisted on looking for other candidates for the new
committee. He threatened to leave the task force if others decided to support the candidacy
of Fatima. In order to ensure Fatima was not elected, Henk also stood candidate for
Treasurer, under the condition that he would not have any formal committee
responsibilities. In a private conversation between task force members Frank, Kees,
Henk and the intended new Chair, Martin, it was decided that Fatima should be advised not
to nominate herself. Frank was tasked with advising her of this, arguing that she was
unable to commit herself for 3 years. A few days later Fatima told one of us that she had
had a meeting with Frank in which he had discouraged her nomination. She was
disappointed, but informed the task force that she still intended to pursue her nomination,
arguing that 'there are enough members who support me'.

Henk and other club members argued that they doubted Fatima's commitment to the club.
Although she had been a volunteer for 4 years, and her son represented the club at junior level,
the interactions demonstrate that she was still considered an 'outsider'. Fatima, who had
expressed her willingness to work for the club, encountered a negative attitude, while Henk,
who was not willing to take full responsibility, did not encounter any resistance. Henk's
petitioning was an attempt to stigmatize Fatima. Like the act of resistance by Ari, described in
the second incident, Henk also gave voice to a sense of community 'loss'. This illustrates how,
when the transition unfolded, the cultural meaning making of the 'established' white Dutch
members with its 'boundaries of belonging and exclusion' was at stake.[63]

In June 2008, notwithstanding the resistance by the 'established' members (using
stigmatizing efforts as well as their key positions), Fatima and Aziz were elected by the
majority of the members as new committee members. Together with one white Dutch

senior member and an externally experienced white Dutch club manager as the new Chair, they formed the new ethnically mixed committee of *Among Ourselves*. From outside, the intervention seemed to have been a success. However, along with the transition, the club's power balance had changed. This was not without consequence however. These are discussed in the final key incident which concerns the exclusion of the last remaining 'established' white Dutch team from the club.

The exclusion of the last remaining all-white Dutch team

The name of the club works illustratively in our studies. 'Among Ourselves' refers to Dutch ideas of familiarity, of being together in a friendly, intimate and safe atmosphere.[64] These ideas were expressed on the club's website: 'Among Ourselves is a small, intimate and cozy football club where you can always enter the canteen and coffee is always ready'. However, apart from giving expression to the idea of a community based on shared understandings, the phrase 'Among Ourselves' also indicates a clique that excludes others. In 2010, two senior teams were playing in the regional football league. The first team, *Among Ourselves* I, had only started that year and consisted predominantly of Moroccan Dutch players. We depict this team as the 'outsiders' team. The second team, *Among Ourselves* II, was the only remaining all-white Dutch team. It consisted mainly of players who were children of elder members and who were aged between 20 and 35 years. We depict this team as the 'established' team. In a meeting with the new committee, the potential new coach for the 'established' team declared: 'I do not want to desert these lads'. As a former player, trainer and committee member, he was a renowned club member. At the end of the meeting, he reiterated that he was willing to take up the coaching position, but under the condition of receiving improved support from the club's committee. Somewhat surprisingly, he then blatantly expressed his disdain for the 'outsiders' and the (not present) new committee member Aziz when he emphasized:

> And I am not communicating with that Moroccan, only with you guys.[65]

The new Chair, Martin, reacted with surprise: 'You mean Aziz?' The coach confirmed with a telling look. Comments such as these, though not representative of all the respondents, do demonstrate the inveterate and institutionalized 'us' and 'them' dynamic which existed within the organizational culture of *Among Ourselves* throughout the research period.

During the season, six of the players of the 'established' team lost their jobs in construction work due to the economic crisis. They stopped paying their membership fees and, moreover, grew very agitated because of their own situation and what they described as: 'Among Ourselves is not the club it used to be'. After several quarrels with players and fans of opposing (also white Dutch) teams, the Dutch Football Association fined the club and banned the players involved. Finally, the newly installed mixed club committee forced the second team to leave the league. Its players and other club members reacted angrily and planned to go to another club. However, for acceptance, they needed a 'termination form'. The Chair, Martin, refused to cooperate and said:

> I will only give you that form once I receive the membership fee. This applies for all members.

One of the players promptly reacted with a phrase that sidelined all Moroccan Dutch members:

> Which members? When we are not playing for you, you do not have members anymore and Among Ourselves does not exist any longer.

When the municipal official was informed about the potential exit of the team, he was certainly not amused as he saw the potential for white flight across the club. Indeed, as expected, as white players of *Among Ourselves* II left the club, so too did most of the remaining white Dutch members and volunteers.

The official's disappointment indicates that the exclusion of the last white Dutch team, as a symbol of the 'established' club culture, did not match the aims of the municipal intervention. Despite the club's financial betterment, its increasing youth membership, the participation of Moroccan Dutch parents and the representative management, the municipal official seemed to conclude that the intervention had failed. The statement of the white Dutch player that sidelined all Moroccan Dutch members affirms the sharp us–them division in the club. Indeed, an organizational culture had developed that operated in an exclusionary fashion towards particular ethnic groups.

The final key incident shows how the domination of white Dutch practices in the club's culture did not prevent the exclusion of the white Dutch team. The 'oldness of association', as the predominant source of power of the 'established', no longer connected to the positions in the club's committee.[66] For the first time in its history, it seemed that white Dutch meaning-making processes had lost their dominance in the club culture of *Among Ourselves*.

Discussion

The four key incidents demonstrated how meaning-making processes of organizational culture produced us–them divisions between different ethnic groups. The photos of white Dutch players, the absence of photos of Moroccan Dutch players and the importance of the bar with beer taps in the canteen represented a white Dutch embodied space. The 'oldness of association' enabled the white Dutch volunteers to monopolize key positions and define the local 'rules of the game'.[67] The encounter between 'outsider' candidate Treasurer Fatima and 'established' candidate Treasurer Henk also showed uneven power relations. However, the municipal intervention with the task force's assignment initiated a change in the existing power balance. At the membership meeting described in the third key incident, the task force assignment and the majority of member votes legitimated Fatima and Aziz to become members of the new committee. The ongoing departure of white Dutch members made 'oldness' a less dominant source of power.[68] Gradually, the Moroccan Dutch members, an ethnic minority in society, became the ethnic majority within the club. The transition was articulated by the selling of Moroccan tea and halal meat, and also by replacing the photos of white Dutch teams with those of Moroccan Dutch (youth) teams. In so doing, the 'outsiders' became the new 'established'.

This paper has explored the making of an ethnically diverse management team for an amateur football club in the Netherlands. As the title suggests, what is formally presented to the outside world as a successful outcome usually has a complex 'making of' process behind the scenes. In our case, the establishment of an ethnically mixed club committee could be viewed as a successful outcome for the local municipality who demanded the integration of two ethnic groups on the level of the club's management. However, as we have demonstrated, the transition was accompanied by conflicts among its members about the meanings that structured the club's organizational culture. We have shown how the 'established', in this case white Dutch members, felt that their space and their sense of being among themselves were being invaded by the Dutch Moroccans as 'outsiders'.[69] We have shown how 'if outsiders trespass in that space … its occupant's own sense of self is felt to be debased and defaced'.[70] We conclude that shared participation and, thus, apparent equity in the club's management did not coincide with the integration of different groups within the club's culture. On the contrary, we argue that the transition towards an ethnically mixed committee reinforced the contestation over cultural meanings and led to an intensification of us–them divisions between the groups.

The implications of our findings are twofold. First, sports club cultures are oriented towards integration and consensus, due to their histories as voluntary organizations established along the lines of existing communities.[71] As a result, within sports club cultures, members prefer to be among themselves. Deviations from the cultural codes and meanings are rarely accepted. Hence, sports club cultures put limits to the bridging capacities of sport in general. Our second implication points at the fact that organizational cultures are relatively immune for outside interventions aimed at social integration. As others have pointed out, although it may be possible to change an organization's formal structure, it is very hard to change its culture.[72] Our study of *Among Ourselves* articulated a discrepancy between the formal structure of the club – where, eventually, ethnic mixing took place in the committee – and its organizational culture – which showed a continuation of the contestation over meaning and the reproduction of differences between ethnic groups. As a consequence, it is important to rethink the relevance of formal power positions. Ethnic equity cannot simply be achieved by changes in the formal power positions at the management level, as this would neglect the informal day-to-day cultural processes in sport organizations that find their expression in deeply ingrained symbolic practices and artefacts. As our research has shown, outside interventions which aim at establishing equity between different groups may result in a situation in which the players change, but the game remains the same.

Acknowledgements

We would like to thank the guest editors for their wonderful work on this volume. We would also like to thank those involved in the Dutch Sport & Society network.

Notes

1. In this paper, we use the signifiers 'Moroccan Dutch' and 'white Dutch' to distinguish between the two groups within *Among Ourselves*, based on ethnicity. Currently, these labels are considered the most politically correct way of referring to members of these groups in the Netherlands. We apologize to readers who may take offense to these essentialist labels.
2. Ministry of Health, Welfare and Sport, *Samen voor Sport*, 17.
3. Donnelly, 'Approaches to Social Inequality'.
4. Beutler, 'Sport Serving Development and Peace'; Spaaij, 'Social Impact of Sport' and Vermeulen, 'Organizing Sport in Public Space'.
5. Verweel, Janssens and Roques, 'Kleurrijke Zuilen' and Ramsahai, *Thuiswedstrijd in een Vreemd Land*.
6. Burdsey, '"Forgotten Fields"?'.
7. Blommaert and Jie, *Ethnographic Fieldwork*.
8. cf. Lake, 'They Treat Me Like I'm Scum' and Sands, *Sport Ethnography*.
9. Lake, 'They Treat Me Like I'm Scum', 114.
10. Bryman, *Social Research Methods*, 410.
11. Alvesson, 'Leadership Studies', 467.
12. The fragments of email texts were obtained with consent by the informants.
13. Emerson, 'Working with "Key Incidents"', 427. According to Emerson, a key incident 'attracts the field researcher's immediate interest, even if what occurred was mundane and ordinary to participants'.
14. Koster and Mulderij, *Gezellig en Gewend*.
15. Municipality of Utrecht, *Wijkenmonitor 2009*.
16. Municipality of Utrecht, *Wijkenmonitor 2009*.
17. Statistics Netherlands, *Annual Report on Integration*.
18. Entzinger, 'Changing the Rules'.
19. Entzinger, 'Changing the Rules', 2.

20. Statistics Netherlands, *Annual Report on Integration*.
21. Fletcher, 'All Yorkshiremen are from Yorkshire', 235.
22. Long, Robinson and Spracklen, 'Promoting Racial Equality'.
23. Vermeulen and Verweel, 'Participation in Sport' and Stokvis, 'Social Stratification and Sports'.
24. MacClancy, *Sport, Identity and Ethnicity* and Burdsey and Chappell, 'Soldiers, Sashes and Shamrocks'.
25. Burdsey, '"Forgotten Fields"?', 716.
26. cf. Verweel, Janssens and Roques, 'Kleurrijke Zuilen' and Ramsahai, *Thuiswedstrijd in een Vreemd Land*.
27. Cohen, *The Symbolic Construction of Community*.
28. See also Fletcher, 'All Yorkshiremen are from Yorkshire', 229.
29. Cohen, *Symbolic Construction of Community*, 70.
30. Cohen, *Symbolic Construction of Community*, 70.
31. Cheska, 'Sport as Ethnic Boundary Maintenance'.
32. e.g. Collins, *Sport and Social Exclusion*; Elling and Knoppers, 'Sport, Gender and Ethnicity' and Elling and Claringbould, 'Mechanisms of Inclusion'.
33. Verweel, 'Sport Maakt Verschil'.
34. Stokvis, 'Social Stratification and Sports', 512.
35. Donnelly and Young, 'Construction and Confirmation of Identity'.
36. Burdsey, '"Forgotten Fields"?' and Donnelly and Young, 'Construction and Confirmation of Identity'.
37. Woodward, '*Identity and Difference*'.
38. Anderson, '*In the Game*'; Shaw, 'Scratching the Back of "Mr X"'; Fletcher, 'All Yorkshiremen are from Yorkshire' and Vermeulen and Verweel, 'Participation in Sport'.
39. Woodward, *Identity and Difference*, 15.
40. Brewis, 'Culture' and Martin, *Organizational Culture*.
41. Martin, *Organizational Culture*, 3 and Yanow, *How does a Policy Mean?*
42. Fineman, Gabriel and Sims, *Organizing & Organizations*.
43. Parker, *Organizational Culture and Identity* and Martin, *Organizational Culture*.
44. Fineman, Gabriel and Sims, *Organizing & Organizations*, 149–62.
45. Parker, *Organizational Culture and Identity*, 217.
46. Puwar, *Space Invaders*.
47. Puwar, *Space Invaders*, 58.
48. Ruijter, 'Invoegen en Uitsluiten' and see also Strauss, *Negotiations*.
49. Elias and Scotson, *Established and the Outsiders*; for application of their insights in a study on sports clubs, see Lake's '"They Treat Me Like I'm Scum"'.
50. Elias, *What is Sociology?*
51. Elias, 'Foreword – Towards a Theory of Communities'.
52. Elias and Scotson, *Established and the Outsiders*, xvii–xviii; see also Lake, 'They Treat Me Like I'm Scum', 116.
53. Elias and Scotson, *Established and the Outsiders*, 199.
54. Elias and Scotson, *Established and the Outsiders*, 27.
55. On behalf of anonymity, the names of the described and quoted informants are pseudonyms.
56. Municipality of Utrecht, *Plan van Aanpak Voetbalvereniging Onder Ons*.
57. For a discussion of the exclusionary effects of sport and alcohol consumption, see Fletcher and Spracklen, 'Cricket, Drinking and Exclusion'.
58. Elias and Scotson, *Established and the Outsiders*.
59. Cohen, *Symbolic Construction of Community*.
60. Fletcher, 'All Yorkshiremen are from Yorkshire'.
61. The football league season starts in September and ends in June. The season is divided by a Winter break.
62. Fragment of email sent to the task force members.
63. Long, Robinson and Spracklen, 'Promoting Racial Equality', 43.
64. Besamusca and Verheul, *Discovering the Dutch*.
65. Besamusca and Verheul, *Discovering the Dutch*.
66. Elias and Scotson, *Established and the Outsiders*, xvii–xviii.
67. cf. Puwar, *Space Invaders*, 152.

68. Elias and Scotson, *Established and the Outsiders*, 155.
69. Puwar, *Space Invaders*.
70. Cohen, *Symbolic Construction*, 109.
71. Martin, *Organizational Culture*, 120.
72. Fineman, Gabriels and Sims, *Organizing & Organizations* and Grieves, *Organizational Change*, 183ff.

References

Alvesson, Mats. 'Leadership Studies: From Procedure and Abstraction to Reflexivity and Situation'. *Leadership Quarterly* 7, no. 4 (1996): 455–85.

Anderson, Eric. *In the Game: Gay Athletes and the Cult of Masculinity*. New York: State University of New York Press, 2005.

Besamusca, Emmeline N. and Jaap Verheul, eds. *Discovering the Dutch. On Culture and Society of the Netherlands*. Amsterdam: Amsterdam University Press, 2010.

Beutler, Ingrid. 'Sport Serving Development and Peace: Achieving the Goals of the United Nations Through Sport'. *Sport in Society* 11, no. 4 (2008): 359–69.

Blommaert, Jan, and Dong Jie. *Ethnographic Fieldwork*. Bristol: Multilingual Matters, 2010.

Brewis, Jo. 'Culture'. In *Introducing Organizational Behaviour and Management*, ed. David Knights and Hugh Wilmott, 344–74. London: Thomson Learning, 2007.

Bryman, Alan. *Social Research Methods*, 410, 3rd ed. Oxford: Oxford University Press, 2008.

Burdsey, Daniel. '"Forgotten Fields"? Centralizing the Experiences of Minority Ethnic Men's Football Clubs in England'. *Soccer and Society* 10, no. 6 (2009): 704–21.

Burdsey, Daniel, and Robert Chappell. 'Soldiers, Sashes and Shamrocks: Football and Social Identity in Scotland and Northern Ireland'. *Sociology of Sport Online* 6, no. 1 (2003): 1–16. http://www.physed.otago.ac.nz/sosol/home.html (accessed April 24, 2013).

Cheska, Alyce Taylor. 'Sport as Ethnic Boundary Maintenance: A Case of the American Indian'. *International Review for the Sociology of Sport* 19, no. 3–4 (1984): 241–57.

Cohen, Anthony. *The Symbolic Construction of Community*. London: Tavistock, 1985.

Collins, Michael. (with Tess Kay) *Sport and Social Exclusion*. London: Routledge.

Donnelly, Peter. 'Approaches to Social Inequality in the Sociology of Sport'. *Quest* 48, no. 2 (1996): 221–42.

Donnelly, Peter, and Kevin Young. 'The Construction and Confirmation of Identity in Sport Subcultures'. *Sociology of Sport Journal* 5, no. 3 (1988): 223–40.

Elias, Norbert. 'Foreword – Towards a Theory of Communities'. In *The Sociology of Community – A Selection of Readings*, ed. Colin Bell and Howard Newby. London: Frank Cass and Company Limited, 1974.

Elias, Norbert. *What is Sociology?* London: Hutchinson, 1978.

Elias, Norbert, and John Scotson. *The Established and the Outsiders – A Sociological Enquiry into Community Problems*. London: Sage Publications, 1994.

Elling, Agnes, and Annelies Knoppers. 'Sport, Gender and Ethnicity: Practises of Symbolic Inclusion/Exclusion'. *Journal of Youth and Adolescence* 34, no. 3 (2005): 257–68.

Elling, Agnes, and Inge Claringbould. 'Mechanisms of Inclusion and Exclusion in the Dutch Sports Landscape: Who Can and Wants to Belong?' *Sociology of Sport Journal* 22, no. 4 (2005): 498–515.

Emerson, Robert. 'Working with "Key Incidents"'. In *Qualitative Research Practice*, ed. Clive Seale, Giampietro Gobo, Jaber F. Gubrium, and David Silverman, 427. London: Sage, 2004.

Entzinger, Han. 'Changing the Rules While the Game is on: From Multiculturalism to Assimilation in the Netherlands'. In *Migration, Citizenship, Ethnos*, ed. Y. Michal Bodemann and Gökce Yurdakul, 121–44. New York: Palgrave MacMillan, 2006.

Fineman, Stephen, Yiannis Gabriel, and David Sims. *Organizing & Organizations.*, 4th ed. London: Sage Publications, 2010.

Fletcher, Thomas. 'All Yorkshiremen are from Yorkshire, But Some are More "Yorkshire" than Others': British Asians and the Myths of Yorkshire Cricket'. *Sport in Society: Cultures, Commerce, Media, Politics* 15, no. 2 (2012): 227–45.

Fletcher, Thomas, and Karl Spracklen. 'Cricket, Drinking and Exclusion of British Pakistani Muslims?' *Ethnic and Racial Studies* (2013). doi:10.1080/01419870.2013.790983.

Grieves, Jim. *Organizational Change. Themes and Issues*. Oxford: Oxford University Press, 2010.

Koster, Martijn, and Karel Mulderij. *Gezellig en Gewend: Jongeren over Wonen en de Toekomst in een Herstructureringswijk* [Cosy and Accustomed: Youth, Their Lives and Futures in a "Restructuring Area"]. Amsterdam: SWP, 2011.

Lake, Robert. "'They Treat Me Like I'm Scum': Social Exclusion and Established-Outsider Relations in a British Tennis Club'. *International Review for the Sociology of Sport* 48, no. 1 (2011): 112–28.

Long, Jonathan, Paul Robinson, and Karl Spracklen. 'Promoting Racial Equality Within Sports Organizations'. *Journal of Sport and Social Issues* 29, no. 1 (2005): 41–59.

MacClancy, Jeremy, ed. *Sport, Identity and Ethnicity*. Oxford: Berg, 1996.

Martin, Joanne. *Organizational Culture: Mapping the Terrain*. Thousand Oaks, CA: Sage Publications, 2002.

Ministry of Health, Welfare and Sport. *Samen voor Sport* [Together for Sport]. The Hague: VWS, 2006.

Municipality of Utrecht. *Plan van Aanpak Voetbalvereniging Onder Ons (VVOO)*. [Strategic Plan VVOO]. Utrecht: Gemeente Utrecht/DMO, 2008.

Municipality of Utrecht. *Wijkenmonitor 2009* [Neighborhood Survey 2009]. Utrecht: Gemeente Utrecht/DMO, 2009.

Parker, Martin. *Organizational Culture and Identity: Unity and Division at Work*. London: Sage Publications, 2000.

Puwar, Nirwal. *Space Invaders: Race, Gender and Bodies Out of Place*. Oxford: Berg, 2004.

Ramsahai, Sieuwpersad. *Thuiswedstrijd in een Vreemd Land* [Home Match in a Foreign Country] PhD diss., Utrecht University 2008.

Ruijter, Ariede. *Invoegen en Uitsluiten: De Samenleving als Arena* [Inclusion and Exclusion: Society as Arena] *Multiculturalisme* [Multiculturalism], ed. Karin Geuijen. Utrecht: Lemma, 1998.

Sands, Robert. *Sport Ethnography*. Champaign, IL: Human Kinetics, 2002.

Shaw, Sally. 'Scratching the Back of "Mr X": Analyzing Gendered Social Processes in Sport Organizations'. *Journal of Sport Management* 20, no. 4 (2006): 510–34.

Spaaij, Ramón. 'The Social Impact of Sport: Diversities, Complexities and Contexts'. *Sport in Society* 12, no. 9 (2009): 1109–17.

Statistics Netherlands. *Annual Report on Integration 2012*. The Hague: Statistics Netherlands, 2012.

Stokvis, Ruud. 'Social Stratification and Sports in Amsterdam in the 20th Century'. *International Review for the Sociology of Sport* 47, no. 4 (2012): 511–25.

Strauss, Anselm. *Negotiations: Varieties, Contexts, Processes and Social Order*. San Francisco, CA: Jossey-Bass, 1978.

Vermeulen, Jeroen. 'The Bridge as Playground: Organizing Sport in Public Space'. *Culture and Organization* 17, no. 3 (2011): 231–51.

Vermeulen, Jeroen, and Paul Verweel. 'Participation in Sport: Bonding and Bridging as Identity Work'. *Sport in Society* 12, no. 9 (2009): 1206–19.

Verweel, Paul. *Sport Maakt Verschil* [Sport Differentiates] *Samenspel: Studies over Etniciteit, Integratie en Sport*, ed. Fons Kemper, 299. Bennekom: Nederlands Instituut voor Sport & Bewegen, 2010.

Verweel, Paul, Jan Janssens, Colette *Kleurrijke Zuilen: Over de Ontwikkeling van Sociaal Kapitaal Door Allochtonen in Eigen en Gemengde Sportverenigingen* [Colourful Pillars: About the Development of Social Capital by Allochthones in Ethnic and Mixed Sports Clubs] Roques, *Vrijetijdstudies* 23, no. 4 (2007): 7–21.

Woodward, Kathryn. *Identity and Difference*. London: Sage, 1997.

Yanow, Dvora. *How does a Policy Mean? Interpreting Policy and Organizational Actions*. Washington, DC: Georgetown University Press, 1996.

Sport controversy, the media and Anglo-Indian cricket relations: the 1977 'Vaseline incident' in retrospect

Souvik Naha

Centre for Historical Studies, Jawaharlal Nehru University, New Delhi, India

This article argues that the increasingly hybrid and transnational nature of contemporary sports has diversified subjectivities of exclusion. It analyses an instance of inclusion/exclusion, the 'Vaseline incident', which transcended the First World/Third World or black/white polarities that were at the forefront of contemporary culture during the 1970s. Having set out the controversy in detail, it interprets the agency of the Indian and British news media and cricket administrators in precipitating and/or subverting the inclusive nature of sport. By studying official and media polemics, it draws attention to the simultaneous production of hegemonic and counter-hegemonic models of marginalization in response to operations of individual exclusions within team sports.

Introduction

> It is said that once when playing a Test [Ranji] hit a mighty six off an Australian bowler. An English spectator proudly clapped and turning on to the Australian sitting next to him said, 'He is a prince, you know. Do you have a prince in your team?' The Australian had to admit, defensively, that Australia did not. The very next ball Ranji was clean bowled. This time the Englishman muttered under his breath, 'Bloody nigger'.[1]

The story may not be authentic, but the subtext alludes to the fact that inclusion and exclusion, as evident in practices and ideologies of sport and physical activities, are not mutually exclusive. The introduction of cricket to India is an example *par excellence* of the diversity, and more importantly, intertexture of inclusive and exclusive policies towards regulation of sport and leisure. Cricket was believed to promote the 'English' qualities of sportsmanship and fair play among the 'natives', and enlighten them adequately to experience the altruism of the British Empire. A number of scholars, notably among them Allen Guttmann, claim that the British governors such as Lord Harris and Lord Brabourne patronized cricket with the hope that the sport might 'bond together India's religiously, linguistically and ethnically diverse population'.[2] Lord Harris, governor of Bombay from 1890 to 1895, went on to say, 'I really do not know a sight really more creditable to the British capacity for administration than that of a cricket match on the parade ground between the Presidency European Eleven and the Parsis'.[3] The pedagogy of inclusion was limited to the efforts of a small number of institutions and individuals. Not all British civilians and military personnel in India subscribed to this grand idea either. Not only did they prefer to establish exclusive European clubs, but they also considered the appearances and playing styles of Indian cricketers highly inappropriate. An army regiment, when pressed hard to play against a Parsee club, agreed on the condition that the match would be played as 'officers with umbrellas versus natives with bats'.[4] The situation in other British colonies such as the Caribbean Islands or Australia was no different. The Victorian virtues of moral masculinity attributed to sports, added with a keen sense of nationalism, generated 'white' egalitarian sporting cultures in nineteenth-century Australia. In this culture, sportspersons from the tribes, clans and far-flung regions whose skin colour was not too light in comparison to Caucasians, collectively termed as Aboriginals, were deliberately kept out of the mainstream.[5]

In colonial India, the disdain or patronizing attitude towards the 'natives' was not too evident. This is evident in the employment of English county professionals Joe Vine (Sussex), George Cox senior (Sussex) and Frank Tarrant (Middlesex) as coaches and players under 'native' princes' sponsored teams. New ambivalences emerged after India's independence in 1947. The uneasy relationship of a former colony and its erstwhile sovereign reflected in the cricket field. The Marylebone Cricket Club's (MCC) reluctance to send strong England teams to tour India and the Anglo-Australian media's criticism of the material conditions of cricket-playing in the country characterize the reception of post-independence Indian sport until the early 1970s. English cricket administrators and sport media started to take India seriously after the latter won its first away series in England in 1971, defeating England 2–1. As a result, the frequency of bilateral cricket tours between the countries increased. However, so did off-field disputes. This article refers to one such controversy during a Test cricket match between England and India in 1977, focusing specifically on the complexity of media response in the aftermath.

In the existing research on inclusion/diversity in sport, much emphasis has been given to the reciprocity of sporting structures and policies related to multiculturalism/class concerns, integration/marginalization, gender bias/equality, etc. which are implemented by public/private agencies. Racism has been a primary determinant of diversity and exclusion in sports, so much so that Ellis Cashmore is positive about the feasibility of writing a history of racism through sports which would include elements of exclusion, prejudice, stereotyping, exploitation and ideology.[6] Cricket has a long history of racism. Jack Williams' masterly study shows how the image of cricket had been organized around racial stereotypes which reproduce psychosomatic differences between players of various nationalities and 'races'.[7] The media's central role in framing inclusion/marginality through categorization of players, playing styles, etc. has been acknowledged by academics.[8] Recent writings have addressed the anomalies of spectatorship, discriminatory nature of cricket governance, the steps taken towards equity of participation and the concomitant ideological disjunctives in different national or global frameworks.[9]

This article argues that the increasingly hybrid and transnational nature of contemporary sports has diversified subjectivities of exclusion. It analyses an instance of inclusion/exclusion, the 'Vaseline incident', which transcended the First World/Third World or black/white polarities that were at the forefront of contemporary culture during the 1970s.[10] Having set out the controversy in detail, it interprets the agency of the Indian and British news media and cricket administrators in precipitating and/or subverting the inclusive nature of sport. By studying official and media polemics, it draws attention to the simultaneous production of hegemonic and counter-hegemonic models of marginalization in response to operations of individual exclusions within team sports.

The Chepauk journal of John Lever

The incident, which was to stir up one of cricket's most talked about scandals, took place on 16 January 1977 at the Chepauk Stadium, Madras. In response to England's first innings total of 262, India was trying to stage a comeback after collapsing to 126 for 7. At the end of an over bowled by John Lever, the England fast bowler, umpire Judah Reuben picked up a strip of gauze that had fallen off his forehead during bowling. Reuben suspected the presence of some greasy substance on the gauze and immediately held a short conference with Tony Greig, the England captain, and Lever. The match ball was inspected and found to be greasy too, leading Reuben to report the incident as a possible breach of the note on fair play in Law 46 which prohibits the use of any foreign substance to shine the ball.[11]

Crucially, England's explanation of how the strip of surgical gauze, daubed in Vaseline, came to be on Lever's body was different from the version offered by the umpire. Reuben maintained that the offending piece of gauze flew out of Lever's body as he was about to deliver a ball. Ken Barrington, the England manager, suggested on the contrary that Lever had used the gauze for medical reasons. He had reportedly disposed of the gauzes on the field of play because the Vaseline, when mixed with the sweat off his forehead, hindered his grip on the ball. Barrington accepted that this might have represented a breach of the laws of the game, but insisted at the same time that it was not a premeditated ploy to gain leverage in performance, as had been suggested by the Indian team. Indeed, England's strong position in that particular session of play, where they had reduced India to 147 for 7 certainly did not warrant the adoption of unfair methods.[12]

After the day's play, Ghulam Ahmed, the Board of Control for Cricket in India (BCCI) secretary, told the press that the umpires had reported Lever to have been constantly 'applying two fingers' to this 'band aid' and polishing the ball.[13] The 'rogue' ball was sent for chemical analysis to the Tamil Nadu Forensic Science and Chemical Laboratory. Journalists thought little of the action as controversies had been 'invented' in the past to distract away from the team's miserable performances. After Australia's Bob Massie had captured 16 wickets on debut, England's Ted Dexter had accused Massie of tampering with the ball by applying chapstick, a brand of lip balm.[14] K.N. Prabhu wrote in *The Times of India* that the Indian authorities' decision to send the ball to the laboratory was pointless since the law book had specified no penalty for polishing the ball with external agents. He lamented that 'a series which had been played in good spirit, has been vitiated by this incident'.[15]

Bishan Singh Bedi, captain of the Indian team at the time, created a stir a day after when he said during the press conference that:

> I suspected something funny in the first Test in New Delhi though I did not know what it was. When I came in to bat in the first innings I was surprised that a ball over 40 overs old could wobble so much. At the end of the innings I asked the umpire's permission to see the ball and found one side glossy and slippery too. I am not squealing. We are playing much below our ability and I am disappointed. But if there has been an infringement of the law it is for the authorities to decide on the action which should be taken.[16]

In the previous Test at Delhi, in reply to England's first innings total of 381, India were cruising at 43 without loss when the ball was replaced on the pretext of it having gone out of shape. Bowlers, especially Lever, generated unexpected swing with the replaced ball, and bowled India out cheaply, for only 122.[17]

Bedi's comments raised suspicion for the England team among the Indian spectators. When play resumed after the customary rest day, the crowd put up banners which read: 'Cheater Lever Go Home, Tony Greig down down!' The laboratory results were available to the public later that afternoon.[18] The report confirmed the presence of Vaseline smears, with more shine on one surface. The tour committee, comprising R.P. Mehra, S.K. Wankhede, Fatesingh Rao Gaekwad, M.A. Chidambaram and P.M. Rungta, held discussions to determine the course of action to be taken. They considered the testimonies of the umpires and other witnesses, but could not arrive at a conclusion whether the application of Vaseline had been a deliberate act to gain unfair advantage. Unable to take any action, the BCCI despatched the report to the Test and County Cricket Board in London for consideration.[19]

Barrington promptly convened a press meeting and thanked the BCCI for accepting England's explanation. The way he termed his address suggested that the two Boards had similar perspectives on the incident, with the Indian captain, Bedi, being a lone voice of dissent. Indian officials did not contradict Barrington, nor did they support their captain. In a later interview, Bedi condemned the umpires for failing to show enough courage to control the situation. The ball sent to the laboratory had 58% oily deposits. Bedi, on the other hand, claimed vehemently that the measurement should have been closer to 90% in Delhi. After the Delhi Test, he reportedly asked umpire Reuben to see the ball and subsequently scraped one side with a car key. Large quantities of grease were removed during the process. After which, Bedi claimed that, 'after the complaint, they [the English bowlers] could not swing the ball at all'.[20] India won the next Test match and drew the last.

Letters between England and India

As the administrators laid the matter to rest, it was the journalists' turn to decipher the 'incident'. The Indian and British sports media had a history of clashes. During the MCC's tour in 1962, Indian sports journalist Barry Sarbadhikary had criticized the British press' uninformed attacks on Indian cricket and its administration.[21] After the riot at the Eden Gardens Stadium, Calcutta, on 1 January 1967, during a match contested between India and West Indies, in which approximately 200 persons, including 52 police personnel, were injured, the British press launched a full-fledged attack on Indian sporting culture.[22] Most of the British dailies published the story on the front page with pictures of the 'battle of Eden Gardens' across five columns. Beneath a blow-up of a radiophoto of a 'bonfire' on the pitch, *The Sun* commented sardonically that the incident had given West Indies and India their own home-grown ashes to play for.[23] Another photo carried the caption that good cricket like this sparked life in a dull audience.[24] The reports ascribed a generic inferiority to Third World spectatorship, invoking Neville Cardus' famous dictum that a nation's approach to playing cricket manifests its national character. The Indian dailies argued that this was a deliberate tactic to humiliate Indian cricket which was then poised to take over from England as the biggest venue of world cricket.[25] Sarbadhikary responded by saying that good cricket in the next few days would silence foreign critics.[26] However, the 'Vaseline incident' elicited a slightly different culture war between the national media of Britain and India.

Reaction to the 'Vaseline incident' from the respective Cricket Boards was not wholly successful. Since there was no provision for judging intentions, the BCCI in particular, should either have confronted the MCC about the trace of Vaseline or promptly put an end to the matter. The forming of investigatory committees and then not acting demonstrated a degree of political impotence on behalf of the BCCI. According to Rajan Bala, a sport journalist who later wrote a book on the history of cricket techniques, the fundamental question was how the ball ended up with more shine on one side.[27] However, by the time of this reaction, the BCCI had already devolved the responsibility to the MCC. They had not exactly endorsed England's public statement, but when Barrington thanked them for their support, they did not counteract either. When the discrepancy between the BCCI and England was pointed out, Greig remarked that the MCC would take into account only the version provided by their players.

The sport press in India generally gave the benefit of doubt to Lever. They resented the BCCI's actions and the British press' criticism. Sunder Raj, on behalf of *The Times of*

India, criticized the BCCI for failing to protect its captain against adverse comments made by foreign press. The BCCI, he said, kept the Indian media in the dark whereas England sought help of their national press to vindicate their claims. Barrington, for example, gave his side of the story immediately after the post-lunch session. Although he was defensive, his account appeared first and the British journalists 'immediately started pounding on their typewriters'.[28] In contrast, the Indian version of the story, circulated only four hours later, revealed little more than a perfunctory announcement of a review of the incident. When the Board finally declared itself unable to determine whether the act of smearing Vaseline on the ball was deliberate, a British journalist dismissed the entire incident as a non-story. Raj further claimed, incorrectly, that the readers in England had been informed nothing about Lever. The British press, he said, emphasized Bedi's character assassination: 'The British writers gave full vent to their inventive genius and made their stories ring true by adding for good measure that Bedi's accusation was born out of despair'.[29]

The response from British cricket correspondents also differed significantly. They mostly concurred that the anguish of losing the first two Tests and the imminent loss in the third had caused Bedi to lose his mind and cry foul of England's achievements. Indian dailies such as *The Hindu*, *The Statesman* and *The Times of India* published extracts from the British media's critical remarks. Henry Calthorpe of the *Financial Times* and John Woodcock of *The Times* had reportedly criticized Bedi for unfairly targeting Lever to divert the public attention away from his team's underperformance. Woodcock saw little significance in the incident and expected that attention would soon be deflected away from it: 'The special branch was not called in, and though an unfortunate episode, I doubt whether we shall hear anything more about it'.[30] Stressing the cultural diversities of India, the *Daily Telegraph*'s Michael Melford noted that the pressure of losing the series in a South Indian city had reduced the North Indian captain to making fanciful allegations in an attempt to save face.[31]

Henry Blofeld's account in the *Guardian* was comparatively less sardonic.[32] The evidence, he claimed, would acquit Lever. He argued that the MCC management would be fully justified in demanding an apology from the Indian Board.[33] Writing in the *Daily Express*, Pat Gibson attacked Bedi for making 'hysterical accusations', appealing to the MCC to step in and protect the honour of a young bowler. He reportedly said that Bedi's accusation was 'an affront to the game that gives Lever a living – and an insult to his intelligence'. The same daily published a highly racist cartoon in which Bedi was drawn with and without his *patka* (a form of headgear frequently worn by Sikhs), with a caption that made a number of speculations about the function of his knot of hair and headgear: whether it was a shelter for illegal immigrants, or a leprechaun cursing England, or carried a radar station or a bowl of steam pudding to nourish him between lunch and tea intervals. The ridicule ended with a comment that the MCC should contemplate the legality of Bedi's clothing.[34]

Some journalists went as far as to legitimize unfair play ('ball tampering' as it is contemporaneously known) as part of the game. In a book chronicling the tour's events, Christopher Martin-Jenkins wrote that applying foreign substances to the ball has been part of cricket (with varying legality) since time immemorial:

> [Such] aids had been known about by those playing the game and, I suppose, reluctantly accepted as one of the 'unacceptable faces' of cricket. Law 46 prohibits the use of oils, waxes, resins etc., but the plain fact is that lip salve and sun cream are frequently used by cricketers genuinely seeking to protect skin from getting cracked or burnt by the hot sun, and bowlers of all nationalities have from time to time taken advantage of them to add a little extra shine to the ball.[35]

The responses, however, amounted to more than counter-allegations from two national media. *The Hindu* published an article by Robin Marlar, the British cricketer-turned-journalist, in which Lever was absolved. Marlar was critical of the placards proclaiming that Lever was a cheat. He summed up his view, writing that, 'cheat' 'is a nasty word in English, a word over which duels have been fought and libel suits won'.[36] Discontent with Lever was not confined to the media. While Lever was fielding on the boundary, the crowd pelted him with paper balls, darts, orange skins and bottles. Any captain would have led his team off the field, but Greig pacified the crowd with folded hands instead. His plea worked and the crowd ceased to be hostile. In fact, the crowd was documented to have applauded good pieces of fielding by Lever. Marlar confessed to have been touched by this 'precious moment for fair play'.[37]

In an article in the *Observer*, Dilip Rao presented the Indian perspective on the turn of events to the British audience. According to Rao, the Indian team had suspected Lever from the Delhi Test. The ball with which Lever took seven Indian wickets was taken from the umpire after the third day's play and sent to the BCCI's technical committee. Indian team captain, Bedi, had played cricket in Delhi since his childhood, and believed that the ground conditions would not permit such exaggerated movement without illegal intervention from the fielding team. Members of the Selection and Technical Committees had discussed the matter, but took no action. He was amazed that even after 50 overs of play the replaced ball looked newer than the original which had previously been discarded after only 10 overs. C.D. Gopinath, Chairman of the Selection and Technical Committees, wanted to have the ball examined by the forensic laboratory in Madras. The BCCI wanted to do the tests in Delhi, but this did not happen in the end. Rao concludes that a lot of controversy could have been avoided had the tests been done immediately. Indians found solace in the fact that Lever's strike rate declined dramatically in the wake of the Madras incident.[38] And, for some, this reinforced their belief that he had tampered with the ball.

Two letters from Indian readers were published by the *Observer*. The first one, from Gopal Ranesh of Delhi, set down that 'Bedi's humiliation by the British Press, when the laboratory tests showed him 100 per cent in the right, represents a shameful episode'. He added that the MCC should apologize to the BCCI. In the opinion of Arundhati Mukherjee of Calcutta, 'Bedi's ridicule by the British Press is of poor taste and shows great personal malice'. A cricketer, she believed, should be above suspicion, like Caesar's wife.[39] The two letters, which reiterated the perspective of Indians on the incident in the British press, are significant evidences of the increasing displacement of what was previously criticized by Indian journalists as the imperial blinker.

There were also testimonies from ex-cricketers and administrators published on the use of illegal substances. Chris Lander, writing in the *Daily Mirror*, quoted Ray Illingworth and John Snow, saying that medium-pacers had used Vaseline and lip salve in the past. Illingworth had suspected that Australian bowlers used lip ice (a similar product to lip salve) during the MCC tour of Australia in 1970–1971. As a result, and on his insistence, some of the England bowlers experimented with lip salve during practice ahead of the 1972 Leeds Test. Years earlier, Australia's Arthur Mailey used to carry resin in his pocket, and often used the bird lime in Bert Oldfield's wicket-keeping gloves. The umpire, Bill Alley, who had played 400 First Class matches, came forward in Bedi's support: 'Bedi is respected by players and umpires in English cricket. He is a great fellow and I cannot believe he would kick up such a fuss without justification'.[40] Indeed, the testimonies of Illingworth and Snow reinforce the idea that introducing foreign substances to facilitate the shining of the ball was not universally rejected.

A survey of newspapers in India reveals that the primary aim of Indian journalists was to amass public opinion in support of the national team. There were little venom against Lever; the criticism was directed primarily at the British media's handling of the affair. They hardly reflected the asymmetry of response in and against India's favour among the public, the press and the administration. Ridicule towards Bedi's religious outfit in the *Daily Express* represented the height of racist rhetoric emerging from the incident. Yet, newspapers such as the *Observer* and the *Daily Mail* defended Bedi against what they interpreted as unfair accusations. Notwithstanding a few exceptions, journalists in England were perhaps less intent on stereotyping Indian sporting culture and focused more on objective analysis of evidence. The fact that an Indian was allowed the space to vindicate Bedi and the BCCI in a popular newspaper such as the *Observer* speaks of the growing entitlements of the Indian diaspora in England at the time. The plural attitude in the press signalled increasing democratization of sporting practices.

On the other hand, the MCC's actions over the next few months demonstrated that equity in elite sport management was still a pipe dream. In his review of the Test series, Blofeld noted that since Bedi did not apologize for the unwarranted remarks, he should be prepared to come up against hostility during his upcoming appointment with English County Championship side Northamptonshire County Cricket Club (NCCC).[41] As the following section illustrates, while cricket fans and journalists lined up to enjoy Bedi's bowling for another season, the authorities ensured that they could not.

The ghastly ordeal of Bishan Bedi

The first group of people to feel the pressure of the controversy were the umpires. Judah Reuben, whose report initiated the chain of events, retired after this Test match as he had reached the compulsory retirement age of 55. He was not to be heard of again, even in domestic circles. His colleague M.S. Sivasankariah, however, was only 50, and had another five years of service left in him. But he did not officiate in a Test match ever again. Machinations of the authorities were in motion.

Soon after Bedi returned to play in the English County Championship competition, the legality of his bowling action was officially questioned; the MCC actually analysed photographs of his bowling. They announced months later as having reached 'no adverse conclusion'.[42] This entire exercise, apparently the brainchild of former captain Ray Illingworth, was interpreted as a way of returning the compliment (for questioning the integrity of England cricketers). It came as a shock since Bedi was widely considered as 'paragon of the perfect action: rhythmic, flowing, gentle, almost lazy'.[43] Indeed, when he had first arrived to play domestic cricket in England six years earlier, the MCC had filmed his bowling and used his action as an example *par excellence* for budding left-arm spinners to learn from. As if this controversy was not enough, on the same day that Bedi was cleared by the MCC, and was enjoying a sterling performance against county champions Middlesex, his contract with Northamptonshire was terminated.[44]

Bedi's release was said to be a part of the club's retrenchment and reorganization policy, but it puzzled cricket fans, journalists and Bedi as well. Although the official reason given was Bedi's recent underperformance and long-term unavailability in the near future, there was widespread suspicion within large portions of cricket followers that something far more insidious was occurring.[45] The public in India, for example, saw it as retribution for the 'Vaseline incident'.[46] A supporter of NCCC wrote in a local newspaper: 'If the club couldn't afford the world's best spinner, why don't they raise the membership fee in order to keep him? I would willingly pay'.[47] Frank Keating wrote in the *Guardian* that it was unfair to dismiss Bedi, whose skill was still unmatched.[48] Indeed, on hearing of his release, two other counties, Glamorgon and Warwickshire, expressed interest in signing Bedi. Negotiations with these clubs came to an abrupt halt, causing Bedi to suspect that 'instructions had come from Lord's (former administrative home of the MCC): "Keep your hands off"'.[49]

In retrospect, Suresh Menon summed up the events as, 'Three decades after independence, no Indian could hope to speak up against the old colonial powers and hope to get away with it, especially since his own administrators were in no mood to pursue the matter'.[50] Consequently, the 'Vaseline incident' and its aftermath are a telling narrative of the coexistence of equity and exclusion within the sport of cricket.

Conclusion

The response to a controversy from two national sport organizations and newspapers indicates the diversity within agents of exclusionary practices. The spate of events signifies the growth of post-nationalist sentiment in sports representation and (post)colonial identities. Additionally, the pluralization of mediation can be explained with reference to multicultural and transcultural influences and expansion of the Indian diaspora. Moreover, whereas previously the Indian media's criticism of the British press had little chance to circulate outside the country, the Indian perspective was now more freely expressed in the British media. This multiplicity of subjectivities indicates an increasing appreciation of diversity within the sports media. On this occasion, however, this outlook did not extend to the managerial level.

The events explored in this article affirm that elite sport bodies held the authority to enforce decisions without sufficient reason or fear of reaction. Drawing on a causal connection between the 'Vaseline incident' and Bedi's persecution by the MCC and dismissal by NCCC alone is not appropriate to sufficiently unpack what forces were at play here. However, the MCC's race policies were none too subtle. Their drive to host the 1970 home Test series against South Africa against nationwide protests, mass actions and the possibility of expulsion from the Commonwealth and Olympic Games is a case in point. They hardly accepted the isolation of Apartheid regimes, which is evident in the frequent Rebel tours organized by leading England cricketers and their token punishments.[51] Hence, covert racial motivation behind Bedi's harassment cannot be ruled out. Moreover, a residual effect of imperial hegemony was visible in the BCCI's unwillingness to confront the MCC over the breach of fair play laws (Law 46 in particular) and the defamation of Bedi's bowling action. The disparity of responses between the media and the authorities reduced in later decades as the non-west and the non-white grew in financial power and performative capacity. The power shift in Anglo-Indian cricket relations was incontrovertibly established by a recent event: 'Vaselinegate'.

Moving forward over 30 years and there is evidence that similar issues continue to haunt the sport. During the Nottingham Test in 2011, India's V.V.S. Laxman survived a close appeal for a catch. The incident led television commentator and ex-England captain Michael Vaughan to tweet: 'Has Vaseline on the outside edge saved the day for Laxman?' Vaughan was referring to the belief that the application of Vaseline on the bat can deceive the infrared imaging technology, Hot Spot, which is used to settle uncertain dismissals.[52] The comment raised a furore among Indian fans and cricket officials. While fans spewed venom on Vaughan's twitter page, the Indian media minced no word to attack Vaughan and English cricketers. Ex-cricketers such as Sunil Gavaskar openly suggested that Vaughan be sued.[53] Vaughan played down the incident with another tweet. But the incident lingered among the television commentators: in particular, India's Ravi Shastri and England's Nasser Hussain were noted to have had heated exchanges, with Shastri claiming that followers of England were only jealous of India's predominance on the world stage.[54] The British media hit back at Shastri saying that it acknowledges India's contribution to world cricket, with one journalist even writing, with a touch of irony, that 'without the current Indian ascendancy cricket would feel strangely empty, bereft of colour and contrast'.[55] The controversy was resolved after BBG Sports, the proprietor of Hot Spot, conducted experiments to determine if Vaseline could indeed reduce the technology's efficiency. The investigation concluded that it could not.[56] This was no reconciliation, however, as no one on either side of the debate apologized for the allegations. However, the incident did imply a new post- or neo-colonial period in Anglo-Indian cricket relations, with the former colony exercising increasing power to their former colonizer over issues of inclusion and marginalization.

Acknowledgements

I would like to thank the editors and the anonymous referees for their useful suggestions on earlier drafts, and to Manikarnika Dutta and *Cloud Atlas* for giving me company through the writing week. The sections are named after the book's chapters.

Notes

1. Nandy, *Tao of Cricket*, 57. Ranjitsinhji, later the prince of Jamnagar in India, was a leading cricketer during what is known as cricket's 'Golden Age' (1890–1914).
2. Guttmann, *Games and Empires*, 33.
3. Lord Harris, 'Bombay', 70, cited in Luhrmann, *Good Parsi*, 119. The Parsis are Zoroastrians who migrated from Iran to the western coast of India to escape Muslim occupation. For a millennium, they remained socially and cultural insular from the rest of the Indian society. The British rule was an opportunity for them to reinforce a strong community identity, which they did by adopting British customs and collaborating with the government, with exceptions of course.
4. Guha, *Corner of a Foreign Field*, 17.
5. Mandle, 'Cricket and Australian Nationalism', 241.
6. Cashmore, *Sports Culture*, xii.
7. Williams, *Cricket and Race*.
8. For instance, Karen Farquharson and Timothy Marjoribanks' examination of the Australian print media's coverage of two incidents of racial abuse, one by an Australian cricketer and the other uttered against his teammate, foregrounds the white/black binary still operational in world cricket, 'Representing Australia'. Rowe's article, 'Televised Sport', on a similar controversy explicates the reversal of the traditional balance of power in the media and sport administrations in the wake of the South Asianization of world cricket.
9. The best work related to cricket is definitely Marqusee's book, *Anyone But England*, which surveys England's disenchanted negotiation with the world after the collapse of their empire and cricket supremacy. Among works on administrative policies concerning equality and diversity in cricket, see Gemmell, *Politics of South African Cricket*; Malcolm, 'Clean Bowled?'; Miller, 'Clean Bowl Racism?'. Among more recent works on everyday migrant identity and administrative discourses ranging from the 'Tebbit test' to 'colour blindness' in the context of cricket-playing British Asians, see Fletcher, 'Who Do "They" Cheer For?'; 'Making of English Cricket'.
10. Vaseline is a petroleum-jelly-based skincare product manufactured by the Anglo-Dutch company Unilever.
11. Bowlers shine one or both sides of the cricket ball so that it swings in the air towards or away from the batsman according to the laws of aerodynamics. For basic knowledge of ball shining, see Mike Whitney's tutorial available at http://www.cricketcoach.com/cricket-basics/bowling-tips/shining-the-ball/ (accessed January 17, 2013).

12. *The Times of India* (hereafter *TOI*), January 17, 1977, 11.
13. Ibid.
14. Ibid.
15. Ibid.
16. *The Hindu*, January 18, 1977, 14.
17. The scorecard is available at http://www.espncricinfo.com/ci/engine/series/60463.html
18. Martin-Jenkins, *MCC in India 1976–77*, 90.
19. *TOI*, January 19, 1977, 11.
20. *TOI*, November 17, 1991, 13.
21. *Weekly Mail*, January 4, 1962, 8.
22. *Hindustan Times*, January 3, 1967, 4.
23. Ibid.
24. *Ananda Bazar Patrika*, January 3, 1967, 1.
25. *The Statesman*, January 3, 1967, 14.
26. Ibid., 7.
27. *The Hindu supplement*, January 22, 1977, 6.
28. *TOI*, January 26, 1977, 19.
29. Ibid.
30. *The Hindu*, January 18, 1977, 14.
31. *TOI*, January 20, 1977, 11.
32. *Guardian*, January 17, 1977, 15.
33. *Guardian*, January 18, 1977, 19.
34. *TOI*, January 20, 1977, 11.
35. Martin-Jenkins, *MCC in India 1976–77*, 89.
36. *The Hindu supplement*, January 22, 1977, 5.
37. Ibid.
38. *Observer*, February 20, 1977, 22.
39. *Guardian*, February 16, 1977, 24.
40. *TOI*, February 1, 1977, 11.
41. *Guardian*, February 19, 1977, 17.
42. *TOI*, August 18, 1977, 8.
43. Menon, *Bishan*, 128.
44. *TOI*, August 18, 1977, 8.
45. *Guardian*, August 20, 1977, 20.
46. Menon, *Bishan*, 126.
47. Ibid.
48. *Guardian*, August 19, 1977, 16.
49. Menon, *Bishan*, 130.
50. Ibid., 116.
51. Marqusee, *Anyone But England*, 189–91.
52. http://www.guardian.co.uk/sport/2011/jul/31/michael-vaughan-twitter-vaseline (accessed January 3, 2013).
53. http://articles.timesofindia.indiatimes.com/2011-08-01/top-stories/29838333_1_faint-edges-vvs-laxman-hot-spot (accessed January 3, 2012).
54. http://www.mid-day.com/sports/2011/aug/010811-Zaheer-Khan-Michael-Vaughan-Nasser-Hussain-Ravi-Shastri.htm (accessed January 3, 2012).
55. http://www.guardian.co.uk/sport/blog/2011/aug/05/ravi-shastri-india-england (accessed January 3, 2013).
56. http://www.espncricinfo.com/england-v-india-2011/content/story/525671.html (accessed January 3, 2013).

References

Cashmore, Ellis. *Sports Culture: An A–Z Guide*. London/New York: Routledge, 2002.
Farquharson, Karen, and Timothy Marjoribanks. 'Representing Australia: Race, the Media and Cricket'. *Journal of Sociology* 42, no. 1 (2006): 25–41.
Fletcher, Thomas. 'The Making of English Cricket Cultures: Empire, Globalization and (Post) Colonialism'. *Sport in Society* 14, no. 1 (2011): 17–36.

Fletcher, Thomas. '"Who Do 'They' Cheer For?" Cricket, Diaspora, Hybridity and Divided Loyalties among British Asians'. *International Review of the Sociology of Sport* 47, no. 5 (2012): 612–31.

Gemmell, Jon. *The Politics of South African Cricket*. London/New York: Routledge, 2004.

Guha, Ramachandra. *A Corner of a Foreign Field: The Indian History of a British Sport*. London: Picador, 2002.

Guttmann, Allen. *Games and Empires: Modern Sports and Cultural Imperialism*. New York: Columbia University Press, 1994.

Luhrmann, Tanya. *The Good Parsi: The Fate of a Colonial Elite in a Postcolonial Society*. Cambridge, MA: Harvard University Press, 1996.

Malcolm, Dominic. '"Clean Bowled?" Cricket, Racism and Equal Opportunities'. *Journal of Ethnic and Migration Studies* 28, no. 2 (2002): 307–25.

Mandle, William F. 'Cricket and Australian Nationalism in the Nineteenth Century'. *Journal of the Royal Australian Historical Society* 59, no. 4 (1974): 225–45.

Marqusee, Mike. *Anyone But England: Cricket and the National Malaise*. London: Verso, 1994.

Martin-Jenkins, Christopher. *MCC in India 1976–77*. London: MacDonald & Jane's, 1977.

Menon, Suresh. *Bishan: Portrait of a Cricketer*. New Delhi: Penguin, 2011.

Miller, Nick. 'Clean Bowl Racism? Inner-City London and the Politics of Cricket Development'. In *Cricket and National Identity in the Postcolonial Age: Following On*, ed. Stephen Wagg, 233–50. Abingdon: Routledge, 2005.

Nandy, Ashis. *The Tao of Cricket: On Games of Destiny and the Destiny of Games*. New Delhi: Viking, 1989.

Rowe, David. 'The Televised Sport: "Monkey Trial", "Race" and the Politics of Post-Colonial Cricket'. *Sport in Society* 14, no. 6 (2011): 792–804.

Williams, Jack. *Cricket and Race*. Oxford: Berg, 2001.

Social inclusion through football fandom: opportunities for learning-disabled people

Kris Southby

School of Applied Social Science, Durham University, Durham, UK

In Britain, within the contemporary drive of using sport to tackle the isolation of socially excluded groups, association football (football) fandom has been implicated in many policy documents as a possible site for learning-disabled people to become more socially included. However, whilst there is some evidence of the benefits of playing football for learning-disabled people, there is little evidence to support these claims. Drawing on empirical data, this paper aims to provide a critical analysis of the opportunities to tackle social exclusion that football fandom provides to learning-disabled people. Evidence suggests that whilst football fandom offers social benefits to learning-disabled people – including a sense of belonging and a shared social identity – that go some way towards tackling their social exclusion, football fandom is unlikely to result in the 'social inclusion' characterized by the government.

Introduction

There is considerable confusion over definitions and applications of the term 'learning disability'. Devlieger suggests that changes in terminology reflect a different logic of the understanding about the phenomenon of disability.[1] Historically, underpinned by a medical model, terms such as 'mental retardation', 'mental handicap', 'intellectual retardation' and 'intellectual handicap' have been used to describe people with an apparently scientifically measurable incomplete development of mind. Following the appeals of advocates and many learning-disabled people themselves from the 1970s onwards, an alternative social model of disability has replaced medicalized and stigmatizing language with terms such as 'intellectual disability', 'learning difficulty' and, most commonly, 'learning disability' to emphasize the social, physical and political barriers that *disable* people with intellectual impairments. Following the example of Mencap – the prominent British learning disability charity – and the British Institute of Learning Disabilities, the term 'learning disability' is used throughout this article in reference to those people who 'find it harder than others to learn, understand and communicate'.[2] 'Learning-disabled' is preferred to 'person with a learning disability' in recognition of the understanding of the social, political and physical barriers that people with intellectual impairments face.

Learning-disabled people have always occupied a marginal position in British society, whether in spatially separated institutions or absent from wider social opportunities.[3] Until relatively recently, learning-disabled people were seen as out of place in mainstream British society and subject to institutionalization.[4] Although no longer viewed as objects of fear, ridicule or segregation, and despite a raft of integrative social policies, learning-disabled people continue to face unseen barriers to participation and are more likely to live their lives on the fringes of society.[5]

In contemporary political discourse, the social isolation of learning-disabled people has been articulated through the language of social exclusion, attributed to individuals lacking social capital and social networks, and being disconnected from their communities.[6] Tackling this social exclusion has been described in political rhetoric as a simple matter of 'creating routes back into society and giving people a chance to integrate' into their communities.[7] The 2001 white paper *Valuing People*[8] and its later incarnation *Valuing People Now*[9] were undeniably positive in their intentions to enable learning-disabled people to 'lead their lives like any others with the same opportunities and responsibilities'. However, rather than attempting to address the structural inequalities at the heart of social exclusion, the aim of these policies has been truncated into promoting 'inclusion' into prescribed institutions of society,[10] principally paid employment and economic activity. Official documents and government discourses aim to involve learning-disabled people in pre-defined social spaces. This ignores the complex social interactions that characterize social exclusion and of learning-disabled peoples' frequent negative experiences of being 'included'.[11]

Primarily, on the basis of the theoretical ideas of Robert Putnam[12] and the research of Collins, Henry, Houlihan and Buller,[13] participation in sports-based leisure activities has been increasingly championed as a source of continuous engagement with one's community and decreasing the risk of becoming socially excluded.[14] As the most popular sport in Britain, association football (football) has been at the forefront of the drive to use sport to tackle the social exclusion of learning-disabled people. Policies bestowed by the national governing body for football, The Football Association (FA), and implemented within individual football clubs, such as 'Football for Disabled People',[15] 'The Disability Football Strategy: 2004–2006'[16] and 'Football for All',[17] have all highlighted the benefits of being involved in football 'whether as a player, referee, administrator, coach or spectator'.[18] However, as yet there is little evidence to substantiate all the claims of such football-based inclusion policies.[19] Whilst some health and social benefits have been recognized for learning-disabled people playing football,[20] there is currently no empirical evidence as to the social benefits of being a fan for learning-disabled people.

I have theorized elsewhere as to the potential for football fandom to help tackle the social exclusion of learning-disabled people.[21] In short, policies encouraging football fandom as a route out of social exclusion adopt a romanticized view of learning-disabled peoples' past experiences of 'inclusion' and appear to ignore the challenges faced by learning-disabled people attempting to fully participate or integrate into mainstream leisure settings.[22] Policies such as 'The Disability Football Strategy: 2004–2006'[23] and 'Football for All'[24] also fail to acknowledge the contemporary nature of football fans as a fragmented group of consumers navigating a transient market place.[25] As such, assumptions about the positive outcomes of football fandom for learning-disabled people lack any evidence base, and a direct linear effect between simple participation and social inclusion cannot be assumed.

Drawing on empirical data from ethnographic research conducted with learning-disabled football fans, this paper aims to provide a critical analysis of the opportunities to overcome social exclusion that football fandom provides to learning-disabled people. Following this introduction, the paper begins with a discussion of the chosen methodology. Learning-disabled people's experiences of football fandom are then analysed. The paper moves on to consider the ability of football fandom to help tackle the social exclusion of learning-disabled people, including examining the social benefits of attending live football matches for learning-disabled people and of being a football fan in everyday life. Finally, the paper concludes that football fandom offers learning-disabled people many social benefits, particularly in relation to generating feelings of belonging and a shared identity with other fans, which may go some way towards tackling their social exclusion. However, these social benefits are unlikely to enable learning-disabled people to gain the necessary social capital to become 'socially included'.

Research methodology

Ascertaining whether football fandom helped tackle the social exclusion of learning-disabled people required an understanding of the experiences of learning-disabled people as football fans and any social benefits they achieve. Following a purposive sample, the research was based on three professional English football clubs, referred to in this article by their pseudonyms Rovers, United and Athletic. All three clubs played in one of the three divisions of the Football League, which enabled conclusions about this administrative body to be drawn. Gaining access to a club in the Premier League would have been useful for understanding the possible effects of hyper-commodification on the experience of football fandom for learning-disabled people, but this was not possible within the constraints of a doctoral research study.

Using an 'institutional definition',[26] learning-disabled fans were conceptualized as anyone attending the football training sessions for Rovers', United's or Athletic's learning-disability football teams and who volunteered themselves as a 'fan'. Referring to 'learning-disabled people' or 'learning-disability' collectively in this way reflects the policy approach of classifying such individuals as a demographic group. Also, commonalities between individuals – possibly stemming from these institutional groupings – meant that theorizing between their experiences 'carries the most weight and biggest impact' in informing discussion and facilitating the policy agenda.[27] Although this sampling frame limited the potential sample to those learning-disabled people who played football, ignoring those fans that did not, it was not feasible to sample participants another way. As Bauer and Aarts suggest, most qualitative research is ultimately constrained by the practicalities of actually having to *do* the research.[28]

Thirteen learning-disabled fans volunteered to participate in the research and to share their experiences of football fandom. Each participant was given a pseudonym. They were Gavin, Mark, Gary, Hannah, Paul, Joe, Sam, Alex, Sanjay, Tom, Steven, Daniel and David. Represented within the sample were a range of impairments, and each person had his/her own individual support needs. Individuals with profound or complex learning impairments were precluded from the study because, as a neophyte researcher, I did not feel I had the necessary skills to gain valid data from these people. Ten of the participants lived at home with their parents. Sam, Alex and Steven lived in private supported housing. The ages of the sample ranged from 18 to 41, with a mean age of 27. Arguably, this precluded drawing any conclusions from the sample about the experiences of older learning-disabled fans that may, for example, have different support needs associated with age. The minimum age for participation was purposefully set as 18 so as to focus solely on the experience of adults and to avoid any additional ethical issues related to involving children in social research.[29] Only one female (Hannah) and one person who was not white British (Sanjay) participated in the research. This limited the sample's representation of female and ethnic minority learning-disabled football fans. Eight of the participants – 61% – had season tickets to attend all of Rovers', United's or Athletic's home matches, whilst only two participants regularly attended their clubs' away fixtures. Limitations or variation in the sample can be attributed to the difficulty of accessing and recruiting learning-disabled fans.

Being concerned fundamentally with the participants' subjective experiences of football fandom, data collection was conducted in the qualitative tradition. Whilst qualitative data collection has often been considered inappropriate for research with learning-disabled people,[30] this was overcome by investing time, gradually building a rapport with each participant before data collection took place.[31] Like Williams, I spent time 'hanging around' Rovers', United's and Athletic's learning-disability football training sessions, getting to know each of the participants.[32] Spending time with participants during training sessions ensured that the participants felt safe and secure,[33] created opportunities to openly discuss personal experiences and feelings,[34] and helped to elicit more valid data.[35] Spending time interacting with the participants prior to data collection also contributed towards the ethical basis of the research as part of an inclusive ethos.

Over the last 30 years, reflecting the changing status of learning disability in society more generally, the role of learning-disabled people in social research has evolved from non-consenting victim to consenting participant.[36] More recently, the role of learning-disabled people has expanded further with many researchers and self-advocates challenging their status as 'subjects' or 'informants' only.[37] The term 'inclusive research' has thus been coined to describe the new discourse of research participation and inclusion in which learning-disabled people are involved as more than just subjects; as equal partners, experts or researchers. Within the confines of this study, it was not possible to implement a fully 'participatory' or 'emancipatory' approach. However, as far as possible I attempted to adhere to the three core beliefs of inclusive research that: (1) the conventional research–research participant relationship is inequitable; (2) people have the right to be consulted in research about their own lives; and (3) the quality of research improves when people are involved in research about their own lives.[38]

The primary tool of data collection was the semi-structured interview. A minimum of three interviews were undertaken with each participant over the course of the 2010/2011 football season, with each interview planned to focus on one aspect of the participants' fandom. The first round of interviews focused on the participants' reasons and motivations for being fans, the second on their experiences of attending live matches (or the experiences of consuming football through an alternative medium) and the third on their perceived benefits of being a football fan. The interviews were conducted by myself and usually took place in the participant's homes (with the presence of a parent or carer), although Hannah and Gary chose to be interviewed at a local leisure centre whilst they attended a weekly social club. In an attempt to empower the participants, interviews were first arranged with participants before specific details were confirmed with their parents or carers. With the participants' consent, interviews were recorded using a Dictaphone, ready to be transcribed immediately after.

In an attempt to stimulate more in-depth conversation during interviews, six of the participants also agreed to take part in a photo-elicitation exercise.[39] After the first interviews, Hannah, Gary, Paul, Joe, Sam and Alex were each given a disposable camera and asked to take pictures of things that were important to them at live football matches. The resultant photographs were very effective conversational prompts during interviews. In addition, with Gavin, Mark, Paul, Joe, Sam and Alex, a participant observation exercise was undertaken. Similar to Stalker's 'guided tour',[40] this involved attending a live football match with each participant and recording the experience in a research diary. This exercise provided some first-hand experience of attending live football matches for the learning-disabled participants to complement and enrich the interview data.

The resultant data – interview transcripts and field notes – were analysed collectively in a process of coding. Using NVivo, the data were examined in a very detailed and methodical manner. Specific words, phrases and paragraphs that categorized a theme in the data were highlighted as a 'code'. Following an inductive research design, codes were not preconceived but based on an emerging interpretation of what participants had said in interviews or what had been seen during participant observations.[41] The most important codes formed the basis of categories and concepts. The two highest order categories were 'How are learning-disabled people included as supporters' and 'Learning-disabled people's experiences of support – do they feel included'. Other codes were either merged into a hierarchical structure or deleted. Being grounded in the data this way – as opposed to trying to fit the data into a broader theoretical framework – locates the data analysis as part of grounded theory.[42] In this way, the resultant findings offered some 'explanatory power … the ability to explain what might happen' with regard to learning disability, football fandom and social inclusion/exclusion.[43]

The experience of football fandom for learning-disabled people

Over the past 20 years, as a result of the switch to all-seater stadia,[44] the growth of televised live football[45] and the increasing commercialization of football clubs,[46] football fandom has undergone a 'cultural revolution'. Whilst much of the sociology of sport literature laments the disruption caused to 'traditional' fans,[47] these changes have benefited those people previously excluded from football fandom. The experience of the learning-disabled fans involved in this research is a novel example of the equality and diversity increasingly pervading contemporary football fandom.

Just as non-learning-disabled football fans are not a homogenous group, there is a wide variety in the way the participants in this research support their favoured teams. The stories told by the participants demonstrate a wide variation of football fandom in terms of duration, intensity and participation. For some, it was a lifelong passion inherited from family members, whilst for others football fandom was merely a sporadic hobby. Giulianotti's 'Supporters, Followers, Fans and Flaneurs' taxonomy of football fans provides perhaps the best visual illustration of the 'changes and cultural differences experienced by [individual learning-disabled fans] in their relationships with identified clubs' (see Figure 1).[48]

Figure 1 illustrates where each of the sample of learning-disabled fans fits onto Giulianotti's[49] taxonomy based on a subjective interpretation of their fandom after spending time with each participant, talking to them and in some cases attending live football matches together. This analysis takes into account, for example, the number of live matches – both home and away – participants attend, duration of fandom, amount and motivation for purchasing club merchandize, and level of identification with their chosen team. Whilst there is not an even distribution, the diagram demonstrates how, just like non-learning-disabled football fans, learning-disabled people are able to operate as supporters, followers, fans or flâneurs.

Out of the 13 participants in this research, 11 can be seen to exhibit 'hot' forms of identification with their chosen clubs. This means that, to a lesser of greater extent, these people experience 'intense kinds of identification and solidarity with the club'.[50] Gary even suggested that being a fan of United is so important to him that 'it's like a religion'. Only Steven and David displayed a mostly 'cool' relationship with Rovers and Athletic, respectively. Along the 'traditional'/'consumer' horizontal axis, greater variation between participants was evident. The number of live matches participants attended was a key

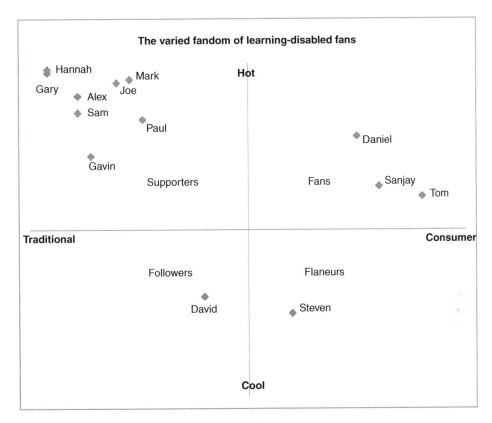

Figure 1.   The varied fandom of learning-disabled football fans.

factor in their placement along this continuum. For example, Sanjay, Tom and Daniel were considered to be the most 'consumer' fans because they attend the least number of live matches on average. They instead had to rely on the 'cool' mediums of television, radio and the Internet. Conversely, Hannah and Gary, who occupied the most 'traditional' positions, had season tickets to attend all of United's home games as well as travelling to many away games throughout the football season.

Amongst the variety of fandom displayed by the participants in this study, however, much of their conduct echoed the 'traditional' fan behaviour idealized in many quarters of the football fan literature.[51] For example, as well as regular match attendance, many of the learning-disabled fans were acutely aware of the binary distinction between the supposedly 'authentic' and 'inauthentic' fan.[52] Those positioned at the 'hot' and 'traditional' ends of Giulianotti's[53] taxonomy – the 'Supporters' – differentiated themselves as 'proper supporter[s]' (Mark) away from other 'glory hunters' (Hannah).

The observed variation in fandom is significant as it suggests that the participants have been able to exercise a choice – a key goal of *Valuing People* and *Valuing People Now* – and therefore, to some extent, they demonstrated the ability to overcome their social exclusion. Attending live matches or consuming certain products possibly empowers learning-disabled fans by giving them control over their own leisure time. For example, Mark described becoming an Athletic fan as a way for him to be '[his] own person'. However, to view the participants' football fandom entirely in this way is to fall prey to the 'utopian vision' of *Valuing People* of learning-disabled people making 'choices about activities in pleasant neighbourhoods with plentiful resources'.[54]

Just as learning-disabled people's opportunities to engage in leisure activities in general are widely constrained and socially patterned,[55] the reality for all the participants was that their fandom was in some way inhibited. Besides the increasing financial costs affecting most football fans,[56] the learning-disabled fans in this research also faced obstacles as a result of their impairments, the most obvious infringement being the inability of some participants to independently attend live matches. Social support – typically from parents or other family members – is an influential factor for learning-disabled people in engaging in leisure activities,[57] and this was evidently the case with regard to attending live football matches. Of course, not all the participants in this research were affected in the same way. Those with less severe impairments, such as Gary, Mark and Gavin, were able to exercise more choice about their fandom by attending matches independently. However, even for the more able participants, their football fandom was still affected – often in more subtle ways – by their impairments. As such, it is perhaps only appropriate to suggest that the football fandom of the learning-disabled participants in this research was a reflection of their personal and social circumstances – their 'capabilities' as Sen would say[58] – and not necessarily their own choices.

Part of the crowd: the social benefits of attending live matches

Despite rising media coverage of football, which has resulted in a proliferation of alternatives to attending live matches in person,[59] amongst the learning-disabled fans involved in this research watching one's team in person continued to be the preferred medium of consuming football. 'Being there' to experience the immediate pleasure and excitement of the live event was overwhelmingly associated with feeling 'excited' (Gavin) and 'really happy' (Daniel), even if 'it's against a really rubbish team!' (Mark). Even for those participants who did not have season tickets, the chance to attend a live football match was a 'happy' (Sanjay) experience. David explained about the few matches he had been to:

> It feels … it feels quite exciting to be honest. I mean, seeing all the team training and that it puts a smile on my face and … uhh … I just like watching 'em and stuff like that.

The pleasure of watching Rovers, United or Athletic compete live in their stadia can be associated with the physical proximity the participants were able to achieve between themselves and both the match itself and to the other fans. This resonates with how football stadia are often conceptualized in the sociology of sport literature:

> Historical social spaces where people's implicit understanding of these particular geographical areas could lead to a deep identity formation and the development of a sense of place within the stadium itself.[60]

This was described by the participants through the notion of the stadium atmosphere, which began to build 'when everybody's coming in and [the team] are in the tunnel and everybody's screaming and shout[ing]' (Paul). During Athletic matches, Gavin said the atmosphere is created when 'all the Athletic fans bang on [the stadium]', 'blow whistles' or generally engage in carnivalesque behaviour.[61] The choreographed football chant or song was perhaps the most powerful expression of collective identity, enabling the participants to demonstrate how 'proud' (Gavin) they were to be fans. Through these activities, the participants were able to participate in the highly symbolic aspects of cultural ritual, which distinguished 'us' from 'them'. Even when the participants were unable or chose not to engage in these activities, other actions could be substituted. The simple act of clapping emerged as a popular alternative for learning-disabled fans to become part of the luminal events that drew fans together in a sense of shared space.[62]

As much of the football fan literature highlights the decline or sterilization of atmosphere in British football stadia,[63] so too did some of the learning-disabled fans involved in this work. Although travelling to away matches appeared to offer a solution to this problem because 'everybody seems more up for away games' (Joe), these benefits were limited to learning-disabled people with the capabilities to attend away matches. Whilst all the fans enjoyed it when the stadium became 'noisy', there was a general concern about there being too much atmosphere with other fans, for example 'getting drunk', 'swearing', 'arguing', 'fighting', 'throwing things' (Joe). However, unlike other contexts where similar negative experiences have been shown to result in learning-disabled people withdrawing further from a particular social space,[64] the participants in this research chose to ignore these experiences in order to keep supporting their teams.

Besides the positive emotions generated by going to games, attending live football matches had many social benefits in terms of the opportunities for social interactions it presented. Compared to other examples where learning-disabled people have entered 'mainstream' locations only to remain absent from social networks,[65] interacting with 'other supporters' whilst attending football matches was a common occurrence. Opportunities for interactions occurred whilst travelling to matches 'in the car' (Alex) or 'sometimes on the bus' (Mark), and then within the stadium with 'the people [sat] around' (Sam). These interactions served to both strengthen the participants' existing social ties with those they attended matches with (i.e. family and friends) and inspire novel interactions with other fans. Through 'having something in common' (Mark), the perceived subordinate role of learning-disabled people appeared to be diminished and relationships of more equal status created.

Like Giulianotti's analysis of the Tartan Army,[66] these interactions can be conceptualized as a form of 'sociability', as a 'play form of association' that pushes individuals into an association with each other.[67] Conversations were focused almost exclusively on the football team or the match at hand: people predicting scores, discussing team selection or asking about previous performances. By following the conversation rules of sociability, the participants ensured their interactions remained 'interesting, gripping, even significant'.[68] Arguably, it is because of the specificity of the conversation that the learning-disabled fans were able to contribute. Whilst they may have missed out on other social 'rites of passage' (i.e. full-time employment, buying a house, raising a family),[69] learning-disabled fans were able to accumulate the necessary subcultural capital (i.e. knowledge of their team) to have their opinions valued. This is in stark contrast to the typical experience of learning-disabled people in mainstream leisure settings. Participants were also able to display 'good form' in their interactions by engaging in what is commonly referred to as 'banter' or 'crack'.[70] Even for those less articulate learning-disabled fans, basic forms of sociability were established through swapping essential terminology, such as the names of favourite players.

None the less, reflecting Hall's concern about the successful involvement of learning-disabled people in specific leisure settings being limited to those contexts,[71] it was apparent that the 'bridging' relationships formed by learning-disabled fans at football matches only existed within the stadia. Gavin coined the moniker 'season ticket friends' to describe how relationships were formed for 90 minutes, when it feels like you have got a 'couple thousand mates' (Tom), only for these to dissolve before recommencing at the next game. These relationships reflect the contemporary understanding about football fan communities, as like-minded individuals who come together to form 'neo-tribes' or 'emotional communities' characterized by 'occasional gatherings and dispersal'.[72] In terms of tackling social exclusion, attending live football matches offered the participants in this research an opportunity for 'intense effective bonding' with other like-minded individuals before they go back to their solitary lives after the final whistle.[73]

The ability of learning-disabled fans to become part of these 'imagined' or 'emotional' communities, however, appeared to be dependent on their capabilities to attend live matches.[74] A common idea identified by the learning-disabled fans in this study was that having a season ticket created more opportunities to 'get to know people' (Mark), not just because season ticket holders were able to attend all home games, but also because they were always sat in the same place, surrounded by the same people. In addition, having a season ticket and attending live matches regularly carried associated subcultural capital amongst other fans and allowed learning-disabled fans to feel 'more part of it', like a 'more dedicated supporter', and 'higher up the ranks of supporters' (Sam).[75]

In this sense, football stadia can be seen as a kind of 'semi-institutional' space where learning-disabled fans are able to feel included in, and make a valued contribution to, the fan 'community'. Whilst other 'refuges' or 'safe spaces' that learning-disabled people have created for themselves are often judged to be isolating or exclusionary,[76] the semi-institutional space of the football stadium allowed the learning-disabled participants to be within a 'correct' mainstream location without being exposed to the oppressive 'normality' of mainstream society. It brought dissimilar people together who otherwise would not have met. Also, because live football matches involve alternative forms of behaviour and participation to mainstream society, the stadium 'camouflage[s] society's typical response to individuals with disability'.[77] This is unlikely to lead to 'social inclusion' in the form of paid employment and economic participation, but it was a positive social experience for the learning-disabled people involved.

After the whistle: the social benefits of football fandom away from live matches

Whilst attending live football matches was evidently an important aspect of the participants' fandom – a site to experience the thrill of being surrounded by like-minded individuals, contribute to the spectacle and interact with other people in ways that might not normally be possible – the participants' fandom was not confined to the 90-minute match. That is to say, to varying degrees, their experience of football fandom was not spatially or temporally bounded (i.e. to the football stadium during a live match), but persisted across their whole lives.[78]

For those fans more 'hotly' identified with their clubs, being a fan of Rovers, United or Athletic endured more strongly into their everyday lives. For example, Hannah indicated how she was a fan of United 'all the time', and Joe is similarly a 'Rovers fan the whole time, not just for one match'. This reflects the findings of numerous other scholars that fandom can become a central feature in one's life.[79] Reflecting Robson's empirical research on fans of Millwall FC,[80] the 'hottest' participants arguably reached a level of commitment where being a fan of Rovers, United or Athletic became an essential element for negotiating everyday life. Comparatively, the fandom of the 'cooler' fans in this study, such as David and Steven, was more likely to be based on 'discrete or isolated socio-cultural 'event[s]'' and not 'an extension of the everyday'.[81] David, for example, referred to being a fan of Athletic as a 'new kind of hobby that's kind of something to do if I'm bored'. He liked going to live matches to 'enjoy the football and try and encourage the team' (David), but the result of the match did not affect his sense of self.

The significance of the persistent fandom of some participants was that it presented opportunities – just like at live matches – to interact with other like-minded individuals in 'everyday life'.[82] Although the day-to-day lives of learning-disabled people are likely to be different from their non-learning-disabled counterparts,[83] to varying degrees the participants in this research successfully interacted with other fans in many of the 'everyday' locations identified by Stone.[84] However, because only one of the participants regularly went to the pub and only two had voluntary employment positions, this predominantly occurred in the home and in other 'transitional' spaces.

Interactions occurred predominantly with people already known to the participants, such as family members and friends. Sanjay described how he interacted with his elder brother about Rovers:

> Then he talk to me and say 'we won'. I say 'yeah'. I said 'they lose'. He said 'Argh'. He said 'They will win next time'. I said 'They won't'. Then my brother just smiling happy. (Sanjay)

Like the relationships formed during live matches, the advantage of such interactions was in enabling the participants to reaffirm and strengthen their existing 'bonding' social relationships. Persistent fandom also presented opportunities for 'bridging' interactions to occur between the participants and their fellow fans. This varied from simply saying 'hello' to other members of the public who appeared to be football fans to having more in-depth conversations with them about the team. Hannah explained that when greeting previously unknown United fans she often asked '"what did you think for the game?" and I just ask 'em how they think they played and that'. An opportunity for interaction emerging from enduring football fandom could be seen in Gavin's account of when he went shopping with his mother. He said:

> He went 'which team do you support?'. We went 'Athletic'. He went 'Nice one'. I went down the road today, I were waiting for me mum in this shop, I was sat outside and this guy came out, he went 'nice, nice, best, best, best Athletic shirt son'. I started laughing. (Gavin)

Paralleling the participants' experiences of attending live matches, being a football fan was evidently an effective 'ice-breaker', providing a source of interaction that might otherwise be missing from the lives of learning-disabled people.[85] Being a football fan can be seen to have brought the participants of this research and other fans together, briefly, as a performative 'cloakroom' community around their shared interest, without entering into 'thick' reciprocal relationships.[86] Whilst these interactions may not have been as 'intensive' as those formed within the emotion and excitement of the stadium,[87] conducted away from any 'discrete ... socio-cultural "event[s]"',[88] these interactions were evidently more 'mobile and flexible'.[89]

The enduring nature of many of the participants' football fandom indicates that it may be considered as a form of 'serious leisure'.[90] Although Patterson and Pegg explicitly refer to 'people going to see their favourite football team' as 'casual leisure',[91] this is to misunderstand the significance of football fandom in the lives of football fans.[92] For the most 'hotly' identified participants, being a fan of Rovers, United or Athletic was 'substantial and interesting enough in nature for the participant to find a career ... acquiring and expressing ... its special skills, knowledge, and experience'.[93] This is significant for two reasons. First, it contravenes previous notions that learning-disabled people do not have the commitment or perseverance to engage in leisure activities long enough for them to be positive or meaningful.[94] Second, and more substantively, engaging in football fandom as serious leisure enabled the participants in this research to enhance their self-concept, self-actualization, self-enrichment, self-expression, feelings of accomplishment, enhanced self-image and self-esteem, and social interaction around 'our' team.[95]

As a medium to access the personal and social benefits of leisure participation, football fandom appears more effective than the majority of leisure programmes offered to learning-disabled people, which tend to be more 'casual', passive and solitary.[96] However, it would be inappropriate to suggest that through football fandom learning-disabled people are likely to gain the skills to effectively participate in Western society (e.g. paid employment) in the way advocates of leisure, such as Rojek,[97] might suggest. Of course, not all participants in this study engaged in fandom as a serious leisure activity. Whilst for some this was through choice – they just were not that into it – for others it was questionable how much their 'capability poverty' prevented them from attaining these benefits.[98]

Football fandom, especially for those engaging in it as serious leisure, also appeared to offer a source of personal identity. Mark explained the personal significance of being an Athletic fan:

> Umm … it is, like, a big part of my life, being a Athletic supporter. So, like, if people accept me for who I am then stuff like that. One of the things is that I'm a Athletic supporter and it's, like, a big part of me.

This identity is transmitted to other people through displaying appropriate symbols, such as wearing clothing emblazoned with club logos, intended to show other people they were a fan of Rovers, United or Athletic.[99] The most common item of clothing to demonstrate fan identity was the clubs' official playing shirt; something that all the participants possessed. Other items of clothing included Rovers, United or Athletic branded coats, raincoats, hats, caps, gloves, scarves and tracksuits. Whilst some fan subcultures reject consuming/wearing branded clothing in favour of a more 'casual' style, this was not evident in this research.

As a form of identity, football fandom appeared to be particularly beneficial for the participants, principally in relation to breaking down the 'stigma' of learning disability.[100] This confirms previous suggestions that football fandom enables the construction of resistant identities amongst marginalized groups.[101] Effectively, displaying their club symbols allowed the participants in this research to be seen, first and foremost, as fans of Rovers, United or Athletic. Participants generally felt that there was 'no difference really' (Gary) between themselves and other non-learning-disabled fans. Instead, there was a feeling of being 'together' (Paul) and 'all together as one' (Gary). Daniel described his feelings about himself as a learning-disabled fan: 'Part of being a Rovers supporter, just like everyone else, and that and just being a person whose there to watch'.

Finally, whilst football fandom was unlikely to result in the permanent expansion of social networks and social capital necessary for 'social inclusion', as a source of personal and social identity, football fandom did appear to offer the participants a location in which they could feel a sense of belonging. The historical starting point for learning-disabled people is that they are 'in varying degrees "other"',[102] unable to seek the dominant routes through which a sense of 'we' can be negotiated, such as employment and independent living, and are denied the opportunity to compare themselves favourably to other social groups. However, just as sports participation in general, and football fandom in particular, is considered to offer non-learning-disabled people a sense of belonging and security increasingly absent in other aspects of life, football fandom appeared to provide learning-disabled fans an environment in which they can fulfil their desire to be 'deeply understood and deeply accepted'.[103] This was true for fans who regularly attended matches as well as those who did not. Joe, for example, spoke about how, as a Rovers fan, he felt part of 'a big group', whilst Hannah described her fellow United fans as 'like a family'. This is comparable to the social acceptance that excluded 'others' can achieve in specially designed inclusive leisure spaces.[104] However, the ubiquity of football in British society means that learning-disabled people are able to experience belonging and a sense of insiderness during both 'isolated socio-cultural events' (i.e. live matches) and in their day-to-day lives.[105]

Conclusions and future research

Ignoring the lived reality of learning-disabled people themselves, 'social inclusion' has come to be synonymous with participation in paid employment. Despite the implications of numerous sport and football policies, the potential social inclusion benefits of football fandom for learning-disabled people have been largely unknown. Drawing on empirical evidence exploring, for the first time, learning-disabled peoples' experience of football fandom, this paper has shown that football fandom can have numerous social benefits for learning-disabled fans. The benefits of football fandom for learning-disabled people are the increased opportunities to interact with other football fans, become part of an imagined community, establish a personal and social identities other than being 'disabled', and bond and feel a sense of belonging amongst other like-minded individuals. These benefits are often absent in the lives of learning-disabled people.

The social benefits of football fandom for learning-disabled people are most palpable inside football stadia during live football matches. The reason for this is because football stadia can be seen as 'semi-institutional' spaces in which the typical norms of mainstream society, which normally serve to stigmatize and exclude learning-disabled people, are suspended in favour of an alternative set of subcultural rules and expectations based on fandom. Where learning-disabled fans were able to display the necessary symbols of fandom through their behaviour (i.e. chanting and singing) and attire (i.e. wearing club colours/kit), they became included in the fan 'community'. Not all learning-disabled fans had the 'capabilities' to regularly attend live football matches, however. Fortunately, because of the ubiquity of football in British society, the social benefits of being a fan were also available to learning-disabled people whose fandom persisted in their everyday lives. Whilst interactions with other football fans, for example, were perhaps more fleeting, the feeling of belonging – of being 'deeply understood and deeply accepted'[106] – still remained.

Evidence in this paper suggests that football fandom is unlikely to result in learning-disabled people becoming more 'socially included' into wider/mainstream society. The relationships and social networks that learning-disabled people are likely to engage with as football fans are only fleeting and content specific. They are unlikely to conduct the transfer of social capital necessary for learning-disabled people to become included in the mainstream social spaces (i.e. paid employment) and economic activity characteristic of 'inclusion'. However, being a football fan can be seen to contribute towards learning-disabled people being less socially excluded. At an individual level at least, football fandom provides learning-disabled people with opportunities for increased social interaction and feelings of belonging within mainstream society frequently missing from their everyday lives. At a societal level, learning-disabled football fans – interacting with non-learning-disabled fans – may help challenge and reduce the stigma of 'learning-disability' ascribed to those with learning impairments.

Whilst this paper has presented an almost entirely positive picture of learning-disabled peoples' experiences of football fandom, this is only the opening foray into this topic. Before drawing any definitive conclusions about the potential of football fandom to help tackle the social exclusion of learning-disabled people, there needs to be further exploration, analysis and discussion around the experience of football fandom for learning-disabled people. This paper is limited by a restricted sample size, ignoring the experiences of people with profound or complex learning impairments, of different demographics already excluded from football fandom (i.e. women and ethnic minorities) and of learning-disabled people who are not already established football fans. An imperative for future research will be to consider the perception of non-learning-disabled football fans about their learning-disabled counterparts. Particular attention should be paid to the possibility of hate crimes occurring between fans as this will contribute towards understanding the appropriateness of football fandom being advocated as a suitable site to reduce the social exclusion of learning-disabled people. In addition, in terms of building up an understanding of what might be done to better facilitate learning-disabled people's football fandom – and to possibly encourage more learning-disabled people to become football fans – it is essential to gain a greater understanding of (1) how individual capabilities impact on football fandom and (2) what, if anything, is already being done (i.e. by football clubs) to enable the involvement of learning-disabled people as fans.

Notes

1. Devlieger, 'From Handicap to Disability'.
2. MENCAP, 'What is a Learning Disability?'
3. Hall, 'Spaces of Social Inclusion'.
4. MacIntyre, *Learning Disability and Social Inclusion*.
5. Ibid.
6. Baron, 'Social Capital in British Politics'.
7. Social Exclusion Unit, *Preventing Social Exclusion*, 109.
8. Department of Health (DH), *Valuing People*.
9. DH, *Valuing People Now*, 11.
10. Labonte, 'Social Inclusion/Exclusion'.
11. Secker et al., *Mental Health, Social Inclusion*.
12. Putnam, *Bowling Alone*.
13. Collins et al., *Sport and Social Inclusion*.
14. Waring and Mason, 'Opening Doors'; Vermeulen and Verweel, 'Participation in Sport'.
15. The FA, *Football for Disabled People*.
16. The FA, *Disability Football Strategy*.
17. The FA, *Football for All*.
18. Ibid.
19. Tacon, 'Football and Social Inclusion'.
20. Collins and Buller, 'Social Exclusion'.
21. Southby, 'Football Fandom'.
22. Solish, Minnes and Kupferschmidt, 'Integration of Children'.
23. The FA, *Disability Football Strategy*.
24. The FA, *Football for All*.
25. Brown et al., *Football and Its Community*.
26. Patterson and Pegg, 'Serious Leisure'.
27. Fawcett and Hearn, 'Researching Others'.
28. Bauer and Aarts, 'Corpus Construction: A Principle for Qualitative Data Collection'.
29. See Bryman 2008.
30. Cleaver, Ouellette-Kuntz and Sakar, 'Participating in Intellectual Disability'.
31. Williams, 'Researching Together'.
32. Ibid.
33. Baxter, 'Learning to Interview'.
34. Morris, 'Including All Children'.
35. Munford et al., 'Looking Inside the Bag'.
36. Cleaver, Ouellette-Kuntz and Sakar, 'Participating in Intellectual Disability'.
37. Walmsley, 'Normalisation, Emancipatory Research'.

38. Stalker, 'Some Ethical and Methodological Issues'.
39. Booth and Booth, 'In the Frame'.
40. Stalker, 'Some Ethical and Methodological Issues'.
41. Charmaz, 'Grounded Theory'.
42. ; Strauss and Corbin, *Basics of Qualitative Research*.
43. Strauss and Corbin, *Basics of Qualitative Research*, 267.
44. Fawbert, 'Gentrification of Football Fandom'.
45. Weed, 'Pub as a Virtual Football Fandom Venue'.
46. Brown et al., *Football and Its Communities*.
47. Giulianotti, 'Supporters, Followers, Fans, and Flaneurs'; Williams, *Is It All Over?*
48. Giulianotti, 'Supporters, Followers, Fans and Flaneurs', 231.
49. Ibid.
50. Ibid., 231.
51. Williams, *Is It All Over?* 35.
52. Robson, *No One Likes Us*.
53. Giulianotti, 'Supporters, Followers, Fans and Flaneurs'.
54. Burton and Kagan, 'Decoding Valuing People', 305.
55. Buttimer and Tierney, 'Patterns or Leisure Participation'.
56. Fawbert, 'Gentrification of Football Fandom'.
57. Frey, Buchanan and Sandt, 'I'd Rather Watch TV'.
58. Sen, 'Disability & Justice'.
59. Weed, 'Pub as a Virtual Football Fandom Venue'.
60. Penny and Redhead, 'We're Not Really Here', 757.
61. Giulianotti, 'Football and the Politics'; Giulianotti, 'Scotland's Tartan Army'; Armstrong and Young, 'Fanatical Football Chants'.
62. Armstrong and Young, 'Fanatical Football Chants'; Kytö, 'We Are the Rebellious Voice'.
63. Armstrong and Giulianotti, 'From Another Angle'.
64. Mathers, 'Hidden Voices'.
65. Pinfold, 'Building Up Safe Havens'; O'Brien, *Paying Customers Are Not Enough*; Bray and Gates, *Community Participation for Adults*; Emerson and McVilly, 'Friendship Activities of Adults'.
66. Giulianotti, 'The Sociability of Sport'.
67. Simmel, 'The Sociology of Sociability', 255.
68. Ibid., 259.
69. Bray and Gates, *Community Participation for Adults*.
70. Giulianotti, 'The Sociability of Sport'.
71. Hall, 'Social Geographies of Learning Disability'; 'Spaces of Social Inclusion'.
72. Maffesoli, *The Time of the Tribes*, 76.
73. Crabbe, 'Post Modern Community', 436.
74. Sen, 'Disability & Justice'.
75. Giulianotti, 'Supporters, Followers, Fans and Flaneurs'; Weed, 'Exploring the Sport Spectator'.
76. Burton and Kagan, 'Decoding Valuing People'.
77. Devine and Parr, 'Come On In but Not Too Far', 402.
78. Stone, The Role of Football.
79. Giulianotti, 'Football and the Politics'; Giulianotti, 'Supporters, Followers, Fans and Flaneurs'; Robson, *No One Likes Us*; Armstrong and Harris, 'Football Hooligans'.
80. Robson, *No One Likes Us*.
81. Ibid., 9.
82. Stone, The Role of Football.
83. Hall, 'Spaces of Social Inclusion'.
84. Stone, 'The Role of Football'.
85. Hall and Hewson, 'The Community Links'.
86. Crabbe, 'Post Modern Community'.
87. Ibid., 436.
88. Robson, *No One Likes Us*, 9.
89. Crabbe, 'Post Modern Community', 436.

90. Stebbins, *Amateurs, Professionals, and Serious Leisure*; 'Serious Leisure'; 'Serious Leisure for People'.
91. Patterson and Pegg, 'Serious Leisure', 390.
92. Giulianotti, 'Supporters, Followers, Fans and Flaneurs'; Crabbe, 'Post Modern Community'; Millward, *Getting 'into' Europe*.
93. Stebbins, *Amateurs, Professionals, and Serious Leisure*, 3.
94. McGill, *Developing Leisure Identities*.
95. Patterson and Pegg, 'Serious Leisure'.
96. Buttimer and Tierney, 'Patterns of Leisure Participation'.
97. Rojek, 'Leisure and Emotional Intelligence'.
98. Burchardt, 'Capabilities and Disability'.
99. Sandvoss, *Fans: The Mirror of Consumption*; Clark, I'm Scunthorpe 'til I die'; Crabbe, *Fishing for Community*.
100. Lesseliers, Van Hove and Vanderveld, 'Regranting Identity'.
101. Giulianotti, 'Popular Culture, Social Identities'.
102. Sibley, *Geographies of Exclusion*, 61.
103. Goble, *The Third Force*, 30.
104. Parr, *Mental Health and Social Space*; Hall, 'Spaces of Social Inclusion'.
105. Robson, *No One Likes Us*, 9.
106. Goble, *The Third Force*, 30.

References

Armstrong, G., and R. Giulianotti. 'From Another Angle: Police Surveillance and Football Supporters'. In *Surveillance, Closed Circuit Television and Social Control*, ed. C. Norris, J. Moran, and G. Armstrong, 119–141. Aldershot: Ashgate, 1998.

Armstrong, G., and R. Harris. 'Football Hooligans: Theory and Evidence'. *Sociological Review* 39 (1991): 427–58.

Armstrong, G., and M. Young. 'Fanatical Football Chants: Creating and Controlling the Carnival'. In *Football Culture: Local Contests, Global Visions*, ed. G. Finn and R. Giulianotti, 173–211. London: Frank Cass, 1999.

Baron, S. 'Social Capital in British Politics and Policy Making'. In *Politics, Trust and Networks: Social Capital in Critical Perspective*, ed. J. Franklin, 5–16. London: London South Bank University, 2004.

Bauer, M., and B. Aarts. 'Corpus Construction: A Principle for Qualitative Data Collection'. In *Qualitative Research with Text, Image & Sound: A Practical Handbook*, ed. M. Bauer, and G. Gaskell (2000), pp. 19–33. London: Sage.

Baxter, V. 'Learning to Interview People with a Learning Disability'. *Research Policy and Planning* 23 (2005): 175–80.

Booth, T., and W. Booth. 'In the Frame: Photovoice and Mothers with Learning Difficulties'. *Disability & Society* 18 (2003): 431–42.

Bray, A., and S. Gates. *Community Participation for Adults with an Intellectual Disability: Review of the Literature Prepared for the National Advisory Committee on Health and Disability to Inform Its Project on Services for Adults with an Intellectual Disability*. Wellington: National Health Committee, 2003.

Brown, A., T. Crabbe, G. Mellor, T. Blackshaw, and C. Stone. *Football and Its Communities: Final Report*. London: Football Foundation, 2006.

Bryman, A. *Social Research Methods*. 3 ed. Oxford: Oxford University Press, 2008.

Burchardt, T. 'Capabilities and Disability: The Capabilities Framework and the Social Model of Disability'. *Disability & Society* 19 (2004): 735–51.

Burton, M., and C. Kagan. 'Decoding Valuing People'. *Disability & Society* 21 (2006): 299–313.

Buttimer, J., and E. Tierney. 'Patterns of Leisure Participation among Adolescents with Mild Intellectual Disability'. *Journal of Intellectual Disabilities* 9 (2005): 25–42.

Charmaz, K. 'Grounded Theory: Objectivist and Constructavist Methods'. In *Handbook of Qualitative Research*, ed. N. Denzin and Y.S. Lincoln, 509–535. Thousand Oaks, CA: Sage, 2000.

Clark, T. 'I'm Scunthorpe 'til I Die': Constructing and (Re)negotiating Identity through the Terrace Chant'. *Soccer & Society* 7 (2006): 494–507.

Cleaver, S., H. Ouellette-Kuntz, and A. Sakar. 'Participating in Intellectual Disability Research: A Review of 20 Years of Studies'. *Journal of Intellectual Disability Research* 54 (2010): 187–93.

Collins, M., and J. Buller. 'Social Exclusion from High-Performance Sport'. *Journal of Sport and Social Issues* 27 (2003): 420–42.

Collins, M., I. Henry, B. Houlihan, and J. Buller. *Sport and Social Inclusion: A Report to the Department for Culture, Media and Sport.* Leicestershire: Loughborough University, 1999.

Crabbe, T. 'Post Modern Community and Future Directions–Fishing for Community: England Fans at the 2006 FIFA World Cup'. *Soccer & Society* 9 (2008): 428–38.

Department of Health. *Valuing People: A New Strategy for Learning Disability for the 21st Century.* London: The Stationary Office, 2001.

Department of Health. *Valuing People Now: A New Three Year Strategy for People with Intellectual Disabilities, Making It Happen for Everyone.* London: HMSO, 2009.

Devine, M., and M. Parr. '"Come On In, but Not Too Far": Social Capital in an Inclusive Leisure Setting'. *Leisure Sciences: An Interdisciplinary Journal* 30 (2008): 391–408.

Devlieger, P. 'From Handicap to Disability: Language Use and Cultural Meaning in the United States'. *Disabilities and Rehabilitation* 21 (1999): 346–54.

Emerson, E., and K. McVilly. 'Friendship Activities of Adults with Learning Disabilities in Supported Accommodation'. *Journal of Applied Research in Intellectual Disabilities* 17 (2004): 1–7.

Fawbert, J. 'Gentrification of Football Fandom?'. In *Delivering Equality in Sport and Leisure*, ed. J. Long, H. Fitzgerald, and P. Millward, 35–48. London: Leisure Studies, 2011.

Fawcett, B., and J. Hearn. 'Researching Others: Epistemology, Experience, Standpoints and Participation'. *International Journal of Social Research Methodologies* 7 (2004): 201–8.

Frey, G., A. Buchanan, and D. Sandt. '"I'd Rather Watch TV": An Examination of Physical Activity in Adults with Mental Retardation'. *Mental Retardation* 43 (2005): 241–54.

Giulianotti, R. 'Football and the Politics of Carnival: An Ethnographic Study of Scottish Fans in Sweden'. *International Review for the Sociology of Sport* 30 (1995): 191–220.

Giulianotti, R. 'Popular Culture, Social Identities and Internal/External Cultural Politics: The Case of Rangers Supporters in Scottish Football'. *Identities: Global Studies in Culture and Power* 14 (2007): 257–84.

Giulianotti, R. 'Scotland's Tartan Army in Italy: The Case for the Carnivalesque'. *Sociological Review* 39 (1991): 503–27.

Giulianotti, R. 'The Sociability of Sport: Scotland Football Supporters as Interpreted through the Sociology of Georg Simmel'. *International Review for the Sociology of Sport* 40 (2005): 289–306.

Giulianotti, R. 'Supporters, Followers, Fans and Flaneurs: A Taxonomy of Spectator Identities in Football'. *Journal of Sport and Social Issues* 26 (2002): 25–46.

Goble, F. *The Third Force: The Psychology of Abraham Maslow.* New York: Washington Square Press, 1970.

Hall, E. 'Social Geographies of Learning Disability: Narratives of Exclusion and Inclusion'. *Area* 36 (2004): 298–306.

Hall, E. 'Spaces of Social Inclusion and Belonging for People with Intellectual Disabilities'. *Journal of Intellectual Disability Research* 54 (2010): 48–57.

Hall, I., and S. Hewson. 'The Community Links of a Sample of People with Learning Disabilities'. *Journal of Applied Research in Intellectual Disabilities* 19 (2006): 204–7.

Kytö, M. '"We Are the Rebellious Voice of the Terraces, We Are Çarşı": Constructing a Football Supporter Group through Sound'. *Soccer & Society* 12 (2010): 77–93.

Labonte, R. 'Social Inclusion/Exclusion: Dancing the Dialectic'. *Health Promotion International* 19 (2004): 115–21.

Lesseliers, J., G. Van Hove, and S. Vanderveld. 'Regranting Identity to the Outgraced–Narratives of Persons with Learning Disabilities: Methodological Considerations'. *Disability & Society* 24 (2009): 411–23.

MacIntyre, G. *Learning Disability and Social Inclusion.* Edinburgh: Dunedin Academic Press, 2008.

Maffesoli, M. *The Time of the Tribes: The Decline of Individualism in Mass Society.* London: Sage, 1996.

Mathers, R. 'Hidden Voices: The Participation of People with Learning Disabilities in the Experience of Public Open Space'. *Local Environment* 13 (2008): 515–29.

McGill, J. *Developing Leisure Identities.* Toronto: Brampton Caledon Community Living, 1996.

Mencap. *What is Learning Disability, 2011*. Available at: http://www.mencap.org.uk/page.asp?id =1684 (Accessed 21 January 2011).

Millward, P. *Getting 'into' Europe: Identification, Prejudice and Politics in English Football Culture*. Saarbrücken: VDM Verlag, 2009.

Morris, J. 'Including All Children: Finding Out about the Experiences of Children with Communication and/or Cognitive Impairments'. *Children & Society* 7 (2003): 337–48.

Munford, R., J. Sanders, B. Mirfin-Veitch, and J. Conder. 'Looking Inside the Bag of Tools: Creating Research Encounters with Parents with an Intellectual Disability'. *Disability & Society* 23 (2008): 337–47.

O'Brien, J. *Paying Customers Are Not Enough: The Dynamics of Individualized Funding*. Lithonia, GA: Responsive Systems Associates, 2001.

Parr, H. *Mental Health and Social Space*. Oxford: Blackwell, 2008.

Patterson, I., and S. Pegg. 'Serious Leisure and People with Intellectual Disabilities: Benefits and Opportunities'. *Leisure Studies* 28 (2009): 387–402.

Penny, S., and S. Redhead. 'We're Not Really Here: Manchester City, Mobility and Placelessness'. *Sport in Society* 12 (2009): 755–64.

Pinfold, V. 'Building Up Safe Havens … All Around the World: Users Experiences of Living in the Community with Mental Health Problems'. *Health and Place* 6 (2000): 201–12.

Putnam, R. *Bowling Alone: The Collapse and Revival of American Community*. New York/London: Simon & Schuster, 2000.

Robson, G. *'No One Likes Us, We Don't Care': The Myth and Reality of Millwall Fandom*. Oxford: Berg, 2000.

Rojek, C. 'Leisure and Emotional Intelligence'. *World Leisure Journal* 52 (2010): 240–52.

Sandvoss, C. *Fans: The Mirror of Consumption*. Cambridge: Polity, 2005.

Secker, J., S. Hacking, H. Spandler, L. Kent, and J. Shenton. *Mental Health, Social Inclusion and Arts: Developing the Evidence Base*. London: National Social Inclusion Programme/Care Services Improvement Partnership, 2005.

Sen, A. 'Disability and Justice' (paper presented at the conference on Disability and Inclusive Development: Sharing, Learning and Building Alliances, Washington, DC, November 30– December 1, 2004). Available at: http://siteresources.worldbank.org/DISABILITY/214576- 1092421729901/20291152/Amartya_Sen_Speech.doc

Sibley, D. *Geographies of Exclusion: Society and Difference in the West*. London: Routledge, 1995.

Simmel, G. 'The Sociology of Sociability'. *American Journal of Sociology* 55 (1949): 254–61.

Social Exclusion Unit. *Preventing Social Exclusion*. London: Social Exclusion Unit, 2001.

Solish, A., P. Minnes, and A. Kupferschmidt. 'Integration of Children with Developmental Disabilities in Social Activities'. *Journal on Developmental Disabilities* 10 (2003): 115–21.

Southby, K. 'Football Fandom, Social Inclusion and Learning Disability: Opportunities and Constraints'. *World Leisure Journal* 53 (2011): 322–31.

Stalker, K. 'Some Ethical and Methodological Issues in Research with People with Learning Difficulties'. *Disability & Society* 13 (1998): 5–20.

Stebbins, R. *Amateurs, Professionals, and Serious Leisure*. Montreal: McGill-Queen's University Press, 1992.

Stebbins, R. 'Serious Leisure'. In *Leisure Studies: Prospects for the Twenty-First Century*, ed. T. Burton and E. Jackson, 69–86. Philadelphia, PN: Venture Publishing, 1999.

Stebbins, R. 'Serious Leisure for People with Disabilities'. In *Leisure Education, Community Development and Populations with Special Needs*, ed. A. Sivan and H. Ruskin, 101–108. Oxon: CABI, 2000.

Stone, C. 'The Role of Football in Everyday Life'. *Soccer & Society* 8 (2007): 169–84.

Strauss, A., and J. Corbin. *Basics of Qualitative Research.*, 2nd ed. London: Sage, 1998.

Tacon, R. 'Football and Social Inclusion: Evaluating Social Policy'. *Managing Leisure* 12 (2007): 1–23.

The Football Association. *The Disability Football Strategy: 2004–2006*. London: The Football Association, 2004.

The Football Association. *Football for All*. London: The Football Association, 2006.

The Football Association. *Football for All*. London: The Football Association, 2010.

The Football Association. *Football for Disabled People*. London: The Football Association, 2001.

Vermeulen, J., and P. Verweel. 'Participation in Sport: Bonding and Bridging as Identity Work'. *Sport in Society* 12 (2009): 1206–19.

Walmsley, J. 'Normalisation, Emancipatory Research and Inclusive Research in Learning Disability'. *Disability & Society* 16 (2001): 187–205.

Waring, A., and C. Mason. 'Opening Doors: Promoting Social Inclusion through Increased Sports Participation'. *Sport in Society* 13 (2010): 517–29.

Weed, M. 'Exploring the Sport Spectator Experience: Virtual Football Spectatorship in the Pub'. *Soccer & Society* 9 (2008): 189–97.

Weed, M. 'The Pub as a Virtual Football Fandom Venue: An Alternative to "Being There"?'. *Soccer & Society* 8 (2007): 399–414.

Williams, J. *Is It All Over? Can Football Survive the Premier League?* Reading: South Street Press, 1999.

Williams, V. 'Researching Together'. *British Journal of Learning Disabilities* 27 (1999): 48–51.

Intolerance and joy, violence and love among male football fans: towards a psychosocial explanation of 'excessive' behaviours

Andy Harvey[a] and Agnieszka Piotrowska[b]

[a]Department of Psychosocial Studies, Birkbeck, University of London, London, UK; [b]Research Institute for Media, Art and Design, University of Bedfordshire, Bedfordshire, UK

This paper examines the phenomena of intolerance and violence among male football fans through psychoanalytic theory as read through the sociology of postmodern group life. We think of intolerance and violence as points on a shared spectrum of emotion and (unconscious) desire that incorporates other forms of 'excessive' behaviour, notably public displays of homosocial love and affection. We argue that the notion of 'transference-love' as proposed by Freud and reformulated by Lacan is an important aspect of fans' libidinal investments in players. We maintain that a psychosocial approach to the problem enables a discussion of the ambiguous place of football fandom within postmodern consumer culture, where such identities are necessarily tenuous, but, at the same time, tenaciously held. Uncertainties of identity are exacerbated by the gendered and unconscious (homo)sexual dynamics that exist in the emotional cauldron of the male football crowd. Displays of excessive behaviour can be seen as a defence against the confusion over gender and sexuality that might arise in this cauldron at the time of the match and in the space of the stadium.

Introduction

In this paper, we sketch out what might be the beginnings of an integrated psychosocial theoretical approach to help in understanding the predilection of some football fans for excessive behaviour. This includes not only acts of aggression towards opposition fans, the use of intolerant language (e.g. racist, sexist, homophobic), but also acts of spontaneous and unrestrained joy and love, such as the same-sex hugging and kissing of unknown neighbours in the crowd. In doing so, we foreground the gendered and (homo)sexualized dynamics involved in such behaviour. The Canadian feminist scholar, Varda Burstyn, observes in *The Rites of Men* (1999) that, 'Gangs of soccer fans are hypermasculine "crowds". In these crowds, the intense need to feel liked or loved is a driving force'.[1] We suggest that the notion of 'transference-love', as proposed by Sigmund Freud in his ground-breaking paper, 'Observations on Transference-Love' (1915), is important in these circumstances. As a short Research Insight piece, we are limiting our discussion to the collective experience of male football fans that have traditionally been associated with professional football. We acknowledge that the gender make-up of football is slowly changing with more women attending games now, than in the past, but we leave open the question as to what impact this changing demographic might have on fan behaviour.[2]

Critical contexts – mapping the terrain

Aggression and violence among football fans has been a topic of intense scholarly debate for more than 40 years, with analytic interventions arising from many parts of the academy. From the field of political theory, there have been Marxist approaches that viewed violence as a working-class response to the appropriation of football by large corporations.[3] By contrast, some early sub-cultural explanations linked disorder to the rise in the 'skinhead' style,[4] while social-psychological analyses concluded that 'ritual' displays of aggression rarely resulted in actual violence.[5] Some anthropological studies found that there was very little organized fighting, but concluded that acts of hostility tended to be spontaneous and unplanned.[6] Perhaps most notably, the so-called 'Leicester school' of sociologists claimed that football violence was linked to social exclusion and was largely perpetrated by what they termed the 'rough' working classes.[7] From the field of psychology, there have been attempts to explain aggression as a response to boredom and the seeking of thrills (peak experiences in the jargon).[8] These approaches have been useful in bringing multiple analytic tools to an examination of the issues of antagonism among football fans. However, their focus has been almost solely on the much-studied phenomenon of 'hooliganism' rather than a wider consideration of excessiveness. Each study brings a valuable perspective to the problem, but in doing so tend to be reductive, offering a single explanation for multifaceted behaviours. As a result, they are insufficiently nuanced and fail to incorporate the interaction of both social and psychic aspects as an explanation for excessive behaviour. We acknowledge that this space is problematic because it raises fundamental questions about the role of complex *emotions* that nevertheless need to be understood through the medium of rational scholarship. However, despite these difficulties, it is necessary to try to make sense of the complexities because it may create a rupture between thought and emotion that enables significant transformations of understanding to take place.

We take an approach that thinks of intolerance, aggression and violence as points on a continuum of 'excessive' behaviour that also include other highly emotionally charged actions in which fans often engage, notably displays of physical affection. In *Football Delirium* (2007), his loosely interwoven analysis of football and psychoanalysis, Chris Oakley argues that the chance to be 'excessive' is the *raison d'être* for many fans in going to the match. To illustrate his point, he tells one story as follows:

> On my way in search of the half time cuppa I was roughly apprehended by the local constabulary and told in no uncertain terms that any further swearing on my part (I had taken a particular dislike to, in my not so considered opinion, a rather inadequate linesman) would result in 'immediate ejection'. And there I was, blithely assuming that, for many of us, it was these 'discharges' that was precisely what we, the fraternity of the faithful, had gathered together for.[9]

Oakley cites the philosopher, Johan Huizinga, who, in *Homo Ludens* (1949), asked the question 'why is a huge crowd roused to frenzy by a football match?' and suggests that the answer lies in the 'fun-element that characterizes the essence of play [and] his claim is that this essential aspect, fun, is beyond analysis', by which he means that it 'resists all logical interpretation'.[10] The problem is that, goals and occasional triumphs aside, watching your team is not usually 'fun' in a happy sort of way. It is riven with anxiety, despair and rage, making it the sort of 'fun' that appears to lie 'beyond the pleasure principle'.[11] Furthermore, Oakley argues that football fandom is a kind of self-elected madness that serves a purpose in distracting the fan from the inner turmoil of his life, substituting the collective experience of football for all sorts of more dangerous passions, especially sex. We argue that this displacement of emotions is crucial to an examination of excessive behaviour as suppressed passions erupt in multifarious ways – sometimes not only as aggression, but also as joy, and very often both together.

For our purposes, it is also necessary to locate football fandom within the contemporary moment of the postmodern. An early theoretical pioneer, Jean-Francois Lyotard, proposed the term to signify the end of all over-arching narratives, especially Marxism, as a way of explaining historical or social 'progress'.[12] To simplify somewhat, and to borrow from Hassan's definition, the postmodern condition might be thought of as refusing any final certainty of knowledge, of fragmentation and plurality of identities and of adopting a displaced ironic stance towards knowledge that is performative, immanent and carnivalesque.[13] However, in many ways, football fandom challenges the proposition that we live in a wholly 'liquid modern'[14] age of individual consumerism, with dissolved identities and with only 'simulacra' for 'reality'[15] because for many people, football remains a profound collective experience, and support for a club is often a lifelong endeavour, which constitutes an unwavering sense of identity, and one that often stretches across generations of family members. Perhaps, this is because some fans cling fiercely to football support as a way of maintaining some stability of identity in a world that otherwise appears to them to be in dangerous flux. Football may be a point of resistance to what are so often seen as the social and identificatory fluidities associated with postmodernism, and there is evidence to support a case being made along these lines. For example, the sociologist Garry Robson maintains that Millwall fandom, even in the years approaching the twenty-first century, is intrinsically bound to a specific south-east London working-class culture and identity, and one which acts as a strong social 'glue' for thousands of men.[16]

Although we are not making any assertions in this Research Insight about crowd behaviour in general, it is still necessary to think about why football groups and crowds do often engage in displays of excessive behaviour of many different kinds. To this effect, we introduce the notion of the unconscious and apply psychoanalytical findings to social situations outside of the clinic. Although not entirely new in concept, this is still a pioneering approach that is informing the emerging scholarly discipline of psychosocial studies.[17] In particular, we argue that psychosocial theorizing enables an examination of the gendered and sexualized dynamics of the football crowd, which we are foregrounding in this piece.

The Freudian schema of group psychology

Freud believed that when he is part of a group, a person's 'emotions become extraordinarily intensified, while his intellectual ability becomes markedly reduced'.[18] Freud assigned these qualities to the group as a whole, claiming that, 'some of its features – the weakness of intellectual ability, the lack of emotional restraint, the incapacity for moderation and delay, the inclination to exceed every limit in the expression of emotion – are evidence of a regression of mental activity'.[19] Basing his arguments on an analysis of the Church and the Army, Freud argued that:

> Each individual is bound by libidinal ties on the one hand to the leader (Christ, the Commander-in-Chief) and on the other hand to the other members of the group [such that] if each individual is bound in two directions by such an intense emotional tie, we shall find no difficulty in attributing to that circumstance the alteration and limitation which has been observed in his personality.[20]

According to the Argentinian psychoanalyst, Patricia Montenegro, 'Freud's claim is that libidinal ties are at the heart of any group and he argues that groups are held together by the illusion that the leader loves all group members equally, as substitute "father"'.[21] Freud goes on to link this claim to his controversial idea of a primal Oedipal scene, first suggested in *Totem and Taboo* (1913), that structures whole societies around the libidinal family dynamic. However, it is a libidinal scene that produces violence in the same measure as it incites love.[22]

In *Group Psychology*, Freud took the view that group bonds were libidinous but non-sexual in nature in order to explain the comradely affection of brothers in arms. However, in the view of Christopher Lane, 'the consensus [of later critics] seems clear: Freud's account of group identification is marred by his inability to resolve the sexual – especially the homosexual – status of group bonds'.[23] The issue is crucial because it is clear that Freud recognizes that feelings of being close are inextricably linked to feelings of hostility. As Lane says, 'a similar argument often recurs in contemporary debates about the community, the crowd, and the nation, as homosexuality for these entities tends to be socially foundational yet psychically inadmissible'.[24] Ultimately, in *Group Psychology* Freud tried to make a clean divide between libidinal feelings that are sexual and those that are social in an attempt to retain homosexuality, now non-sexual and sublimated, as an explanation for comradeship or group love, but also for hostility and aggression. Such a clear divide, which possibly arose out of Freud's own often confused understanding of homosexuality, cannot be maintained, and a sexual element of close homosocial ties must be allowed. It is the disturbing effect of these unconscious sexual attachments that may trigger excessive behaviour, as a way of warding off feelings of uncertainty and anxiety.

Another problem with the Freudian schema is that his analysis is predicated wholly on the figure of the 'leader' of the group. Freud argued that the group, or mass, could only be understood by reference to the structuring position of the leader, maintaining that it is 'impossible to grasp the nature of a group if the leader is disregarded'.[25] This goes back to the childhood requirement of having to position oneself in relation to a parent or teacher, which forces the child to identify with other children because the parent/teacher will give each child an equal amount of love and attention. In this way, identification with other members of the group comes into existence in relation to the leader figure, not so much because he or she wants to share the leader's attention, but because envy dictates that no one else should receive a greater amount of attention. It is at this point that the Freudian analysis breaks down in respect to its applicability to the football crowd. The vast majority of people attending games do not affiliate to a longstanding and stable group with a well-defined leader in the sense that Freud envisaged with the Church or the Army.

How might Freud's schema be thought about in situations where there is no identifiable 'leader'? To answer this question, it is necessary to think about the place of football fandom in contemporary society. Above all, to be a fan is to partake in a uniquely collective and intensely emotional experience, especially on the match day when the faithful gather, and become an 'emotional community'. Thus, football fandom seems to occupy a liminal position, caught between an older age of more stable identities and today's supposed postmodern fluidity. What is the nature of this strange position, which, on the one hand, seems to offer a place of sanctuary in a chaotic world, yet, on the other hand, is a product of postmodern culture itself? If Freud claimed to have uncovered the unconscious processes that underpin the psychology of the groups, Max Weber's term, 'emotional community', has been interpreted more recently by the French sociologist, Michel Maffesoli in *The Time of the Tribes* (1996), as a group that 'is unstable, open, which may render it in many ways anomic with respect to the established moral order. At the same time it does not fail to elicit a strict conformity among its members'.[26] Maffesoli implies the existence of social glue within social groupings, a common deno-minator of shared values, particular types of dress and other adornments, which distingui-shes every fan of one club from the fans of all other clubs in a continuous process of identification and identity. For Maffesoli, these groups are often transient and temporary and one person may well be a member of many different groups, shedding one identity and adopting another with ease. We concur with this view but would add that the transience of identity does not mean such groups do not exert a powerful pull on their members.

By announcing the demise of the individual, Maffesoli was keen to promote the meta-narrative implications of the growth and importance of small affinity groups, or 'neo-tribes', in contemporary social life. An attachment to small groups may produce expressive identities, which come into existence solely for their own purpose rather than as indicative of being representative of society as a whole. Football is a good example of this, as fans appropriate a time and space but without a political imperative to change anything forever or to be representative of anything else. Hetherington argues for the importance of the performative nature of such identity work, contending that identity formation occurs 'through recognizable performative repertoires that are expressive and embodied'.[27] Space, place and occasion are central to this process, such as occur when fans invest their part of the terrace with their own localized and temporal structures and meanings, which comes to life on match days as they adopt their collective and expressive 'football identity' in a process that is both conscious and unconscious.

Towards an integrated psychosocial approach

How might Freud's unconscious group ties be thought together in a postmodern world where collective identities are often transient and temporary, yet are often felt all the more keenly as a consequence? To do so means to recognize that Freud's schema does not fit the type of postmodern society described by Maffesoli as 'neo-tribal'. In updating Freud's analysis, the psychoanalyst, Claudia Amorim Garcia argues that in the postmodern world:

> We seldom find natural leaders that can be a role model for the common individual and thus serve as locus of identification in the constitution of the cultural superego, as Freud understood it. Thus in our technological society of excess and waste, individuals are left on their own to perform the arduous task of receiving and elaborating intensities which overwhelm their psychic capacity to deal with stimulation, in the absence of a consistent superego that could facilitate the task. They are, consequently, thrown into a traumatic state of helplessness, in Freudian terms, which brings about intense anguish and subjective paralysis, which interfere with the constitution of the superego.[28]

Garcia's acute analysis is borne out in the football arena. Groups such as football fans are primarily affectual groups, often transient or occasional, and with their own identities that, in turn, help to constitute the identities of other members and the group as a whole. Maffesoli argues that the motive force for the members of such groups is a desire to be together. Football fandom is one way for men to bond and, according to Jonathan Fish, 'the idea of "being together" is closely bound up with Durkheim's religious notions of collective consciousness (*conscience collective*) and the life-affirming Dionysian quality of the transcendent warmth of the collectivity (*divin social*)'.[29] However, Freudian insights tell us that the 'transcendent warmth of the collectivity' is laced treacherously with hostility and aggression.

Fandom and identification

In a postmodern light, while he is at the football match, the fan can be seen as having multiple identifications – with club, with players and with other fans – although none of these are simple or unified. It is now necessary to bring back the gendered and sexualized dynamics of the mass as discussed earlier. A radically reworked Freudian schema takes into account the lack of a single leader and the multiple identifications that follow, while also unearthing any repressed (and not so repressed) homosexual attachments. In this new schema, there is the desire of many fans 'to be' the football player. Such a desire is common for many football fans who would love to be professional footballers themselves if only they were young enough and good enough. In this situation, according to Freud, the 'tie attaches to the subject'.[30] It is a desire shared by fellow fans, many of whom show their desire 'to be' the footballer by, for example, wearing a shirt like his. This collective desire is expressed not only in dress and song, but also in rage and frustration, especially if a player fails to make sufficient effort on behalf of the team, with each fan solid in the knowledge that if *he* had been that player he would have given his all!

Furthermore, by his gaze upon the player(s), there is also the unconscious desire 'to have' the player where the 'tie attaches to the object' of the ego.[31] Chris Oakley sums all this up in the following way when he says, 'What else could we think that is involved in so many of us spending our winter afternoons and evenings watching other men run around in silk shorts, if it was not homoerotic? So fondly gazing, so wanting to be those men'.[32] Oakley's own formulation highlights the confusion between the erotic and the identificatory that occurs at a football match played under the postmodern condition, where the cultural superego has weakened and been replaced by tenuous, yet tenaciously held, identifications with club, players and fans. By wanting 'to be' and wanting 'to have' the players they watch, traces of these disturbing identifications may arise within members of the crowd. The close physical proximity of other male bodies in the crowd reinforces those feelings. One means of dealing with such unsettling emotions is through aggression. Another way might be through expressions of love as men unknown to each other hug each other passionately as their team scores a goal. Often they come together as the joy of celebrating a goal often involves the aggressive taunting of opposition fans.

'Transference-love' and the 'subject supposed to know'

To interrogate further the notion of libidinal investments that may underpin excessive behaviour at the football stadium, we propose to use the psychoanalytic notion of 'transference', which, in its clinical context, is the attachment between the patient and the analyst that enables the analytical work to take place. Even within the emerging discipline of psychosocial studies, the notion of 'transference' outside the clinic is still a new way of thinking of the unconscious and yet there are grounds for suggesting that it might be important in this context too.[33]

Freud originally defined 'transference' as a transfer of archaic emotions from the patient's past onto the psychoanalyst. In his famous paper in 1915 on transference-love, Freud pays attention to the fact that transference can feel very similar to love and he warns of its potential to radically alter the relationship between the analyst and his or her patient. We argue that this altered relationship can also occur in some circumstances outside of the clinic, especially in emotionally charged atmospheres such as a football match. Crucially for our purposes, the French psychoanalyst, Jacques Lacan, connects transference to Freud's *Group Psychology* which we discussed earlier, but develops it in a different way. In the place of a leader, Lacan introduces a notion of 'the subject supposed to know' and he defines transference as 'the enactment of the reality of the unconscious'.[34] His key intervention is that although 'transference' might have some roots in the past, it takes place in an embodied encounter in the present, stating that it is an essential phenomenon in any human communications.

Lacan holds that the analyst is 'the subject supposed to know', whereas on the side of the patient Lacan sees his or her desire as linked to a desire to know, which manifests itself as an urge to find out what goes on in his or her unconscious (which compels the patient to repeat the various things he or she would rather not repeat) and also, possibly, other kinds of knowledge. The Lacanian *le sujet supposé savoir* is thus a powerful concept.[35] It is the idea of power and knowledge inducing desire that makes transference relevant in interrogating relationships outside the clinic too, especially in situations that feature a potential imbalance of knowledge and power.

As Lacan stresses, 'whenever this function may be [the subject supposed to know], for the subject, embodied in some individual, *whether or not an analyst, the transference, according to the definition I have given you of it, is established*'.[36] In Seminar XI, Lacan raises the issue of whether the love that one can feel during 'transference' is false, and he says that Freud did not think it was.[37] In his later work (Seminar XX), Lacan goes further in his description of transference as similar to love, stressing that it is always linked to a demand for knowledge: 'I deemed it necessary to support the idea of transference as indistinguishable from love [...] The person in whom I presume knowledge to exist, thereby acquires my love',[38] [and] 'the question of love is thus linked to the question of knowledge'.[39]

In developing this line of thought further, some scholars argue that transference-love is ubiquitous when issues of power and knowledge are played out. In his paper 'Transference as Deception', Gueguen ascertains the presence of transference outside the clinic, maintaining that 'politicians, educators and leaders would have encountered 'transference' in their work'.[40] Gueguen glosses further: 'Politics, education, medical practice, and psychoanalysis all require some kind of adherence or belief, some kind of risk taking at the beginning and throughout, since the choice has to be renewed every day. Every time you go to your session, you have to ask yourself these questions again because such risks can be taken, not in the name of reason or science, but only in the name of love'.[41]

In applying these concepts to the libidinal investments made by fans in the players they go to watch, it is possible to advance an argument that in the situation of the football match the players are the 'subjects supposed to know' who might be the objects of desire and even love on the part of their fans. First, they possess something that the fan most commonly does not, which is the knowledge and ability to play football to an exceptionally high standard: a standard that the average fan can merely fantasize about. As we stated earlier, many male fans, often amateur players themselves, would desperately like to be that professional player, many of whom also achieve a status of fame. In our postmodern, celebrity-obsessed times, the desire simply to be famous is powerful and acts as an inducement to identification rather than a barrier. Even in the absence of celebrity, the notion of secret knowledge might be assumed; the players have been playing a game at a level far superior to those watching them. As a result, the fans not only love the players but also in part they begin to hate them through transference because the 'subjects supposed to know' are in the possession of that secret something which escapes the rest of us. Such ambivalent feelings are in evidence as adoration of the player who scores a goal can quickly turn to contempt if he fails to live up to the lofty standards that the fans expect. As Lacan says: 'I love you, but, because inexplicably I love in you something more than you – *l'objet petit a* – I mutilate you'.[42] In Lacan, *l'objet petit a* is the object cause of desire, something which makes us desire but also something which emphasizes our own lack, thus creating at times a sense of envy and rage.

It is worth emphasizing here that 'transference' and 'identification' are not the same mechanisms but that it is possible that the two might take place concurrently. There is a fantasmatic quality to the excitement at the football match too; the fans might enter a semi-delirium state in which, in their fantasies, they can escape the mundane ordinariness of everyday life. According to psychoanalytic theory, on a most basic level, the end of this delirium will necessarily always produce a violent negative reaction. There is no space in this short piece to interrogate this further, but one could argue that expressions of rage often take place as a result of an incident on the pitch which somehow disrupts the idealization of the process or the fantasy of perfection. A poor decision (in the view of the fans) by the referee, a bad tackle or just a misplaced pass by one of his own players can lead a fan to curse and swear. Similarly, the heightened emotions during the game are necessarily punctured at the final whistle as fans come to terms with a dizzying array of feelings that can range from exultation, despair and anger, all mixed up with unconscious libidinal desire. As authors such as Nick Hornby have observed, football fandom can be an all-consuming passion in which emotions run high and sometimes out of all control.[43]

Conclusion

In this Research Insight, we have argued that, when viewed through the theoretical lens we have proposed here, the excessiveness of fans' behaviour might be seen as located somewhere along a continuum that includes joy and love, hate and violence. We do not contend that this theory provides a comprehensive explanation for the excessive behaviour of fans; clearly many other sociological and psychological factors are important. However, we offer this insight as a provocative intervention that aims to use recent advances in psychosocial theorizing in the context of the football arena. We acknowledge that numerous questions are left unanswered and which might be the subject of further research. In particular, our claim that the types of behaviours we are describing are a product of the postmodern condition, where football identities are clung to passionately in the face of the dissolution of identity in other parts of the fan's life, needs to be examined in the light of fan behaviour long before the advent of the postmodern era.

We have already acknowledged that we have bracketed the issue of changing gender demographics at football matches: the impact of greater numbers of women attending football matches should also be the focus of future studies. However, it is worth noting in passing that the notion of 'the subject supposed to know' works equally well in mixed-gender situations. Furthermore, we have argued that the notion of transference may help to unpack the particularities of the fans' libidinal investments in players, and the consequent mixed emotions that arise which are often experienced at a football match. However, we recognize that this is a new application of this psychoanalytic concept and, therefore, demands further research. In conclusion, we are suggesting in this paper that unconscious mechanisms, which are 'hidden' might influence, in quite profound ways, the often irrational behaviour of fans in their collective form, especially in our postmodern times.

Notes

1. Burstyn, *Rites of Men*, 197.
2. See BBC News, '"More Diverse" Crowds'.
3. See the work of Ian Taylor for Marxist approaches, especially Taylor, 'Soccer Consciousness', Taylor, 'Spectator Violence Around Football' and Taylor, 'Walking Alone Together'.
4. See Clarke, *Football Hooliganism and the Skinheads*.
5. See especially Marsh, *Aggro: The Illusion of Violence*.
6. See Armstrong, *Football Hooligans*.
7. See Dunning et al., 'Social Roots of Football Hooliganism', 39–56.
8. See Kerr, *Understanding Soccer Hooliganism*. For a useful summary of theoretical approaches to football 'hooliganism', see Frosdick, Marsh, and Chalmers, *Football Hooliganism*.
9. Oakley, *Football Delirium*, 36.
10. Ibid., 37.

11. Freud, *Beyond the Pleasure Principle*. In his later writings, he explicitly implicated the interdependency of the drives into group life, arguing that aggression and hostility are constitutive factors in collective life.
12. Lyotard, *Postmodern Condition*.
13. Hassan, 'Pluralism in Postmodern Perspective', 196–9.
14. See Bauman, *Liquid Modernity*.
15. See Baudrillard, *Simulacra and Simulation*.
16. Robson, *No One Likes Us*.
17. Frosh, *Psychoanalysis Outside the Clinic*.
18. Freud, *Group Psychology*, 33. First published in 1922. All page references are from the 1949 edition. We use the pronoun 'he' here as we are discussing only the male crowd in this piece but we recognise its use as problematic of the 'gender-blindness' of much of Freud's work.
19. Ibid., 81 and 82.
20. Ibid., 45.
21. Montenegro, 'Competing Masculinities', 76.
22. In *Totem and Taboo* (1913), Freud infamously postulated that the primal 'band of brothers' murdered the father, who they loved and hated in equal measure, in order to take from him his sole access to women, thus installing aggression and violence (as well as love) at the heart of group life.
23. Dean and Lane, *Homosexuality & Psychoanalysis*, 147.
24. Ibid., 148.
25. Freud, *Group Psychology*, 85.
26. Maffesoli, *Time of the Tribes*, 15.
27. Hetherington, *Expressions of Identity*, 18.
28. Garcia, 'Superego and Its Vicissitudes', 223.
29. Fish, 'Stjepan Metrović', 269.
30. Freud, *Group Psychology*, 62.
31. Ibid.
32. Oakley, *Football Delirium*, 133.
33. See, for example, Piotrowska, 'Animating the Real', 335–53 and Piotrowska, 'Conman and I', 15–29.
34. Lacan, 'Four Fundamental Concepts', 149.
35. Ibid., 230–3.
36. Ibid., 233 (our emphasis).
37. Ibid., 123.
38. Lacan, 'On Feminine Sexuality', 67.
39. Ibid., 91. Irigaray, Lacan's famous rebel student who was expelled from his school after the publication of *Speculum of the Other Woman* (1974), defines transference as 'the experience of the most extraordinary intimacy: a communication or communion which respects the life of the other whilst still tasting this strangeness of his/her desire'. This is, she says because: 'the transference is not only the projection or a reprojection of a history; it is also *an appropriation of the other* – here, now, the food the analysand partakes of to bring his/her analytic process to a successful conclusion and to live his/her life well' (1997 [1991], 114, our emphasis).
40. Gueguen, 'Transference as Deception', 77.
41. Ibid., 78.
42. Lacan, 'Four Fundamental Concepts', 268.
43. Hornby, *Fever Pitch*.

References

Armstrong, Gary. *Football Hooligans: Knowing the Score*. Oxford: Berg, 1998.

Baudrillard, Jean. *Simulacra and Simulation*. Ann Arbor, MI: University of Michigan Press, 1994.

Bauman, Zygmunt. *Liquid Modernity*. Cambridge: Polity Press /Malden, MA: Blackwell 2000.

BBC News. '"More Diverse" Crowds at Premier League Football'. http://www.bbc.co.uk/news/uk-11079597 (accessed March 3, 2013).

Burstyn, Varda. *The Rites of Men: Manhood, Politics, and the Culture of Sport*. Toronto, ON; Buffalo, NY: University of Toronto Press, 1999.

Clarke, John. *Football Hooliganism and the Skinheads*. Birmingham: Centre for Contemporary Cultural Studies, University of Birmingham, 1973.

Dean, Tim, and Christopher Lane. *Homosexuality & Psychoanalysis*. Chicago, IL: University of Chicago Press, 2001.

Dunning, E. G., J. A. Maguire, P. J. Murphy, and J. M. Williams. 'The Social Roots of Football Hooliganism'. *Leisure Studies* 1 (1982): 39–56.

Fish, Jonathan S. 'Stjepan Metrović and Michel Maffesoli's "implosive" Defence of the Durkheimian Tradition: Theoretical Convergences Around Baudrillard's Thesis on the "end" of the Social'. *The Sociological Review* 51, no. 2 (2003): 257–75.

Freud, Sigmund. *Beyond the Pleasure Principle: Authorized Translation from the Second German Edition*. London: Hogarth Press and the Institute of Psycho-analysis, 1922.

Freud, Sigmund. *Group Psychology and the Analysis of the Ego*. London: Hogarth Press and the Institute of Psycho-Analysis, 1949.

Freud, Sigmund. 'Observations on Transference-Love (Further Recommendations on the Technique of Psycho-Analysis III)'. *Standard Edition of the Complete Psychological Works of Sigmund Freud*. Vol. XII. Trans. J. Strachey, 157–217. London: Hogarth Press and the Institute of Psycho-Analysis, 1915.

Frosdick, Steve, Peter Marsh, and Jim Chalmers. *Football Hooliganism*. Cullompton: Willan, 2005.

Frosh, Stephen. *Psychoanalysis Outside the Clinic: Interventions in Psychosocial Studies*. Hampshire: Palgrave Macmillan, 2010.

Garcia, Claudia Amorim. 'The Superego and Its Vicissitudes in Contemporary Society'. *International Forum of Psychoanalysis* 12, no. 4 (2003): 221–6.

Gueguen, P. G. 'Transference as Deception'. In *Reading Seminar XI*, ed. R. Feldstein, B. Fink, and M. Jaanus, 77–91. New York: State University of New York Press, 1995.

Hassan, Ihab. 'Pluralism in Postmodern Perspective'. In *The Post-Modern Reader*, ed. Charles Jencks, 196–9, Academy Editions London: St Martin' Press, 1992.

Hetherington, Kevin. *Expressions of Identity: Space, Performance, Politics*. London: Sage, 1998.

Hornby, Nick. *Fever Pitch*. Harmondsworth: Penguin, 1992.

Irigaray, Luce. *The Speculum of the Other Woman*. Trans. G.C. Gill. Ithaca, NY: Cornell University Press, 1985 [1971].

Jencks, Charles. *The Post-modern Reader*. Academy Editions. London: St Martin' Press, 1992.

Kerr, John. *Understanding Soccer Hooliganism*. Buckingham: Open University Press, 1994.

Lacan, Jacques. 'The Four Fundamental Concepts of Psychoanalysis'. In *Seminar XI*. Trans. A. Sheridan ed. J.-A. Miller. London: W.W. Norton, 1998 [1973].

Lacan, Jacques. 'On Feminine Sexuality, the Limits of Love and Knowledge'. In *Seminar XX*. Trans. B. Fink and ed. J.-A. Miller. London: W.W. Norton, 1999 [1975].

Lyotard, Jean-François. *The Postmodern Condition: A Report on Knowledge*. Minneapolis: University of Minnesota Press, 1984.

Maffesoli, Michel. *The Time of the Tribes: The Decline of Individualism in Mass Society*. London: Sage, 1996.

Marsh, Peter. *Aggro: The Illusion of Violence*. London: Dent, 1978.

Montenegro, Patricia. 'Competing Masculinities and Homosocial Desire in El Jefe'. *Journal of Romance Studies* 4, no. 2 (2004): 67–83.

Oakley, Chris. *Football Delirium*. London: Karnac Books, 2007.

Piotrowska, Agnieszka. 'Animating the Real – A Case Study'. *Animation: An Interdisciplinary Journal* 6, no. 3 (2011): 335–53.

Piotrowska, Agnieszka. 'Conman and I: A Case Study in Transference in Documentary'. *Studies in Documentary Film* 6, no. 1 (2012): 15–29.

Robson, Garry. *No One Likes Us, We Don't Care: The Myth and Reality of Millwall Fandom*. Oxford: Berg, 2000.

Taylor, Ian. 'Soccer Consciousness and Soccer Hooliganism'. In *Images of Deviance*, ed. S. Cohen. Harmondsworth: Penguin Books, 1971.

Taylor, Ian. 'Spectator Violence Around Football: The Rise and Fall of the "Working-Class Weekend"'. *Research Papers in Physical Education* 4 (1976): 4–9.

Taylor, Ian. 'Walking Alone Together: Football Supporters and Their Relationship with the Game'. In *British Football and Social Change: Getting into Europe*, ed. J. Williams and S. Wagg. Leicester: Leicester University Press, 1991.

The role of mediated sports programming on implicit racial stereotypes

Matthew J. Kobach and Robert F. Potter

Indiana University, Bloomington, IN, USA

Previous content analyses show that televised sports programming attributes athletic success achieved by Black athletes to athleticism whereas success for White athletes is attributed to hard work and intelligence. This research explores whether the amount of such programming a person views affects attitudes held about Black and White athletes. Using a unique version of the Implicit Association Test, a strong association was found between images of White athletes and 'smart' athlete words, whereas Black athletes were more strongly associated with 'natural' athlete words. Furthermore, results from a mediated sports-consumption survey suggest that there is a significant positive correlation with the amount of sports programming a participant is exposed to and the strength of these stereotypical associations.

The ubiquity of mediated sports programming is an undeniable facet of the modern world; sports programming can be seen 24 hours a day, 7 days a week. Furthermore, there appears to be a shift in mediated sports programming from a sole focus of showing sporting events/highlights, to an increase in programming that focuses mainly on the discussion of sports and the athletes themselves. Current sports programming now appears to discuss issues beyond highlights, and often engages in debates over a countless number of sports-related topics. Past research indicates that Black athletes are more often discussed in a stereotypical way when compared with their White counterparts,[1] and the addition of sports-talk programming only increases the chances for similar stereotypical portrayals to be expressed.

This research focuses on the 'brain versus brawn' notion, and further explores athletic achievements in the context of race. Where some research attributes the athletic success of Black athletes to biological factors,[2] other work has dismissed this notion suggesting that there is no direct evidence tying race to athletic proficiency.[3] Instead, culture, class and environment prove much better predictors of athletic success in comparison to race.[4] In contrast, the success of White athletes is more often attributed to the sports they are exposed to, encouragement, role models and family affluence.[5] Furthermore, Coakley noted the issue of 'sports stacking' wherein White athletes are often assigned positions that are perceived as requiring a higher level of intellectual ability (e.g. quarterback and offensive linemen in American football) whereas Black athletes are expected to fill positions that require greater athletic dexterity, but require less cognitive ability.[6] This line of research suggests that not only is the 'brain versus brawn' mentality perpetuated via media creators but also, perhaps, in coaches who make personnel decisions based in part upon these stereotypes. This notion is further bolstered by the fact that 25% of respondents from a 2011 survey noted the influence of media stereotypes in the attribution of racially driven athletic success.[7] However, what researchers are now beginning to explore is whether or not these portrayals have any effect on viewers. This research explores whether a correlation exists between mediated sports viewing and racial associations, taking the 'brain versus brawn' notion as its point of departure. To address this issue, the researchers created a unique version of the Implicit Association Test (IAT)[8] and had participants complete it after answering a survey assessing the amount of sports media they consume.

Stereotypes

The field of psychology contains a thorough history of stereotype research,[9] with media scholars also exploring the issue.[10] Absent from this research is a thorough discussion about the effects of repeated exposure to stereotypical images. Instead researchers appear to assume the existence of these effects with little empirical data to support such claims.[11] That is to say, most of the media research focuses on the presence of stereotypical portrayals in mediated messages, but it does not empirically investigate further whether these depictions result in new and/or reinforced stereotypes.

The favoured method of this research is an empirical systematic examination of media messages showing that one or more particular groups are portrayed in a stereotypical manner.[12] Another method is the sociological exploration of this topic from a reflective critical ontology.[13] In their 2009 book, Carrington and McDonald supplied a contemporary critical socio-cultural analysis of sport and race.[14] In addition, Carrington and McDonald explored the notion of racial bonding that is made possible by sports.[15] In what Feagin refers to as the 'White racial frame' Carrington suggests that current views of race have been shaped by long-standing White supremacy.[16] Carrington expands upon this notion when he discusses the 'White colonial frame' as a centuries-old social and cultural reality, and examines the subsequent political and economic racial ramifications on the Black sporting diaspora.[17]

However, in the communication and sociology literature, it is far less common for researchers to explore whether these stereotypical portrayals and/or the prevalence of sports in society leads to, reinforces, or correlates with specific stereotypes. Testing this requires a different methodology, but doing so allows researchers to consider more thoroughly the relationship between media portrayals of certain groups and public perceptions of those groups. For the purpose of this research, stereotypes are conceptually defined as beliefs or expectations about the qualities and characteristics of certain social groups.[18] This research gives specific attention to the role played by modern media in the stereotype process, and uses a cultivation and social reality theoretical perspective in order to predict the effects.

Cultivation and social reality theory

Cultivation theory suggests that media consumption has an influential cumulative effect on the way an individual views the world.[19] Gerbner and his colleagues suggest that social influences have shifted from education/religion to television because of its mass-produced, repetitive and symbolic nature, which is still prevalent in today's mediated culture.[20] Furthermore, the more one is exposed to mediated messages, the closer their beliefs about the real-world mirror that of the mediated world.[21] This line of research has found that, as exposure to television increases, an individual's beliefs and opinions of the real world become more similar to that of the television world. This research applies this perspective by predicting a correlational relationship between automatic stereotypical associations and the amount of sports programming an individual reports consuming.

Gerbner and his colleagues expanded upon the initial formulation of cultivation theory by including individual differences and other demographic variance that affect the degree of cultivation, especially in adolescents.[22] Furthermore, they suggested that the cultivation effects of television contribute to the conception of social reality in that, it assumes an interaction between a pervasive medium and other subtle, complex and intermingled influences.[23]

The theoretical concept of 'social reality' was developed to extrapolate the psychological and cognitive processes that explain how Gerbner's cultivation effect occurs. People construct their reality by automatically and unconsciously selecting certain events that occur in their world and storing them in long-term memory networks.[24] Because mediated messages may make up a substantial portion of the events individuals selectively choose to expose themselves to, the media plays a large role in what can later be drawn upon to construct a person's conception of reality. A person's cognitive response to a message helps construct the memory of daily events. Information stored as a result of viewing a mediated message goes on to determine – at least partially – how the person will act or react to future events.[25] Social reality does not assume that all media is created equal and understands that it will not have the same effect on everyone. Rather it postulates that several circumstances lead to stronger long-term memory traces than others.

One such circumstance is the repetition of information. The more frequently facts, opinions or attitudes are repeated, the stronger the memory networks associated with those details become.[26] Social reality is a multiple-trace model of memory networks – one that states each repetition of an event results in an independent, yet coexisting, memory trace. These multiple memory traces are then used as heuristic cues that allow people to gauge how frequently an event happens.[27] Thus, the frequency of repeated comments celebrating the natural athletic ability of Black athletes (as opposed to stressing hard work or intelligence) arguably leads viewers to assume this is true, more often than it actually is.

Furthermore, arousal has also been shown to affect the encoding of information and its subsequent storage into the long-term memory system.[28] Things that arouse are better remembered than things that are calm in nature or presented within a calm context. This is an important aspect of social reality theory for the current discussion considering that the very nature of sporting events is often exciting and emotional. In addition, with sport-related programming focusing more on clip shows compared with the competitive events themselves, the impact of excitement on long-term memory formation is even more salient. In sports clip shows, only the most exciting and/or controversial plays are shown and discussed by commentators – professional speakers hired for their ability to create excitement in viewers. Therefore, with respect to stereotyping of athletes based on race, viewers are repeatedly exposed to emotionally charged content that depicts Black athletes as naturally talented and White athletes as hard workers.[29] The media that an individual chooses to consume may have an effect on that individual's beliefs, and possibly their actions. Thus, individuals who are heavily exposed to sports programming have the potential to form long-term memory networks containing information provided in the subtle messages conveyed via sports announcers and commentators.

Certainly, there are exceptions to this phenomenon that are task dependent. Social reality suggests that real-world face-to-face experience will most likely (but not always) trump perceptions obtained from a mediated environment.[30] Furthermore, social reality theory suggests that the most relevant information will be called upon when making a decision. It is possible that a person with little to no experience with members of an out-group (e.g. members of a race different than oneself) would more readily recall the mediated messages he or she has either consciously or unconsciously obtained. Consequently, this would influence his or her social judgement decisions of this individual based solely upon mediated messages. This has been suggested in regard to the stereotyping of Black people in the context of media consumption.[31] Fujioka found that the effects of mass media are more pronounced when the viewer lacks significant face-to-face interactions with Black people. As a result, these data suggest that people will rely on stereotypical media portrayals of Black people if real-world exposure is lacking.

There are many determining factors that influence a person's social reality, and it is not always as simple as a person recalling relevant information to shape their reality. One of the important distinctions to understand is that mediated messages vary on a number of factors (e.g. medium, genre and technology). This is clear when looking at a television drama in comparison with a news broadcast. One is fictional while the latter, if nothing else, has at least an illusion of reality. Social reality theory argues that a person will often deem real events more relevant than fictionalized events.[32] This is important when looking at the discussion of athletes by sports commentators. Sports are unscripted and, therefore, what is said in the context of these sports programmes has the potential to be considered more relevant by viewers, and thus perceived as factual, either consciously or subconsciously.

Under the theory of social reality, the creation and utilization of stereotypes often happens without the individual ever being aware of it.[33] And while it is possible to control these stereotypical views, humans have cognitive mechanisms that make this more difficult than one might assume. The reliance on automatic responses to situations can lead a person to use familiar information even when making decisions about unfamiliar stimuli. When an individual possesses little knowledge about a particular topic he or she will call upon any relevant information within memory to make a judgement. If a person has limited non-mediated exposure to a particular situation, and most of their information about it – be it a person, place or thing – comes from the media, then the media help shape their attitude about that object.

Black athletes in mediated sports

Several content analyses have been conducted to explore how Black athletes are portrayed in the media.[34] A good deal of this research has investigated how the athletic traits of White male athletes are described in comparison with those of Black male athletes, with additional research exploring why differences exist.[35] Results suggest that athletic success achieved by Black athletes is more commonly attributed to athleticism, whereas success for White athletes is more often attributed to hard work and intelligence. Furthermore, Whites are more commonly portrayed as natural leaders in comparison with Black athletes. This difference in the perception of Black and White athletes is not a new phenomenon. According to Carrington, it dates back to the 1930s when the rise of the Black athlete concurrently gave way to the atavistic attribution of Black athletic success.[36] This success 'would disallow any suggestion that such sporting achievements be reflective of any deeper, cognitive and above all intellectual disposition', with contemporary-mediated studies supporting this perception.[37]

While Black athletes may have gained equality on the playing field with regard to participation percentages, at times their accomplishments are undermined by television's biased coverage of sports. Studies suggest that Black athletes are more likely to be characterized in a way that trivializes the amount of work they have put into achieving their athletic status. The more recent content analyses suggest that while these kinds of stereotypes appear to be diminishing, they have not yet disappeared completely.[38] Media presentations of racially fuelled stereotypes have shifted from overt descriptions to covert portrayals. These studies suggest that while sports commentators appear to be increasing equality when it comes to describing athletes of different races, they have yet to achieve an actual balance.

Although the presence of stereotypical attributions in media commentary has been well documented, researchers have only recently considered if and when these presentations lead to stereotypical attitudes on the part of sports viewers.[39] The literature contains far more studies of content analysis of race in sports, and researchers rarely set their focus on people's perceptions of race with regard to sport. One such study empirically explored the relationship between the perception of athletic success and race.[40] The researchers found that 25% of respondents attribute the influence of perpetuated stereotypes to mediated portrayals. In a similar study, Buffington and Fraley found that participants endorse the notion that Blacks and Whites possess different physical and mental skills (in relation to sport).[41] These studies suggest that exposure to television could have partially led to the construction of these responses. The numbers of such studies, however, are few. This research attempts to add to the literature in this area.

Hypotheses

The media has the ability to reach mass audiences with sports and sports-related information, and these messages have been shown to contain stereotypical depictions of race. Furthermore, social reality theory and cultivation theory suggest that the more frequently an individual is exposed to a piece of information through the media, the more likely she/he is to believe it to be true due to an increased number of nodes in long-term memory networks that are developed over time. Therefore, the following predictions were made:

H_1: The more sports programming a person reports viewing in an average week, the greater their level of association of Black athletes as 'natural' athletes.

H_2: The more sports programming a person reports viewing in an average week, the greater their level of association of White athletes as 'intelligent' athletes.

Method

As part of this study, 114 telecommunication students (65 males and 49 females) at a large Midwest university participated in exchange for course credit. All participants were treated according to Institutional Review Board standards. Students ranged in age from 18 to 25 years ($M = 20.10$, $SD = 1.59$), and all but seven self-identified as White.[42]

Predictor and outcome variables

The ways in which people can be exposed to information about sports competition has expanded far beyond broadcasts of the sporting event itself. In order to capture the full range of ways in which participants could be exposed to sports *and* commentary on sports, an original survey was constructed. Participants completed a media-use survey that focused specifically on how much time they spend with all types of mediated sports programming. Furthermore, because sports viewing habits may be different depending upon whether weekdays or weekends are considered, participants were asked about each separately. Specifically, participants were asked: On an average weekday how many hours/mins do you spend: (1) Watching live sports? (2) Watching sports highlights? (3) Watching sports talk? (4) Reading about sports in newspapers or magazines? (5) Surfing the Internet about sports? and (6) Listening to radio stations about sports? The same questions were then asked about an average weekend day. The media sports survey information was further collapsed into three categories: (1) Total time (in minutes) spent with sports media on an average week day, (2) total time (in minutes) spent with sports media on an average weekend day and (3) the overall total time (in minutes) spent with sports.

The topic of racial stereotypes is a very difficult area to address, not only because participants are often unwilling to acknowledge their own stereotypical attitudes but also because they may be unaware that they even possess them. This latter phenomenon has been dubbed 'implicit social cognition', and led to the development of the IAT.[43] The IAT asks participants to rapidly pair various stimuli objects and traits. During this task, decisions are made so quickly that the participant relies on associations that have been learned and reinforced through repetitive exposure. The rapid nature of the IAT response is believed to result in respondents using heuristic processing to provide a more automatic response. The ability to respond quickly is based on the strength of developed long-term memory networks. In the case of this research, it is hypothesized that these memory networks have been developed through repeated exposure to sports media and the information they contain about race and athletic performance. The IAT provides cognitive processing data that self-report survey research might not be able to obtain because many cognitive processes affecting behaviour are unconscious in nature and, therefore, inaccessible by simply asking questions of a participant or even observing their overt behaviors.[44]

In this research, the IAT was administered through a computer programme where participants were asked to associate words describing particular traits with a certain side of the computer screen (left or right), along with images of particular group members. Both the images and the words were chosen to be unambiguously a part of a specific category: individuals in the images were easily recognized as Black or White, and the words were selected to be representative of the categories 'Smart Athlete' or 'Natural Athlete'. The words chosen for the IAT task needed to be short due to the speed of the response task the participants were asked to do. The specific words selected were descriptors that either appeared frequently in previous content analyses of sports content or their synonyms.[45] To decrease confusion, the images and the categories associated with each of the words were shown to the participants before the test began, following proper IAT protocol.[46]

The theoretical underpinnings of the IAT state that pairings that are consistent with a participant's view of the world are called *compatible pairings* and result in much quicker categorizations. Pairings that are inconsistent with a participant's view of the world are called *incompatible pairings* and result in longer reaction times. The IAT is a measure of how closely participants implicitly associate groups of people with a certain identifiable characteristic with particularly valenced words.

The IAT in this study was specially designed to incorporate sports-related racially stereotypical traits and pictures of White and Black people. Furthermore, to test the specific stereotypes of interest, instead of words that were synonymous with 'Good' or 'Bad' (e.g. the typical IAT protocol), it was designed to use adjectives shown to be commonly associated with White and Black athletes in media portrayals. Similar IAT studies in the past have utilized stereotypical words that are not as obviously valenced, such as 'Career' versus 'Family'.[47] This research employs a similar approach in regard to 'natural athlete' words compared with 'smart athlete' words. On the surface, complimenting an athlete for his athletic ability and physical attributes would seem to be a positive reflection on that person; however, bias reveals itself when such commentary is viewed through the lens of race. Previous research has shown that announcers often confine both their descriptions and praise of Black athletes to their athletic abilities and physical attributes. The 14 stereotypical words in this study were broken down into two equal categories: 'natural athlete' and 'smart athlete'. The words in the 'natural athlete' category specifically were tall, strong, quick, fast, good jumper, agile and big. The 'smart athlete' category included: determined, intelligent, disciplined, moral, strategic, prepared and coachable.

Greenwald *et al.* have identified the standard for the number of trials, blocks and order of presentation for the IAT.[48] This study followed the IAT standard to explore whether or not repeated viewing of racially stereotypical sports media is correlated with implicit attitudes towards race.[49] As typically done, the words and the categories were first shown to each participant before the IAT was administered to eliminate confusion.

The template for the IAT used in this study was obtained as part of the DirectRT software program[50] and closely mirrors the online version created by the originators of the IAT (available at: http://www.implicit.harvard.edu). The close-up images of seven Black people and seven White people dressed in casual attire used in this study were also part of the sample IAT included with DirectRT. Stimuli appeared in the centre of the screen against a black background. The words for each category appeared in uppercase letters in a blue font against a black background. Reminder labels were positioned in the upper left and right sides of the screen. These reminders read 'African American' and 'European American'[51] for target-classification blocks and 'Natural Athlete' and 'Smart Athlete' for attribute-classification blocks. As the IAT provides participants beforehand with objective words/images and their appropriate categories, incorrect classifications were followed by a red 'X', signifying that they had pressed the wrong key. Following an incorrect answer (e.g. when a participant categorized an image of a Black individual as White, or when she/he categorized a 'natural athlete' term as 'smart athlete'), participants are still required to press the correct key as soon as possible to continue to the next stimulus. Each participant completed a total of seven blocks and 180 trials. Of these, 100 trials were practised and the remaining 80 recorded for analysis (Table 1).[52]

Participants completed the IAT on individual laptops but were run in groups of 1–5 people. Participants were separated from each other with dividers to reduce the possibility of distractions. Participants were given a brief overview of the media use survey and the IAT by the researcher prior to being left alone to complete the media use survey. After that, each participant contacted the researcher to initiate the IAT.

In accordance with past IATs, to correct for anticipatory responses and momentary inattention, response times less than 300 ms and more than 3000 ms were re-coded as 300 and 3000, respectively.[53] Reaction times from incorrect categorizations were kept as part of the data-set. In other words, if someone initially categorized a word or picture incorrectly they still had to press the correct key to move on to the next picture or word. Pairing the association incorrectly indicates that there in not a strong association between the two stimuli, and to exclude that data would eliminate data suggesting that little or no association exists.[54] In addition, past research suggests that there is only a trivial difference when participants with high error rates – defined by Greenwald as above 17.5% – are eliminated. Therefore, data from the single participant in this study who had error rates above 17.5% (but clearly tried to classify the stimuli) were retained for analysis. However, one participant's data were excluded because of excessively fast (<100 ms) response latencies, consistent with standard IAT protocol.[55] This resulted in data from 113 participants being used in the final analysis.

Table 1. Sequence of trial blocks in the IAT.

Block	Number of trials	Function	Items assigned to left key response	Items assigned to right key response
1	20	Practice	'Natural' athlete words	'Smart' athlete word
2	20	Practice	African American images	European American images
3	20	Practice	'Natural' athlete words + African American images	'Smart' athlete word + European American images
4	40	Test	'Natural' athlete words + African American images	'Smart' athlete word + European American images
5	20	Practice	European American images	African American images
6	20	Practice	'Natural' athlete words + European American images	'Smart' athlete word + African American images
7	40	Test	'Natural' athlete words + European American images	'Smart' athlete word + African American images

Note: For half of the subjects, the positions of blocks 2, 3 and 4 were switched with those of blocks 5, 6 and 7, respectively.

To analyse the IAT scores, the mean latency for African American/Natural Athlete and European American/Smart Athlete ('compatible' responses) was subtracted from the mean latency for African American/Smart Athlete and European American/Natural Athlete ('incompatible' responses). In other words, the equation is as follows: the mean reaction time for incompatible responses minus the mean reaction time for compatible responses. Thus, positive difference scores indicate stronger associations with consistent pairings compared with inconsistent pairings. The next step was to convert the difference between mean latency into D scores.[56] This measure divides the difference between means by the standard deviation of all the latencies, thereby adjusting differences between means for the effect of underlying variability. This adjustment has been recommended for use because it helps account for both higher means and greater variability of latencies.[57] Division of a difference between means by a standard deviation is quite similar to the well-known effect size measure, d.[58] This conversion results in scores that range from 0 to 1, with larger numbers indicating stronger associations and small numbers indicating smaller associations. Lastly, based upon their mediated sports survey, participants were divided into light sports media users and heavy sports media viewers based on a median split of their overall total time spent with mediated sports programming.

Results

Prior to controlling for mediated sports consumption, results show that a heuristic preference for White people associated with 'smart' athlete words and Black people associated with 'natural' athlete words was found (average IAT effect of M difference = 96.21 ms; $SD = 197.62$; $D = 0.48$). As expected, participants were 96.21 ms faster in their associations when presented with a compatible pairing (African

American + 'natural' athlete and White + 'smart' athlete) compared with incompatible pairings (African American + 'smart' athlete and White + 'natural' athlete) resulting in a D score that suggests a 'moderate' relationship. However, when the participants were separated into heavy and light sports media users, the reaction times support the hypotheses. The mean latency difference for light mediated sports users (M difference = 43.78 ms; $SD = 167.39$; $D = 0.26$) was significantly different F (1112) = 8.98; $p = 0.003$) when compared with the mean latency difference for heavy sports viewers (M difference = 151.51 ms; SD = 212.98; $D = 0.71$; Figures 1 and 2). This suggests that participants who fell into the category of heavy sports viewers more easily associated pictures of Whites with 'smart' athlete words and pictures of Blacks with 'natural' athlete words when compared to the alternative.

Additional analysis correlated the D scores with amount of self-reported time spent with mediated sports. As predicted, the results show a significant positive correlation between the D scores and the reported overall total time spent watching sports media on a weekly basis ($r = 0.33$; $p < 0.001$). Further analysis also showed significant positive correlations between D scores and total weekend day sports media use ($r = 0.33$; $p < 0.001$) and the total weekday sports media use ($r = 0.28$; $p = 0.001$). For more detailed analysis, see Table 2.

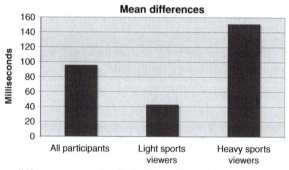

Figure 1. The mean difference scores for the IAT for all participants, and then broken down into light sports viewers and heavy sports viewers.

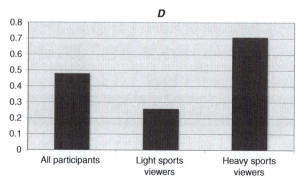

Figure 2. The D score (derived from the IAT) for all participants, and then broken down into light sports viewers and heavy sports viewers.

Table 2. Correlations of sports survey and D scores.

Mediated sport Genres	Average Weekend day	Average Week day
Total time	$r = 0.34; p < 0.001$	$r = 0.28; p = 0.001$
Watching live sports	$r = 0.26; p = 0.003$	$r = 0.25; p = 0.004$
Watching sports highlights	$r = 0.27; p = 0.002$	$r = 0.19; p = 0.023$
Watching sports talk	$r = 0.19; p = 0.024$	$r = 0.19; p = 0.025$
Surfing the internet	$r = 0.41; p < 0.001$	$r = 0.27; p = 0.002$
Reading about sports	$r = 0.17; p = 0.033$	$r = 0.14; p = 0.067$
Listening to sports radio	$r = 0.03; p = 0.375$	$r = 0.08; p = 0.190$

Discussion

This research has examined whether the automatic association of Whites as 'smart' athletes and Blacks as 'natural' athletes (i.e. brain versus brawn) correlates with time spent with mediated sports. Furthermore, we also predicted that people who are light media sports users would show significantly less association with these stereotypes than those who are heavy users. The data support both of these predictions. Results indicate that there is a relationship between overall time spent with mediated sports and associating pictures of Blacks with 'natural' athletic descriptors and pictures of Whites with 'smart' athletic descriptors. When the participants were separated into heavy and light sports media users by a median split, the data suggest that heavy viewers have 'strong' associations compared with light viewers who have a 'small' association. Based on the high correlation between the overall amount of time an individual spends with mediated sports and his/her result on the IAT, this is an area that demands more attention. These data suggest that people who are heavy consumers of mediated sports have, over repeated exposure, formed stronger long-term memory networks and, therefore, more implicitly associate these potentially harmful racial stereotypes with Blacks as a whole. The implicit nature of this association suggests that individuals employ this stereotype in an automatic fashion, and without conscious awareness.

Furthermore, because this IAT drew associations from generic pictures of Black people and White people (i.e. not images labelled as athletes), it is possible that the people who have such strong associations activate these stereotypes when interacting with individuals in general, not solely in the context of sports. The fact that these associations have the potential to transcend sports and seep their way into everyday associations makes them that much more incendiary. As we discuss below, the impact of sports viewership on racially categorized implicit attitudes towards athletes compared with the population at large is an area in need of future research.

If we work from the assumption that the relationship between exposure to mediated sports and racial stereotypes is not correlational in nature, but instead is causal, important contributions can be made to both social reality theory and cultivation theory, as the results are consistent with the tenets of both theories. Cultivation theory suggests that media consumption is cumulative, and that the more an individual is exposed to a particular mediated message, the closer the real-world perspective will mirror the mediated perspective.[59] The effects rely on the mass-produced, repetitive and symbolic nature of television (all arguably present in mediated sports programming). This study found a strong correlation between automatic stereotypical associations and the amount of sports programming a viewer reports consuming. Thus, mediated racial stereotypes are both prevalent in sports programming, *and* are being used by the viewers to shape their view of the world (if only implicitly). And it is this implicitness that is important in contributing to social reality theory. Social reality theory operates under the assumption that media consumers unconsciously select events to construct their conception of reality. The implicit nature of these results suggests that viewers are not consciously adopting these stereotypes, but instead that they are being consumed without the viewer's awareness.[60] It would stand to reason that heavy mediated sports consumers are automatically and unconsciously selecting information from mediated sports programming to construct part of their reality. However, for a more substantial advancement of social reality theory, additional demographic and individual differences data would be necessary.

The preliminary findings from this research leave the possibilities open for future research. While this research suggests that the amount of time spent with mediated sports correlates with certain associations, other correlating demographics could be examined in the future. Specific demographic issues were not controlled for, and could be the subject of future research. Socio-economic status, time spent participating in sports, race, sexuality, gender and interracial interactions are all examples of variables that should come under consideration in future research.

This research found that people associate 'smart' and 'natural' athlete words, respectively, to generic pictures of Whites and Blacks. Future IATs could include pictures of athletic looking individuals (fit individuals dressed in athletic wear), which might increase the effect. Furthermore, IATs have been shown to be significant when as little as five target words are used.[61] By pre-testing 'smart' and 'natural' athlete words researchers could identify the terms that are most closely associated with each category and use only those terms in an IAT, again increasing the effects. In addition, access to participants from minority ethnic backgrounds could allow future researchers to explore whether or not ethnic minorities possess similar implicit stereotypes, and what the role of mediated sports may or may not be in establishing them.

The initial IAT was created to explore sensitive racial issues. The creators of the IAT wanted to ensure that issues of social desirability or unknown implicit attitudes were avoided. However, the association of Whites as 'smart' athletes and Blacks as 'natural' athletes might not fall under this category. It is quite possible that people would openly admit that they endorse these associations. If this were the case, it would be important to investigate whether explicit attitudes correlate with their implicit associations.

Additional research should also be mindful of ways we measured online sports consumption; ideally, that research should add greater specificity to what participants are doing when consuming online sports content. For example, it is possible that Internet users could be watching live sports, reading articles or listening to sports-talk podcasts. It is also possible that sports consumers utilize more than one media outlet at once when getting their mediated sports 'fix'. Specification would result in more in-depth analysis, allowing for a more concrete discussion concerning Internet use. Furthermore, this research was only concerned with overall mediated sports use. Future studies would benefit from an inclusion of a sports survey that addresses the many different types of mediated sports that are consumed by viewers. Previous research has focused primarily on basketball and American football, but has also included Olympic events, covering a wide array of athletes with different abilities. This line of research suggests that these depictions transcend any particular sport, and instead that they exist as a whole in the world of mediated sports.

Finally, data for this research were collected in the USA and it is unclear the extent to which the findings would generalize globally. Attitudes towards race are certainly determined – at least in part – by the specific social milieu in which they are formed.

However, racism in sports is certainly not a problem only in the USA, as similar European-based literature can demonstrate.[62] Future studies should consider using the IAT methodology in global and comparative studies to see the extent to which the amount of sports viewing and implicit stereotypical attitudes are correlated in different cultures.

Notes

1. Billings and Eastman, 'Selective Representation'; Billings and Eastman, 'Framing Identities'; Birrell, 'Racial Relations'; Eastman and Billings, 'Biased Voices of Sports'; McCarthy and Jones, 'Speed, Aggression, Strength, and tactical naïveté'; Rada, 'Colorblind-Sided'; Rada and Wulfemeyer, 'Color Coded'; and Whannel, 'Sport and the Media'.
2. Entine, *Taboo*.
3. Carter et al., 'Success, Race and Athletic Performance'.
4. Lapchick, *Five Minutes to Midnight*.
5. Comeaux and Harrison, 'African American Ballers'; May, Good and Bad'.
6. Coakley, *Sport in Society*.
7. Harrison, Lawrence, and Bukstein, 'White College Students'.
8. Greenwald, McGhee, and Schwarz, 'Measuring Individual Differences'.
9. Allport, *Nature of Prejudice*.
10. Billings and Eastman, 'Selective Representation'; Billings and Eastman, 'Framing Identities'; Birrell, 'Racial Relations'; Eastman and Billings, 'Biased Voices of Sports'; McCarthy and Jones, 'Speed, Aggression, Strength, and tactical naïveté'; Rada, 'Colorblind-Sided'; Rada and Wulfemeyer, 'Color Coded'; and Whannel, 'Sport and the Media'.
11. Gorham, 'Stereotypes in the Media'.
12. Billings and Eastman, 'Selective Representation'; Billings and Eastman, 'Framing Identities'; and Eastman and Billings, 'Biased Voices of Sports'.
13. Carrington, *Race, Sport and Politics*; Carrington and McDonald, *'Race', Sport and British Society*; Carrington and McDonald, *Marxism, Cultural Studies and Sport*; and Feagin, *White Racial Frame*.
14. Carrington and McDonald, *'Race', Sport and British Society*.
15. Carrington and McDonald, *Marxism, Cultural Studies and Sport*.
16. Feagin, *White Racial Frame*.
17. Carrington, *Race, Sport and Politics*.
18. Nelson, Acker, and Manis, 'Irrepressible Stereotypes'.
19. Gerbner, 'Cultivation Analysis'; Gerbner, 'Cultivation Theory'; Morgan and Shanahan, 'State of Cultivation'; and Morgan, Shanahan, and Signorielli, *Living with Television Now*.
20. Gerbner et al., 'Living with Television'.
21. Gerbner et al., 'Living with Television'.
22. Gerbner et al., 'Growing up with Television'.
23. Gerbner et al., 'Living with Television'.
24. Shapiro and Lang, 'Making Television Reality'.
25. Shapiro and Lang, 'Making Television Reality'.
26. Shapiro and Lang, 'Making Television Reality'.
27. Hintzman, 'Schema Abstraction' and Zechmeister and Nyberg, *Human Memory*.
28. Shapiro and Lang, 'Making Television Reality'.
29. Billings and Eastman, 'Selective Representation'; Billings and Eastman, 'Framing Identities'; Birrell, 'Racial Relations'; Eastman and Billings, 'Biased Voices of Sports'; McCarthy and Jones, 'Speed, Aggression, Strength, and tactical naïveté'; Rada, 'Colorblind-Sided'; Rada and Wulfemeyer, 'Color Coded'; and Whannel, 'Sport and the Media'.
30. Shapiro and Lang, 'Making Television Reality'.
31. Fujioka, 'Television Portrayals'.
32. Shapiro and Lang, 'Making Television Reality'.
33. Shapiro and Lang, 'Making Television Reality'.
34. Billings and Eastman, 'Selective Representation'; Billings and Eastman, 'Framing Identities'; Birrell, 'Racial Relations'; Eastman and Billings, 'Biased Voices of Sports'; McCarthy and Jones, 'Speed, Aggression, Strength, and tactical naïveté'; Rada, 'Colorblind-Sided'; Rada and Wulfemeyer, 'Color Coded'; and Whannel, 'Sport and the Media'.

35. Entine, *Taboo*; Carter et al., 'Success, Race and Athletic Performance'; Lapchick, *Five Minutes to Midnight*; Comeaux and Harrison, 'African American Ballers'; and May, 'Good and Bad'.
36. Carrington and McDonald, *'Race', Sport and British Society*.
37. Carrington and McDonald, *'Race', Sport and British Society*, 79.
38. Billings and Eastman, 'Selective Representation'; Billings and Eastman, 'Framing Identities'; and Rada and Wulfemeyer, 'Color Coded'.
39. Harrison, Lawrence, and Bukstein, 'White College Students' and Buffington and Fraley, 'Skill in Black and White'.
40. Harrison, Lawrence, and Bukstein, 'White College Students'.
41. Buffington and Fraley, 'Skill in Black and White'.
42. Data from the seven participants who identified as non-White were included in the final analyses because removing them was found to have no impact on the statistical results. As a result of the extremely low number of non-white participants, any exploration that the race of the participant may have had on the results was left unexplored.
43. Greenwald et al., 'Measuring Individual Differences'.
44. Greenwald et al., 'Measuring Individual Differences'.
45. Billings and Eastman, 'Selective Representation'; Billings and Eastman, 'Framing Identities'; Birrell, 'Racial Relations'; Eastman and Billings, 'Biased Voices of Sports'; McCarthy and Jones, 'Speed, Aggression, Strength, and tactical naïveté'; Rada, 'Colorblind-Sided'; Rada and Wulfemeyer, 'Color Coded'; and Whannel, 'Sport and the Media'.
46. Greenwald, McGhee, and Schwarz, 'Measuring Individual Differences'.
47. Rudman, Greenwald, and McGhee, 'Implicit Self-Concept'.
48. Greenwald, Nosek, and Banaji, 'Understanding and Using'.
49. Jarvis.
50. Greenwald, Nosek, and Banaji, 'Understanding and Using'.
51. Although the authors realize that 'Black' and 'African-American' are not synonyms worldwide, this study was conducted in the USA where the terms are often used interchangeably. Because most of the previous content analyses we relied upon were conducted on US media, and the participants in our experiment were all students in America, this term was used in the administered IAT. Furthermore, the term 'European American' was also used, as is consistent with previous racially based IAT studies.
52. Greenwald, Nosek, and Banaji, 'Understanding and Using'.
53. Greenwald, Nosek, and Banaji, 'Understanding and Using'.
54. Greenwald, Nosek, and Banaji, 'Understanding and Using'.
55. Greenwald, Nosek, and Banaji, 'Understanding and Using'.
56. Greenwald, Nosek, and Banaji, 'Understanding and Using'.
57. Cohen, *Statistical Power Analysis*.
58. Gerbner, 'Cultivation Analysis'; Gerbner, 'Cultivation Theory'; Morgan and Shanahan, 'State of Cultivation'; and Morgan, Shanahan, and Signorielli, *Living with Television Now*.
59. Greenwald, Nosek, and Banaji, 'Understanding and Using'.
60. Feagin, *White Racial Frame*.
61. Billings and Eastman, 'Selective Representation'; Billings and Eastman, 'Framing Identities'; Birrell, 'Racial Relations'; Eastman and Billings, 'Biased Voices of Sports'; McCarthy and Jones, 'Speed, Aggression, Strength, and tactical naïveté'; Rada, 'Colorblind-Sided'; Rada and Wulfemeyer, 'Color Coded'; and Whannel, 'Sport and the Media'.
62. Burdsey, *British Asians and Football*; Carrington, *Race, Sport and Politics*; Carrington and McDonald, *'Race', Sport and British Society*; Carrington and McDonald, *Marxism, Cultural Studies and Sport*; Fletcher, 'Aye, but it were Wasted on THEE'; Fletcher, 'Yorkshiremen are from Yorkshire'; and King, *Offside Racism*.

References

Allport, G. *The Nature of Prejudice*. Reading, MA: Addison-Wesley, 1954.
Billings, A.C., and S.T. Eastman. 'Selective Representation of Gender, Ethnicity, and Nationality in American Television Coverage of the 2000 Summer Olympics'. *International Review for the Sociology of Sport* 37, no. 3–4 (2002): 351–70.

Billings, A.C., and S.T. Eastman. 'Framing Identities: Gender, Ethnic, and National Parity in Network Announcing of the 2002 Winter Olympics'. *Journal of Communication* 53, no. 4 (2003): 369–86.

Birrell, S. 'Racial Relations Theories and Sport: Suggestions for a More Critical Analysis'. *Sociology of Sport Journal* 6 (1989): 212–27.

Buffington, D., and T. Fraley. 'Skill in Black and White: Negotiating Media Images of Race in a Sporting Context'. *Journal of Communication Inquiry* 32 (2008): 292–310.

Burdsey, D. *British Asians and Football*. London: Routledge, 2007.

Carrington, B. *Race, Sport and Politics: The Sporting Black Diaspora*. London: Sage, 2010.

Carrington, B., and I. McDonald. *'Race', Sport and British Society*. London, New York: Routledge, 2001.

Carrington, B., and I. McDonald. *Marxism, Cultural Studies and Sport*. London, New York: Routledge, 2009.

Carter, R., S.N. Cheuvront, K. Harrison, L. Proctor, K. Myburgh, M.D. Brown, and R.M. Malina. 'Success, Race and Athletic Performance: Biology, Belief or Environment?' *Journal for the Study of Sports and Athletes in Education* 4, no. 3 (2010): 207–29.

Coakley, J. *Sport in Society: Issues and Controversies*. New York: McGraw Hill, 1998.

Cohen, J. *Statistical Power Analysis for the Behavioral Sciences.*, revised edition New York: Academic Press, 1977.

Comeaux, E., and C.K. Harrison. 'Labels of African American Ballers: A Historical and Contemporary Investigation of African American Male Youth's Depletion from America's Favorite Pastime, 1885–2000'. *The Journal of American Culture* 27 (2004): 67–80.

Eastman, S.T., and A.C. Billings. 'Biased Voices of Sports: Racial and Gender Stereotyping in College Basketball Announcing'. *The Howard Journal of Communications* 12 (2001): 183–201.

Entine, J. *Taboo: Why Black Athletes Dominate Sports and Why We're Afraid to Talk About It*. New York: Public Affairs, 2000.

Feagin, J. *The White Racial Frame: Centuries of Racial Framing and Counter Framing*. London: Routledge, 2010.

Fletcher, T. 'All Yorkshiremen are from Yorkshire, but Some are More "Yorkshire" than Others: British Asians and the Myths of Yorkshire Cricket'. *Sport in Society* 15, no. 2 (2012): 227–45.

Fletcher, T. '"Aye, but it were Wasted in Thee': Cricket, British Asians, Ethnic Identities, and the "Magical Recovery of Community"'. *Sociological Research Online* 16, no. 4 (2012): 5, http://www.socresonline.org.uk/16/4/5.html

Fujioka, Y. 'Television Portrayals and African-American Stereotypes: Examination of Television Effects When Direct Contact is Lacking'. *Journalism and Mass Communication Quarterly* 76, no. 1 (1999): 52–75.

Gerbner, G. 'Cultivation Analysis: An Overview'. *Mass Communication and Society* 1, no. 3/4 (1998): 175–94.

Gerbner, G. 'Cultivation Theory'. In *A First Look at Communication Theory*, ed. Michael Ryan, 353–4, 7th ed. New York: Frank Mortimer, 2009.

Gerbner, G., L. Gross, M. Morgan, and N. Signorielli. 'Living with Television: The Dynamics of the Cultivation Process'. In *Perspectives on Media Effects*, ed. J. Bryant and D. Zillman, 17–40. Hilldale, NJ: Lawrence Erlbaum Associates, 1986.

Gerbner, G., L. Gross, M. Morgan, and N. Signorielli. 'Growing up with Television: The Cultivation Perspective'. In *Against the Mainstream: The Selected Works of George Gerbner*, ed. M. Morgan, 193–213. New York: Peter Lang, 2002.

Greenwald, A.G., D.E. McGhee, and J.L.K. Schwarz. 'Measuring Individual Differences in Implicit Cognition: The Implicit Association Test'. *Journal of Personality and Social Psychology* 74 (1998): 1464–80.

Greenwald, A.G., B.A. Nosek, and M.R. Banaji. 'Understanding and Using the Implicit Association Test: I. An Improved Scoring Algorithm'. *Journal of Personality and Social Psychology* 85 (2003): 197–216.

Gorham, B.W. 'Stereotypes in the Media: So What?' *The Howard Journal of Communications* 10 (1999): 229–47.

Harrison, C.K., S.M. Lawrence, and S.J. Bukstein. 'White College Students' Explanations of White (and Black) Athletic Performance: A Qualitative Investigation of White College Students'. *Sociology of Sport Journal* 28, no. 3 (2011): 347–61.

Hintzman, D. 'Schema Abstraction in Multiple-Trace Memory Model'. *Psychological Review* 93 (1986): 411–28.

King, C. *Offside Racism*. Oxford: Berg, 2004.

Lapchick, R. *Five Minutes to Midnight: Race and Sport in the 1990s*. Lanham, NY: Madison Books, 1991.

May, R.A.B. 'The Good and Bad of it All: Professional Athletes as Role Models for Young Black Males'. *Sociology of Sport Journal* 26 (2009): 443–61.

McCarthy, D., and R.L. Jones. 'Speed, Aggression, Strength, and Tactical Naïveté'. *Journal of Sport and Social Issues* 21 (1997): 348–62.

Morgan, M., and J. Shanahan. 'The State of Cultivation'. *Journal of Broadcasting and Electronic Media* 54, no. 2 (2010): 337–55.

Morgan, M., J. Shanahan, and N. Signorielli. *Living with Television Now*. New York: Peter Lang, 2012.

Nelson, T., M. Acker, and M. Manis. 'Irrepressible Stereotypes'. *Journal of Experimental Social Psychology* 32 (1996): 13–38.

Rada, J. 'Colorblind-Sided: Racial Bias in Network Television's Coverage of Professional Football Games'. *The Howard Journal of Communications* 7 (1996): 231–40.

Rada, J., and K. Wulfemeyer. 'Color Coded: Racial Descriptors in Television Coverage of Intercollegiate Sports'. *Sports Journal of Broadcasting and Electronic Media* 49 (2005): 5–85.

Rudman, L.A., A.G. Greenwald, and D.E. McGhee. 'Implicit Self-Concept and Evaluative Implicit Gender Stereotypes: Self and Ingroup Share Desirable Traits'. *Personality and Social Psychology Bulletin* 27 (2001): 1164–78.

Shapiro, M., and A. Lang. 'Making Television Reality: Unconscious Processes in the Construction of Social Reality'. *Communication Research* 18 (1991): 685–705.

Whannel, G. 'Sport and the Media'. In *Handbook of Sports Studies*, ed. J. Coakely and E. Dunnings, 291–308. London: Sage, 2000.

Zechmeister, E., and S. Nyberg. *Human Memory; An Introduction to Research and Theory*. Monterey, CA: Brooks/Cole, 1982.

Index

INDEX